NEW STRATEGIES FOR
AMERICA'S WATERSHEDS

Committee on Watershed Management
Water Science and Technology Board
Commission on Geosciences, Environment, and Resources
National Research Council

NATIONAL ACADEMY PRESS
Washington, D.C. 1999

NATIONAL ACADEMY PRESS • 2101 Constitution Avenue, N.W. • Washington, DC 20418

NOTICE: The project that is the subject of this report was approved by the Governing Board of the National Research Council, whose members are drawn from the councils of the National Academy of Sciences, the National Academy of Engineering, and the Institute of Medicine. The members of the committee responsible for the report were chosen for their special competences and with regard for appropriate balance.

Support for this project was provided by the Tennessee Valley Authority under Contract No. TV-93635V, the Environmental Protection Agency under Grant No. GR 823884-01-0 and X826699-01-0, the McKnight Foundation under Grant No. 94-990, the former National Biological Service under Grant Agreement No. 1445-GT09-95-0017, the Natural Resources Conservation Service under Cooperative Agreement No. 68-3A75-5-175, the Forest Service, the Bureau of Reclamation under Grant No. 1425-96-FG-81-07009, and the National Water Research Institute.

New Strategies for America's Watersheds is available from the National Academy Press, 2101 Constitution Avenue, N.W., Box 285, Washington, DC 20418 (1-800-624-6242; http://www.nap.edu).

Library of Congress Cataloging-in-Publication Data

New strategies for America's watersheds / Committee on Watershed
Management, Water Science and Technology Board, Commission on
Geosciences, Environment, and Resources, National Research Council.
    p. cm.
    Includes bibliographical references and index.
    ISBN 0-309-06417-1 (casebound)
    1. Watershed management—United States. I. National Research
Council (U.S.). Committee on Watershed Management.
    TC423 .N46 1999
    333.73—dc21   98-58156

Cover: The watersheds of Arizona appear on this digital map created by Ray Sterner of Johns Hopkins University's Applied Physics Laboratory. The image, with north at the top, shows an area about 200 by 150 miles, with the Colorado River and the Grand Canyon at the top. The Colorado Plateau occupies the top and upper right portions of the view, with the Basin and Range terrain visible in the lower left. Between the two is a northwest-southeast trending transition zone of mountainous terrain. The oblong blue feature in the lower center of the image is Roosevelt Lake, impounded by Theodore Roosevelt Dam. This image, and similar ones for all states, is available on the World Wide Web at http://fermi.jhupal.edu/states/states.html.

COMMITTEE ON WATERSHED MANAGEMENT

WILLIAM L. GRAF, *Chair,* Arizona State University, Tempe
CLIFTON J. AICHINGER, Ramsey-Washington Metro Watershed District, Maplewood, Minnesota
BLAKE P. ANDERSON, Orange County Sanitation Districts, Fountain Valley, California
GABOURY BENOIT, Yale University, New Haven, Connecticut
PETER A. BISSON, USDA Forest Service, Olympia, Washington
MARGOT W. GARCIA, Virginia Commonwealth University, Richmond
JAMES P. HEANEY, University of Colorado, Boulder
CAROL A. JOHNSTON, University of Minnesota, Duluth
LEONARD J. LANE, USDA Agricultural Research Service, Tucson, Arizona
CAROLYN HARDY OLSEN, San Francisco Public Utilities Commission, San Francisco
GARY W. PETERSEN, The Pennsylvania State University, University Park
MAX J. PFEFFER, Cornell University, Ithaca, New York
LEONARD SHABMAN, Virginia Polytechnic Institute and State University, Blacksburg
JACK STANFORD, University of Montana, Polson
STANLEY W. TRIMBLE, University of California, Los Angeles

Staff

CHRIS ELFRING, Study Director
ANGELA F. BRUBAKER, Research Assistant (through May 14, 1997)
ANITA HALL, Senior Project Assistant

The National Academy of Sciences is a private, nonprofit, self-perpetuating society of distinguished scholars engaged in scientific and engineering research, dedicated to the furtherance of science and technology and to their use for the general welfare. Upon the authority of the charter granted to it by the Congress in 1863, the Academy has a mandate that requires it to advise the federal government on scientific and technical matters. Dr. Bruce M. Alberts is president of the National Academy of Sciences.

The National Academy of Engineering was established in 1964, under the charter of the National Academy of Sciences, as a parallel organization of outstanding engineers. It is autonomous in its administration and in the selection of its members, sharing with the National Academy of Sciences the responsibility for advising the federal government. The National Academy of Engineering also sponsors engineering programs aimed at meeting national needs, encourages education and research, and recognizes the superior achievements of engineers. Dr. William A. Wulf is president of the National Academy of Engineering.

The Institute of Medicine was established in 1970 by the National Academy of Sciences to secure the services of eminent members of appropriate professions in the examination of policy matters pertaining to the health of the public. The Institute acts under the responsibility given to the National Academy of Sciences by its congressional charter to be an adviser to the federal government and, upon its own initiative, to identify issues of medical care, research, and education. Dr. Kenneth I. Shine is president of the Institute of Medicine.

The National Research Council was organized by the National Academy of Sciences in 1916 to associate the broad community of science and technology with the Academy's purposes of furthering knowledge and advising the federal government. Functioning in accordance with general policies determined by the Academy, the Council has become the principal operating agency of both the National Academy of Sciences and the National Academy of Engineering in providing services to the government, the public, and the scientific and engineering communities. The Council is administered jointly by both Academies and the Institute of Medicine. Dr. Bruce M. Alberts and Dr. William A. Wulf are chairman and vice chairman, respectively, of the National Research Council.

Preface

"... the belief that the social dilemmas created by the machine can be solved merely by inventing more machines is today a sign of half-baked thinking which verges close to quackery."

Lewis Mumford, Technics and Civilization, 1934.

"[Restoration] will not happen by regulation, changes in the law, more money, or any of the normal bureaucratic approaches. It will only occur through the integration of ecology, economic, and social factors, and participation of affected interests."

Letter creating the National Riparian Service Team, 1996.

The late twentieth century is a time of change in the way Americans perceive and manage water and its associated resources. The nation is poised at the end of an era in which we viewed water and riparian environments as commodities, and in which we spent trillions of dollars building the machines of water control: storage dams, diversion works, canals, levees, and artificial channels. This investment accurately reflected the country's focus on economic development and the control of natural processes.

The last two decades, however, have brought greater emphasis on environmental quality and integrated management. The Clean Water Act strongly expresses this new perspective by establishing as a national goal the restoration and maintenance of the physical, chemical, and biological integrity of the nation's waters. This new goal will not likely be achieved through the construction of additional control works, more regulations, or more money. Rather, the new ethic of sustaining economic prosperity while preserving environmental quality will require management approaches that integrate human and natural systems. What will these new management approaches be? What will they use as scientific underpinnings?

Watershed-based approaches offer a promising way to achieve this integration. By their nature, watershed-based management strategies are integrative, drawing on concepts from the physical, biological, social, and economic sciences. Not surprisingly, they have emerged just as many sciences are beginning to emphasize integrative, system-based approaches to environmental research that examine entire systems rather than analytic approaches that examine only the parts of systems.

Thus we find both science and policy moving toward integrative systems. Unfortunately, communications among scientific disciplines is often difficult, and given the compartmentalized training of many scientists, communications between scientists and policymakers is even more haphazard.

This report grew out of a recognition of the emerging trends toward integrative watershed management and the need to improve communication between scientists and decisionmakers. In 1996, several agencies asked the National Academies of Sciences and Engineering and their investigative arm, the National Research Council (NRC), to provide advice on the utility and limitations of the watershed-based policy-making and management. The Environmental Protection Agency took a prominent role in this request, because the agency was beginning its Watershed Initiative to deal with nonpoint source pollution, a problem inadequately addressed through traditional approaches. The Tennessee Valley Authority, itself defined by the geographic boundaries of a river basin, supported the review effort in part to produce guidance for its Clean Water Initiative, an innovative approach to water-quality problems that is organized according to smaller watersheds within the Tennessee Valley. The Natural Resources Conservation Service (formerly the Soil Conservation Service), an agency with a long and venerable history of watershed management mostly for agricultural purposes, also sponsored the NRC review. The Forest Service provided support because the agency has as part of its charter the requirement to manage watersheds on a significant component of the nation's public lands. Other governmental supporters included the Bureau of Reclamation, an agency charged with development and management of western water resources, and the U.S. Geological Survey, the nation's primary source of data for water science, policy, and management. In addition to these federal agencies, two nongovernmental organizations also provided support. The National Water Research Institute has broad interests in scientific research related to water. The McKnight Foundation is a major stimulant for local involvement in watershed projects in the upper Mississippi.

In response to the request for advice by these organizations, the National Research Council appointed a committee of 15 scientists, planners, and public administrators. Committee members included practitioners from the fields of biology, chemistry, geography, economics, engineering, hydrology, sociology, planning, and administration. The Council and the sponsors agreed upon three specific charges for the committee:

• Review the range of scientific and institutional problems related to watersheds, especially water quality, water quantity, and ecosystem integrity.
• Evaluate selected examples of watershed management in a search for the common elements of successful management.
• Recommend ways for local, state, regional, and federal water managers to integrate ecological, social, and economic dimensions of watershed management.

The committee addressed these charges over a two-year period. Committee members donated their time in five multiple-day meetings, which included field hearings in Chattanooga, Tennessee; Irvine, California; and Minneapolis, Minnesota. In Minneapolis, the committee participated with local, state, and regional managers in a workshop focused on issues in the Upper Mississippi Basin.

During the field investigations, hearings, workshops, and meetings with scientists and administrators, the committee experienced a true adventure in modern America. We met researchers trying to unravel complex natural systems to produce better understanding for public decisions, private citizens who had organized local watershed efforts to meet a variety of goals, and administrators working to realize visions of a quality future. We also met state and local officials overrun with management problems, yet lacking sufficient financial resources to solve them, and federal officials uncertain about the future of their agencies. We saw examples where people ignored the downstream consequences of their pollution. We also met heroes who organized the chaos around them to create successful initiatives to improve both the human and the natural environment.

This report contains the lessons we learned as a committee. Our report is not only for the experts. Instead, we crafted the report to be useful to readers ranging from interested laypersons to working scientists and policymakers at all levels. Underlying the formal lessons recounted here were three more general truths. First, the way we perceive the nation as individual resource users, researchers, and decisionmakers has a direct and major impact on how we perceive problems and solutions. The problems and solutions of watershed management depend on your perspective. As shown in the Figure P1, the continental United States takes on a very different general appearance depending upon whether we use a political or a natural framework. Even different natural frameworks provide us with very different contexts.

Second, watersheds are logical divisions or regions of the natural landscape, and for some purposes they are ultimately the best framework to use for management. Yet it is also true that for every natural watershed there is a "shadow watershed" defined by human and natural components that extend the decision-

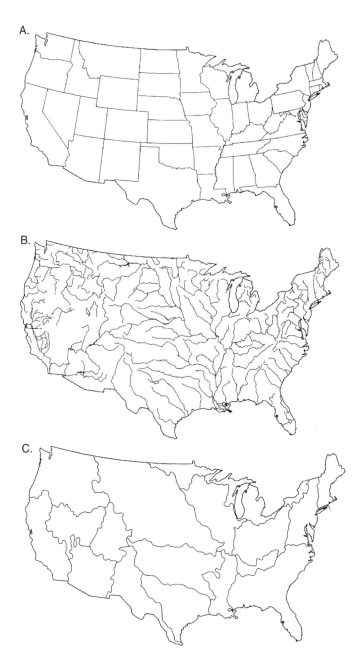

FIGURE P1   Three views of the geographic framework of the continental United States.
(A)   political, state boundaries, (B) major rivers, and (C) major watershed regions and
drainage basins. SOURCE: W. L. Graf.

maker's interest beyond the boundaries of the physical watershed. Whether migratory birds, hydroelectric power grids, or other factors are involved, we must be prepared to perceive watershed space in dimensions other than physical.

Third, the devolution of political power from the federal to regional and local levels in American politics means that we must develop a new "flexible federalism" in which the federal government maintains a newly defined role with some responsibilities while regional and local governments exert greater influence in solving problems. For the federal agencies, this arrangement means efforts increasingly in partnerships with regional and local governments. However, it does not excuse the federal government from its responsibility for representing the interests of the nation as a whole, especially regarding the setting of standards and the management of public land and water.

Our work in creating this report would not have been possible without the constant oversight and contributions of Chris Elfring, who served as Study Director. Her skillful planning, guidance, and management of the committee process was a key to the successful completion of the task. She was a full partner in every respect during the meetings, workshops, debates, and writing processes. Her knowledge of government and science, her ability to work with diverse groups of people, and her professionalism in shepherding the reporting process to completion were magnificent. Angie Brubaker and Anita Hall provided valuable support in making the many complicated arrangements to allow the committee to conduct its business. Barbara Trapido-Lurie of the Department of Geography, Arizona State University, provided indispensable skill and judgment in the design and production of graphics for the report.

This report has been reviewed by individuals chosen for their diverse perspectives and technical expertise, in accordance with procedures approved by the NRC's Report Review Committee. This independent review provided candid and critical comments that assisted the authors and the NRC in making the published report as sound as possible and ensured that the report meets institutional standards for objectivity, evidence, and responsiveness to the study charge. The content of the review comments and draft manuscript remain confidential to protect the integrity of the deliberative process. We wish to thank the following individuals for their participation in the review of this report: Leo M. Eisel, McLaughlin Water Engineers, Inc., Denver, Colorado; Paul Faeth, World Resources Institute, Washington, D.C.; Denise Fort, University of New Mexico, Albuquerque; Debra Knopman, Progressive Policy Institute, Washington, D.C.; Ronald Lacewell, Texas A&M University, College Station, Texas; Thomas S. Maddock, Boyle Engineering Corporation, Newport Beach, California; and Richard Sparks, Illinois Natural History Survey, Havana, Illinois.

While the individuals listed above provided many constructive comments and suggestions, responsibility for the final content of this report rests solely with the authoring committee and the NRC.

While this report represents a consensus and all the committee members contributed to writing it, probably no single committee member agrees with every detail. Our committee members came from diverse backgrounds, ethics, and professional cultures, and all were strong-willed individualists. Despite differences in background, experience, and opinion, however, compromise of divergent positions was a necessity. I express my sincere gratitude to the committee members for their contributions of valuable professional time and their amazing professional talents to this endeavor. To have engaged in this productive, difficult, and demanding enterprise, replete with opportunities for divisive debate, and to have emerged with a cohesive product produced by people with mutual respect and friendship is a success in itself. Collectively, we hope that watershed approaches will resolve part of the puzzle posed by our national desire for developing water-related resources to sustain economic prosperity, while at that same time restoring and maintaining a quality environment.

William L. Graf, *Chair*
Comiittee on Watershed Management

Contents

NEW STRATEGIES FOR
AMERICA'S WATERSHEDS

Summary

Many factors are converging to cause citizens, scientists, resource managers, and government decisionmakers to look increasingly to watershed management as an approach for addressing a wide range of water-related problems. Managing water resources at the watershed scale, while difficult, offers the potential of balancing the many, sometimes competing, demands we place on water resources. The watershed approach acknowledges linkages between uplands and downstream areas, and between surface and ground water, and reduces the chances that attempts to solve problems in one realm will cause problems in others. Watershed management is an integrative way of thinking about all the various human activities that occur on a given area of land (the watershed) that have effects on, or affected by, water. With this perspective, we can plan long-term, sustainable solutions to many natural resource problems. We can find a better balance between meeting today's needs and leaving a sound resource legacy for generations to come.

Management of water and related resources based on a regional perspective is not a new concept, but as the 21st century approaches it has taken on added importance for America's watersheds. National goals of vibrant economic development with simultaneous progress in environmental restoration and preservation emphasize the need to bring together the public, decisionmakers, and scientists in effective strategies. The attainment of these goals is not mutually exclusive, but can be assured only with the integration of ecological, social, and economic approaches to environmental management problems. At the same time, the reinvention of the federal government, with continuing devolution of authority to state and local authorities, demands a more effective integration of administrative levels. Watershed management is one method for addressing these needs for integration.

Government and private sponsors gave the National Research Council's Committee on Watershed Management three tasks: investigate the present state of knowledge about watershed management, investigate representative examples of the application of the approach, and identify barriers to successful implementation of such approaches and means for overcoming them. The committee pursued its work based on the idea that watersheds of all sizes, ranging from small local drainages to large river basins, were part of the charge. The committee's activities included much research as well as efforts to talk to people involved in watershed initiatives at all levels, from large, regional planning approaches to small, local projects. We held meetings or workshops in Washington, D.C.; Tennessee; California; and Minnesota; and met in total five times over our two-year study to deliberate and write this report. The committee hopes this effort will be of value to a wide range of potential users, including watershed managers from local to national levels, researchers, Congress, and the executive agencies of the federal government.

WATERSHEDS AS A BASIS FOR PLANNING AND MANAGEMENT

Watersheds are defined by the "waterscape," the combination of the hydrology and topography of the landscape, and they are ubiquitous units that can be seen as the physical foundation of the nation. The U.S. Geological Survey provides a standardized definition of regions and watersheds that subdivides the nation into hydrologic units averaging about 700 square miles. These units provide a common basis of discussion for the public, planners, decisionmakers, and scientists who deal with water-related issues. Although social and economic data are not collected with respect to these natural boundaries, modern geographic information systems allow reformulating of diverse data sets into common frameworks. This tool increasingly allows managers to use ecological, social, and economic data in concert.

The environmental, social, and economic diversity of the United States dictates that one standard solution is unlikely to be useful in all parts of the country. A huge range of environments occurs between the humid east coast and the progressively dry mid-continent area, between the well-watered Pacific northwest and the arid southwest. Population densities range from the crowded northeast to the sparsely settled inter-mountain regions. Regional variations in wealth are substantial. Any well-designed national policy for watershed management must maintain great flexibility to accommodate these natural and human variations and allow significant local control and input to decisions.

Governmental attempts at watershed management have been ongoing in the United States for more than half a century, but the science of watershed management is still evolving and many of our current activities are, in essence, experiments. As a result, many of the models that link data to concepts in a way that might be useful to managers are not effective. Technology that takes advantage of modern advances in geographic information systems and decision support systems are poorly developed at present. The collection of basic environmental data describing the changing conditions of watersheds is in jeopardy as agencies react to shrinking budgets by eliminating monitoring sites for the hydrologic system. Risk and uncertainty must be adequately accounted for in planning and predictive models. Watershed science in general has yet to develop an effective interface between what we know and how we use that knowledge. Good science is not enough; we need useful science. Watershed management without significant input of new scientific understanding, especially understanding of watershed processes and of the human dimensions, is doomed to inefficiency and eventual loss of credibility; research without input from involved stakeholders and those with real management acumen will always prove less than useful. In the end, watershed management is both institutionally and scientifically complex, and thus inherently difficult to implement.

During most of the mid- to late-20th century, watershed management has been a top-down process, but this approach has led to numerous barriers to effective citizen involvement and to use of locally developed knowledge. A truly effective watershed management effort is most likely to be a bottom-up process, driven largely by citizen concerns about local or regional problems and guided by sound data and information. Successful collaborative planning requires broad participation by those likely to be affected by the outcome. Sometimes these stakeholders are beyond the physical boundaries of the watershed or river basin in question, so that a "problemshed" must be accounted for. In a successful process, scientific analysis is married with public participation, ensuring that decisions based on cultural values are informed decisions with respect to likely consequences and a clear understanding of who benefits and who pays.

Organizations for watershed management are most likely to be effective if their structure matches the scale of the problem. Individual local issues related to site planning, for example, should be the purview of local self-organized watershed councils, while larger organizations should deal with broader issues. These larger organizations, however, must include the nested smaller watershed groups within their areas of interest, and must account for downstream interests. A major barrier to effective watershed management for large basins in the past has been limitations on the transfer of powers. The various levels of government in the United States developed historically with specific authorities and powers, and most governmental entities are unlikely to give up those powers to some larger all-encompassing organization. In addition, large federal agencies defined by their topical missions (flood control for the Army Corps of Engineers and water management and delivery for the Bureau of Reclamation) are antithetical to overarching regional organization. Partnerships among levels of government and various agencies are required for effective watershed management. The era of a large, dominant federal government must give way to an era of flexible federalism where the federal government maintains a role but allows state and local governments to assume substantial rights and responsibilities for watershed management.

Funding for watershed management and science is a continuing problem. Much of the funding for single-purpose watershed efforts, such as control of point source pollution, comes from single purpose agencies, such as a wastewater management district. Because most watersheds are administered under a complex institutional structure, new broadly based funding sources are needed. Potential sources include revenues from hydropower production and user charges for water supply, flood control, recreation, and other uses. These users may be expected to resist increased costs to provide for watershed management, but governments at all levels must ensure that those who benefit from watershed products or services also support the management of the systems. Pricing structures at or near market values may create new revenue sources of this type. The creation of some stable mechanism, such as a revenue-sharing strategy or trust fund, could ensure that there is a way for the federal government to contribute to and encourage watershed management partnerships. In the area of science, reallocation of existing funds from general programs to highly targeted programs can benefit watershed research.

The chapters of this report provide greater detail on many discussions of how implementation of watershed approaches might be improved, from areas where our scientific understanding is lacking to planning and decisionmaking. Ultimately, the Committee on Watershed Management reached conclusions that are described briefly below, supported in greater detail in the chapters, and summarized in Chapter 9. Here we comment specifically on the reauthorization of the Clean Water Act as a key way to improve implementation of watershed management in the United States. We then offer conclusions addressing a range of issues connected to integrating ecological, social, and economic approaches to watershed management.

REAUTHORIZATION OF THE CLEAN WATER ACT

Congress and the President have an historic opportunity to enhance sustainability of resources and the economy through improved watershed management by reauthorizing the Clean Water Act. The original Act and its revisions brought about improved control of point sources of pollution, resulting in impressive improvements in water quality for many streams. However, other waterways, including some of the nation's most important rivers, continue to degrade because of nonpoint source pollution. Such pollution is by its nature "area-based" or regional, so that its control is likely to be watershed-based. Many rivers and watersheds are fragmented physically by dams, while the administration of these systems is also fragmented among sometimes competing agencies and levels of government. Science is also fragmented by a continuing trend to compartmentalize knowledge and to emphasize analysis rather than synthesis.

Integrated thinking must be articulated in the reauthorized Clean Water Act. The Act should allow bottom-up development of watershed agencies that respond to local problems rather than having a rigid institutional structure imposed upon them from the federal level. The reauthorized Act can empower watershed managers at the local and regional levels to consolidate their authorities on a watershed basis, an approach that can increase efficiency and control costs. In management, the Act must recognize that all components of the waterscape are connected and must be managed together, along with their related social and economic considerations. For example, the language of the Act must explicitly link drinking water, ground water, and surface water, just as they are linked in physical reality. The Act must also not avoid the thorny issue of funding, but rather undertake the difficult task of ensuring that those who benefit from watershed products and services also bear the cost. The Clean Water Act should be a visionary statement that gives national emphasis to the conservation and enhancement of watersheds because of the many important functions and values they provide, and it should give authority to the relevant agencies for implementing that goal.

CONCLUSIONS

In addition to stressing the importance of revising and reauthorizing the Clean Water Act, the committee offers the following thoughts about other mechanisms to steer the nation toward improved strategies for watershed management. These conclusions address the basic guiding philosophy, management processes, research, and support functions.

Guiding Philosophy

1. Watersheds as geographic areas are optimal organizing units for dealing with the management of water and closely related resources, but the natural boundaries of watersheds rarely coincide with political jurisdictions and thus they are less useful for political, institutional, and funding purposes. Initiatives and organizations directed at watershed management should be flexible to reflect the reality of these situations. (For more information, see Chapters 2, 6, and 8.)

2. Specific watershed problems must be approached in distinctive ways, and determining the appropriate scale for the resolution of any problem is an essential first step. Both the structure of watershed management organizations and the nature of the activities undertaken should be matched to the scale of the watershed. The range of stakeholders varies with scale and must be clearly defined so that the costs and benefits associated with any plan are fully taken into account.

Watershed approaches are easiest to implement at the local level; they can be most difficult to implement at large scales where the political, institutional, and funding decisionmaking grows especially complex. (For more information, see Chapters 2, 6, and 8.)

Management Processes

3. Risk and uncertainty are parts of the natural as well as institutional settings for watershed management, and they can limit the effectiveness of applying the watershed approach. One important need for advancing watershed management is to develop practical procedures for considering risk and uncertainty in real world decisionmaking. Scientists and managers should strive to educate the public by specifically outlining potential uncertainty so that expectations of research and decisionmaking are reasonable. (For more information, see Chapter 5.)

4. Watershed management plans should be viewed as the starting point and not the end product of a management cycle. The cycle should include formulation of a problem statement, identification of an agreed-upon set of goals, identification of the scope of activities appropriate to the issue in question, negotiated action steps, implementation, feedback, evaluation, and appropriate adjustments made as a result of lessons learned (i.e., adaptive management). (For more information: See Chapter 8.)

5. Scientific and technical peer review of watershed improvement activities conducted by qualified independent professionals can provide objective evaluations of their impact. Scientific or technical review groups can help design, carry out, and evaluate monitoring programs and help prioritize locations for intensive study. Such groups also can inform policymakers about the relative uncertainty associated with implementing management alternatives. (For more information, see Chapter 8.)

6. For too long, agencies have viewed their polices and projects in isolation. In their normal course of work, the U.S. Army Corps of Engineers, Bureau of Reclamation, U.S. Department of Agriculture, and Environmental Protection Agency should examine the watershed-wide implications of their policies, programs, rules, and permitting processes to take into account the regional and downstream ecological, social, and economic consequences of their actions, rather than using a limited project-by-project approach. (For more information, see Chapter 8.)

7. The committee was impressed with the information-gathering aspects of the Western Water Policy Review Advisory Commission. This kind of regionally based analysis of watershed resources provides a comprehensive evaluation

of the current management of American watersheds and guidance for the future, and should be duplicated for other regions as a means of gathering information and evaluating the potential of the watershed approach. (For more information, see Chapter 8.)

8. Watershed management seeks to develop careful, long-term solutions to problems and provide sustainable access to resources and thus it benefits the nation. The President and Congress should consider establishing some stable mechanism to fund the federal contribution to watershed management partnerships, such as a revenue-sharing strategy or trust fund. This funding should be available to state, regional, and local organizations for research, planning, implementation, and ongoing peer evaluation of watershed initiatives. (For more information, see Chapter 7.)

Scientific Research

9. Because water is a strategic national resource and sustainable use of water resources is a national priority, watershed management decisions must be based on the best possible science. More research is needed to provide the data, knowledge, and technology necessary to support effective watershed management, especially work focused on integrating social, economic, and ecological elements. There is a special need for research and monitoring that is long-term and integrated across scales and timeframes, as well as for specific problem-solving research and theory and model development. One specific step to greatly improve scientific understanding of watersheds is for Congress to increase funding for the National Science Foundation in areas that can improve understanding of the human dimensions of watersheds. Moreover, new problems and challenges such as human alteration of watersheds, volatile world economies, and global climate change will require new and innovative centers of research excellence in watershed science and management, and more effective technology transfer and leadership, at scales ranging from local to regional. (For more information, see Chapters 4, 5 and 6.)

10. Although our understanding of fundamental physical, biological, economic, and social processes needs improvement, an even greater need is improved understanding of how all these components operate together within watersheds. Watershed researchers should emphasize the integration of environmental, economic, and social perspectives, with more attention to the linkages and what they imply for management and overcoming barriers to implementation. Science and policy must function together for watershed management to be successful, so there also must be more attention to the role of politics in decisionmaking. (For more information, see Chapter 5.)

11. Process-oriented research is research that extends beyond description and measurement; it addresses structure, function, and the how and why of the processes operating within a watershed. Process-oriented research is particularly valuable because it leads to enhanced predictive capabilities, better understanding of cause-effect relationships, and a firmer foundation for planning and management. The National Science Foundation, Environmental Protection Agency, U.S. Geological Survey, U.S. Department of Agriculture, and other federal agencies involved in process-oriented watershed research should reorient their efforts to close critical information gaps that hamper effective implementation of watershed management. Important gaps include:

- linkages among watershed components (rivers, wetlands, ground water, atmosphere, floodplains, upland areas);
- integration across disciplines (especially biophysical and social sciences);
- feedback among processes operating at different spatial and temporal scales;
- inexpensive, useful indicators of watershed conditions and quantitative methods to evaluate land use and watershed management practices;
- advanced watershed simulation models (especially models that link natural and social attributes) that are useful to and can be operated by managers who are not scientific experts; and
- understanding of risk and uncertainty in the decisionmaking process. (For more information, see Chapter 4.)

12. A solid scientific foundation of basic and applied research is needed to provide the data, information, and tools necessary for effective implementation of watershed management activities. Federal resource management agencies should form partnerships with the National Science Foundation in jointly funded research, with agencies identifying critical areas needing investigation and NSF ensuring high quality, peer reviewed work in both short-term and long-term projects. Agencies might include the Forest Service, Bureau of Reclamation, Corps of Engineers, Bureau of Land Management, National Park Service, U.S. Geological Survey, and Tennessee Valley Authority. Universities and non-governmental research organizations can be key partners in this process. (For more information, see Chapter 4.)

Support Functions

13. The Federal Geographic Data Committee, as the organization charged with primary responsibility for establishing the National Spatial Data Infrastructure, should assume a leadership role in establishing a capability for collecting spatial data on watersheds by creating national data standards, designating a central clearinghouse, and maintaining a single national watershed database. Other

federal agencies should be encouraged to coordinate efforts and electronically link related databases. (For more information, see Chapter 4.)

14. Data collection efforts provide baseline information for increased scientific understanding of watershed processes, for analyses and interpretation of problems and causes, for assessing the status of watershed resources and detecting and predicting trends, and for decisionmaking in watershed management. Stream gaging and monitoring network design should emphasize adequate temporal resolution, sampling of storm events, measurement of appropriate ancillary hydrological and biogeochemical data (e.g., meteorological data with hydrological data or biological surveys with water quality parameters), and should use the highest possible quality of sampling and analysis. It is increasingly expensive to maintain data collection and monitoring efforts. As the U.S. Geological Survey, National Oceanic and Atmospheric Administration, and other federal and non-federal organizations engaged in collecting watershed data evaluate their monitoring sites, they should prioritize the remaining sites to ensure continuation of sites that are most effective in helping managers understand water quality trends. Particular emphasis should go to maintaining sites with exceptionally long-term records. In some instances, monitoring sites should be retained to provide adequate geographic representation, while some geographic areas with dense coverage might lose some sites without loss of data. Sampling schemes should be designed to answer specific questions about the status and trends of watershed resources rather than simply collect broad-based data. (For more information, see Chapters 3 and 4.)

15. Effective watershed management requires integration of theory, data, simulation models, and expert judgment to solve practical problems and provide a scientific basis for decisionmaking at the watershed scale. The engineering and scientific communities should develop better, more user-friendly decision support systems to help decisionmakers understand and evaluate alternative approaches. These improved approaches should help decisionmakers understand and convey the concepts of risk and uncertainty. A decision support system is a suite of computer programs with components consisting of databases, simulation models, decision models, and user interfaces that assist a decisionmaker in evaluating the economic and environmental impacts of competing watershed management alternatives. One of the technical challenges in developing decision support system technology for watershed management is linking models for all of the components of an extremely complex system to estimate the effect of management alternatives on all of the criteria of interest. (For more information, see Chapters 5 and 8.)

Two recurrent themes appeared throughout the committee's deliberations. First, one overarching lesson from the nation's long history of interest in watershed management is that "one size does not fit all." Watersheds in the United States reflect tremendous diversity of climatic conditions, geology, soils, and other factors that influence water flow, flora, and fauna. There is equally great variation in historical experiences, cultural expression, institutional arrangements, laws, policies, and attitudes. No single model could fit with all the existing governmental arrangements found at the state and local levels, and it would be a mistake to impose a standard model from the federal level.

Second, fragmentation of responsibility and lack of clarity about how to resolve disputes caused by conflicting missions among federal agencies inhibits the success of the watershed approach. For example, during the course of this study the committee identified 22 federal agencies that deal with the hydrologic cycle, although often with dramatically different perspectives. To the public, these confusing and sometimes conflicting approaches to water management are baffling. There is no one consistent voice for the water resource.

As an intellectual and organizational tool, watershed-scale management can be useful in many circumstances, especially for managing biological and geophysical resources and for local and some regional applications. The value of watershed management as a means for truly integrated efforts to achieve a balance of ecological, economic, and social goals remains a hypothesis that has not yet been completely proven. But flexible application of watershed principles can improve the joint efforts of researchers, managers, decisionmakers, and citizens in their search for a sustainable economy and a quality environment.

A spring-fed creek in Cunningham Falls State Park, Maryland, makes its way through a forested watershed in the Catoctin Mountains. Credit: USDA-Natural Resources Conservation Service.

1

Why Watersheds?

The belief that watersheds make a sound basis for water resources planning and management is not new, as evidenced by waves of scientific, policy, and public interest going back as far as the 1930s. Yet after many years of high expectations, the nation is still struggling to find ways to implement integrated management at the watershed level. Much of the science and technology needed to provide the underpinnings necessary for integrated water management already exists. Numerous scholarly reports have highlighted the potential benefits to be gained from a watershed approach. But we have fallen short in turning our understanding of watersheds and the benefits of integrated management into action. How can decisionmakers—given the complex social, economic, and environmental setting that is any watershed—put all the pieces together in support of a long-term vision that meets a variety of needs, both social and environmental? How do we judge where a watershed approach is appropriate, and how do we bring together the right mix of people and resources to make it happen?

The National Research Council formed the Committee on Watershed Management in 1996 at the request of a coalition of federal agencies with responsibilities related to watersheds.[1] The committee was asked to study the opportunities and constraints associated with watershed-scale management and provide water resource managers and planners with ideas to improve the implementation

[1]Funding for this study was provided by the Environmental Protection Agency, the Tennessee Valley Authority, the Natural Resources Conservation Service, the Bureau of Reclamation, the U.S. Biological Service (now part of the U.S. Geological Survey), the U.S. Forest Service, the McKnight Foundation, and the National Water Research Institute.

of watershed management activities. The committee reviewed the range of watershed-scale problems faced today; evaluated selected examples of watershed management to identify strengths, weaknesses, and opportunities; and explored the issue of scale in watershed management and the appropriate roles of federal, state, and local decisionmakers.

The committee's members brought a broad range of experience and expertise to this activity, but to broaden their perspective the members designed this study to include opportunities to talk to a wide range of people working on watershed issues. During the course of the committee's five meetings, we talked with grassroots organizations working to restore fisheries, build greenways, and reduce pollution; state and local officials responsible for day-to-day decisionmaking that affects both large and small watersheds; federal agency personnel striving to balance national and local interests; and members of the academic community who have spent years understanding how watersheds and the people and resources within them function. We visited watersheds in different regions and viewed different scales of activity. This report is the result of two years of effort, and while the committee is wholly responsible for the content and conclusions, we express our sincere thanks to the many people who contributed their time and thoughts (Appendix D). This chapter is a brief primer on watershed management, and includes definitions, descriptions of issues, and other overview material to set the stage for the more detailed discussions in later chapters.

The committee began its assessment of watershed management by posing as a hypothesis the proposition that watershed management is an effective method for integrating environmental, economic, and social aspects of water-related problem solving. Throughout our deliberations, we found ourselves returning to this hypothetical base. As will be seen in almost every chapter of this report, we found some evidence to support our hypothesis, but we also found much contrary evidence. In the end, as explored in Chapter 9, we find we cannot prove or disprove the assertion across the broad range of scales we considered, from small local watersheds to large river basins. We consider the assertion philosophically sound but hampered by uncertainty, especially at larger scales and more complex systems.

"WATERSHED THINKING"

There are many ways to define watersheds and watershed management. At the most basic level, a watershed is "a region or area bounded peripherally by a water parting and draining ultimately to a particular watercourse or body of water" (Webster, 1994). Watershed management is a broad concept incorporating the plans, policies, and activities used to control water and related resources and processes in a given watershed. Watershed management activities can range from hands-on guidance to farmers about how to control runoff to multistate initiatives like those under way to improve the health of the Chesapeake Bay.

Watershed management has taken on a large, complex meaning. For instance, the Environmental Protection Agency (USEPA) has been instrumental in developing what has come to be called a "watershed protection approach" (USEPA, 1993), the principles of which provide a solid foundation for watershed thinking. According to this model, watershed management should be an integrated, holistic problem-solving strategy used to restore and maintain the physical, chemical, and biological integrity of aquatic ecosystems, protect human health, and provide sustainable economic growth. It focuses on hydrologically defined drainage basins—watersheds—rather than on areas defined by political boundaries. A watershed encompasses not only the water resource, such as a stream, river, lake, estuary, wetland, aquifer, or coastal zone, but all the land that drains into that resource. The appropriate scale of a watershed management unit depends on the physical, political, and resource conditions of the area of interest.

A watershed management approach typically has several distinguishing characteristics, including:

• It seeks to balance the institutional objectives of the federal, state, and local agencies operating within the watershed to achieve a balanced strategy for the particular area of interest.

• Its decisionmaking processes strive to involve the full range of relevant stakeholders and to use consultation and consensus-building techniques to reach a broadly supported plan that reflects a negotiated balance of interests.

• It uses sound, scientifically based information from an array of disciplines to understand the factors influencing the aquatic and terrestrial ecosystem, human health, and economic conditions of the watershed.

• It attempts to design and use cost-effective methods that are funded by fair cost-share contributions of the stakeholders within the area of interest so that the cost of the projects, both in terms of financial resources and impacts on stakeholders, are distributed in proportion to the benefits received by the different stakeholders.

• It creates a framework of intergovernmental and interagency agreements that guarantee implementation of the plans developed in the decision-making process and which rely on a partnership approach rather than laws or ordinances.

• It includes steps to evaluate the effects of watershed management with easily defined measurements and standards.

USEPA's watershed approach has three major cornerstones. First is problem identification, which identifies the primary threats to human and ecosystem health within the watershed. Second is stakeholder involvement, which involves the people most likely to be concerned or most able to take action. And third is the integration of actions, that is, corrective efforts taken in a comprehensive, integrated manner once solutions are determined. The approach evaluates success and refines actions as necessary (USEPA, 1993).

USEPA views this approach as placing a heavy emphasis on the many elements that affect water quality, including chemical composition (toxics and conventional pollutants), physical water quality (temperature, flow, and circulation), habitat quality (channel morphology, composition, and health of biologic communities), and biodiversity (species number and range). The approach encompasses all waters—surface and ground, inland and coastal—and is seen as a framework for integrating existing programs (USEPA, 1993). Chapter 8 contains more discussion of USEPA's watershed approach.

The National Resource Conservation Service (NRCS) (formerly the Soil Conservation Service or SCS) also has been heavily involved in developing watershed management approaches. The NRCS approach provides ecosystem-based assistance to its clients (mostly farmers), and focuses on scientific management of natural systems and processes. Ecosystems are defined in space and time with subsystems that address inputs, processes, and outputs. This ability to conceptually nest smaller ecosystems within larger ecosystems offers tremendous flexibility. One method of nesting is along defined hydrologic boundaries, where ecosystems can be nested from subfield to field to large watershed. However, NRCS also advocates using functional boundaries that recognize socioeconomic, political, and legal constraints as a framework for analyzing ecosystem conditions and delivering technical and financial assistance to clients. The NRCS planning process encourages public involvement in identifying problems, evaluating the effects of alternative solutions, and implementing actions at the appropriate level (SCS, 1994).

The advantages of the NRCS approach is that it creates awareness of the interrelationships that sustain life, considers the effects of its planned actions over time, at interrelated scales (e.g., in large and small watersheds, interconnected planning areas, farms, fields, etc.), and considers interactions among the soil, water, air, plant, animal, and human resources to achieve environmentally and economically sustainable use of natural resources. NRCS calls for an interdisciplinary approach that recognizes risk or uncertainty while still acting on the best available science and technology. The goal is to help clients sustain and or enhance ecosystems in harmony with social, cultural, and economic considerations (SCS, 1994). Chapter 8 contains more on NRCS's watershed planning approach.

As seen in both the USEPA and NRCS efforts, watershed thinking puts great emphasis on involving stakeholders in both identifying issues and problems and creating and implementing solutions (see Box 1.1). Stakeholders include all those people, groups, corporations, local governments, and state and federal agencies that have some authority over the watershed or its processes, or interest in its condition. In the past, when government alone tried to solve the problems, it often created resistance from the people who lived, earned their living, or recreated in the watershed. Individuals and groups often lacked the resources or authority to accomplish their goals for the watershed. Only by bringing all these groups together in a collaborative planning effort can lasting agreements be reached that restore or prevent further degradation of the watershed.

MANAGING WATERSHEDS TO BENEFIT PEOPLE

Since passage of the Clean Water Act, the federal government has invested more than $100 million to improve the quality of the nation's waters. Despite this investment, which focused on point discharge of pollutants, the goal of swimmable and fishable waters has not been attained for all surface water bodies. The remaining problems stem primarily from nonpoint sources, related mainly to farms, transportation systems, and urban runoff. Such uses greatly influence the quality and quantity of the water resource, emphasizing the need for a geographically anchored or place-based approach to water quality.

The nation also needs a more productive approach to both the quality and quantity of its ground water supplies. Ground water quality impacts surface water quality because most of the base flow of rivers and streams is from ground water, springs, and seeps. And surface waters percolate into ground water through wetlands, recharge areas, and stream bottoms. The frequent interchange between surface and ground water ensures that what pollutes one pollutes the other. The more we learn about the paths water travels—over land, picking up sediments and pollutants, underground, dissolving salts and minerals, sitting in lakes and ponds, dropping sediment in wetlands, and being aerated in streams running over rocks—the more we appreciate the complexity of the interactions.

Because many of the problems leading to water pollution are complex and interrelated, many piecemeal attempts to specific problems have actually exacerbated or created other problems. Watershed-based approaches offer a more integrated way to address these issues. Comprehensive management programs can affect the full range of goods and services that watersheds provide. These benefits include water supply, water quality, flood control, sediment control, navigation, hydroelectric power generation, fisheries, biodiversity, habitat preservation, and recreation. These various purposes are often intertwined, and they can at times be in competition. To some extent, the purposes for which a watershed can be managed are controlled by the physical environment. Beyond that, the choice of benefits desired is made based on human needs and societal goals—a situation that sets the stage for a complex and sometimes contentious process.

Water Supplies

As the receiver, collector, and conveyer of precipitation, the watershed is a logical central component of management efforts to provide adequate water supplies to users. Land uses in the watershed directly affect how much and how quickly water runs off the surface into downstream rivers and reservoirs. The importance of watersheds to urban water supplies has long been recognized in the

Box 1.1
Involving Stakeholders:
The Phalen Chain of Lakes Watershed Project

The Phalen Chain of Lakes watershed project illustrates an effort that integrates the interests of a wide range of stakeholders. Located in the northeast section of St. Paul, Minn., in the Mississippi River basin, it is a 25-square-mile (40.225 sq. km.) urban watershed that has undergone a comprehensive planning process to develop an integrated resource management plan. The plan addresses water quality, wetland protection, vegetation and wildlife management, fisheries, and river corridor protection and restoration. The effort is governed by a citizen-based steering committee composed of local elected officials and commissioners, lakeshore owners, business representatives, environmental organizations, and neighborhood representatives. While the initial project partners included the Ramsey-Washington Metro Watershed District, the Minnesota Department of Natural Resources, the City of St. Paul, and the University of Minnesota Department of Landscape Architecture, it now also includes seven city governments and two counties. A technical advisory committee, composed of city and county staff from involved resource agencies, was

United States, especially in relatively dry western areas where cities depend on water originating in distant mountain areas. The demand for water has become so great that local supplies have been augmented by water imported from hundreds of miles away (NRC, 1992). Some eastern cities rely on similar arrangements, such as New York City's use of water from upstate watersheds. In fact, one of the initial justifications for establishing national forest reserves (now called National Forests) included watershed management to protect downstream urban water supplies.

Abundant water fuels the U.S. economy and standard of living. Public water systems provide about 160 gallons per person per day, for a total of approximately 40 billion gallons. In 50 years, water demand is expected to be 50 billion gallons per day if per capita use remains constant. At the household level, a typical family of four each day uses 10 gallons for drinking and cooking, 15 gallons for dish washing, 98 gallons for toilets, 80 gallons for bathing, 35 gallons for laundry, and 100 gallons for watering the lawn and car washing. This comes

formed to help assemble information and comment on issues and recommendations of the steering committee. Planning funding was provided
by the McKnight Foundation and in-kind services from agencies and the
Watershed District.

The planning process identified seven major issues of priority to the
stakeholders: declining water quality, loss of wetlands, need for ecosystem-
level management, reduced biodiversity, need for balance between natural resources protection and growth, recreation, and conflicts between levels of government. A seven-point action plan was developed:

1. Improve, restore, and protect water quality in area lakes, wetlands,
and creeks.
2. Improve, restore, and protect wetlands and creeks on a watershed
basis.
3. Manage land use in the watershed to protect ground water resources and local drinking water supplies.
4. Develop a corridor system that links the wetlands, creeks, lakes,
parks, and natural areas in the watershed.
5. Restore and expand the urban forest and diversify plant communities to protect water quality and increase biodiversity.
6. Increase public awareness and involvement in improving water
quality and natural resources in the watershed.
7. Establish a local watershed natural resources advisory board to
promote and monitor implementation of the plan.

to 338 gallons per day, or 84.5 gallons per day per person. In arid regions the per
capita use is higher due to use of water in cooling and higher needs for lawn
watering and gardening (Naiman et al., 1995).

Water is an indispensable component of industrial production. About
100,000 gallons of water are required to produce one automobile, 60,000 gallons
to produce a ton of steel, and 280 gallons to produce one Sunday newspaper
(World Resources Institute, 1992).

Water is also critical to agriculture. While irrigation is concentrated in western states, it is remarkably widespread, from Hawaii's sugar fields to the rice
fields of Arkansas to southern Florida's truck gardens. In the 1980s, irrigation
accounted for 1 of every 8 acres under cultivation and nearly $4 of every $10 of
the value of crop production (U.S. Department of Agriculture, 1986). And while
irrigation occurs on just 14.8 percent of all harvested cropland, that cropland
produces 37.8 percent of the value of U.S. crops (Bajwa et al., 1992). Care should
be taken, however, not to equate consumptive use with water withdrawals. Not

all water withdrawn is consumed; in fact, much is returned to the system as return flows and reused downstream. So even if conservation practices are adopted and withdrawals are reduced by a significant amount, it does not necessarily hold that this "conserved" water is available for reallocation.

Water Quality

Water quality is a reflection of the chemical, physical, and biological constituents that are suspended or dissolved in the water. These constituents are contributed by both natural processes and human activities. Natural factors that influence water quality include geology, soils, topography, vegetation, wildlife populations, and climate. But far more important in causing most water quality problems are human activities and land use in the watershed (see Box 1.2).

Water quality problems and our progress in combating them vary considerably around the nation. Overall, significant strides have been made over the past 30 years in ameliorating water quality problems caused by point sources, largely as a result of the Clean Water Act. Sources of contamination include point sources, such as municipal wastewater and industrial discharges. But little progress has been achieved to combat nonpoint sources, such as agricultural cropland, livestock, urban development, forest management, mining, recreation, roads, and atmospheric deposition. On a national scale, nonpoint sources are responsible for most of the contaminants introduced to waterways (Robbins et al., 1991)—so much so that to many people the term watershed management means primarily the management of nonpoint pollution, although this report takes a broader view.

Flood Control

The United States has a long history of managing watersheds to reduce problems caused by floods, primarily via engineering structures such as dams, levees, and reservoirs. In fact, providing reliable water supplies and concurrent protection against floods was perhaps the most important motivator of this nation's earliest watershed management efforts. But rapid accumulation of runoff from storms or snowmelt also can be controlled at least in part by upland land-use practices, riparian zone management, and other strategies. Integrated approaches to watershed management that include attention to source areas and protection of wetland areas offer real potential as a tool in the flood protection toolbox.

Sediment Control

Stream sedimentation caused by the erosion of surface materials is a significant chemical and physical issue for any watershed management effort. Sediment can affect water quality, natural habitat, navigation, flood control, and recreational uses of the downstream reaches of the watershed. Accordingly, federal and state regulations consider sediment to be a pollutant, despite the fact that it is a natural component of functional rivers. Many chemical pollutants adhere to the surfaces of sedimentary particles, so that sediment-rich discharges usually carry higher loadings of pollution than water alone. The sediment itself also poses problems for the physical integrity of streams because it fills downstream reservoirs, consuming space that was originally designed to store water. Sedimentation in channels alters their configuration and destabilizes them, making management and use more difficult as well as increasing their flood potential as channel capacity is reduced. Sedimentation also affects fish by silting over gravel beds necessary for spawning and covering benthic organisms important in the food chain.

Navigation

Many American waterways serve as transportation corridors for large quantities of bulk goods. For instance, the Ohio, Missouri, and Mississippi rivers have huge upstream service areas to ocean ports and carry barge traffic of coal, grain, natural gas, and other bulk commodities. The system of dams and locks that makes this commerce possible requires a consistent flow of water made possible only by basinwide management. On the Columbia River system, and many others, barge traffic must compete for management attention with fisheries, recreational, and hydroelectric objectives. The resolution of such competition among uses must take into account local as well as national interests.

Economic Development with Hydroelectric Power

The United States has long used watershed management to accomplish economic development goals, primarily but not exclusively in the West. That is, we have used construction of large dams and associated structures to provide water and water-dependent services (e.g., drinking water, irrigation water, and power) to our citizens, first to encourage people to settle the West and through time to sustain the farms and industry of western communities. Hydroelectric power generation is a classic example. At least two large efforts—the Tennessee Valley Authority (TVA) in the southeast and the Bonneville Power Administration (BPA) in the Pacific Northwest—originated during the Great Depression and were part of a vast federal initiative to restore economic vitality. The spirit of these programs was captured in the words of folk singer Woody Guthrie, who in 1941 wrote the following on commission for BPA about the new Columbia hydropower system (Lee, 1993):

> . . . roll along, Columbia, you can ramble to the sea,
> But river, while you're rambling, you can do some work for me.
> . . . Lots of folks around the country,

Box 1.2
A Model of Success in Watershed Management:
The Flathead River-Lake Ecosystem

Watershed management has been the centerpiece of community-based efforts to protect water quality in the Flathead River Basin in north-western Montana and Southeastern British Columbia, Canada. Some 42 percent of this 22,250 km^2 water-shed is virtually pristine because of its location in Glacier National Park and adjacent National Forest wilderness areas. The remainder is extensively roaded for timber harvest, and the very scenic valley bottoms contain large tracts of agricultural lands, which are rapidly becoming semi-urban. The sixth order Flathead River discharges a mean annual flow of 360 cms into 480 km^2 Flathead Lake, which is the largest lake in the western United States and has extremely high quality water on par with Lake Superior and Lake Tahoe.

In 1977, research was initiated to determine potential impacts of a coal strip mine in British Columbia on water resources downstream in Montana. Concern about mining impacts on native trout and nutrient and metal pollution prompted funding from the Environmental Protection Agency to a local board composed of agency heads, tribal and community leaders, and private citizens. This watershed management board, which later was designated the Flathead Basin Commission (FBC) by the Montana legislature, coordinated funding of water quality monitoring and research and mediated public participation in the watershed manage-

Politicians and such,
Said the old Columbia wouldn't 'mount to much.
But with all their figures and all their books
Them boys didn't know their Royal Chinooks.
. . . It's a good river.
Just needs a couple more dozen big power dams
Scattered up and down it,
Keepin' folks busy.
. . . Well the folks need houses and stuff to eat,

ment effort. The mine plan was scrapped when the high likelihood of severe pollution of the pristine waters of the Flathead was demonstrated. The FBC continued to coordinate management efforts to reduce nutrient loading to Flathead Lake from human sources.

Three interactive threats to water quality have been demonstrated through research conducted by the University of Montana Flathead Lake Biological Station: eutrophication from nutrient loading, food web change caused by introduction of non-native biota, and flow and lake level regulation by hydroelectric dams on Flathead Lake and the South Fork of the Flathead River. Eutrophication has been curtailed substantially by a 10 percent reduction in the Flathead Lake nutrient load as a result of construction of urban sewage treatment systems with nutrient removal technologies, a basinwide ban on sale of phosphorus-containing detergents, and encouragement of best management practices for timbering and agriculture. The FBC adopted total maximum daily load targets for Flathead Lake to reduce nonpoint loading by at least 30 percent. State legislation now forbids introduction of non-native fishes, and the large dams are being retrofitted and reregulated to minimize downstream effects of hydropower operations. The National Park Service received a federal reserve water right under an unprecedented agreement with the state that protects in perpetuity the virgin flow of the north and middle forks of the Flathead River.

Successful watershed conservation and management in the Flathead was largely a product of proactive and voluntary actions mediated by the FBC and other citizen-based organizations, and by the use of basic research on ecosystem processes to demonstrate threats and solutions. More information may be obtained from the FBC at the Office of the Governor, Helena, Montana, or from the Flathead Lake Biological Station web page (http://www.umt.edu/biology/flbs).

And the folks need metals and the folks need wheat.
Folks need water and power dams.
And folks need people and people need the land.
. . . This whole big Pacific Northwest up here out to be run,
The way I see it,
By electri-sigh-tee.

The generation of hydroelectric power requires a dependable water supply that can be released from control and storage structures on demand. Because of the need for significant infrastructure and careful operation, hydroelectric power generation is generally compatible with two other watershed benefits—provision of water supplies and flood protection. But hydroelectric power is not always compatible with other watershed objectives. For instance, depending on the design and operation of the facilities, a dam often creates a stretch of river below it with little or no water present until the water is returned from the bypass structures, thus eliminating fish habitat and recreation. Dams also create barriers to the upstream migration of species such as salmon, and fish ladders and other methods for moving populations upstream are less than ideal. Upstream, dams create flatwater reservoirs where moving water species once lived. Downstream, fish populations can change, and native species can be threatened with extinction, because the water released from dams may be much colder or different in other ways from pre-dam conditions.

Dam operation also can have environmental effects. Many dams operate to produce what is called "peaking power," that is, they produce power only when it is most needed—a practice that causes rapid and sometimes major fluctuations in flows. For instance, the Colorado River below Glen Canyon Dam has seen river level fluctuations up to 13 feet per day in the Grand Canyon, leading to accelerated erosion of beaches and loss of critical habitat along the river corridor. Beach replacement is slow because the sediment that once muddied the river is trapped above the dam; native species like the humpback chub are endangered because of the many changes to the environment (NRC, 1996a). As a result of careful study and societal pressure, in 1996 Glen Canyon Dam operators released an experimental high flow designed to rectify some of these problems, and early indications are that future operation of the dam will be altered to better balance the benefits and costs of the dam.

Biodiversity

Scientific studies of terrestrial and aquatic ecosystems during the last two decades have drastically altered our understanding of their composition, structure, function, and complexity (Franklin, 1992), and increased our awareness of the value of biodiversity in ecosystems. As explained by the noted scientist E.O. Wilson (Wilson, 1988):

> The diversity of life forms, so numerous that we have yet to identify most of them, is the greatest wonder of this planet. . . . Biological diversity must be treated more seriously as a global resource, to be indexed, used, and above all, preserved. Three circumstances conspire to give this matter an unprecedented urgency. First, exploding human populations are degrading the environment at an accelerating rate, especially in tropical countries. Second, science is discovering new uses for biological diversity in ways that can relieve both human suffering and environmental destruction. Third, much of the diversity is being irreversibly lost through extinction caused by the destruction of natural habitats. . . .

From a watershed perspective, riparian habitats in particular have come to be seem as diverse and essential habitats for many organisms and processes, and they provide a critical link between aquatic and upland ecosystems. Riparian vegetation, for instance, controls much of the environmental regime of stream ecosystems (although this is less true of larger streams and rivers), and plays a vital role in determining the quantity and timing of flows as well as stream temperature, which is strongly influenced by shadows cast by riparian vegetation. Riparian zones are the source of woody debris, an extremely important structural component of the aquatic ecosystem; such debris creates a structural complexity vital to the stream's ability to store sediments, detain water, and create a variety of specialized habitats supporting biological diversity. Wetlands play similar important roles in maintaining biodiversity and watershed processes.

Watershed management can be used as a tool to enhance wildlife objectives, one element of ecological diversity. Although not relevant in all cases, watershed planning can include attempts to avoid degradation of critical wildlife habitat or restore habitat lost to past decisions. For example, the current phase of relicensing nonfederal hydropower facilities now gives attention to restoring minimum water flows below dams where appropriate, thus restoring fish habitat. Communities rehabilitating waterways through urban areas often attempt to restore fish habitat, for instance by placing logs or other debris in strategic locations to serve as cover for fish.

The artificial introduction of exotic species, in some cases for the express purposes of manipulating watershed processes such as erosion, can have a negative effect on ecological diversity. Kudzu and water hyacinths in the southeastern United States, tamarisk in Western states, purple loosetrife in New England, arrundo in California, and Russian olive in many sections of the country were well-intentioned introductions that have escaped control and now infest many watersheds in undesirable densities, eliminating native species and reducing overall diversity.

Increased attention to diversity and the related issue of habitat protection often calls for making hard decisions about trade-offs involving other watershed benefits—for instance, accepting some lost power opportunities in exchange for increased flows below dams.

Fishes and Other Aquatic Biota

Overall the threat to aquatic biodiversity in North American is great. In the United States, aquatic organisms are among the nation's most imperiled (Table 1.1). Of the entire flora and fauna, the four groups with the greatest percentage of species currently extinct or at risk of extinction are aquatic.

Our nation's historical approach to managing of watershed resources has reduced the populations of native fishes in American streams. New England mill dams eliminated shad runs on many streams by the early 1800s, and two thirds of

TABLE 1.1   The Percent of Species of Conservation Concern (Vulnerable, Imperiled, Critically Imperiled, or Extinct) in Each of 13 Major Plant and Animal Groups in the United States.

	Percent of Species Currently at Risk
Fresh Water mussels	67.9 %
Crayfish	50.9 %
Amphibians	40.5 %
Fresh Water fishes	38.7 %
Flowering plants	33.3 %
Conifers	26.1 %
Ferns	21.6 %
Tiger beetles	20.0 %
Dragonflies/damselflies	18.4 %
Reptiles	18.0 %
Butterflies/skippers	16.8 %
Mammals	16.5 %
Birds	14.6 %

NOTE: Italics denote groups requiring fresh water for all or part of their life cycles.
SOURCE: Reprint, with permission, from Stein and Flack, 1997. © 1997 by The Nature Conservancy.

the species of the Illinois River watershed had experienced elimination or declines by 1850. By 1950, the fish catch in the Illinois system had declined nearly to zero (Doppelt et al., 1993). In the Southwest, conversion of sections of warm, sediment-laden streams to cool, clear water conditions by the installation of numerous large dams has eliminated or endangered all the native fishes, and in the Pacific Northwest, the annual salmon catch in some systems has plummeted from millions to thousands of fish in the past few decades because of the impoundment of millions of acre-feet of water behind extensive dam systems and because of poor watershed management (NRC, 1996b).

Despite a nationwide effort to improve water quality sparked by passage of the Clean Water Act in 1972, of the 251 species of fish classed as being at risk of extinction in 1979, none were removed from the list by 1989 except those that actually became extinct (Williams et al., 1989). To date, not a single aquatic species has been delisted through Endangered Species Act procedures because of implementation of a successful recovery plan. The majority of listed aquatic species do not even have formalized recovery plans.

Many factors, usually in combination, have contributed to the decline of aquatic organisms. Some of the most important include habitat loss (migration blockages, draining and filling, impounding rivers, diversion of flow to other watersheds, channelization, and other effects of human activities) and exotic species introductions. Miller et al. (1989) estimated the relative importance of different factors to the extinction of North American fishes and estimated that habitat alteration was a major factor in 73 percent of the cases of extinction of native North American fishes; introduced species were a factor in 68 percent, water pollution a factor in 38 percent, hybridization in 38 percent, and overfishing in 15 percent.

Over geologic time periods, fish populations evolved in response to prevailing watershed conditions, including seasonal variations in flow, sediment concentrations, streambed particle sizes, riparian vegetation, and water chemistry. Land uses, engineering structures, and water management have altered all these basic conditions. Naiman et al. (1995) estimate that wetlands in the United States have declined by 40 to 60 percent, and riparian forests along approximately 70 percent of the rivers have been lost or severely altered. It is only through integrated watershed management addressing these varied influences that fisheries can be improved and restored to desirable levels.

Habitat Preservation

Most watersheds in the United States have been altered by human activities, with only five percent of the surface area still in its original natural condition, and about 2.5 percent in designated wilderness areas. Preserved watersheds serve multiple purposes, including recreation, the protection of wildlife habitat, and the filtration and storage of water. Wilderness areas in the Colorado Rockies, for example, yield water for the urbanized Front Range cities such as Denver while also serving as major outdoor recreation areas. Pursuit of preservation in mountain or upstream watersheds is fairly straightforward, but the issue becomes more complex when considering the Wild and Scenic River system, where some river segments are developed while others downstream are designated as wild. Preserving some segments is difficult because they receive pollutants and altered hydrologic regimes from upstream areas not managed primarily for preservation.

Preserve boundaries rarely conform to watershed boundaries, with political considerations playing an important role. A cursory examination of boundaries in the National Park system suggests that parks are usually centered around a landscape feature of interest, such as a mountain range, rather than drainage basins. However, there are some exceptions; for example, Great Basin National Park, and the designation by the Forest Ecosystem Management and Assessment Team (FEMAT, 1993) of 162 "key watersheds" covering 8.7 million acres in the Pacific Northwest in which conservation of spotted owls and aquatic resources was given priority over other development activities on federal lands.

Recreation

Water provides a great range of recreational opportunities that can be enhanced by watershed management. For instance, upstream watershed management activities designed to help ensure adequate supplies and protect water quality can also benefit downstream reservoirs, increasing their value for flatwater recreation such as boating and fishing. Similarly, hydroelectric facilities can be operated in a way that balances economic and recreation values—for example, scheduling releases of whitewater flows on weekends when paddlers most desire access and when power demands are low, or requiring minimum flows below dams to maintain recreational fisheries. While managing watersheds to accomplish such goals may involve land-use decisions, dam operating rules and licenses, and other complex social and institutional issues, recreation's social and economic importance make it a "stakeholder" in any integrated watershed planning effort.

BARRIERS AND CHALLENGES TO IMPLEMENTATION

Although watershed planning and management offers great potential and can draw on a technical foundation that has evolved tremendously in recent years, implementation has proven extremely difficult. Some of the reasons for this include (Heaney, 1993):

- Watershed planning, and planning in general, is often perceived as a static process that leads to the formulation and adoption of a restrictive master plan. Groups of people, especially those with diverse interests, can seldom agree to accept a master plan that will bind them to a single course of action.
- Watershed boundaries typically do not coincide with political boundaries, creating problems in establishing a watershed authority or commission.
- Planning models often have been based on weak databases, and thus the results were not realistic and had little credibility.
- Watershed planning involves great complexity, especially when environmental impacts are included (see Box 1.3).
- The planning process is slow, and people grow impatient waiting for answers, agreement, and especially action.

Any efforts to manage resources at a watershed level must account for and try to overcome these challenges.

In addition, both the national movement toward watershed management and any individual watershed-level efforts must deal with the fragmentation of authority that is still common in the water resources field. Different federal agencies that play a role in water resource decision-making have different agency goals. For instance, on a federal level, the Environmental Protection Agency is concerned about water quality under the Safe Drinking Water Act, and "fishable and swimmable" issues under the Clean Water Act. The U.S. Army Corps of Engineers concerns itself with navigation, flood control, and wetlands preservation. The Bureau of Reclamation develops and delivers water supplies and hydropower in western states. The Natural Resources Conservation Service is con-

---

Box 1.3
The Chesapeake Bay: Watershed Management Meets
Airshed-Scale Problems

The restoration of the Chesapeake Bay has been the focus of intense effort over the last 20 years. The hydrologic watershed covers 64,000 square miles (102,979 sq. km.), encompassing parts of the states of New York, Delaware, Pennsylvania, Maryland, Virginia, and all of Washington, D.C. Three of these states, (VA, MD, PA) and the District of Columbia, together with the USEPA, have joined together in a cooperative effort to clean up the Bay. They have set a goal to reduce the phosphorus and nitrogen entering the Bay by 40 percent. Each state has planned its own approach to meet the goal, using techniques such as a ban on phosphates in detergents; vegetated buffers along streams, wetlands, and bay edges; and more stringent regulations on septic tank placement and operation. But when the Chesapeake Bay Commission modeled the nutrient inputs from the various land and water sources and compared them to the amounts found in the Bay, they could not balance the equation. Researchers finally realized that the unaccounted for nitrogen (25-33 percent) was coming from air pollution.

The airshed for the Chesapeake Bay covers 350,000 square miles (563,150 sq. km.) and ranges north to Ontario, to Indiana, and to Tennessee and North Carolina. Atmospheric deposition is also the Bay's leading source of toxic pollutants such as zinc, lead, and mercury. The smallest particles, which are not regulated at this point and which carry the greatest concentration of toxics, are washed out of the air by rain. This enriched rainwater falls directly into the Bay as well as onto the land that drains into the Bay.

This illustrates the difficulty of defining boundaries when dealing with environmental problems. What are the boundaries that we need to be concerned with if we are working to restore the Chesapeake Bay to a healthy aquatic system with an abundance of crab, oysters, and rock fish?

---

cerned with soil erosion within small watersheds, particularly agricultural areas. And the U.S. Fish and Wildlife Service is responsible for enforcing the Endangered Species Act, and is concerned about the health of natural aquatic and terrestrial communities. Often these agencies disagree with one another on the correct approach to managing water resources. They compete with one another for federal dollars to carry out their missions. Often the states, local governments, tribes, and private parties are caught between these federal agencies, and rarely is there a path of action that satisfies all.

FRAGMENTATION OF AUTHORITY AND FUNDING

Fragmentation of decision-making is not limited to the federal level. The problem is mirrored in the states with competing agencies such as water quality regulators, wildlife agencies, public health agencies, and land management agencies. Frequently, for management purposes ground water is separated from surface water, point sources are treated separately from nonpoint sources of pollution, and watershed impacts from agriculture, forestry, and mining are addressed by separate agencies. Local governments may have departments that deal with different aspects of water resources, with one department for drinking water and another for wastewater, and still another for wetlands and riparian areas. Local governments must often depend on the science that comes from the federal government, follow state and federal laws and regulations, and seek funds from a myriad of sources to help them solve their water resource problems. Private enterprises must obtain permits from local, state, or federal government agencies, or even all three. Identifying solutions to management problems that are satisfactory as well as economically feasible to all these groups is difficult.

A continuum of regulatory interest thus runs from the federal government through the state to the local entities. Each has its sphere of influence over land and water resources. Each has strengths and weaknesses in its ability to deal with all the aspects of a watershed system. Integrating this continuum into the reality of the physical resource and political context is an unmet challenge.

Funding of watershed projects is also fragmented and complicated. A number of federal and state programs make some funds available for watershed-level planning and implementation, but the funds are often narrowly focused leaving many needs unmet. Local governments experience considerable difficulty balancing the equation of who pays and who benefits. Headwaters communities are reluctant to pay for projects that primarily benefit those downstream. Communities in the lower reaches of watersheds may be willing to contribute to headwaters projects, but if the effort is in a different county, state, or even country, legal arrangements may prohibit such investments. Similarly, when multiple jurisdictions benefit from a project, contributions can be complicated. Some watershed groups have been organized with taxing authority that cuts across jurisdictions, but such arrangements are uncommon and not necessarily a panacea for funding problems.

As interest in the watershed approach grows and the problems of water quality and quantity increase, there are more cooperative efforts to solve these challenges. Problem identification is usually the first, and easiest, step. Defining feasible and achievable goals and moving to the planning stage are more difficult. Measurements and assessments of outcomes are rare. Many watershed projects require several years of effort, a time period that may outlast the terms of important elected officials or funding.

WHY WATERSHEDS AGAIN?

Given these challenges why revisit the watershed approach now? Do we really possess new ideas, tools, and opportunities available today that we lacked in the past? Many past watershed efforts met with limited success, so what is different this time around? The committee believes that a combination of factors have coalesced to spark renewed interest today. These include (Heaney, 1993):

• frustration with the fragmented "command and control" approach that has been in favor for more than a decade;
• a significant shift of power, with nonfederal entities emerging as important partners due at least in part to the federal government's withdrawal of financial support for planning activities;
• growing concern over cost-effectiveness, especially with regard to environmental management and in light of tight budgets;
• related planning approaches that have demonstrated success, such as in the electric energy field where integrated resources planning is an accepted approach; and
• growing realization that decentralized water markets can be an effective alternative to central control over water allocation.

The committee believes that these and other changes make this an especially propitious point in the evolution of watershed management. First, the scientific foundation necessary to build watershed activities has advanced greatly, both in the depth and breadth of information and in the tools and techniques of analysis available. Perhaps more important, public awareness of watershed issues has increased, as has the public's desire to participate in decision-making. Changes in government funding mechanisms and new methods for conflict resolution also increase interest in a watershed approach. This means that a watershed approach can offer real help to decision-makers working in ever more complex settings.

Increased Public Awareness

The public's interest in environmental protection, signaled by the first Earth Day in 1970, has provided a political and funding base that has created many changes in the nation's laws and in people's behavior. The nation underwent an unprecedented shift in values, and calls for a cleaner, safer environment continue, along with an apparent willingness to pay the necessary costs. Political efforts made in the mid-1990s to relax environmental standards provoked a backlash. Public opinion polls consistently indicate a widespread interest in enhancing and protecting the environment. Public interest and support are especially necessary if we are to produce new successes in watershed management, since nonpoint source pollution reduction, water conservation, and aquatic habitat protection will require broadly based activity at the grassroots level.

New Technical Tools

Watershed-level environmental management may be desirable, but it often has been impractical because of the complexity of integrating biological, hydrological, chemical, economic, and social considerations into decision-making, particularly at large scales. Many recent developments, however, allow faster and better gathering, organization, and manipulation of data. Remote sensing from satellites allows land use and land cover to be analyzed with relative ease and great accuracy. Locations in the field can be specified within a few meters rapidly and cheaply, thanks to Global Positioning Systems (GPS). Automated sampling and analytical methods can provide fine-resolution data of high quality, and telemetry can pass this information to users in real time. Geographic Information Systems (GIS) allow for storage, manipulation, and visualization of large and complex data sets. Many of these tools have been combined with field expertise in a technique called Rapid Ecological Assessments, which provide quick but relatively complete pictures of the system being studied. GIS also makes spatially distributed modeling accessible to a much larger segment of the management community, and the maps produced can be understood by the general public.

The power and ease of use of computers is another dramatic advance. For instance, there are now software programs for stormwater modeling, surface water modeling, groundwater modeling, and watershed modeling that provide guidance on water quality and quantity, erosion, and sediment transport. Finally, the expansion of the Internet and the World Wide Web greatly facilitate the dissemination of information.

Governmental Funding

Unprecedented cost-cutting by the federal government in recent years has led to the restructuring of several agencies with key water resource responsibilities. In some instances, tight budgets have hampered watershed management efforts. For example, reductions in the scope of the USGS monitoring of water quality and quantity is creating a serious data gap to emerge (see Chapter 5). At the same time, however, restructuring may provide an opportunity to enhance watershed management, as agencies realign to prevent duplication. Restructuring therefore may provide an opportunity to remodel some activities along watershed lines within or among agencies. The USEPA has already reorganized some programs with an explicit watershed focus, and significant changes in agencies like the NRCS and Army Corps of Engineers allow them to address issues on a watershed level.

New Approaches to Conflict Resolution

Much has been learned over the past two decades about how to mediate environmental and other public policy disputes, and alternative dispute resolution has grown into an important tool in a wide variety of resource-management planning activities. Increasingly, environmental planning strives to include all stakeholders, and this list becomes longer and more complete when the environment is considered as a whole, as in watershed management. Thus the watershed management approach can facilitate conflict resolution by fostering more complete inclusion of interested parties. This is not to underplay real conflicts that may exist, nor to imply that all discord is simple misunderstanding that can be corrected by increased dialogue. But it is to recognize that by bringing all the parties to the table, undertaking negotiations. and conducting research needed contentions to answer questions, we can often get closer to a solution.

CHOOSING TERMS:
WATERSHED VERSUS ECOSYSTEM MANAGEMENT

As noted earlier, interest in watershed management is not new and the term has been in use since at least the 1930s. In recent years, much emphasis has been devoted to a similar, related concept: ecosystem management. Ecosystem management has been defined in different ways, but in general the goal is "sustaining healthy ecosystems . . . to ensure ecosystem viability indefinitely" (Iverson, 1993). It is, according to The Keystone National Policy Dialogue on Ecosystem Management (1996) "a collaborative process that strives to reconcile the promotion of economic opportunities and livable communities with the conservation of ecological integrity and biodiversity." It requires the integration of social, economic, and ecological considerations at broad spatial and temporal scales (Moote et al., 1994). Ecosystem management is a management philosophy which focuses on desired conditions, rather than system outputs, and which recognizes the need to protect or restore critical ecological components, functions, and structures in order to sustain resources in perpetuity (Cortner et al., 1996).

Ecosystem management and watershed management share some important elements: a focus on socially defined goals and management objectives; use of integrated, holistic science; focus on a broad range of spatial and temporal scales, often larger and longer than has been the norm in resource management; reliance on collaborative decision-making; and a call for more flexible, adaptable institutions in which decisions are continuously reviewed and revised, and thus where planning and decision-making can go forward even in the face of uncertainty (Cortner et al, 1996). Despite these similarities and the many merits of an ecosystem approach, this committee elected to focus on watershed management in part because our focus is on solving water-related problems rather than restoration/ conservation, and in part for the clarity of communication we believe comes with thinking about watersheds, which are fairly obvious, understandable landscape units. Ecosystems are far harder to draw on a map with any precision and even federal agencies have drawn different lines in dividing the nation into ecoregions (GAO, 1994). As Adler (1996) points out:

> . . . ecological boundaries often cannot be identified with precision, and depending on the aquatic resources of greatest concern, a variety of potential aquatic ecosystem boundaries exist— "salmonsheds" versus "ducksheds," for example. After adding terrestrial ecosystems, the situation becomes even more complex. should programs focus on the boundaries of aquatic ecosystems (watersheds, ducksheds, or salmonsheds), on plant ecosystems (forestsheds), or on the ring of key terrestrial species (bearsheds).

Of course, neither ecosystem boundaries nor watershed boundaries are matched to the political boundaries that are the most common basis for resource management decision-making, which leads to many difficulties in implementing such approaches. In fact, rivers were often used as boundaries in creating political divisions, thus actually cutting watersheds in half. Political boundaries are important in delineating the areas by which much of the demographic, cultural, and economic data are collected and analyzed in the nation. They also set the limits of political and legal authority, and set the policies by which natural resources of the area are governed. Awareness of boundaries—political and physical—is thus essential for both understanding the advantages and disadvantages of a watershed approach to decision-making and for overcoming barriers to implementation of such approaches.

CONCLUSION

The notion of watersheds as the basic unit for management of water resources is not new and a watershed approach is being used in many places in the United States to protect and enhance natural resources. However, watersheds are rarely the primary unit used for management because neither national nor local decision-making infrastructures are designed to address the complex biophysical, sociological, and economic interactions that occur within watersheds.

Over the past 20 years, the nation's greatest achievement in the field of water management has been enormous reduction in pollution from point sources, with some notable water quality improvements. Yet major portions of our lakes, rivers, wetlands, estuaries, and coastlines do not meet current water quality standards. The unfortunate results of continued impairment can be seen in the decline of fisheries, loss of biodiversity, and curtailment of commercial and recreational activities in watersheds across the country (Wayland, 1993). Programs focused on addressing particular problems, contaminants, or types of activities can be helpful, but are by definition limited. Lasting solutions to many remaining water quality and environmental problems require an integrated management approach that addresses all water-related issues within hydrologic boundaries. Such an approach must recognize that all resources within natural (hydrologically defined) watershed boundaries are part of interconnected systems and are dependent on the health of the ecosystem as a whole.

The committee believes that watershed science and management needs a broad endorsement by government at all levels as the primary mechanism for dealing with strategic issues of conservation and enhancement of natural resources, particularly water resources. In the following chapters we attempt to provide guidance for reaching this goal.

REFERENCES

Adler, R. W. 1996. Addressing barriers to watershed protection. Environmental Law 25:973-1106.

Bajwa, R. S., W. M. Crosswhite, J. E. Hostetler, and O. W. Wright. 1992. Agricultural Irrigation and Water Use. Washington, D.C.:ERS/USDA. Agricultural Information Bulletin No. 638.

Cortner, H. J., M. A. Shannon, M. G. Wallace, S. Burke, and M. A. Moote. 1996. Institutional Barriers and Incentives for Ecosystem Management: A Problem Analysis. U.S. Department of Agriculture, Forest Service. Pacific Northwest Research Station.

Doppelt, B., M. Scurlock, C. Frissell, and J. Kerr. 1993. Entering the Watershed: A New Approach to America's River Ecosystems. Washington, D.C.: Island Press and the Pacific Rivers Council.

Forest Ecosystem Management Assessment Team (FEMAT). 1993. Forest ecosystem management: an ecological, economic, and social assessment. Report of the Forest Ecosystem Management Assessment Team. Portland, Oregon: USDA Forest Service.

Franklin, J. F. 1992. Scientific basis for new perspectives in forests and streams. In Watershed Management: Balancing Sustainability and Environmental Change, edited by R. J. Naiman. New York: Springer-Verlag.

General Accounting Office (GAO). 1994. Ecosystem Management: Additional Actions Needed to Adequately Test a Promising Approach. GAO/RCED-94-111. Washington, DC: U.S. General Accounting Office.

Heaney, J. P. 1993. New Directions in Water Resources Planning and Management. Water Resources Update, no.93, Autumn 1993.

Iverson, D. 1993. Framework for a shared approach to ecosystem management. On file with: Water Resources Research Center, 350 North Campbell Ave., Tucson, Ariz.

Lee, K. N. 1993. Compass and Gyroscope: Integrating Science and Politics for the Environment. Washington, D.C.: Island Press.

Miller, R. R., J. D. Williams, and J. E. Williams. 1989. Extinctions of North American fishes during the past century. Fisheries 14:22-38.

Moote, M. A., S. Burke; H. J. Cortner; and M. L. Corn. 1994. Principles of ecosystem management. Tucson, Ariz.: Water Resources Research Center, University of Arizona.

Naiman, R. J., J. J. Magnuson, D. M. McKnight, and J. A. Stanford. 1995. The Freshwater Imperative: A Research Agenda. Washington, D.C.: Island Press.

National Research Council. 1992. Water Transfers in the West: Efficiency, Equity, and the Environment. Washington, D.C.: National Academy Press.

National Research Council. 1996a. River Resource Management in the Grand Canyon. National Academies Press. Washington, D.C.

National Research Council. 1996b. Upstream: Salmon and Society in the Pacific Northwest. Washington, D.C.: National Academy Press.

Robbins, R. W., J. L. Glicker, D. M. Bloen, and B. M. Niss. 1991. Effective Watershed Management for Surface Water Supplies. Denver, Colo.: American Water Works Association.

Soil Conservation Service (SCS) 1994. Action Plan: Providing Ecosystem Based Assistance for the Management of Natural Resources: A Soil Conservation Service Strategic Initiative for the 1990s. Washington, D.C.: United States Department of Agriculture.

Stein, B. A., and S. R. Flack. 1997. 1997 Species Report Card: The State of U.S. Plants and Animals. Arlington, Va.: The Nature Conservancy.

The Keystone Center. 1996. The Keystone National Policy Dialogue on Ecosystem Management. Final Report. The Keystone Center, Colorado.

U.S. Department of Agriculture. 1986. Agricultural Resources: Cropland, Water, and Conservation. Washington, D.C.: Economic Research Service.

U.S. Environmental Protection Agency (USEPA). 1993. The Watershed Protection Approach, Annual Report 1992. USEPA 840-S-93-001. Washington, D.C.: Environmental Protection Agency.

Wayland, R. H. 1993. Comprehensive Watershed Management: A view from USEPA. Water Resources Update, No. 93.

Webster. 1994. Webster's Ninth New Collegiate Dictionary. Springfield, Mass.: Merrian-Webster, Inc.

Williams, J. E., J. E. Johnson, D. A. Hendrickson, S. Contreras-Balderas, J. D. Williams, M. Navarro-Mendoza, D. E. McAllister, and J. E. Deacon. 1989. Fishes of North American: Endangered, threatened, or of special concern. Fisheries 14:2-20.

Wilson, E. O., and F. M. Peter, editors. 1988. Biodiversity. Washington, D.C.: National Academy Press.

World Resources Institute. 1992. Environmental Almanac. Boston: Houghton Mifflin Company.

2

Spatial and Temporal Scales for Watersheds

Successful strategies for the management of America's watersheds must take into account an immense range of scales in the natural environment as well as in decision-making. Watersheds partition the natural landscape into units ranging in size from a few square meters to more than 3 million square kilometers (1.15 million square miles) for the Mississippi River basin, and decision-making for their management occurs in venues ranging from neighborhood groups serving a few dozen people to the federal government, which represents the interests of more than 260 million citizens. Meanwhile, natural forces affecting watersheds also occur at a range of scales (see Figure 2.1). Effective watershed science and policy require understanding the effects that variations in scale and scope have on watershed management efforts. This chapter explores the implications of scale, scope, and structure by (1) outlining the influence of scale on both physical and human processes related to watersheds, (2) exploring connections between temporal and geographic scales of change, and (3) reviewing an established scale-based system that defines watersheds in the United States for general application.

DEFINING WATERSHEDS

In general usage, the term *watershed* often connotes a relatively small drainage area, while the term *river basin* is reserved for very large areas. These terms are not scale-specific and should not be limited to particular size classes, however, because each term properly applies to regions ranging in size from less than a small field to almost a third of the North American continent. A more precise lexicon for watershed science and policy adopts specific meaning for several

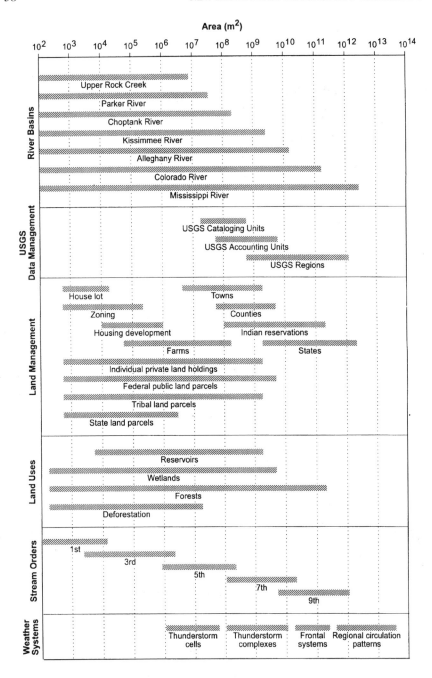

FIGURE 2.1 Spatial scales for watersheds.

terms and concepts that are often commingled: a *drainage basin* is a portion of the surface of the earth where all water falling on its surface collects in a network of channels and exits the watershed at a single point. The basin may terminate in a lake that has no outlet (in some arid regions), the ocean, or another larger river. Drainage basins have perimeters defined by relatively high portions of the topography that form drainage divides. The vertical projection of the basin outline onto a horizontal plane is the *drainage area*. Except for a few rare exceptions, the entire earth surface is divided into drainage basins. Each basin contains smaller sub-basins with their own identities, with minor *interbasin areas* where slopes drain directly to large channels. Drainage basins therefore have two topologic properties important to their investigation and management: they completely divide the earth's surface into naturally defined subunits, and they are also nested areas, with larger basins subsuming smaller ones (Figure 2.2).

The term *watershed* is now a wide-ranging label. Originally it referred only to the line of high ground separating two basins (now referred to as the *interfluve*), but in the twentieth century watershed came to denote the drainage area (Bates and Jackson, 1980). In general usage (if not formal definition) in the late twentieth century, watershed refers to a drainage area along with its associated water, soils, vegetation, animals, land use, and human activities.

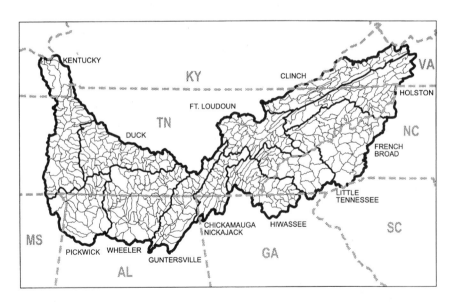

FIGURE 2.2 The watersheds of the Tennessee River basin, showing nesting of the smallest basins within larger sub-basins, all contained with the outline of the Tennessee River drainage. Modified from original map by TVA.

The defining geographic characteristic of the watershed is its topography, but it is a dynamic system with inputs, outputs, and interactive ecosytem components. An ecosystem is a distinctive collection of life forms and their physical support systems within a particular region, a concept that is a foundation in modern environmental management (National Research Council, 1994). Numerous laws and operating regulations use the ecosystem concept as a foundation for management goals that generally strive to sustain flows of goods and services for human welfare while maintaining the long-term health and integrity of the natural system (Jensen et al., 1996). Ecosystem management is difficult to put into practice because ecosystems are geographically difficult to define from a scientific standpoint, and even more troublesome from an administrative perspective because many citizens do not have a mental picture of such a system (Fitzsimmons, 1996).

The watershed, however, provides a logical boundary system and conceptual unit for ecosystem management because it is based on the geographic characteristics of the ecosystem's hydrology. It thus recognizes the dominant role that water plays in the biological relationships. In addition, a watershed is easily perceived and recognized. People understand it. From a legal perspective, watershed boundaries are more easily defined than many other boundaries in the natural environment.

Using of watershed boundaries for ecosystem management provides an advantage for measuring and monitoring of basic physical and chemical ecosystems components, since water is the fundamental transporter of nutrients through ecosystems. Each stream gauge with its measurements of quantity and chemical quality of water, specifically reveals variations in processes in the watershed that drains to it. Our understanding of geographical budgets for water, energy, and nutrients is therefore predicated on watershed outlines, and this understanding is most readily applied to management decisions on the same watershed basis. Climatic data in the United States are also organized according to major watersheds because of the importance of precipitation to runoff estimates. The National Weather Service organizes its climatic, precipitation, and drought data according to climatic regions with boundaries corresponding to watershed boundaries. Data sets for very large river basins can be constructed in additive fashion by cumulating the data for smaller climatic regions.

Although economic and social data are not intentionally collected and reported according to watershed boundaries, nearly coincidental economic and social regions can be defined at least for the large water regions of the United States. This congruity occurs because the nation's economic and social data are arranged by the Bureau of the Census according to the boundaries of more than 3,000 counties and the county boundaries in many parts of the country are partially aligned with drainage divides. Where such intentional correspondence does not occur, the mismatch is rarely so large as to be problematic. County data can therefore be aggregated into regions approximating large and medium scale watersheds. Agricultural data is also compatible with watershed boundaries because the Census of Agriculture (of the U.S. Department of Agriculture), reports production data and livestock populations according to counties. For smaller watersheds, census data collected on divisions smaller than counties are also available, with data aggregated according to census tracts and census blocks that have resolution to a scale equal to about four city blocks. Watershed approaches are therefore geographical perspectives that can integrate of physical, chemical, some biological, economic, and social data.

The use of watershed boundaries is less effective for wildlife and vegetation applications. Many types of ecosystems do not have boundaries determined by drainage divides, but this problem should not be detrimental to watershed approaches. For small ecosystems, vegetation patches, and limited habitats for some wildlife species, even small watersheds will completely contain the area of concern. In the case of bald eagle nesting places, for example, some watershed will contain the critical habitat, while others do not, and so the management issue will be present for some watersheds and not others. Some ecosystems are either larger than easily defined watersheds, or they span several, such as the greater Yellowstone ecosystem. In these cases, special considerations will be required to account for the overlap.

Watersheds are open systems, with mass and energy being exchanged with places outside the defined area. Groundwater, for example, migrates along groundwater gradients that do not always respect the surface configuration, so that an aquifer may transcend watershed boundaries. The hydroelectric power generated in one watershed may be conducted to distant markets, so that the consumers of that power become legitimate stakeholders in the management of the watershed of origin, even if they never see it. Water may also be diverted from the watershed of origin and transported by artificial means into neighboring watersheds. These interbasin transfers occur commonly in the United States, and they extend the interests of managers beyond the nearest drainage divide. In effect, most watersheds circumscribe areas of primary interest containing most of the environmental resources and human users, but in many cases a secondary, larger region also merits consideration, a sort of expanded shadow of the original watershed. In some cases, the watershed is not the appropriate model. Airsheds, for example, with their attending issues of air quality and visibility, define regions that do not depend on watersheds. For these issues, the watershed may not be the appropriate framework for management, and other administrative regions must be constructed.

These exceptions not withstanding, the watershed is clearly useful a scientific and administrative tool for organizing the natural and human landscape. The watershed approach provides an organizational framework that integrates natural, social, and economic components shared in a geographic area.

GEOGRAPHIC SCALES FOR WATERSHEDS

Underlying the watershed's human and biological components are the basic physical foundations of landforms, water, sediment, and chemicals (including nutrients and contaminants). The landforms of the watershed are associated either with hillslopes or channels. Hillslopes (non-channel parts of the landscape) contribute water from runoff, sediment from erosion, and chemicals carried in solution in the water or attached to particles of sediment. The slopes serve as the platforms for human use of the watershed, ranging from agricultural to urban, and they are the primary sources of the watershed's physical constituents. The channels are conduits for water, sediment, and chemicals, with their shapes and configurations reflecting a temporary balance among mass, hydraulic energy, and geomorphology.

As assemblages of hillslopes and channels, watershed sizes have specific functions. The smallest drainage basins, ranging from a few square meters to perhaps a square kilometer, often resemble simple hillslopes in their behavior, and they are source areas for water, sediment, and chemicals. Their behavior, is heavily influenced by soil characteristics, with respect to runoff, especially because if the soils of a small watershed have a high infiltration capacity, little runoff occurs. Small basins with soils that have low infiltration capacity, either naturally or because of construction, agriculture, or urbanization experience high runoff rates and accelerated erosion, sending large quantities of sediment downstream.

Natural and human controls on hillslope and stream channel behavior can create physical changes in small watersheds over short time periods (from hours to months). Thunderstorm cells up to 3 kilometers (1.9 miles) across may completely cover a small watershed, and within an hour release literally overwhelming amounts of rainfall that cause the watershed to change its surface configuration in an hour or two. For example, the maximum recorded rainfall in the United States is 305 millimeters (12 inches) in less than an hour during a thunderstorm at Holt, Missouri, in 1947 (Dingman, 1994), but the event covered only a few square kilometers. Human controls can also radically change small watersheds, such as reshaping the surface for urban development or by managing vegetation or agricultural practices.

Intermediate-size watersheds (ranging from a few square kilometers to a few thousand square kilometers) subsuming more complex terrain systems host a larger variety of processes, because unlike the smallest watersheds they have space for temporary storage of water, sediment, and associated chemicals. These intermediate watersheds have complex slopes with space for sediment storage in their lower portions, and the channels often include floodplains as major temporary depositories for sediment. The floodplains also temporarily store water during flood events, draining their overflows back into channels after the highest stages of discharge. Intermediate-size rivers therefore experience considerable changes and adjustments even under entirely natural conditions, and human-induced alterations can amplify these changes.

Intermediate-size watersheds and rivers are often such large enough to absorb, without adjustment, the precipitation released by individual thunderstorm cells. Frontal systems or decaying tropical storms, however, can produce enough runoff to generate widespread changes in hillslopes and channels. Erosion in some parts of the watershed may be counterbalanced by deposition of sediment in other downstream areas, so that floodplains in central and lower parts of the channel network lose or gain materials. Human attempts to control water flow begin to reach their effective limit in watersheds and rivers of this size; large dams, channel engineering, and floodplain protective works such as levees can influence the processes and results of most events short of large "50-year" or "100-year" extremes, but larger and rarer events may be beyond direct human control.

Large watersheds—those with areas greater than 10,000 square kilometers (3,860 square miles)—include extensive areas of deposition for sediment and chemicals from upstream areas. The lower reaches of their rivers include large valleys partially filled with alluvium or deltaic areas either extending into the sea or confined by valley walls in areas subjected to rising sea levels. These largest watersheds span multiple geologic and vegetation provinces and include the widest variety of land uses. They are so large that they change mostly one part at a time rather than as an entire system, and their overall adjustments are related to global hydroclimatic changes. Human activities cannot control such systems, as evidenced by the extensive floods in the Mississippi River Basin in 1993. Despite the investment of billions of dollars in flood protection, the 1993 flood event on the Mississippi produced a river several kilometers wide in its lower reaches. The flood was remarkably similar to one observed by the Spanish explorer Hernando de Soto when he crossed the river below present-day Memphis in 1541, when the basin was essentially in its natural condition.

An important property of watersheds is that their characteristics and processes are not strictly additive. That is, measurements made on a series of small watersheds cannot necessarily be extrapolated to a larger watershed that includes the smaller ones. For example, sediment yield on a unit area basis is very different for small watersheds than large ones in the same region, because the small basins may not store sediment along their channels, while storage does occur in the larger watersheds in the form of floodplains. As a result, average measurement of sediment yield from drainage areas less than 26 square kilometers (10 square miles) in extent for the United States is 1,800 cubic meters per square kilometer (about 9 tons/acre), but for areas larger than 2600 square kilometers (100 square miles) the average yield is only 240 cubic meters per square kilometer (1 ton/acre). Many fluvial and hydrologic processes have similar connections to scale, so that measurements of small area processes may not be added together to assess the behavior of the larger sum of the areas (see Box 2.1).

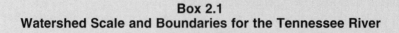

Box 2.1
Watershed Scale and Boundaries for the Tennessee River

The Tennessee Valley Authority (TVA) is an independent federal agency created in 1933 and given responsibility for flood control, navigation development, electric energy production, natural resource conservation, and general economic development within the Tennessee River Basin. The agency seeks to manage the 652-mile long Tennessee River and its a drainage basin, which includes 125 counties in 7 states (Figure 2.2). TVA has recently increased its emphasis on water quality and has adopted the goal of making the Tennessee the cleanest and most productive commercial river system in the United States by the year 2000 (Ungate, 1996).

To help accomplish this objective, TVA established the Clean Water Initiative using a watershed approach. With the concept of nested functions, TVA divided the basin into 12 watersheds named for major tributaries of the main stream. Each is divided into still smaller watersheds defined by TVA as hydrologic units (HUCs). Typical sizes encompassed by these various divisions include:

SIZE SCALE FOR CHANNELS

Researchers and administrators often characterize the stream channels using an ordering system to describe channel topology (Figure 2.3). In the Strahler ordering system, a first-order channel is the smallest fingertip tributary that begins in a hillslope area and terminates at the confluence with another channel. A second-order stream forms where two first-order channels join; a third-order stream forms where two second order streams join; and so on. A channel changes order only when joined by another of equal order. Therefore, many second order channels are joined by numerous small, first-order tributaries without changing the order of the main stream. As a result, change in order rarely occurs in the downstream direction after the trunk stream achieves an order of six or seven. The Mississippi River in its lower reaches is probably tenth order. Investigators sometimes label a drainage basin with an order number corresponding to the highest order stream within its boundary, as in "first-order basin." Because of the geometric arrangement of stream networks, the smallest order streams are by far

River Basin   Tennessee River   106,000 km^2 (41,000 mi^2)
Watershed   Hiawassee River Watershed 7,000 km^2 (2,700 mi^2)
Hydrologic Unit Fightingtown Creek HUC   186 km^2 (72 mi^2)

For each hydrologic unit, TVA collected and reviewed aquatic resource data based on existing agency reports, U.S. Environmental Protection Agency's computerized STORET data base, TVA water quality data, aerial photography, and interviews with state and federal natural resource management agencies, local governments, county health departments, and planning commissions. TVA used these data to rate each hydrologic unit for its degree of degradation and to identify areas needing remediation. TVA also uses data from rapid bioassessments and conventional physical and chemical stream measurements to assess ecological conditions of streams. Geographic information systems (GIS) provide computerized tools for storing and analyzing the data. Assessments are action-oriented, with decisions on remediation strategies taken with the best information available, rather than waiting until all the data are available. By using an adaptive management approach, decisions can be changed to reflect new information as it develops. In this process, resource value and resource condition have separate assessments, so that a resource can be degraded but still be very valuable. A small improvement in a very valuable resource may be more desirable than a large improvement in a not-so-valuable resource.

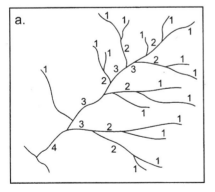 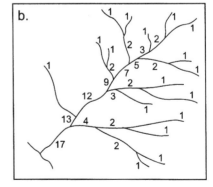

FIGURE 2.3 Two examples of stream ordering systems for a hypothetical small stream: (a) the typically used Strahler method, and (b) the more useful but less commonly applied Shreve method that shows increases in stream order more closely associated with hydrologic reality. Modified from Doornkamp and King (1971).

the most numerous (Table 2.1), and roughly represent the "local" point of intersection between natural processes and public policy. Of necessity, the less numerous highest order streams require regional or national policy and management.

Whether applied to channels or basins, the ordering scheme provides a relative index to size or scale, but its utility is limited to description. Stream orders are mathematically related to numbers of channels, channel lengths, and drainage areas, for example, but these connections do not provide any scientific explanation of river or watershed behavior. The relationships are the geographic products of random space-filling processes, and their application is not limited to channels or drainage areas. The same mathematical relationships apply to veins in a leaf or arteries in the human circulation system, both of which can be "ordered" in the same way as a branching stream system. Stream and basin orders are firmly anchored in the geomorphologic and management literature, however, and are likely to see continued use for general descriptive purposes.

Although the properties and processes of small watersheds do not necessarily accumulate arithmetically to the larger basins that contain them, there is a clear direction of causality up the scale system. Smaller watersheds obviously influence the larger ones, but not the reverse. Watershed management may be successful for certain purposes at the small scale (for example, erosion control), and transmit changes to the larger system (for example, through changes in sediment yield). Local land-use rules in small watersheds cumulatively (but in a nonlinear fashion) influence channel behavior of the larger watersheds in which they are nested. In the reverse, however, dams and levees on large rivers have no

TABLE 2.1 Estimated Number and Length of River Channels in the United States.

Order	Number	Mean Length (mi)	Total Length (mi)	Mean Drainage Area (mi^2)	Example River
1	1,570,000	1	1,570,000	1	Runway Area, St. Louis Airport, Mo.
2	350,000	2.3	810,000	4.7	Upper Rock Creek, D.C.
3	80,000	5.3	420,000	23	Parker River, Mass.
4	18,000	12	220,000	109	Choptank River, Maryland
5	4,200	28	116,000	518	Upper Iowa River, Iowa
6	950	64	61,000	2,460	Kissimmee River, Florida
7	200	147	30,000	11,700	Allegheny River, Penn.
8	41	338	14,000	55,600	Gila River, Ariz. and N.M.
9	8	777	6200	264,000	Columbia River
10	1	1,800	1,800	1,150,000	Mississippi River
Total			3,249,000		

SOURCE: Modified from Leopold, Wolman, and Miller, 1964, p. 142.

influence on smaller watersheds upstream. Causality, like water, generally flows downstream.

TEMPORAL SCALES FOR WATERSHEDS AND CHANNELS

Temporal scales also provide a framework for considering natural and human processes in watersheds (Figure 2.4). Geographic and temporal scales are closely related to each other in processes related to watersheds. The magnitudes of events in a natural environmental system are usually linked to the frequency with which they occur, with the smallest events occurring most often and the largest events very seldom. When considering any group of natural events such as floods, the smallest ones have a high probability of occurring in any given year, and the length of time between events is relatively short. The larger events and the extensive changes that accompany them have a low probability of occurring in any single year, and (on average) their return interval is relatively long. In the natural sciences, the connection between size and probability is expressed in the concepts of magnitude and frequency, which quantify particular statistical relationships (see Figure 2.5). Although the concept appears most often in hydrology, it applies equally well to events in geomorphology, meteorology, and the life sciences.

Magnitude and frequency of relationships have important implications for change in watersheds. For example, the mean maximum annual flood (the average size of the largest flood that occurs in any one year) usually remains within well-defined channels. However, floods that are larger than this reference size and that have a frequency of occurrence of less than once a year spill out of the channel and inundate the floodplain (Williams, 1978). For this reason, watershed and river management to control runoff and discharge events in channels must seek to constrain the unusual rather than the ordinary hydrologic event—a difficult task, since those events with moderate return intervals (20 to 50 years) are usually large enough to cause considerable economic damage, but are infrequent enough to be overlooked in short-term planning.

Physical factors change their roles in watershed processes depending on the temporal scale of analysis. For example, if an analyst considers watershed changes on a time scale of decades to centuries, the drainage network morphology (numbers and arrangements of channel segments) is seen as variable, subject to the influences of geology, climate, vegetation, relief, and other factors. But if the analyst considers a time span of only a year or two, the drainage network morphology is relatively unchanging, and rather than being a responding variable it is a control that influences hydraulic behavior of the stream system.

Three commonly considered time scales in geomorphology and hydrology are *steady state time* (years to about a decade), *graded time* (decades to centuries), and *cyclic time* (greater than a millennium). Regulators often deal with only a year or two, yet the natural processes in watersheds are better understood and

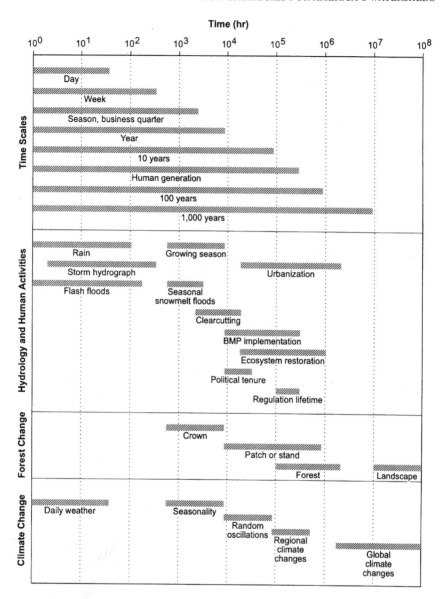

FIGURE 2.4 Temporal scales for watersheds.

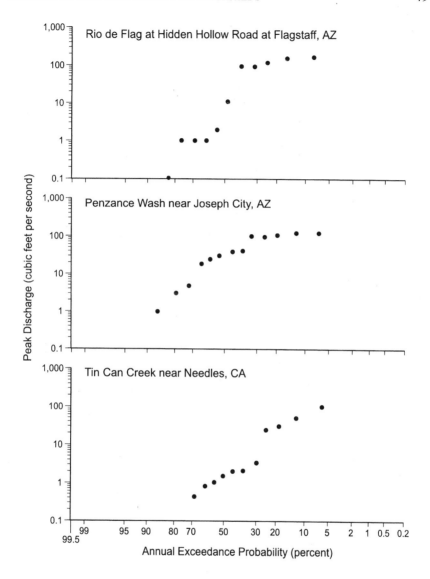

FIGURE 2.5 Examples of magnitude and frequency relationships, showing how the smallest floods have the greatest probability of occurrence. SOURCE: Thomas et al., 1994.

managed on at least a decade scale. As we consider increasingly long time scales, we must account for increasing numbers of variables that change within those scales (Table 2.2). At the scale most often addressed in watershed management, decades, three vital components of physical watershed systems are likely to respond as dependent variables: the drainage network morphology, hillslope forms, and the discharges of water and sediment. These three variables are most susceptible to management.

From a management perspective, the role played by each watershed variable within the temporal scale of the management effort must influence measurements and their interpretation. Depending on the time span, a variable might not be relevant, might change under the control exerted by other variables, or might change independently of other variables. Watershed problems are often detected by measured changes in dependent variables, particularly changes in the channel discharge of water or sediment. Effective watershed managers identify the independent controlling variables and try to manipulate them while recognizing that some variables are beyond human control but must be accounted for. For instance, on a one-to-ten time scale (the one managers most often encounter), the manager might manipulate primarily the runoff and sediment yield per unit area and hillslope morphology (managed by land use controls), and the drainage network morphology (managed by sewers or drains and building-site regulations), but can not respond to other controlling variables such as climate or geology.

Human action can sometimes modify natural relationships between the magnitude and frequency of watershed events. Sometimes such modifications are

TABLE 2.2 The Status of Drainage Basin Variables During Various Time Spans.

Drainage Basin Variables	Status of Variables During Designated Time Spans		
	Greater Than a Millennium	Decade to Centuries	Year to Decade
Time	Controlling	Not Relevant	Not Relevant
Initial Relief	Controlling	Not Relevant	Not Relevant
Geology	Controlling	Controlling	Controlling
Climate	Controlling	Controlling	Controlling
Vegetation	Responding	Controlling	Controlling
Local Relief	Responding	Controlling	Controlling
Hydrology (runoff and sediment yield per unit area)	Responding	Controlling	Controlling
Drainage network morphology	Responding	Responding	Controlling
Hillslope morphology	Responding	Responding	Controlling
Hydrology (channel discharge of water and sediment)	Responding	Responding	Responding

SOURCE: Modified from Schumm and Lichty, 1969.

intentional, such as the construction and maintenance of a large dam to control the return interval of large floods. More often, however, modifications occur as unplanned and unanticipated outcomes of watershed activities. Urbanization of watersheds ranging up to about 10 square kilometers (4 square miles), with attendant installation of impervious surfaces, streets, and drains, causes floods of a given magnitude to become more frequent than under previous natural conditions. During construction in urban watersheds, previously frequent sediment discharges of small amounts temporarily become much larger before declining in magnitude again after construction. In every case, small watersheds react to both natural and human changes more rapidly than large watersheds. Thus management plans for medium to large watersheds may not have immediately visible effects. Over periods of several years or decades, however, the fruits of wise watershed management become more apparent.

HYDROLOGIC UNITS

Organization of policy-making bodies along the geographic lines of watersheds is not as difficult in its conception as it is likely to be in implementation. The boundaries of the nation's drainage areas have been precisely delineated and are available in printed and digital form. During the 1970s, the U.S. Water Resources Council devised a framework for dividing the nation into *water resources regions* wherein all the regional boundaries are hydrologic and topographic except where blocked by international boundaries (U.S. Water Resources Council, 1978). The regions contain either the drainage area of a major river, such as the Missouri Region, or the combined drainage areas of a series of closely related rivers and their watersheds, such as the South Atlantic-Gulf Region which includes a number of watersheds draining directly into the Atlantic Ocean or the Gulf of Mexico (Figure 2.6). Note that from a hydrological view, these water resource regions do not stop at international borders, as the map implies, which complicates both policy-making and implementation efforts.

The Water Resources Council's second level of classification divides the regions into 222 *planning subregions*. A planning subregion includes that area drained by a river system, a reach of a river and the tributaries in that reach, a closed basin, or a group of streams forming a coastal zone. All the planning subregion boundaries are hydrologic except where discontinued at international boundaries. In 1974 the U.S. Geological Survey, in cooperation with the U.S. Water Resources Council, published maps for each state showing the locations of the boundaries, as well as a national map. A few years later during the Second National Water Assessment, the Council reclassified the 222 planning regions into 106 *assessment subregions*, which have hydrologic boundaries that can be approximated by county boundaries. This connection between the physical landscape and the political landscape is critical, because it eases the aggregation and analysis of both environmental and social and economic data. The primary

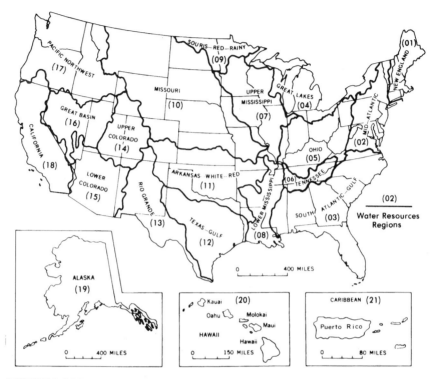

FIGURE 2.6 Map showing the water resources regions of the United States. Seaber et al., 1987.

method for collecting and collating the social and economic data is the U.S. Census, which uses counties as a basic grouping mechanism for its data. The U.S. Geological Survey uses *accounting units* for designating and managing the National Water Data Network. These units are a further refinement of the water resource regions based on size and hydrologic conditions. There are 352 hydrologic accounting units that nest within or are equivalent to the planning subregions.

The smallest division in the system is the *cataloging unit*. It is a geographic area representing part or all of a drainage basin, a combination of basins, or a distinct hydrologic feature. These 2,150 units, each with an average area of about 1,750 square kilometers (700 square miles), combine to form planning subregions and accounting units (Figure 2.7). The entire group of divisions are referred to collectively as hydrologic units, and they form a hierarchy of geographic divisions of the nation (Figure 2.8).

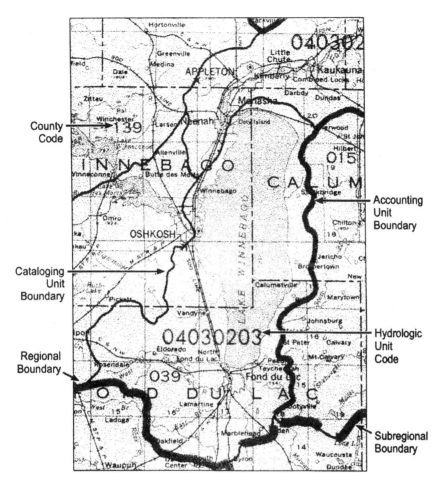

FIGURE 2.7 Section of a hydrologic unit map of a portion of north-central Wisconsin, showing the various boundaries and the association of hydrologic unit code numbers with the areas. Similar maps are available from the U.S. Geological Survey on paper or in digital format, from either the Survey or the National Resource Conservation Service. (See Appendix C for Web addresses.) SOURCE: Seaber et al., 1987.

CONCLUSIONS

Watersheds are natural topographic units of the earth's surface, usually with easily defined boundaries. The U.S. Geological Survey and U.S. Water Resources Council have defined watershed boundaries within the United States, providing a nested series of 2,150 small hydrologic units within 222 subregions, all subsumed by 21 water resource regions or large river basins. The boundaries of these units

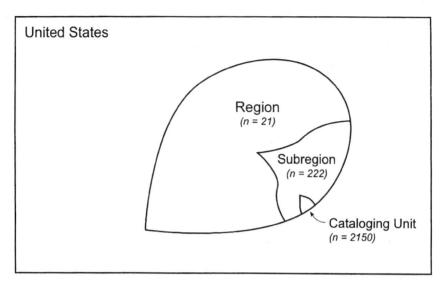

FIGURE 2.8 A schematic diagram showing the hierarchy of hydrologic units, where n = the number of units of each type in the entire nation. Data from Seaber et al., 1987.

are useful geographic delineations for ecosystems, and especially for the hydrologic components of ecosystems. In addition, much of the economic and social data collected by federal and other governments is collected in spatial units such as counties that can be often be aggregated to approximate watershed boundaries, which allows managers to further integrate ecologic, economic, and social data in their management efforts. Watershed concepts, when used in conjunction with ecosystem concepts, provide the geographic context and structure for scientific investigations and some management functions for water and water-related resources.

The consideration of scale is exceptionally important in the science and management of watersheds, and managers will be less likely to make effective use of scientific information if the scale of the information is not matched to the scale of decisionmaking. Studies of mass (water and sediment), energy, nutrients, or contaminants are not necessarily directly additive as small watersheds combine into successively larger watershed scales, because smaller systems have internal storage. Management efforts must also consider the temporal scale of the various watershed processes they seek to respond to.

REFERENCES

Bates, R. L., and Jackson, J. A. 1980. Glossary of Geology. Falls Church, Virginia: American Geological Institute.

Dingman, S. L. 1994. Physical Hydrology. New York: Macmillan Publishing Company.

Doornkamp, J. C., and King, C. A. M. 1971. Numerical Analysis in Geomorphology: An Introduction. New York: St. Martin's Press.

Fitzsimmons, A. K. 1996. Sound Policy or Smoke and Mirrors: Does Ecosystem Management Make Sense? Water Resources Bulletin 32:217-227.

Jensen, M. E., Bourgeron, P. B., Everett, R., and Goodman, I. 1996. Ecosystem Management: A Landscape Ecology Perspective. Water Resources Bulletin 32:203-216.

Leopold, L. B., Wolman, M. G., and Miller, J. P. 1964. Fluvial Processes in Geomorphology. San Francisco: W. H. Freeman.

National Research Council. 1994. Review of EPA's Environmental Monitoring and Assessment Program. Washington, D.C.: National Academy Press.

Schumm, S. A., and Lichty, R. W. 1969. Time, space, and causality in geomorphology. American Journal of Science 263:110-119.

Seaber, P. R., Kapinos, F. P., and Knapp, G. L. 1987. Hydrologic Unit Maps. U.S. Geological Survey Professional Paper 2294. Washington, D.C.: U.S. Geological Survey.

Thomas, B. E., Hjalmarson, H. W., and Waltemeyer, S. D. 1994. Methods for estimating magnitude and frequency of floods in the southwestern United States. U.S. Geological Survey Open-File Report 93-419. Tucson, Ariz.: U.S. Geological Survey.

Ungate, C. D. 1996. Tennessee Valley Authority's Clean Water Initiative: Building Partnerships for Watershed Improvement. Journal of Environmental Planning and Management 39:113-122.

U.S. Water Resources Council. 1978. The Nation's Water Resources: The Second National Water Assessment by the U.S. Water Resources Council. Washington, D.C.: Government Printing Office.

Williams, G. P. 1978. Bank-full discharge of rivers. Water Resources Research 14:1141-1154.

3

Regional Variations

The United States contains an extraordinarily diverse landscape, with tremendous variation in physical geography, climate, and ecology, as well as parallel diversity in the political and economic landscape. As a result, approaches to watershed management differ, too. This chapter describes regional variations in physical hydrology, ecology, and human impacts. These regional variations and human aspects significantly affect the functioning of watersheds, and managers must consider them when creating plans and regulations and when implementing watershed approaches. This chapter demonstrates that no single approach to watershed planning can fit the wide range of conditions present, and sets the stage for understanding why site-specific research planning will always be necessary for watershed management.

PHYSICAL HYDROLOGY

Physical hydrology sets the limits within which the watershed operates. The physical hydrology includes precipitation, evaporation, the amount of water held in the soil, streamflow, groundwater, and water quality.

Precipitation

The contiguous United States receives an average of approximately 75 centimeters (30 inches) precipitation per year, but there is great spatial variability (Figure 3.1). The heavy precipitation of the Pacific Northwest is a function of cool eastward-moving wet and cool air masses, mid-latitude cyclones, and oro-

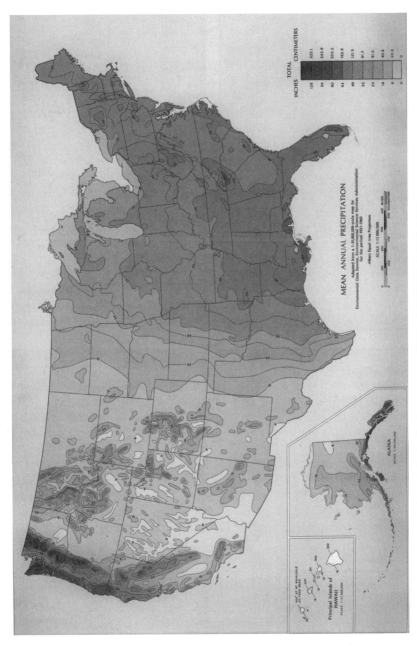

FIGURE 3.1 Mean annual precipitation in the continental U.S. SOURCE: USGS, 1970.

graphic lifting by coastal mountains. The same mountains, along with the dominant high pressure in the Southwest, block most Pacific moisture from the continental interiors, creating an arid effect extending eastward to mid-continent. The humid East is affected by warm, moist air from the Gulf and South Atlantic, with mid-latitude and tropical cyclones and strong convection.

Average annual precipitation is only a crude guide to natural water supply, given its high annual and monthly variability (Figure 3.2). First, there is an annual pattern in the timing of precipitation. On the West Coast, a strong summer minimum of precipitation exists while the North-Central states and East show a summer maximum. Second, there is a great deal of long-term variance of total amounts received on a monthly and annual basis. There is also great spatial variation in the frequency of precipitation, with the Northeast and Northwest having more rainy days. While there is a general spatial correlation between amount and frequency of precipitation (Figure 3.1), the Southeast often receives great amounts of precipitation in fewer days while the Northeast has more precipitation days with smaller amounts.

The frequency and magnitude of rainfall events have important implications for flood control aspects of watershed management. For any given return period (that is, the time between events of the same magnitude), the magnitude of those events varies with geography. Magnitudes are highest in the Southeast, followed by small areas in the mountains of the far West (Figure 3.3). Minimum values are found in the intermountain basins of the West. An example showing these distributions is the map of 100-year, 24-hour values of precipitation (Figure 3.4), which shows the maximum 24-hour rainfall amounts expected on average every 100 years. Watershed planning often uses this 24-hour maximum value. A complete set of similar maps is available showing the distribution of small events (a minor 1-year, 30-minute storm) to major 100-year, 10-day events (Miller, 1964; Hershfield, 1961). These frequency-magnitude values are on an annual basis, but monthly probabilities are also available for the eastern United States (Hershfield, 1961).

Another important characteristic of precipitation in watershed management is its erosivity, or ability to erode soil, expressed in units of 100 foot-tons per acre-year (Figure 3.5). These values, in conjunction with the other factors of the Revised Universal Soil Loss Equation (RUSLE), give a prediction of annual sheet and rill erosion in tons per acre for any location in the nation (Renard et al., 1995).

Evaporation

Evaporation is important to water supply and watershed management because it represents the natural loss of otherwise available water. One measure of the concept is the combination of potential evaporation and transpiration, known as potential evapotranspiration or PET. PET data are very sparse, but a suitable

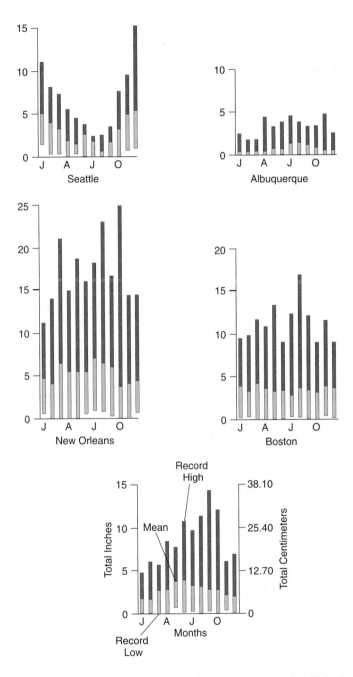

FIGURE 3.2 Monthly precipitation: means and extremes. SOURCE: U.S. Geological Survey (USGS) 1970.

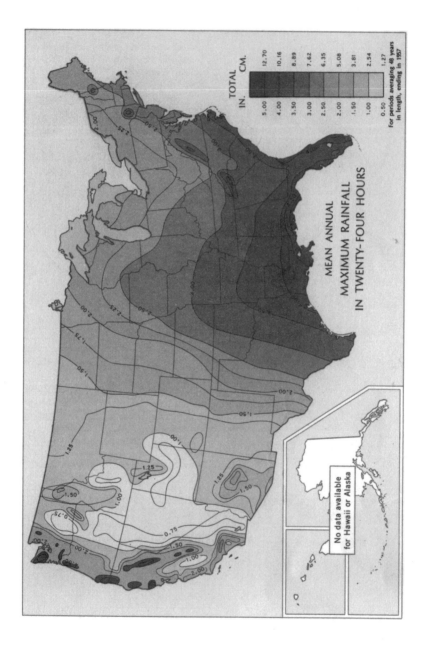

TOTAL

IN.	CM.
5.00	12.70
4.00	10.16
3.50	8.89
3.00	7.62
2.50	6.35
2.00	5.08
1.50	3.81
1.00	2.54
0.50	1.27

For periods averaging 48 years
in length, ending in 1957

MEAN ANNUAL
MAXIMUM RAINFALL
IN TWENTY-FOUR HOURS

No data available
for Hawaii or Alaska

FIGURE 3.3 Mean annual maximum rainfall in 24 hours. SOURCE: USGS, 1970.

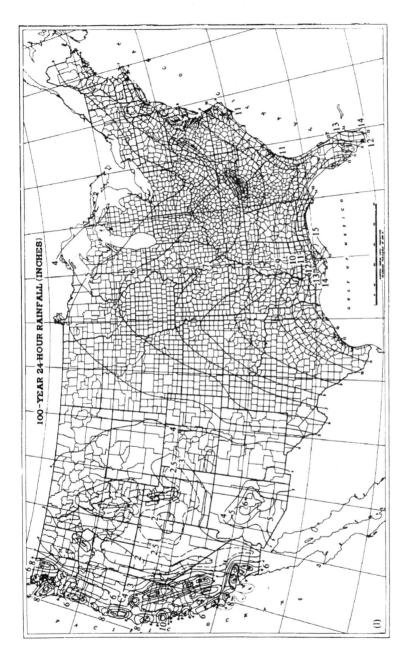

FIGURE 3.4 100-year 24-hour rainfall. SOURCE: Hershfield, 1961.

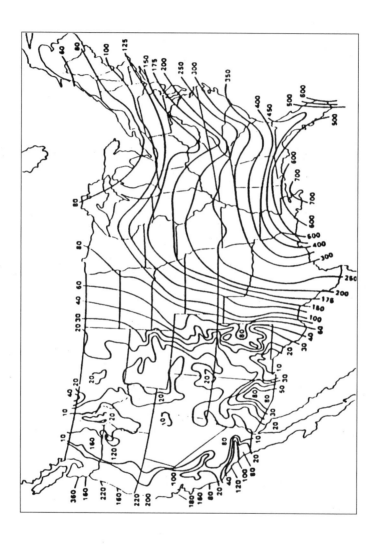

FIGURE 3.5 Rainfall erosion index. SOURCE: Modified from Renard et al., 1991.

surrogate is lake evaporation. Annual average values range from 50 centimeters (20 inches) in northern Maine to 215 centimeters (86 inches) in Southwest California (Figure 3.6). The amount of mean annual lake evaporation reflects the major physical controls of latitude, altitude, and relative humidity. Like precipitation, PET has an annual temporal pattern (systematic variance through the course of the year) as well as year-to-year variation. One important consideration in watershed management is what proportion of the year's moisture loss occurs during the growing season (May to October). Values range from a high of more than 80 percent in the northern U.S. to below 60 percent in south Florida (Kohler et al., 1959).

Soil Water Budgets

Soil water—that is, water contained in soil—is necessary for most plant and animal life. The availability of soil water is a function of both precipitation (counted as income) and evapotransporation (counted as expenditures). These budgets or balances can be expressed in diagrammatic form to show soil water surpluses, deficits, recharge, and utilization of stored soil water (Figure 3.7). Such water budgets not only give insight into a major control on natural processes, they also provide information relevant to irrigation and other water requirements. Amounts of water that exceed a soil's holding capacity move down through the soil into groundwater for aquifer recharge. Some of the groundwater provides baseflow for streams and leaves the region as runoff. Representative soil water budgets for the United States show that the magnitude of deficits and surpluses varies greatly by region and season. The greatest deficits occur in the Southwest, while the strongest surpluses occur in the Pacific Northwest and the East. Short but significant soil water deficits may occur, even in humid areas, near the end of the growing season. Given variations in precipitation and evaporation, water budgets can vary significantly from year to year. "Drought" occurs when precipitation is far enough below the long-term average to create a soil water deficiency great enough to adversely affect economic and social systems. There are great regional differences in the United States regarding the severity of drought (USGS, 1970).

Streamflow

Streamflow plays an important role in water supply, flooding, navigation, pollution, and recreation. It is composed of two major components: baseflow and stormflow. Baseflow is the more or less continuous flow that results from groundwater and a surplus of soil water. Stormflow results from rainfall or snowmelt events. In soils with high infiltration capacities and hydraulic conductivities, most stormflow may be subsurface except where soil is absolutely saturated. Where infiltration and/or conductivity is low, as in areas affected by compaction

64

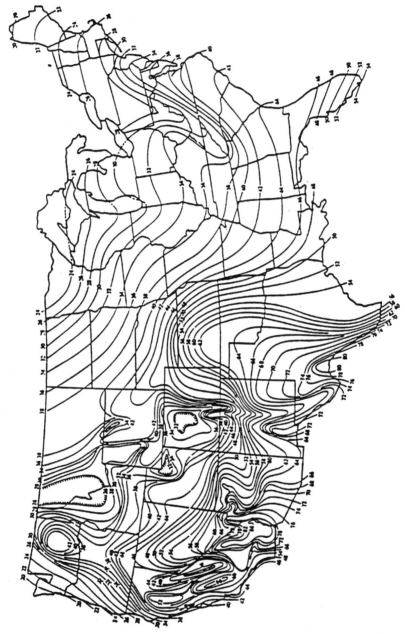

FIGURE 3.6 Mean annual lake evaporation (in inches for 1946 to 1955). SOURCE: Kohler et al., 1959.

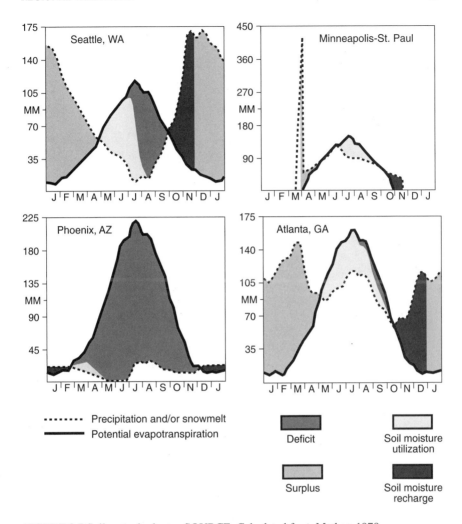

FIGURE 3.7 Soil water budgets. SOURCE: Calculated from Mather, 1978.

and/or deterioration of soil structure, rainfall from intense storms may be forced to move toward streams as overland flow, increasing the risk of soil erosion and downstream flooding. Similarly, urbanized areas are effectively "waterproofed" with roofs and pavement so that surface runoff is greatly increased.

The average annual runoff for the contiguous United States is approximately 30 centimeters (12 inches), but varies greatly by region (Figure 3.8), with rates ranging from less than 0.6 centimeter (0.25 inches) in some western areas to over 50 centimeters (20 inches) in some parts of the East. The runoff rates are roughly predicted by the soil water budgets.

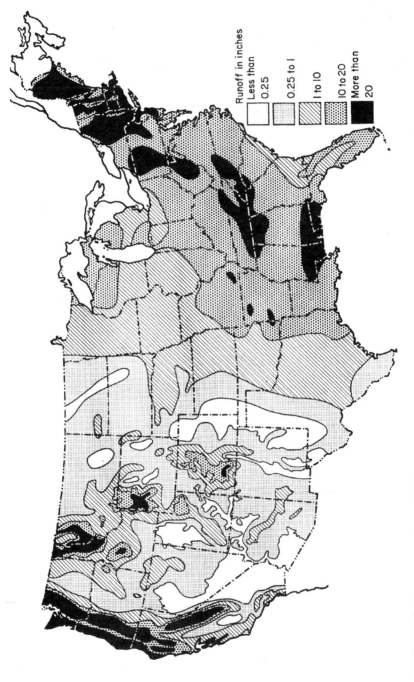

FIGURE 3.8 Average annual runoff. SOURCE: Leopold, 1964.

In addition to their geographic variability, precipitation, evaporation, and runoff usually vary considerably in monthly patterns and from year to year. Regime (or normal) monthly distribution of runoff, somewhat resembles the precipitation regimes discussed earlier. However, these are modified everywhere by evaporation regimes and by snowmelt in the mountainous West.

As with precipitation and evaporation, runoff can vary greatly from year to year, with one-year amounts ranging from less than 10 percent of the long-term average to over 400 percent (Figure 3.9 and Figure 3.10). Standardized to the coefficient of variation, the variance is greatest in the central U.S. and the Southwest, and least in the Northwest and Northeast (USGS, 1970). Given the greater average annual runoff (Figure 3.8), there is greater river flow in the eastern half of the country and in the Northwest than elsewhere (Figure 3.11).

One of the most important considerations in watershed management is dealing with floods. High flood potential is caused by a combination of intense rainfall, high antecedent soil moisture, steep topography, and less permeable land conditions (Figure 3.12).

Climate Change

While year-to-year variation in precipitation and runoff can be significant, some changes occur on a scale of decades or centuries, and climatologists have only recently begun to appreciate how important these changes can be to local and regional weather patterns. The gradual warming of the earth's atmosphere over the last century has been the subject of a tremendous amount of scientific investigation, and there are models that predict how global warming will change the amount and timing of snow and rain. In the last 40 years there have been seven significant El Niño events generated by water circulation anomalies in the tropical Pacific Ocean, including very large El Niño events in 1982-1983 and 1997-1998 (Figure 3.13) that resulted in severe flooding and erosion along both the west and east coasts of North America. The frequency of occurrence of each El Niño event has apparently increased following a shift in the intensity of regional low pressure systems in the northern and southern Pacific Ocean that occurred in 1976-1977. Such events should remind us that yearly patterns of variability in precipitation and runoff are superimposed on decades-long or even centuries-long climate cycles about which much remains to be learned.

Ground Water

Ninety-seven percent of all fresh water on earth is subsurface; only 2 percent of the total is contained in lakes and rivers (Gleick, 1993). Scientists and water managers have studied the geohydrology of ground waters for decades, trying to define and exploit ground water supplies in aquifers for human uses (U.S. Water Atlas, 1973; Figure 3.14). Nationwide we obtain at least 23 percent of our

68

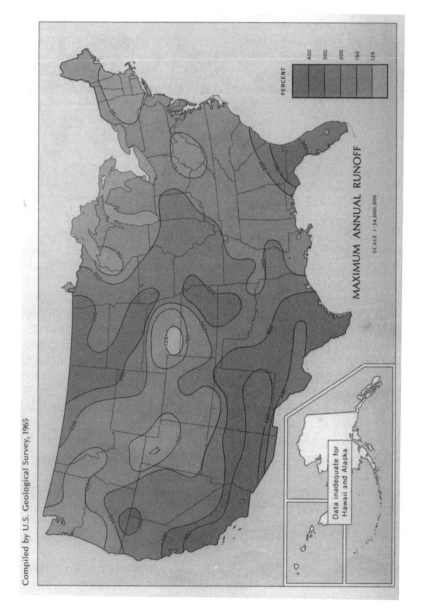

FIGURE 3.9 Maximum annual runoff. SOURCE: USGS, 1970.

69

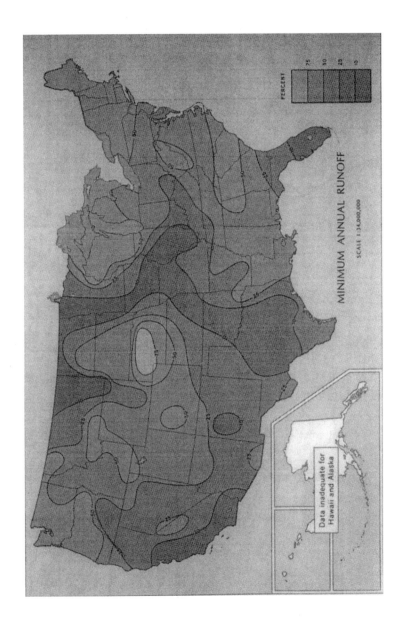

FIGURE 3.10 Minimum annual runoff. SOURCE: USGS, 1970.

70

FIGURE 3.11 Average annual discharge in main rivers. SOURCE: Council on Environmental Quality, 1981.

71

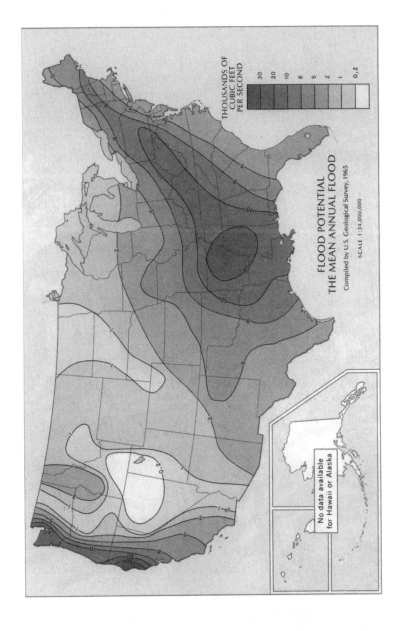

FIGURE 3.12 Flood potential. SOURCE: USGS, 1970.

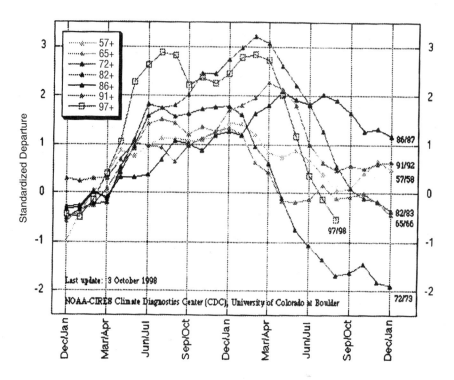

FIGURE 3.13 Comparison of a multivariate index of the strength of several El Niño events from 1957 to 1998. SOURCE: National Oceanic and Atmospheric Administration, 1998.

domestic and industrial water supply from local and regional aquifers, many of which are restored (recharged) at rates often less than 0.2 percent per year by volume (Pimentel et al., 1997). Almost all rural homes and many cities depend heavily on ground water. As a consequence, aquifers have been thoroughly mapped and are extensively mined, especially for irrigation supplies (Figure 3.15). Throughout the western and midwestern states, large aquifers have declined substantially because rates of extraction exceed recharge rates (e.g., Ogalala Aquifer).

While ground water basins do not always coincide with watersheds, there are important interactions between surface water and ground water. In most watersheds, surface water and ground water flow paths are interconnected (Gibert et al., 1994a). The recharge areas may be wetlands or simply areas in the watershed where there are very permeable soils and sometimes a shallow water table. While the regional flow of water in aquifers generally reflects the general surface topography above, ground water resources in one watershed may also be fed by surface

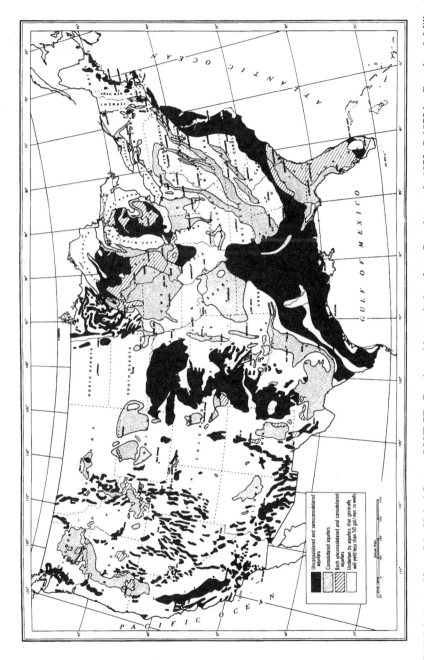

FIGURE 3.14 Aquifers of the United States. SOURCE: Reprint, with permission, from Geraghty et al., 1973. © 1973 by Geraghty & Miller, Inc.

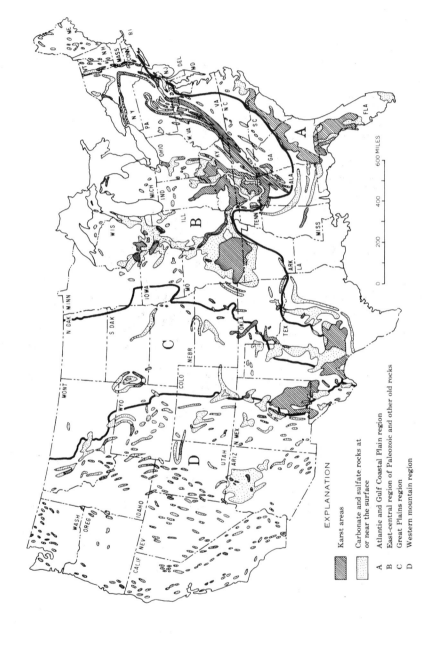

FIGURE 3.15 Generalized groundwater regions and major karst areas in the United States. SOURCE: LeGrand and Stringfield, 1973.

sources in an adjacent watershed. Watershed-scale issues therefore must be examined above and below ground. To date, management has generally under-emphasized ground water problems and responses as a component of water resource conservation and rehabilitation (GAO, 1991). Indeed, watershed management too often focuses only on surface waters, or if ground water resources are recognized only volume and accessibility receive notice whereas quality and biologic characteristics are also important.

Research has established at least five important attributes of groundwater ecology that are essential to a holistic view of watersheds (Gibert et al., 1994b). First, there is a continuum of geohydrologic units involving surface and ground-water flow pathways. For example, in one area surface runoff may flow into caves and fissures and that ground water may then feed directly into a river via large springs. In another, water from a river may penetrate alluvial soil at the upstream end of a floodplain, flow through unconfined aquifers within the flood-plain and upwell back into the channel via a network of springbrooks at the down-stream end (Jaffe and Dinovo, 1987). In either case, surface water becomes ground water that then re-enters the surface systems. This simply illustrates that geohydrologic units should be viewed as a diverse, interconnected mosaic.

A second essential ecological feature of ground water is that as water and materials move from one underground unit to the next, significant biogeochemical transformations usually occur. Types and concentrations of solutes change as the geomorphology and hence flow rate changes along the geohydrological gradient. Likewise, biotic species composition and abundance may change significantly along the geohydrological gradient. Thus we recognize biophysical (e.g., flow, temperature, redox, ion concentration, biodiversity, bioproduction) gradients as water moves through the geohydrological continuum. Gradients may be very steep (i.e., conditions may change very quickly) at boundaries or ecotones between different units (Vervier, 1992).

Third, virtually all ground water has some sort of biotrophic (food) web composed of microbes (bacteria and protozoa) as well as larger, more complex organisms, except in situations where oxygen is insufficient. As in surface water, the food web relies on microbial activity that uses dissolved or particulate organic matter as the primary energy source (Stanford and Ward, 1993). Since photosynthesis cannot occur in ground water, a supply of organic matter from soils or surface waters upstream is critical. Limited supplies of this organic matter generally makes ground water much less productive than surface waters. Nonetheless, ground water can support food webs (including in some cases vertebrates) that play vital ecological roles in transforming solute concentrations (including pollutants) in waters moving through the ground.

Fourth, water's movement through ground water systems and its associated biogeochemical transformations adds complexity to our view of landscapes. For example, we now examine river ecosystems in four dimensions: upstream-down-stream (longitudinal), channel-riparian (lateral), channel-groundwater (vertical), and temporal (time) (Ward, 1989). The penetration of river water into floodplain gravels defines the *hyporheic* zone, a ground water-surface water ecotone that occurs throughout river corridors of gravel-bed rivers. The hyporheic zone contains a community of organisms having both ground and surface water affinities that greatly influence local and regional biodiversity patterns. For instance, chemical transformations within the hyporheic zone and the dynamics of hyporheic discharge may actually control bioproduction within the river channel of gravel-bed rivers and the distribution and abundance of riparian vegetation throughout the river corridor (Stanford and Ward, 1993). Clearly, ground water is an interconnected component of riverine landscapes and corollaries apply to wetlands, lakes, and near-shore marine systems.

Finally, most ground water systems are naturally more biophysically constant than surface water environments. Ground water organisms are rather nonresilient in that they have evolved in conditions that, in many cases, have not changed for long periods of geologic time. Therefore, groundwater organisms are not likely to be resistant to environmental change. Yet, in many cases they have been subjected to such change, in the form of massive ground water pollution—a worldwide problem that threatens endemic ground water biota (Notenboom et al., 1994). It may be that many groundwater systems have been destroyed or severely damaged by abstraction and diversion, either for irrigation and potable use, or by disposal of wastes, before their natural integrity was recognized. If ground waters are connected components of river, lake, and marine ecosystems, vital ecosystem linkages may have been disconnected by ground water abstraction and pollution.

Watershed management must consider subsurface water resources and influences of land-use activities, especially ground water abstraction and subsurface injection of waste water and other pollutants, on these resources. Underground flow pathways provide recharge routes for aquifers and primary sites for the natural attenuation of pollution by microbes. Surface water simply cannot be effectively managed without detailed understanding of its biophysical connections to ground water.

Water Quality

Among the most important considerations in watershed management is water quality. Several aspects of water quality follow regional trends, although a patchwork of local inputs can greatly alter the regional pattern in many locations. Water contaminants can be broadly divided into dissolved and suspended constituents, although their causes and sources are often interrelated. A key component of water quality, not always detrimental, is concentration of dissolved inorganic substances. Although many minerals may be included, the dominant constituents by mass are generally salt (NaCl) and calcium carbonate ($CaCO_3$), the latter resulting in "hard water." For reasons described below, the highest dissolved surface water mineral concentrations tend to occur in the arid West (Figure 3.16), while the highest ground water mineral concentrations tend to occur in the central and southern U.S. (Figure 3.17). This difference can occur because ground waters in the West are less diluted by rain when they enter surface streams.

Sediment is generally the most common water pollutant. Not only can it fill stream channels and harbors, but it can also degrade habitat by reducing the amount of light that reaches stream bottoms and covering spawning beds and submerged aquatic vegetation. Additionally, chemical pollutants often sorb to sediment particles and thus move through and contaminate the environment.

A broad range of factors cause marked differences in water composition and quality at various locations in the United States. First, precipitation varies in chemical composition. For instance, rain near the coasts contains a much higher concentration of sea salts than further inland. However, only in areas with no anthropogenic pollution and very slow weathering rates does this have a significant effect on stream composition. More important, acid rain created by fossil fuel use has dramatically reduced pH and acid neutralizing capacity (ANC) and increased levels of sulfate and nitrate. In areas lacking carbonate bedrock, serious acidification of surface waters can result. In the United States, acid sources are concentrated in the Ohio River Valley. Downwind from this region is a broad area underlain mainly by granitic bedrock (New York and New England) which is especially vulnerable to the atmospheric acid inputs.

Lead added to gasoline and released during combustion was the dominant source of this metal to aquatic ecosystems during most of the 20th century. The historical record of trace-metal analyses of fresh waters is so riddled with contamination artifacts that it is impossible to know whether streams contained significant lead levels before the days of the automobile—a question further complicated by the ability of natural processes to greatly attenuate lead as it passes through soil (Wang et al., 1995). Yet substantial documentation suggests that lead from gasoline combustion significantly increased lead levels in surface waters of the world's oceans (Flegal and Patterson, 1983) and in soils throughout the United States. The elimination of lead in gasoline has caused a dramatic decline in atmospheric delivery, and surface waters now contain almost immeasurably low amounts, especially in bioavailable dissolved forms (Windom et al., 1991; Benoit, 1994).

Changes in forest ecosystems can also change water quality. For instance, gypsy moth defoliation of forested uplands in Virginia led to dramatic increases in concentrations of nitrates in stream waters. Other solute changes included increasing concentrations of calcium, magnesium, potassium, and hydrogen ions as well as decreasing concentrations of acid-neutralization capacity and SO_4^{2-}. After several years, the composition of the study stream returned to predefoliation concentration levels. Short-term effects of the defoliation included an increase in the frequency and severity of episodic acidification. Long-term effects included reduction of base nutrient supplies in the catchment basin (Webb et al., 1997).

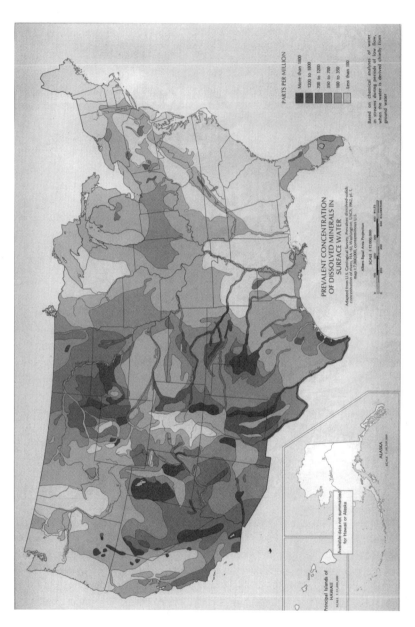

FIGURE 3.16 Prevalent concentration of dissolved minerals in surface waters. SOURCE: USGS, 1970.

79

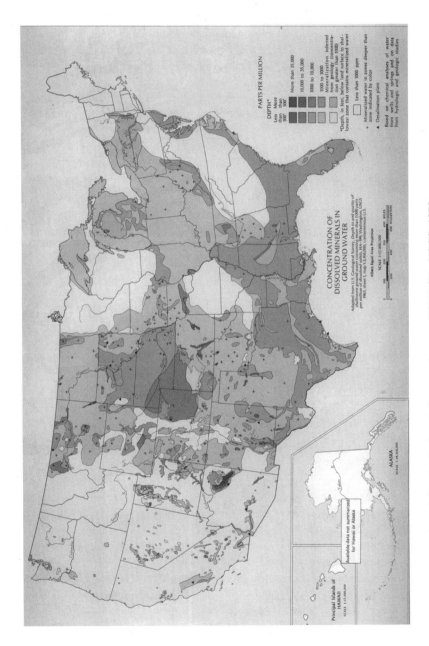

FIGURE 3.17 Concentration of dissolved minerals in ground water. SOURCE: USGS, 1970.

Climate can induce significant regional water-quality variations. Warmer areas undergo more rapid and complete weathering, generating large quantities of cation-depleted clays. Easily transported by running water, abundant clays contribute to the load of suspended particulate matter (SPM) and can carry contaminants. Differences in mean annual temperature thus explain indirectly (through the connection between temperature and evapotranspiration) much of the variation in extent of soil weathering and in the amount of suspended load in East Coast rivers, where SPM tends to increase as one moves south. The arid climate of the West meanwhile, enhances evapotranspiration, which can concentrate dissolved and suspended matter carried by streams and rivers.

Differences in bedrock cause most of the evident differences in regional water composition. Carbonates weather much more extensively and rapidly than silicates. Watersheds underlain mainly by silicate bedrock tend to have rivers with low ANC, pH, hardness, and total dissolved solids (TDS), and are dominated by the anions chloride and sulfate. In areas where carbonate rocks are common, hard water with high TDS occurs, and the most common anion is bicarbonate. The larger a watershed, the more likely it is to contain areas of carbonate bedrock. Thus large rivers tend to have chemistry reflecting carbonates dominating over silicates.

If evaporites (halite, gypsum) occur in a watershed, water may have high concentrations of chloride or sulfate, but pH is unaffected. Because of their very high solubility, evaporites are less common in humid regions, so they are more abundant in the West, but they underlie broad regions of the country. Finally, if reduced minerals are plentiful, their oxidation releases protons that cause stream acidification. An extreme example is found in the vicinity of mining operations, where coal and metal ores are found in association with metal sulfides. Streams in these areas can have pH as low as 3.

Land use and land cover, which influence water quality, also tend to have regional patterns. Many of these represent human-induced perturbations (e.g., agriculture and urbanization) as discussed later in this chapter. Populous regions and those where agriculture is extensive are likely to have degraded water quality. Another land cover, natural wetlands, covers a large portion of the landscape in several states (e.g., Minnesota, Maine, Florida). Waters from wetlands tend to have high levels of dissolved organic matter (humic and fulvic acids). Arid regions lack vegetation, which retains particulate matter, the combination of low vegetative cover and high evapotranspiration tend to cause high concentrations of SPM in western rivers.

Wide variations in the chemical composition of water are a natural consequence of regional differences in soils, bedrock, atmospheric inputs, and climate. In each region, aquatic ecosystems have adapted to local chemical conditions. Measurements of water quality in undeveloped headwater streams provide local benchmarks against which watershed managers can compare water quality degradations. Differences between ambient water quality and the local baseline are

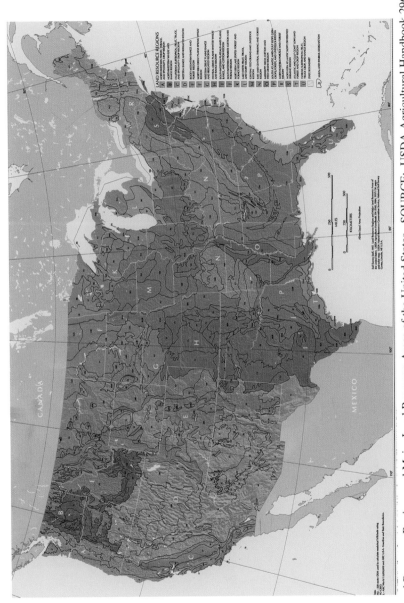

Plate 1: Land Resource Regions and Major Land Resource Areas of the United States. SOURCE: USDA Agricultural Handbook 296, 1997. USDA Natural Resources Conservation Service, National Soil survey Center, Lincoln, Nebraska.

Soil Drainage Class

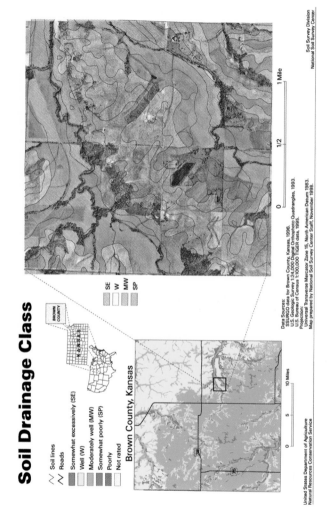

Legend:
- ∧ Soil lines
- ∧ Roads
- Somewhat excessively (SE)
- Well (W)
- Moderately well (MW)
- Somewhat poorly (SP)
- Poorly
- Not rated

Brown County, Kansas

0   5   10 Miles

United States Department of Agriculture
Natural Resources Conservation Service

SE
W
MW
SP

Data Sources:
SSURGO data for Brown County, Kansas, 1996.
U.S. Geologic Survey 1:24,000 Digital Orthophoto Quadrangles, 1993.
U.S. Bureau of Census 1:100,000 TIGER data, 1995.
Projection:
Universal Transverse Mercator Zone 15, North American Datum 1983.
Map prepared by National Soil Survey Center Staff, November 1998.

0   1/2   1 Mile

Soil Survey Division
National Soil Survey Center

Plate 2: Geographic information systems (GIS) can provide access to information across multiple scales, giving decisionmakers both an overall view of the issue and specific information to guide site-specific planning. This map of soil drainage class combines information about topography and land use with soil drainage characteristics to provide a detailed, field-by-field perspective on drainage patterns. Farmers can use such maps to plan cropping systems and minimize erosion potential as well as groundwater vulnerability. This image shows field boundaries and water retention dams in Brown County, Kansas. Photo image tones can be seen through the soil drainage class thematic overlay in shades of red, yellow, green, and blue. SOURCE: Brown County, Kansas Soil Survey Geographic Data Base (SSURGO), 1996. USDA–Natural Resources Conservation Service, Salina, Kansas.

Groundwater Vulnerability Map

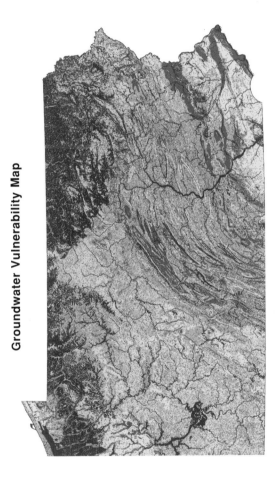

Plate 3: Geographic information systems (GIS) make decisionmaking more efficient and can help reduce the costs of environmental protection. For instance, as a result of regulatory requirements, water suppliers must test their source waters for a substantial list of possible chemical contaminants unless they can clearly justify that there is no reason to do so. In an effort to obtain a waiver for a suite of synthetic organic chemicals (most related to pesticide use), resource managers in Pennsylvania developed a strategy to determine the likelihood of a pesticide being applied in a given area and a measure of the risk posed. Using the location of all water supply facilities, they developed a GIS strategy that incorporated the amount of agricultural land, the most likely crops crown, and water movement through the environment (based on terrain factors such as geology, soil type, and topography). The result was this map of inherent ground water vulnerability. The map shows clearly where certain pesticides were not in use, and thus provides scientific support for waiving the testing of certain potentially problematic chemicals. This combined watershed and GIS initiative saved Pennsylvania taxpayers $7 million. (SOURCE: Barry Evans, Environmental Resources Research Institute, The Pennsylvania State University.)

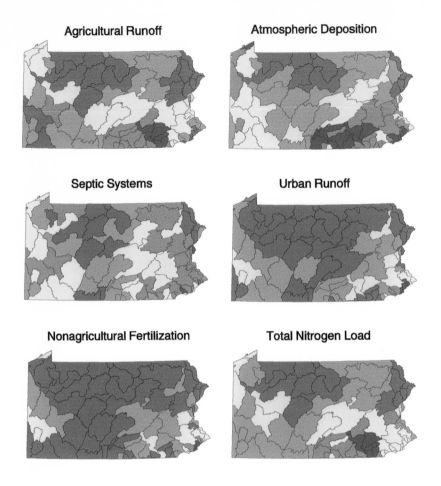

Agricultural Runoff

Atmospheric Deposition

Septic Systems

Urban Runoff

Nonagricultural Fertilization

Total Nitrogen Load

Plate 4: Geographic information systems (GIS) can be used to compile information in ways to help decisionmakers set priorities. In Pennsylvania, for example, legislation requires increased control of nitrogen and phosphorus as part of a multi-state effort to control nutrient loads to the Chesapeake Bay. But to reduce its contributions, Pennsylvania needed to understand the base levels of each pollutant in surface and ground water. The Department of Environmental Protection used a GIS strategy to quantify loads in different watersheds and estimate the fraction contributed by different nonpoint sources. With this information, the state developed mitigation strategies to address the most significant contributors. These maps show the nitrogen loads (in kg/ha) delivered to surface water by source category. Dark green indicates the lowest per unit area loads and dark red indicates the highest loads. (SOURCE: Barry Evans, Environmental Resources Research Institute, The Pennsylvania State University.)

usually caused by point and nonpoint sources of pollution (discussed later in this chapter). Watershed managers must decide what level of water quality is desired in relation to the inevitable costs, and design strategies to achieve those water quality goals.

ECOSYSTEMS

Plant and animal communities are interdependent and interact with their physical environment (soil, water, and air) to form distinct ecological units called ecosystems. The structures, components, processes, and even the boundaries, of ecosystems vary over time as a result of disturbances such as fires, floods, and climatic variations. However, ecosystem functions are generally resilient to the normal range of these disturbances, commonly referred to as the historic range of natural variability. In many cases, ecosystems depend on such disturbances for their regeneration and continued functioning.

The wide variation in climate and hydrology across the United States contributes to variation in its terrestrial and aquatic ecosystems. Such regional variation imposes inherent limits on attainable water quality, biotic assemblages, and trophic states that should be considered in watershed management. For example, stream-water quality in 107 watersheds across Ohio varied substantially among five ecological regions, even though all were minimally disturbed by human activity (Larsen et al., 1988). Similarly, there are distinct regional differences in water quality among Minnesota lakes, indicating that no single total phosphorus concentration should be used for setting standards across the state (Heiskary et al., 1987). Such regional differences also affect the assemblages of fish and other aquatic organisms present in lakes and streams (Larsen et al., 1986; Hughes et al., 1987; Rohm et al., 1987; Whittier et al., 1988). Watershed managers should take these regional variations into consideration in plans and regulations.

A number of maps have been developed to show ecological variation across the country using various combinations of climatic, physiographic, soils, land use, and vegetation characteristics to regionalize the landscape. Some of these maps show conditions that would exist if human influence were absent from ecosystems (Küchler, 1970). However, for most of the United States, particularly in regions of cultivated cropland, it is unrealistic to expect that water and land resources could attain the level of quality possible prior to major human settlement. Thus regionalization schemes by the U.S. Department of Agriculture (USDA, 1981) and the U.S. EPA (Omernik, 1987; USEPA, 1996) take into account the influence of human activities. Similarly the U.S. Geological Survey's "Seasonal Land Cover Regions" (USGS, 1994) represents actual rather than potential vegetation, dividing the conterminous United States into 154 different phenological vegetation groups through analysis of multitemporal satellite imagery, elevation, and climate data.

Omernik's (1987) "Ecoregions of the Conterminous United States" is notable in that it was compiled specifically "to give managers of aquatic and terrestrial resources a better understanding of the regional patterns of attainable quality of these resources" (Omernik and Gallant, 1990). It consists of a map and accompanying tables that describe 76 regions of relative homogeneity in ecological systems based on land use, land surface form, potential natural vegetation, and soils (Figure 3.18). Tests in Arkansas, Minnesota, Ohio, and Oregon have shown this system to have practical application for water resource management (Larsen et al., 1986; Heiskary et al., 1987; Hughes et al., 1987; Omernik, 1987; Rohm et al., 1987; Hughes and Larsen, 1988; Larsen et al., 1988; Whittier et al., 1988).

There are two initiatives to coordinate ecological regionalization schemes within North America. The first is a joint effort among Canada, the United States, and Mexico, to develop a hierarchical set of ecoregions across North America, for which draft "Level I" and "Level II" ecoregions has been developed. The second effort is a U.S. interagency effort to develop a hierarchical and common set of ecoregional boundaries that will bring greater uniformity to the different ecoregion maps the various land and water management agencies have created as they have adopted ecosystem-based approaches. For example, the U.S. Forest Service uses an ecosystem approach to forest management, considering an area's physiography, soils, and understory vegetation as indicators of the most suitable forest practices (Figure 3.19). The Service believes that maintaining or restoring ecosystems—rather than managing legislatively or administratively established land units and individual natural resources—would better address declining ecological conditions and ensure the sustainable long-term use of natural resources (GAO, 1994). The U.S. EPA has also delineated ecoregions (Omernik, 1987) and proposed their use for managing environmental resources (Hughes and Larsen, 1988; Gallant et al., 1989) (Figure 3.18). The Natural Resources Conservation Service (NRCS) (formerly the Soil Conservation Service) has divided the country into 27 Land Resource Regions based on physiography and crop potential (see color plate 1) (USDA, 1981), that form the basis for the NRCS's regional organizational structure. In March 1994 the U.S. Fish and Wildlife Service adopted an ecosystem management approach to fish and wildlife conservation and identified 52 ecosystems (Figure 3.20).

The effort to better coordinate these ecoregion designations was created by an interagency memorandum of understanding (MOU) that established an interagency team, designated as a work group of the Federal Geographic Data Committee (FGDC), to develop a common framework of ecological regions for the nation. Achieving this common regionalization scheme required recognition of the differences in the conceptual approaches and mapping methodologies that have been used to develop the agencies' various ecoregion frameworks.

These efforts reflect the strong push toward coordinated ecosystem management called for by an Interagency Ecosystem Management Task Force formed by the White House Office on Environmental Policy in 1993. The Task Force was asked to find ways to implement an ecosystem approach to environmental man-

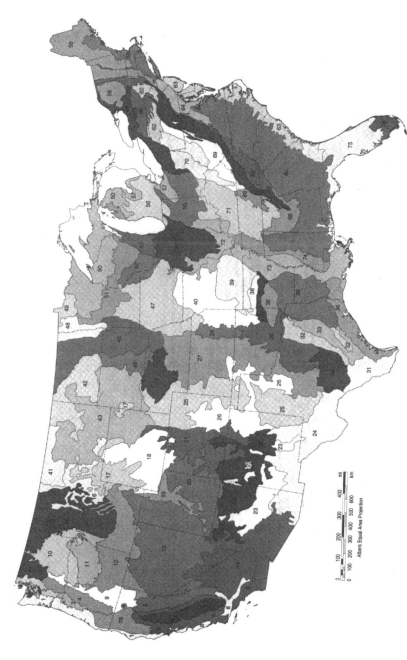

FIGURE 3.18 Ecoregions of the conterminous United States. SOURCE: Reprint, with permission, from Omernik, 1987. © 1987 by Association of American Geographers.

84

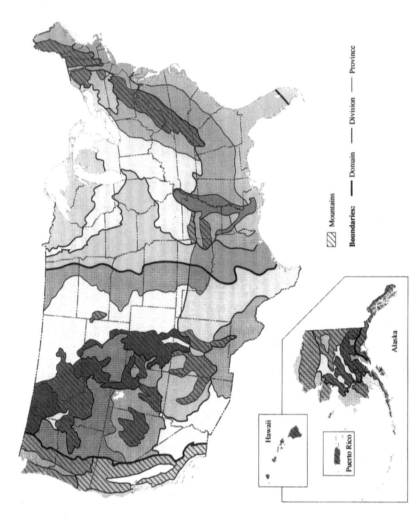

Mountains

Boundaries: —— Domain —— Division —— Province

FIGURE 3.19 Ecoregions as identified by U.S. Forest Service. SOURCE: GAO, 1994.

agement, establish overarching goals for all federal agencies, and remove barriers that frustrate more effective, efficient interagency cooperation (GAO, 1994). The Task Force's report made the case for use of ecosystem concepts of environmental management:

> The ecosystem approach is a method for sustaining or restoring natural systems and their functions and values. It is goal driven, and it is based on a collaboratively developed vision of desired future conditions that integrates ecological, economic, and social factors. It is applied within a geographic framework defined primarily by ecological boundaries. The goal of the ecosystem approach is to restore and sustain the health, productivity, and biological diversity of ecosystem and the overall quality of life through a natural resource management approach that is fully integrated with social and economic goals. This is essential to maintain the air we breath, the water we drink, the food we eat, and to sustain natural resources for future populations (Interagency Ecosystem Management Task Force, 1995).

It is a common sense way for public and private managers to carry out their mandates with greater efficiency.

DEMOGRAPHY

Patterns of human settlement have a variety of environmental impacts related to watersheds. In urban environments, watershed management issues range from the efficiency and effectiveness of high-volume water treatment to concentrated runoff from extensive impervious surfaces. In more sparsely populated areas, control of nonpoint source pollution becomes a central watershed management issue. Agricultural land use and on-site residential waste disposal pose water quality concerns. Thus while watershed management is needed across the entire landscape, specific watershed management problems vary depending on the type of land use and the pattern of population settlement within a given area.

Until the 1970s, urban population growth rates had long exceeded rural growth rates in the United States. In the 1970s, however, population growth rates in rural, nonmetropolitan areas exceeded those in metropolitan areas, demonstrating a national pattern of population dispersal. Not only did small towns grow, but there were high rates of population growth in nonurban areas, driven mostly by migration. Though the earlier pattern of higher urban growth rates reappeared in the 1980s, evidence from the early 1990s indicates that rural growth may again exceed urban rates (Fuguitt, 1985; Fuguitt et al., 1989; Johnson and Beale, 1994).

Human population is most dense in the eastern half of the nation, especially in the cities of the East Coast. A comparison of the nation's largest cities illustrates the contrast between the East and West. In 1992, the density of New York City's population was 22,900 persons per square mile, while the density of Los Angeles' population was 6,300 (U.S. Bureau of Census, 1995). These radically

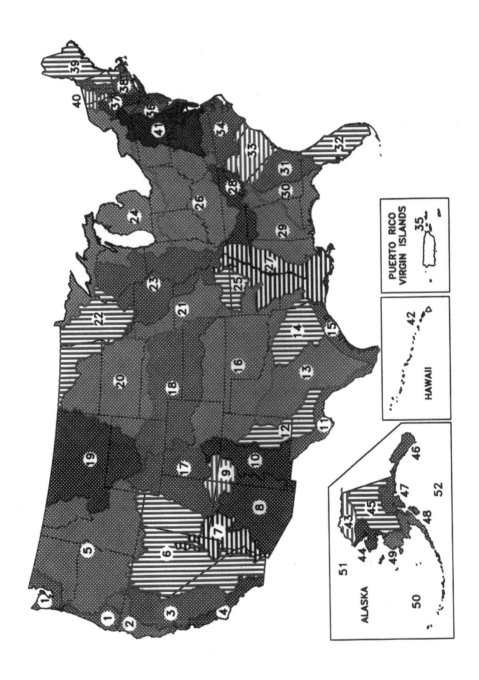

PUERTO RICO
VIRGIN ISLANDS   35

HAWAII   42

ALASKA
51
50
44
43
45
47
49
48
46
52

1. North Pacific Coast
2. Klamath/Central Pacific Coast
3. Central Valley of California/San Francisco Bay
4. South Pacific Coast
5. Columbia River Basin
6. Interior Basins
7. Lower Colorado River
8. Gila/Salt/Verde River
9. San Juan
10. Middle and Upper Rio Grande
11. Lower Rio Grande
12. Pecos River
13. Edwards Plateau
14. East Texas
15. Texas Gulf Coast
16. Arkansas/Red Rivers
17. Upper Colorado River
18. Platte/Kansas Rivers

19. Upper Missouri/Yellowstone Rivers
20. Main Stem Missouri River
21. Lower Missouri River
22. Mississippi Headwaters/Tallgrass Prairie
23. Upper Mississippi River/Tallgrass Prairie
24. Great Lakes
25. Ozark Watersheds
26. Ohio River Valley
27. Lower Mississippi River
28. Tennessee River
29. Central Gulf Watersheds
30. Florida Panhandle Watersheds
31. Altamaha/Sunwanee Rivers
32. Peninsular Florida
33. Savannah/Suntee/Pee Dee Rivers
34. Roanoke/Tar/Neuse/Cape Fear Rivers
35. Caribbean

36. Delaware River/Delmarva Costal Area
37. Hudson River/New York Bight
38. Connecticut River/Long Island Sound
39. Gulf of Maine Rivers
40. Lake Champlain
41. Chesapeake Bay/Susquehanna River
42. Pacific Islands
43. Arctic Alaska
44. Northwest Alaska
45. Interior Alaska
46. Southeast Alaska
47. South Central Alaska
48. Bristol Bay/Kodiak
49. Yukon - Kuskokwim Delta
50. Bering Sea/Aleutian Islands
51. Beaufort/Chukchi Seas
52. North Pacific/Gulf of Alaska

FIGURE 3.20 Ecoregions as identified by U.S. Fish and Wildlife Service. SOURCE: GAO, 1994.

different densities demand different management strategies for resources (such as watersheds) closely related to human populations.

Federal lands have low population density. For example, 41 percent of the land base of six Western states (Montana, Wyoming, Colorado, Utah, New Mexico, and Arizona) is federally held land with few permanent residents (Figure 3.21).

The dispersal of population to more rural areas creates new watershed management challenges. Population growth rates from 1980 to 1990 were highest along the East, South, and West Coast. Sparsely populated areas in Texas and Nevada also had high growth rates, but this arises from population change. It is important to note that this change takes different forms, including high density urban development, rural/urban fringe, dispersed moderate density settlement, and extensive population dispersal into rural areas.

HUMAN EFFECTS ON WATERSHEDS AND STREAMS

Humans affect watersheds and streams in two basic ways. First, they alter the land surface of watersheds, affecting both quantity and quality of streamflow and lakes. Second, streams and streamflow are directly affected by channel and floodplain alterations, dams, and water transfers, while water quality is affected by point sources. Many researchers have addressed these impacts (Leopold et al., 1964; Dunne and Leopold, 1978; Turner et al., 1990; Maidment, 1993; Goudie, 1994; Whitney, 1994; and Mays, 1996).

Land Use

Land use and land cover exert a powerful influence on the quantity and quality of runoff (Potter, 1991; Calder, 1993; McCutcheon et al., 1993; Malina, 1996). The primary land uses are forest, urban, agricultural, and wetlands.

A forest is usually the most hydrologically benign of land uses. First, the canopy and vegetative litter protect the soil from erosion. Second, the forest promotes permeable soils that often can accept even the most intense rains and convey the water downslope by subsurface routes. Forests thus prevent erosion, infiltrate most water, mitigate smaller floods, and yield clean streamflow. The general exception is after extensive tree harvesting when temporary erosion and nutrient export can occur; most forest erosion occurs as a result of poor harvesting practices. Although forests give many benefits, there is a cost: forests consume water (Calder, 1993) (see Box 3.1). An area of forest annually consumes a depth of water about 326 millimeters (13 inches) greater than other vegetation such as crops or grass. Thus, cutting an acre of forest will produce more than an acre-foot (1234 m^3, or 326,000 gallons) of water that would otherwise be transpired by the trees. In water-short areas (where an acre-foot of water costs $200-$300) forest management for water may become common in the future (Trimble

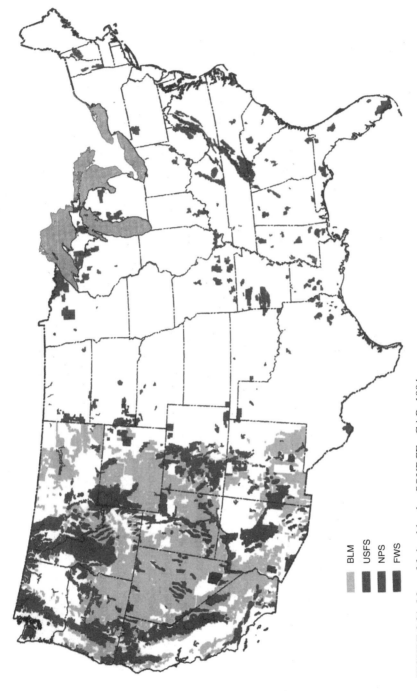

FIGURE 3.21 Map of federal lands. SOURCE: GAO, 1994.

BLM

USFS

NPS

FWS

Box 3.1
Watersheds of the Southern Piedmont:
Forest vs. Water Supply

Water yields from watersheds in the Southern Piedmont region, which spans parts of Georgia, Alabama, and South Carolina, illustrate the interaction between forest management and water yield. With the decline of agriculture in the Southern Piedmont during this century, forests have succeeded cotton, corn, and other crops. This recovering forest has decreased erosion, but it has also significantly decreased streamflow. Between 1919 and 1967, forested areas in this region increased in size between 10 to 28 percent, bringing about average annual decreases of streamflow ranging from 4 to 21 percent. The inclusive water-yield model shows that complete afforestation can decrease annual yield by about 13 inches, while 100% deforestation can increase it by the same amount. Such changes can be significant in a region like the Piedmont where streamflows average only about 15 inches. Another factor makes the impact of trees even more significant: forest-induced water deficits become greater with less rainfall. The net effect is that natural droughts are exacerbated while the forests have little impact in very wet years. Since water supply management is often based on minimum flows, forest management for increased water yield may become significant as water-supply demands increase. This is true not only for the Piedmont, but also for much of the forested Eastern United States.

SOURCE: Trimble et al., 1987.

et al., 1987). Although forests reduce small floods, they cannot control the larger ones. The Mississippi River was in flood and 60 miles wide when a member of the expedition of the Spanish explorer De Soto first saw it in 1541 (Frankenfield, 1927).

Fire has long been perceived as the enemy of the forest and especially of its watershed values. For many years, the official policy of the U.S. Forest Service and other governmental agencies was to suppress fires. However, long experience showed that this policy allowed the accumulation of fuel so that when fire eventually occurred, the accumulated fuel created a much worse fire than had nature been allowed to run its course. The Forest Service has therefore changed its policy to allow forest fires to burn, and even prescribes periodic fires to help prevent fuel accumulation.

Forest fires in the deciduous forests of the humid eastern United States are normally ground fires, and rarely disturb the hydrologic values of watersheds. In coniferous forests, especially in the West, complete or crown fires are more common, and these fires can significantly affect hydrologic qualities. Fire's effects are strongest in the chaparral scrub forest of the Southwest, where the waxy vegetation burns furiously and can create hydrophobic (water repellent) soil so that runoff and erosion are dramatically increased (De Bano, 1969).

The antithesis of forest is an urbanized area, where a large percentage of the surface is impermeable and pipes and sewers augment natural channels (Leopold, 1968; Loganathan et al., 1996). The runoff process in such areas is so efficient that stream discharge peaks may be several times those of comparable rural areas. Urbanization's greatest effects on floods are for smaller events; larger magnitude, lower frequency floods may be less affected. Thus urban areas and forests will produce greatly disparate 1-year and 10-year flood levels while producing the 100-year flood events or more similar magnitude.

The "waterproofing" caused by pavement in urban areas can actually "harvest" water, producing a much greater volume of surface water than unpaved areas. However, urban runoff may be of extremely poor quality because it may contain such pollutants as pet wastes, air pollution fallout, and the wastes of vehicular traffic such as antifreeze, oil, gasoline, lead, asbestos, and some exhaust products (Heaney, 1986; Makepeace et al., 1995) (see Table 3.1 and Box 3.2). Road salt is a common additional pollutant in snowy regions. Particulate matter concentrations from air pollution and street abrasion may approach levels from

TABLE 3.1 Comparison of Stormwater Quality from Various Sources for Selected Parameters

Study Location	BOD (mg/l)	Total solids (mg/l)	Suspended solids (mg/l)	Phosphate (mg/l)	Chloride (mg/l)	Fecal coliforms (MPN/100 ml)[a]
Durham, North Carolina	2-232	194-8860	27-7340	0.15-2.5	3-390	7000-86000
Cincinnati, Ohio	1-173	—	5-1200	0-02-7.3	5-705	500-76000
Coshocton, Ohio	0.05-23	—	5-2074	0-08	—	2-56000
Detroit, Michigan	96-234	310-914	—	—	—	25000-930000
Seattle, Washington	10	—	—	43	—	16000
Morristown, New Jersey	3-17	—	56-550	0.02-4.3	—	—
Ann Arbor, Michigan	28	—	2080	0.8	—	100

[a]MPN—Most probable number.

Box 3.2
Quinnipiac River Watershed, Connecticut:
Urban Water Pollution

The Quinnipiac River watershed, draining 429 square kilometers in 15 towns in south-central Connecticut, is a typical New England coastal river basin in the densely populated eastern United States. Its case illustrates the problems associated with highly urbanized watersheds and the pollution they generate. Millions of gallons of treated municipal, domestic, and industrial wastewater are discharged into the river every day, and two U.S. Superfund sites are located on the banks of the Quinnipiac river. The Quinnipiac was once badly polluted, but regulation of point source discharges has improved water quality, and now thousands of anglers and boaters use the stream. Thousands of people rely on aquifers within the watershed for drinking water.

While the health of the river is steadily improving, there are continuing threats to its water quality and habitat integrity. Nonpoint source (NPS) pollution is likely to be a major contributor to water quality degradation within the watershed and in Long Island Sound, at the river's outlet. Urban land uses near the Sound and in its major tributaries, including the Quinnipiac, contribute the greatest amount of nonpoint source pollution to the coastal waters. A study of Long Island Sound identified subbasins of the Quinnipiac watershed as of the highest priority for managing nonpoint sources of nitrogen.

Priority nonpoint source problems in the watershed include water quality impacts associated with seasonally low flows, on the one hand, and high volume stormwater runoff on the other. These phenomena result in

rural areas. Urban pollution can accumulate during dry periods and be flushed out in a highly concentrated burst during the first minutes or hours of a storm. Levels of some pollutants in urban runoff are worse than raw domestic sewage (Table 3.2). Roads, including highways, are often rural extensions of the urban phenomena, and can affect outlying areas.

In their effects on the quantity and quality of runoff, agricultural fields usually lie somewhere between forest and urban land (Calder, 1993). The variance depends on soil condition, type of crop or vegetation, and level of management.

Cropland, ranging from close-grown grasses to row crops with much bare water pollution, habitat impairment, severe erosion, and sedimentation. However, many aspects of the degradation process are poorly understood. For example, salt- and fresh-water wetlands may play a critical role in mitigating the effects of NPS pollution by removing excess nitrogen, heavy metals, and suspended solids from the river before they reach the Sound. On the other hand, badly degraded marshes may themselves become sources of contamination.

With funding from a Nonpoint Source Pollution Grant under Section 319 of the Clean Water Act, a local consortium has organized to resolve NPS problems in the Quinnipiac Watershed. The Yale School of Forestry and Environmental Studies, University of New Haven's Environmental Sciences Program, Qunnipiac River Watershed Association, and the Peabody Museum of Natural History joined forces with the Connecticut Department of Environmental Protection, U.S. Environmental Protection Agency, the Regional Water Authority, Natural Resources Conservation Service, municipal personnel, and concerned citizens. The consortium has initiated data collection, technical advisory activities, planning processes, and the development of a GIS database. The consortium also strives to raise community awareness of the issues because the majority of the population is unaware of the river, the resources it provides, and the threats to its health.

The next major step is a proposed broad, multi-objective planning and management initiative under the Connecticut Multiple Use Rivers Act. The approach will integrate solutions to a wide range of issues, including water quality, water supply, habitat, and land use, all focused on the watershed. The nonpoint source pollution project, with its assessment, prioritization, and implementation of abatement measures, will be the model for resolution of other problems. The Quinnipiac experience shows how a variety of interested groups can organize around the watershed concept, and how the solution of one problem leads to confidence in dealing with a broad array of issues.

soil exposed, usually shows the greatest variance in the quantity of runoff. Cropland receives the bulk of agricultural chemicals such as fertilizers (especially nitrates), herbicides, and pesticides. The movement of these chemicals into streams is enhanced because they often adsorb onto soil particles, and soil erosion is usually greatest from cropland. The need to reduce erosion from cropland has led to greatly improved management techniques, including minimum- and no-till farming.

Irrigation of cropland, especially in the Southwest, leads to great water losses from infiltration and evaporation. Without careful management, soils can become

TABLE 3.2 Comparison of Contaminant Profiles for Urban Surface Runoff and Raw Domestic Sewage, Based on Surveys Throughout the United States

Constituent[a]	Urban surface runoff	Raw domestic sewage
Suspended solids	250-300	150-250
BOD[b]	10-250	300-350
Nutrients		
(a) Total nitrogen	0.5-5.0	25-85
(b) Total phosphorus	0.5-5.0	2-15
Coliform bacteria (MPN/100ml)[c]	10^4-10^6	10^6 or greater
Chlorides	20-200	15-75
Miscellaneous substances		
(a) Oil and grease	Present	Present
(b) Heavy metals	(10-100) times sewage conc.	Traces
(c) Pesticides	Yes	Seldom
(d) Other toxins	Potential exists	Seldom

[a]All concentrations are expressed in mg l^{-1} unless stated otherwise.
[b]Biochemical oxygen demand.
[c]MPN—Most probable number.

SOURCE: Reprint, with permission, from Burke, 1972. © by Academic Press.

salinized. Excess water from irrigated fields (return flow) often contains excess salts, nutrients, and other chemicals that can pollute streams and groundwater.

Because it is vegetated and usually untilled, pasture may be a relatively benign use of land. Heavy grazing with soil compaction and vegetative damage, however, can transform the hydrologic characteristics of pastures into something near those of a parking lot. Such poorly managed pasture produces more overland flow, which causes soil erosion and allows animal wastes to be washed into streams. Because of sparse vegetation and poorly developed soil, semi-arid rangeland is even more fragile than pasture, and has been heavily abused and eroded in the past (Cooke and Reeves, 1976; Branson et al., 1981).

Aside from their value as wildlife habitat, wetlands are also generally valuable as sinks for sediment and nutrients (Johnston et al., 1984, 1990; Johnston 1991, 1993; NRC, 1995; Richardson, 1996). Both empirical and modeling studies have also demonstrated the value of wetlands for reducing flood peaks (Novitzki, 1979; Jacques and Lorenz, 1988), although the location of wetlands in relation to stream order influences how far downstream their flood peak reduction effects are observed (Ogawa and Male, 1986).

Large areas of wetlands have been drained for urban development and agricultural purposes, especially in the Midwest. The purpose of wetland drainage is to lower the water table and move water faster off the wetland surface. This reduces or eliminates their wildlife habitat, nutrient retention, and flood peak reduction capability. Lowering the water table may mitigate runoff from small rainfall events by increasing water storage in the soil (Goudie, 1994), but this mechanism ceases to be effective once the soil becomes saturated. Drainage also increases oxidation and subsidence of organic soils.

Strong state and federal efforts have been made in the last two decades to save the remaining American wetlands. Additionally, large areas of wetlands have been created in the eastern United States from the effects of historical soil erosion and associated sedimentation.

Changes of Streams and Streamflow

Many United States streams have undergone significant changes of morphology and/or streamflow during the past two centuries (Schumm, 1977; Goudie, 1994; Chapra, 1996). Some of these changes were deliberate, some unintentional. Land use, channelization, changes in riparian vegetation, dams and reservoirs, water transfers, and changes in groundwater depths all helped create changes in streams and streamflow.

Some of the greatest impacts on streams have come from the land-use changes discussed earlier. Generally, the greatest impact on runoff and floods is from urban land use (Leopold, 1968) (see Box 3.3). Greatly enhanced floods can cause severe channel erosion, while decreased soil-infiltration rates leave little base flow between storms so that water often collects in stagnant pools (Wolman, 1967; Graf, 1975, 1977; NRC, 1997).

On agricultural land, accelerated soil erosion over the years has streams and valleys to aggrade (fill with eroded sediment and other detritus) in some cases over at depths over 5 meters. Frequently, streams were aggraded more rapidly than floodplains, creating wetlands. Such large amounts of sediment take centuries or millennia to move through watersheds (Happ et al., 1940; Meade, 1982) (Figure 3.22). The management of migrating sediment can be an important aspect of watershed management (Trimble, 1993). In other cases, runoff has increased disproportionately to sediment, causing tributary stream channels to erode and enlarge and sending sediment downstream to be deposited in larger valleys with lower gradients (Happ et al., 1940; Meade, 1982). With the implementation of soil conservation measures since the 1930s, both runoff and erosion have been reduced (Trimble and Lund, 1982; Potter, 1991). As a result, formerly deposited sediment has been eroded and transported farther downstream and redeposited (Figure 3.22). Stream sediment loads therefore do not necessarily indicate current upland erosional processes—which makes sediment management more complex than just managing upland land use.

Channelization with a combination of open surface ditches and subsurface feeder drains is a common means of wetland drainage that has been employed to

Box 3.3
San Diego Creek, California:
Urban Channel Erosion

While stream-channel erosion in urbanizing watersheds has been documented in humid regions, few studies have examined such erosion in arid or semi-arid locales (Graf, 1988). San Diego Creek came to the attention of the public in the late 1970s when it was realized that sediment from the watershed was filling New-port Bay, a large and important estuarine habitat. An extensive and expensive 208 study attributed the problem to upland erosion (Boyle Engineering, 1982). Research since then, however, has shown that stream channel erosion has been responsible for much of the sediment moving toward Newport Bay (Trimble, 1997a). Most channel erosion is in tributaries while the broad, downstream trunk channels are usually sediment sinks. Both situations present controversial management problems. Despite attempts to control channel erosion, many tributaries have had their cross-sectional area increased by a factor of two to ten during the past one to seven decades. This erosion not only sends vast amounts of sediment to Newport Bay, but can also remove significant areas of expensive real estate as channels widen. Undermined trees and other debris fall into the channel, sometimes blocking the channel and increasing flood damage. These processes lead to a major management question: Should such channels be left in their earthen condition to presumably erode at high rates, or should the channels be paved or armored with rip-rap? Paved channels prevent erosion and convey floodwaters more efficiently, but many people oppose them on both cost and aesthetic grounds.

Downstream trunk channels have been vastly enlarged to transport the expected 500-year flood. However, these broad channels have become sediment traps because they do not efficiently transport the smaller, sediment-laden flows. The resulting sediment deposits are rapidly colonized by trees and brush which, in turn, quickly become wildlife habitat. These deposits, along with their trees and brush, reduce the flood conveyance capacity of the trunk channels. Additionally, large floods could remobilize these materials, sweeping them downstream where the vegetation can snag on bridge piers, thus decreasing openings and potentially increasing flooding. Regular maintenance would remove these deposits, but local pressure has been brought to protect the incipient wildlife habitat. Thus, the management question in the lower reaches becomes wildlife habitat versus public safety.

GENERALIZED EVOLUTION OF THE PIEDMONT LANDSCAPE, 1700–1970

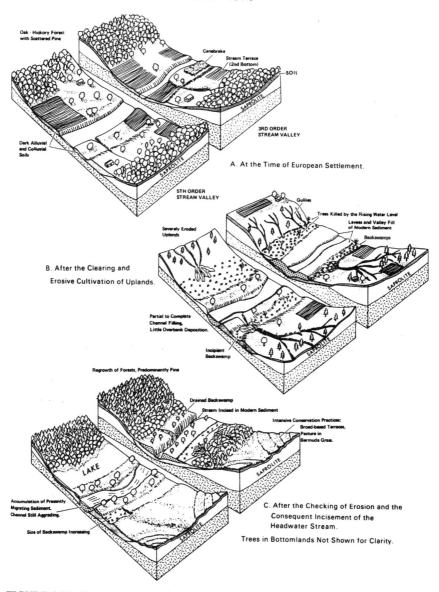

A. At the Time of European Settlement.

B. After the Clearing and Erosive Cultivation of Uplands.

C. After the Checking of Erosion and the Consequent Incisement of the Headwater Stream.
Trees in Bottomlands Not Shown for Clarity.

FIGURE 3.22 Severe erosion and sedimentation from poor agricultural land use in the Southern Piedmont, 1700-1970. Note the aggradation of streams, the transformation of flood-plain into swamps, and the transfer of sediment downstream and its relation to land use. SOURCE: Reprint, with permission, from Trimble, 1974. © by Soil Conservation Society of America.

drain large wetland areas stream valleys that had been swamped by historical sedimentation. Such channels were usually deep, straight, and inherently unstable (Keller, 1976; Brookes, 1985). Some channels have eroded laterally or vertically, or both, with the sediment being redeposited further downstream (Schumm et al., 1984). In cases where hillside and upstream erosion have not been curtailed, the enlarged channels have simply filled with sediment. Ditching these mainstream channels lowers the base level of tributaries, thus destabilizing them and causing channel erosion which helped fill the trunk channel (Happ et al., 1940). Such complications make management of such channels a growing art (Shields et al., 1995; Wang et al., 1997).

Managers also channelize streams as a flood protection measure. This is especially true in urban areas where rapidly eroding channels are straightened to increase a stream's slope, reshaped into a hydraulically efficient cross section with a uniform grade, and paved. Although not aesthetically pleasing, paving is important to (a) reduce hydraulic friction and thereby lower flood stages, (b) prevent channel erosion, and (c) maintain a uniform grade (Loganathan et al., 1996). One problem with paved channels in arid regions is that recharge of groundwater through the channel floor is prevented. Thus, such areas need recharge basins in or next to urban channels.

Where streams are too large for channelization by excavation, some flood control may be gained by building levees. In addition to being very expensive to build and maintain, levees lead to two additional problems. First, they keep floods out of the storage zones on floodplains, thus increasing the floodwave downstream. Second, by reducing the flood-channel width by restricting it between the levees, levees cause flood stages to be higher. If levees fail or are overtopped, the resulting flood is locally much higher than it would have been without the levees. Both effects were apparent in the 1993 Midwest flood (Interagency Floodplain Management Review Committee, 1994).

The most striking historic changes in streamflow and stream channels have occurred in the Southwest, where exotic rooted plants, especially salt cedar (*Tamarix chinesis*), have colonized stream channels, transpiring huge amounts of water and causing streams to aggrade and braid (Graf, 1978). In coastal streams, giant reed (*Arundo donax*) causes similar problems. Channelization measures that remove all vegetation along streams without stabilizing them somehow have left many streambanks especially vulnerable to erosion, creating a highly unstable stream environment (Keller, 1976; Schumm et al., 1984; Gregory, 1985; Madej et al., 1994).

Stream morphology and the quality of habitat for aquatic organisms are strongly influenced by the presence of large woody debris (Harmon et al., 1986; Sedell et al., 1988). As riparian trees grow and die, they fall into channels or onto stream banks and the floodplain. Large woody debris also results from environmental disturbances such as floods, windstorms, wildfires, and landslides (Keller and Swanson, 1979; Benda, 1990). Large woody debris deflects streamflow, causing scour of the bed and banks and creating pools that are used by many species of fish and other animals (Bisson et al., 1987). In addition to creating pools, large woody debris in small streams may store sediment and organic matter, regulating the rate of movement of these materials downstream (Naiman and Sedell, 1980; Bilby, 1981; Megahan, 1982; Triska and Cromack, 1982). The structural and ecological diversity created by large woody debris in many streams is critical to the support of rich and diverse communities of plants and animals (Gregory et al., 1991; Reice, 1994).

Large woody debris has historically been removed from streams to aid river navigation (including log drives) and to facilitate upstream fish migrations (Bisson et al., 1987; Hicks et al., 1991). As a result, many streams across the nation now hold much less large woody debris than existed a century ago (Sedell and Luchessa, 1982; Sedell and Beschta, 1991) and a considerable amount of habitat diversity has been lost (Gregory et al., 1991; Bisson et al., 1992; Bayley, 1995).

Large woody debris also can be problematic. Accumulations can cause streambank erosion and damage to structures such as bridges, fences, and buildings. Large woody debris from forested floodplains may destabilize streams causing channel widening and enlargement with a loss of sediment to downstream reaches. Conversely, grassy floodplains can cause storage of sediment resulting in smaller and narrower channels (Davis-Colley, 1997; Montgomery, 1997; Trimble, 1997b).

Dams and reservoirs also can have profound influences on streams and streamflow (Baker, 1996; Stanford, 1997). Perhaps their foremost effect is to make streamflow downstream of the dam more regular by increasing low-flow discharges and decreasing the magnitudes of most floods. This downstream effect is beneficial in many ways, but there are areas in the West where coarse sediments from tributaries accumulate downstream from large dams because flows are inadequate to transport them away (Graf, 1980).

Additionally, because periodic high flows are necessary for the ecological integrity of rivers (Stanford et al., 1996), a certain degree of flooding may be desirable. Another problem, common in more populated areas of the humid East, is that although reservoirs may control smaller floods, they rarely can control the larger ones. Thus, people are lulled into economic activity on floodplains, only to be periodically flooded out with grave economic consequences.

Another characteristic of reservoirs is that they trap much of the entering sediment (Dendy and Champion, 1978; Trimble and Bube, 1990; Baker, 1996). Such sediment can displace part of the usable reservoir volume. In addition much of the sediment is usually deposited at the head of the reservoir, creating a rise in base level that sometimes causes the river to aggrade for several miles upstream. Furthermore, while the trapping of sediment by a reservoir may improve downstream water quality, the sediment-starved water may degrade channels for many miles downstream (Williams and Wolman, 1984). Wildlife habitat may be changed significantly upstream and downstream from a reservoir (Pitlick and Van Steeter, 1994; Ligon et al., 1995).

Large reservoirs are vulnerable to evaporative losses. In the humid East, these losses are often not much larger than otherwise would have been lost to vegetative transpiration. In the arid West, however, gross evaporative losses are net losses and can amount to as much as 7 feet (2 m) per year from an entire reservoir area. Evaporation also concentrates salt and other minerals in the remaining reservoir waters.

Reservoirs can affect water temperature. Shallow reservoirs allow warming during the summer, while deep reservoirs may become so cold at the greatest depths that released water may be unsuitable for irrigation and contain less dissolved oxygen level, impacting aquatic life. Stratification of deep reservoirs can also cause undesirable changes in water quality, such as when bottom water isolated from the atmosphere suffers oxygen depletion.

Whether caused by dams, water transfer, or land use alteration, changes of stream flow regimes can have significant effects on aquatic and terrestrial ecosystems. Evaluating such changes can sometimes make mitigation measures possible (Richter et al., 1996).

Because significant distances often separate areas of high water demand from those areas of water surplus, water transfers play an important role in the United States (NRC, 1992). One example is the Colorado River. Fed from the mountains, the Colorado once flowed through the deserts of the Southwest and emptied into the Gulf of California. By compact, the entire flow was apportioned to seven states including California, Nevada, and Arizona, and the river's water has been transported to regions outside the river's watershed. Indeed because of erroneous long-term streamflow measurements, more water was apportioned than would normally be available! A series of reservoirs made the water readily available for consumption so that little flow now reaches the ocean (Graf, 1985). Between 1935 and 1965, water storage in western U.S. reservoirs increased from about 5 million acre-feet to 270 million acre-feet (Graf et al., 1997).

Southern California is the nation's largest importer of water; its imported water is used extravagantly for both urban and agricultural uses, especially irrigation (Hundley, 1992). This water is brought not only from the Colorado River, but also from Northern California and the Owens River Valley on the east side of the Sierra Nevada Mountains.

Significant ground water extraction, another form of water transfer, may have any of several impacts (Graham et al., 1996). First, as the water table drops, pumping of ground water becomes increasingly difficult and expensive. Second, declining ground water can often cause depleted streamflow and local surface-water supply. Finally, excessive ground water extraction can cause the ground to subside. Subsidence of more than 9 meters has been recorded in Southern California (Figure 3.23), and some formerly inhabited areas along the Gulf Coast are now inundated.

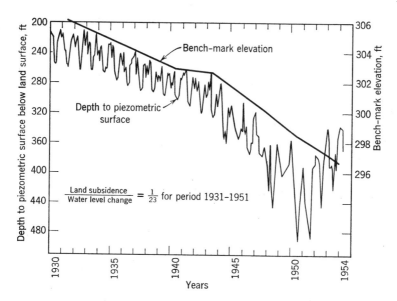

FIGURE 3.23 Changes in ground water surface and piezometric surface (ground water surface from confined aquifer) north of Bakersfield, California. SOURCE: Reprint, with permission, from Todd, 1959. © 1959 by John Wiley and Sons, Inc.

Because of heavy irrigation, some areas have too much ground water recharge. As water tables rise close to the surface, the slightly saline ground water can move to the surface by capillary action and evaporate. This concentrate salt and other minerals at the surface, often damaging the soil and polluting local ground water.

Point Sources of Pollution

Unlike the nonpoint sources considered earlier in this section, point sources of water pollution are released, often deliberately, into a stream at an identifiable place. Thus, prerelease treatment usually becomes more practicable for point sources than nonpoint sources of pollution (Malina, 1996; McCutcheon et al., 1993). The main point-source dischargers are wastewater treatment systems, industrial plants, feedlots, and mining operations.

Wastewater treatment plants put sewage from residential, commercial, and industrial areas through primary, secondary, and in some cases tertiary treatment processes that remove organic material, nitrogen, phosphorus, and pathogens. With present technology, increased public awareness, and increasingly stringent discharge permit requirements, wastewater can be treated to better-than-ambient condition and the effluent released into rivers, lakes, and oceans, or recharged

Box 3.4
Santa Ana River Watershed, California:
An Effluent-Dominated Stream

The Santa Ana River of Southern California exemplifies effluent-dominated streams and their watershed management problems. The 2,800 square-mile watershed is home to 4.5 million people, and spans ecological zones with little rainfall, ranging from arid lowlands and coastal areas to pine forests in the San Bernardino Mountains. Water users consume twice as much water as is available naturally, with the deficit made up by water imported from northern California and the Colorado River. Land uses include residential, commercial, industrial, military bases, airports, agriculture (crops, orchards, and high-density dairy farms), open spaces and parks (including Disneyland and Knott's Berry Farm), tourism and recreation (skiing, sailing, swimming, boating, marinas, hunting, and hiking), wildlife habitats for rare and endangered species, water reclamation, groundwater recharge, and major flood control facilities.

The Santa Ana River is an intermittant stream, and for most of the year, 45 wastewater treatment plants contribute 85 to 90 percent of its surface flows. Many sections of the river are concrete lined and the river serves as a dry flood control channel. Because of discharges from National Pollution Discharge Elimination System (NPDES) permitted point sources, the Santa Ana River was listed by EPA on the 304 (l) "toxic hot spots" list of impaired waterways. Water quality problems would continue to exist even if all permitted dischargers met all their discharge requirements. Nitrogen and total dissolved solids exceed water quality objectives mostly due to nonpoint source discharges from agricultural and dairy practices. Polluted urban runoff, which is growing from increasing urbanization, exacerbates the problem. This watershed illustrates the failure of the "one-size-fits-all" water quality criteria developed at the national and state governmental levels, for those criteria do not fit the unique conditions of the Santa Ana River watershed. If federally mandated "Individual Control Strategies" are added to the NPDES permits of the dischargers to the Santa Ana River, as required under the 304(l) listing, the cost (an estimated $6 billion) would have a substantial adverse effect on the economy of the region.

The Santa Ana Watershed Project Authority, a joint powers agency made up of the five major water districts in the watershed that coordinate and implement projects to improve water quality in the region, and the Santa Ana River Dischargers Association, an organization of the upstream dischargers into the Santa Ana River, initiated a "Use-Attainability Analysis" for the basin. Their objective was to evaluate the physical, biological, chemical, and hydrological conditions of the Santa Ana River, and to determine what specific beneficial uses the river could support. The Santa Ana Watershed Planning Advisory Committee was also formed. It was made up of agricultural and dairy interests, city and county governments, wastewater and water supply agencies, coastal and environmental interests, stormwater and flood control interests, water quality regulators, and state and numerous federal government resource agencies. The study developed and made scientifically grounded recommendations on establishing a new beneficial-use designation based on the effluent-dependent, concrete-lined conditions of the river. The Californian Regional Water Quality Control Board's Basin Plan for the watershed designated portions of the river as "Limited Warm Fresh Water Habitat," with new water quality criteria based on the site-specific characteristics of the Santa Ana River. However, the new beneficial use and water quality criteria were rejected by EPA.

The use-attainability analysis was a technical success, an excellent example of a thorough, scientifically based study of the physical, biological, chemical, and hydrological conditions of a watershed. It made a strong a case for rejecting the "one-size-fits-all" regulations and instead developed a beneficial use designation designed for the site-specific characteristics of effluent-dominated streams in arid areas. However, the study was a bureaucratic failure. It was accepted at the regional and state levels, but rejected by the EPA regional and national offices. It is a prime example of the jurisdictional disputes that arise among local, state, and federal agencies over the authority to establish water quality control standards for a river (Anderson, 1996, personal communication).

SOURCE: O'Connor, 1995.

into aquifers. In some parts of the Southwest, sewage effluent may constitute the major portion of streamflow (Stanford, 1997), making the management of such streams problematic (see Box 3.4). In most parts of the country, the effluent is discharged into reservoirs and rivers that serve as drinking water sources for people living downstream. The effluent may also be used for irrigation and industrial purposes.

In non-seaward urban and rural areas, wastewater is treated on-site septic systems. Increasingly stringent public health codes and inspections are reducing the ground water and surface water pollution caused by these systems. However, in many places, septic systems are still placed too close to the ground water table, leading to ground water pollution, or in soils that are too thin, allowing the effluent to move along bedrock into springs and streams.

Industrial wastes (heat, chemical, infectious agents, and radiation) are treated prior to release into the waters of the United States. Some industries pretreat their wastewater and then release it into the wastewater treatment system. Other industries treat the waste themselves to National Pollution Discharge Elimination System (NPDES) permit standards prior to releasing it into streams and rivers. The 1995 Toxic Release Inventory Report (TRI) shows that 630,000 tons of toxins were released into the waters of the United States and 120,000 tons transferred to wastewater treatment plants (USEPA, 1997).

Air emissions from industrial sources carry many pollutants. These airborne pollutants fall directly into the rivers and lakes ("dry fall") or are collected by precipitation and brought to earth. Sulfur oxides from burning of coals have been implicated in acid precipitation, which has heavily affected both terrestrial and aquatic ecosystems. Many streams of the Northeast, where poorly buffered acidic soils predominate, have been rendered sterile. Air currents have carried pollutants, including DDT, dioxins, and other carcinogens, into all parts of the globe, so that there are no places that do not have measurable concentrations of these and other toxic chemicals. The TRI data for 1995 show a release of approximately 631,000 tons of toxic chemicals into the air (USEPA, 1997). Some of these chemicals eventually get into the water, although many are retained in the soils.

Feedlots are important point sources of pollution from agriculture. They may range from isolated barnlots for small herds to very large feeding areas where thousands of animals are kept in relatively small areas. The runoff from feedlots is toxic, high in biochemical oxygen demand (BOD), looks and smells bad, and carries a high load of nitrogen and phosphorus. Confined feeding operations must now treat their wastewater, but problems remain.

Mining can create both sediment and chemical pollution. Environmental laws have greatly curtailed impacts from present-day mining, but past mining activity has left a harsh legacy. In areas of high relief, spoil from mining often was sufficient to aggrade streams and floodplains, while clearing of forests for ore smelting caused stream erosion elsewhere (Graf, 1979). Perhaps the most dramatic example of mining impacts was from hydraulic mining for gold in

California's Sierra Nevada, where mountain valleys were sometimes buried to depths of 25 meters (Gilbert, 1917). Even though hydraulic mining was outlawed in the mid-19th century, sediment has continued to move down the rivers toward San Francisco Bay. A continuing problem is the mining of sand and gravel from streams.

The mining of minerals and fuels, especially of coal, expose such compounds and minerals as iron sulfides, pyrite, and marcasite (ferrous sulphide). The result is often acidification with high sulfate and iron concentrations that may not only be toxic, but also unsightly. In some cases, mining may release toxic metals into the environment. In the past, air pollution from ore processing has affected vegetation and soils over a large area. Wastes from the mining and processing of uranium and thorium may pollute the water and sediments of rivers for miles downstream (Graf, 1994).

CONCLUSIONS

The physical and hydrologic components of our environmental systems are tremendously variable from one place to another and from one time to another. The ecological systems that depend on that hydrology are also variable, giving rise to great diversity in the life forms and processes across the continent. Our human population is part of this vast and changeable ecosystem, and it too shows great variability, especially with respect to the density of settlement. Humans affect the physical behavior of hydrologic systems through engineering works, and their chemical characteristics through pollution. Watershed managers need to be aware of the regional variation of environmental systems and take it into account as they plan activities.

The variability in natural systems is matched by variability of the institutional landscape created to manage our water and watershed resources, and this diversity is described in Chapters 6 and 7. Because of the great variability in natural resources and institutional structures, it is unlikely that a standard solution for watershed problems imposed from the national level will be workable in all localities. Rather, it appears that partnerships involving a range of governmental levels, citizens, businesses, and nongovernmental organizations are necessary to accommodate the variability.

REFERENCES

Baker, L. 1996. Lakes and reservoirs. Chap. 9 In Mays, L. (ed.) Water Resources Handbook. New York: McGraw-Hill.

Bayley, P. B. 1995. Understanding large river-floodplain ecosystems. BioScience (45(3):153-158.

Benda, L. E. 1990. The influence of debris flows on channels and valley floors in the Oregon Coast Range, USA. Earth Surface Processes and Landforms 15:457-466.

Benoit, G. 1994. Clean technique measurement of Pb, Ag, and Cd in fresh water: A redefinition of metal pollution. Environ. Sci. Technol. 28:1987-1991.

Bilby, R. E. 1981. Role of organic debris dams in regulating the export of dissolved and particulate matter from a forested watershed. Ecology 62:1234-1243.

Bisson, P. A., R. E. Bilby, M. D. Bryant, C. A. Dolloff, G. B. Grette, R. A. House, M. L. Murphy, K. V. Koski, and J. R. Sedell. 1987. Large woody debris in forested streams in the Pacific Northwest: past, present, and future. Pp.143-190 in E. O. Salo and T. W. Cundy (eds.) Streamside Management: Forestry and Fishery Interactions. Contribution Number 57, Institute of Forest Resources, University of Washington, Seattle, Washington.

Bisson, P. A., T. P. Quinn, G. H. Reeves, and S. V. Gregory. 1992. Best management practices, cumulative effects, and long-term trends in fish abundance in Pacific Northwest river systems. Pages 189-232 In R. B. Naiman (ed.) Watershed Management: Balancing Sustainability and Environmental Change. Springer-Verlag, New York, N.Y.

Boyle Engineering Co. 1982. Sediment source analysis and sediment delivery analysis, Newport Bay Watershed - San Diego Creek comprehensive stormwater sedimentation control plan. San Diego, CA.

Branson, F., G. Gifford, K. Renard, and R. Hadley, 1981. Rangeland Hydrology, 2nd Ed. Dubuque, Iowa: Kendall-Hunt.

Brookes, A. 1985. River channelization: traditional engineering methods, physical consequences and alternative practices. Prog. in Phys. Geog. 9: 44-73.

Burke, R. 1972. Stormwater runoff. Pp. 727-733 in R. T. Oglesby, C. A. Carlson, and J. A. McCann (eds.) River Ecology and Man. New York: Academic Press.

Calder, I. 1993. Hydrologic effects of land use change. Chap. 13 In Maidment, D. (ed.) Handbook of Hydrology. New York: McGraw-Hill.

Chapra, S. 1996. Rivers and streams. Chap. 10 In Mays, L. (ed.)Water Resources Handbook. New York: McGraw-Hill.

Cooke, R. U., and R. Reeves. 1976. Arroyos and Environmental Change in the American Southwest. Oxford: Oxford Univ. Press.

Council on Environmental Quality. 1981. Environmental Trends. Washington, D.C.: U.S. Government Printing Office.

Davies-Colley, R. J. 1997. Stream channels are narrower in pasture than in forest. New Zealand Journal of Marine and Freshwater Research 31:599-608.

Dendy, F. E., and W. A. Champion. 1978. Sediment deposition in U.S. reservoirs: Summary of data reported through 1975. U.S. Dept. Agr. Misc. Pub. 1362.

Dunne, T., and L. B. Leopold. 1978. Water in Environmental Planning. San Francisco, Calif.: Freeman.

Ellis, J. B. 1975. Urban Stormwater Pollution. Middlesex Polytechnic Research Report 1.

Flegal, A. R., and C. C. Patterson. 1983. Vertical concentration profiles of lead in the central Pacific at 15N and 20S. Earth Planet. Sci. Lett. 64:19-32.

Frankenfield, H. C. 1927. The floods of 1927 in the Mississippi Basin. Monthly Weather Review Supp. 29:10.

Freeze, R. A., and J. A. Cherry. 1979. Groundwater. Englewood Cliffs: Prentice-Hall.

Fuguitt, G. V. 1985. The Nonmetropolitan population turnaround. Annual Review of Sociology 11:259-280.

Fuguitt, G. V., D. L. Brown, and C. L. Beale. 1989. Rural and Small Town America. New York: Russell Sage Foundation.

Gallant, A. L., T. R. Whittier, D. P. Larsen, J. M. Omernik, and R. M. Hughes. 1989. Regionalization as a Tool for Managing Environmental Resources. EPA Research and Development Report EPA/600/3-89/060. Corvallis, Ore.: U.S. EPA Environmental Research Laboratory.

GAO. 1991. Water Pollution: More emphasis needed on prevention in EPA's efforts to protect groundwater. Washington, D.C.: U.S. General Accounting Office.

GAO. 1994. Ecosystem Management: Additional actions needed to adequately test a promising approach. GAO/RCED-94-111. Washington, D.C.: U. S. General Accounting Office.

Gibert, J., D. L. Danielopol, and J. A. Stanford (eds.). 1994a. Groundwater Ecology. San Diego, Calif.: Academic Press, Inc.

Gibert, J., J. A. Stanford, M. J. Dole-Oliver, and J. V. Ward. 1994b. Basic attributes of groundwater ecosystems and prospects for research. Pp. 7-40 in Groundwater Ecology. San Diego, Calif.: Academic Press, Inc.

Gilbert, G. K. 1917. Hydraulic Mining Debris in the Sierra Nevada. U.S. Geological Survey Professional Paper 105.

Gleick, Ph.H. (ed.). 1993. Water in Crisis: A Guide to the World's Fresh Water Resources. Oxford: Oxford University Press.

Goudie, A. 1994. The Human Impact on the Natural Environment. Cambridge: MIT Press.

Graf, W. L. 1975. The impact of suburbanization on fluvial geomorphology. Water Resources Research 11:690-692.

Graf, W. L. 1977. Network characteristics in suburbanizing streams. Water Resources Research 13: 459-63.

Graf, W. L. 1978. Fluvial adjustments to the spread of Tamarisk in the Colorado Plateau Region. Geol. Soc. Am. Bull. 89: 1491-1501.

Graf, W. L. 1979. Mining and channel response. Ann. Assoc. Am. Geogr. 69: 262-275.

Graf, W. L. 1980. The effect of dam closure on downstream rapids. Water Resources Research 16: 129-136.

Graf, W. L. 1985. The Colorado River: Instability and Basin Management. Washington, D.C.: Association of American Geographers.

Graf, W. L. 1994. Seasonal Land Cover Regions (map, scale 1:11,000,000). Sioux Falls, SD: USGS EROS Data Center.

Graf, W. L., K. K. Hirschbock, R. A. Marston, J Pitlick, and J. C. Schmidt. 1997. Sustainability and changing physical landscapes. Pp. 1-13 In McKindley, W.L. (ed.) Aquatic Ecosystem Symposium in Western Water Policy. Tempe, Ariz.: Arizona State University.

Graham, M., J. Thomas, and F. Metting. 1996. Groundwater. Chap. 11 In Mays, L. (ed.) Water Resources Handbook. New York: McGraw-Hill.

Gregory, K. J. 1985. The impact of river channelization. Geogr. 151: 53-74.

Gregory, S. V., F. J. Swanson, and W. A. McKee. 1991. An ecosystem perspective of riparian zones. BioScience 40:540-551.

Happ, S. C., G. Rittenhouse, and G. Dobson. 1940. Some Principles of Accelerated Stream and Valley Sedimentation. U.S. Dep. of Ag. Tech. Bull. 695.

Harmon, M. E., J. F. Franklin, F. J. Swanson, P. Sollins, S. V. Gregory, J. D. Lattin, N. H. Anderson, S. P. Cline, N. G. Aumen, J. R. Sedell, G. W. Lienkaemper, K. Cromack Jr., and K. W. Cummins. 1986. Ecology of coarse woody debris in temperate ecosystems. Advances in Ecological Research 15:133-302.

Heaney, J. P. 1986. Research needs in urban-storm water pollution. Journal of Water Resources Planning and Management 112:36-47.

Heiskary, S. A., C. B. Wilson, and D. P. Larsen. 1987. Analysis of regional patterns in lake water quality: Using ecoregions for lake management in Minnesota. Lake and Reservoir Management 3:337-344.

Hershfield, D. M. 1961. Rainfall frequency atlas of the United States. U.S. Weather Bureau Technical Paper.

Hicks, B. J., J. D. Hall, P. A. Bisson, and J. R. Sedell. 1991. Response of salmonids to habitat changes. American Fisheries Society Special Publication 19:483-518.

Hughes, R. M., and D. P. Larsen. 1988. Ecoregions: an approach to surface water protection. J. Water Pollut. Control Fed. 60:486-493.

Hughes, R. M., E. Rextad, and C. E. Bond. 1987. The relationships of aquatic ecoregions, river basins, and physiographic provinces to the ichthyogeographic regions of Oregon. Copeia 2:423-432.

Hundley, N. 1992. The Great Thirst. Berkeley, Calif.: University of California Press.

Interagency Ecosystem Management Task Force. 1955. The Ecosystem Approach: Healthy ecosystems and sustainable economies, Volume 1-Overview. Washington, D.C.: Council on Environmental Quality.

Interagency Floodplain Management Review Committee. 1994. Sharing the Challenge: Floodplain Management into the 21st Century. Report to the Administration Floodplain Management Task Force. Washington, D.C.: U.S. Government Printing Office.

Jacques, J. E., and D. L. Lorenz. 1988. Techniques for estimating the magnitude and frequency of floods of ungaged streams in Minnesota. U.S. Geological Survey Water Resources Inv. Rep 87-4710.

Jaffe, M., and F. Dinovo. 1987. Local Groundwater Protection. Chicago, Ill: American Planning Association.

Johnson, K. M., and C. L Beale. 1993. The recent revival of widespread population growth in nonmetropolitan areas of the United States. Rural Sociology 59:655-667.

Johnston, C. A. 1991. Sediment and nutrient retention by fresh-water wetlands: Effects on surface and quantity. Critical Reviews in Environmental Control 21:491-565.

Johnston, C. A., G. D. Bubenzer, G. B. Lee, F. W. Madison, and J. R. McHenry. 1984. Nutrient trapping by sediment deposition in seasonally flooded lakeside wetlands, Journal of Environmental Quality 13:283-290.

Johnston, L. A., N. E. Detenbeck and G. J Niemi, 1990. The cumulative effect of wetlands on stream quality and quantity: a landscape approach. Biochemistry 10:105-147.

Johnston, C. A., 1991. Sediment and nutrient retention by fresh-water wetlands: Effects on surface and quantity. Critical Reviews in Environmental Control 21:491-565.

Keller, E. A. 1976. Channelization: Environmental, geomorphic and engineering aspects. In Coates, D. R. (ed.) Geomorphology and Engineering. Stroudsburg, Penn.: Dowden, Hutchinson and Ross.

Keller, E.A., and F.J. Swanson. 1979. Effects of large organic material on channel form and fluvial processes. Earth Surface Processes 4: 361-380.

Kohler, M. A., T. J. Nordenson, and D. R. Baker. 1959. Evaporation maps for the United States. U.S. Weather Bureau Technical Paper 37.

Küchler, A. W. 1970. Potential Natural Vegetation (map, scale 1:7,500,000). Pp. 89-91. In the National Atlas of the United States of America. Washington, D.C.: U.S. Geological Survey.

LeGrand, H. E., and V. T. Stringfield. 1973. Concepts of karst development in relation to interpretation of surface runoff. J. of Research of the U.S. Geological Survey 1(3):351-360.

Larsen, D. P., R. M. Hughes, J. M. Omernik, D. R. Dudley, C. M. Rohm, T. R. Whittier, A. J. Kenney, and A. Gallant. 1986. The correspondence between spatial patterns in fish assemblages in Ohio streams and aquatic ecoregions. Environmental Management 10:815-828.

Larsen, D. P., D. R. Dudley, and R. M. Hughes. 1988. A regional approach to assess attainable water quality: an Ohio case study. J. Soil Water Conservation 43:171-176.

LeGrand and Stringfield. 1973. Concepts of Karst development in relation to interpretation of surface runoff. J. of Research of the U.S. Geological Survey 1(3):351-360.

Leopold, L. B., M. G. Wolman, and J. G. Miller. 1964. Fluvial Processes in Geomorphology. San Francisco: W.H. Freeman and Co.

Ligon, F. K., W. E. Dicterom, and W. J. Thrus. 1995. Downstream ecological effects at dams: a geomorphic perspective. BioScience 45:183-192.

Loganathan, D., D. Kibler, and T. Grizzard, 1996. Urban stormwater management. Chap. 26 in L. Mays (ed.) Water Resources Handbook. New York: McGraw-Hill.

Madej, M. A., W. E. Weaver, D. K. Hogans. 1994. Analysis of bank erosion on the Merced River, Yosemite Valley, Yosemite National Park, U.S.A. Environmental Management 18:235-250.

Maidment, D. (ed.) 1993. Handbook of Hydrology. McGraw-Hill, New York.

Makepeace, D. K., D. W. Smith, S. J. Stanley. 1995. Urban stormwater quality: summary of contaminant data. Critical Reviews in Environmental Science and Technology 25:93-139.

Malina, J. 1996. Water quality. Chap. 8 in L. Mays (ed.) Water Resources Handbook. New York: McGraw-Hill.

Mather, J. R. 1978. The Climatic Water Budget in Environmental Analysis. Lexington, Mass: Lexington Books.

Mays, L. M. ed. 1996. Water Resources Handbook. New York: McGraw-Hill.

McCutcheon, S., J. Martin, and T. Barnwell. 1993. Water quality. Chap. 11 In Maidment, D. (ed.) Handbook of Hydrology. New York: McGraw-Hill.

Meade, R. H. 1982. Sources, sinks, and storage of river sediment in the Atlantic drainage of the United States. J. Geol. 90:235-252.

Megahan, W.F. 1982. Channel sediment storage behind obstructions in forested drainage basins draining the granitic bedrock of the Idaho Batholith. Pp. 114-121 in F.J. Swanson, R.J. Janda, T. Dunne, and D.N. Swanston, editors. Sediment budgets and routing in forested drainage basins. United States Forest Service, Research Paper PNW- 14 1, Pacific Northwest Forest and Range Experiment Station, Portland, Oregon, USA.

Miller, J. F. 1964. Two-to-ten-day precipitation for return periods of 2 to 100 years in the contiguous United States. U.S. Weather Bureau Technical Paper 49.

Montgomery, D. 1997. What's best on banks? Nature 338:328-329.

Naiman, R. J., and J. R. Sedell. 1980. Relationships between metabolic parameters and stream order in Oregon. Canadian Journal of Fisheries and Aquatic Science 37:834-847.

National Oceanic and Atmospheric Administration. 1998. CIRES Climate Diagnostics Center. http://www.cdc.noaa.gov/ENSO/enso.current.html).

National Research Council (NRC). 1995. Wetlands: Characterization and boundaries. Washington D.C.: National Academy Press.

National Research Council (NRC). 1997. Watershed Research in the U.S. Geological Survey. Washington, D.C.: National Academy Press.

Notenboom, J., S. Plenet, and M.J. Turquin. 1994. Groundwater contamination and its impact on groundwater animals and ecosystems. Pp. 477-504 in J. Gibert, D. L. Danielopol, and J. A. Stanford (ed.) Groundwater Ecology. San Diego, Calif.: Academic Press.

Novitzki. R. P. 1979. Hydrologic characteristics of Wisconsin: Wetlands and their influence on floods, stream flow, and sediment. Pp. 377-388 in R. E. Greeson, J. R. Clark, and J. E. Clark (eds.) Wetland Functions and Values: The state of our understanding. Minneapolis, Minn.: American Water Resources Association.

O'Connor, K. A. 1995. Watershed Management Planning: Bringing the Pieces Together. M.S. Thesis, California State Polytechnic University, Pomona. 166 pp.

Ogawa, H., and Male, J. W. 1986. Simulating the flood mitigation role of wetlands. Journal of Water Resources, Planning, and Management 112:114-128.

Omernik, J. M. 1987. Ecoregions of the coterminous United States. Ann. Assoc. Am. Geogr. 771:118-125.

Omernik, J. M., and A. L. Gallant. 1990. Defining regions for evaluating environmental resources. Pp. 936-947 in Global Natural Resource Monitoring and Assessments: Preparing for the 21st Century, Vol. 2. Bethesda, Md.: American Society for Photogrammetry and Remote Sensing.

Pimentel, D., J. Houser, E. Preiss, O. White, H. Fang, L. Mesnick, T. Barsky, S. Tariche, J. Schreck. and S. Alpert. 1997. Water resources: agriculture, the environment, and society. BioScience 47:97-106.

Pitlick, J., and M. Van Streeter. 1994. Changes in morphology and endangered fish habitat, the Colorado River. Colorado Water Resources Institute Compliance Report 144. Fort Collins, Colo.: Colorado Water Resources Institute.

Potter, K. W. 1991. Hydrological impacts of changing land management practices in a moderate-sized agricultural catchment. Water Resources Research 27:845-855.

Reice, S. R. 1994. Nonequilibrium determinants of biological community structure. American Scientist 82(5):424-435.

Renard, K. G., G. R. Foster, and G. A.Weesies. 1991. Predicting soil erosion by water: A guide to conservation planning with the Revised Universal Soil Loss Equation. U.S. Department of Agriculture, Agricultural Handbook 703.

Richardson, C. 1996. Wetlands. Chap. 13 in Mays, L. (ed.) Water Resources Handbook. New York: McGraw-Hill.

Richter, B. D., J. V. Baumgartner, J. Powell, and D. Braun. 1996. A method for assessing hydrologic alteration within ecosystems. Conservation Biology 10:1163-1174.

Rohm, C. M., J. W. Giese, and C. C. Bennett. 1987. Evaluation of an aquatic ecoregion classification of streams in Arkansas. J. Freshwater Ecology 4:127-140.

Schumm, S. 1977. The Fluvial System. New York: John Wiley.

Schumm, S., M. D. Harvey, and C. C. Watron. 1984. Incised Channels: Morphology, Dynamics, and Control. Littleton, Colo.: Water Resources Publications.

Sedell, J.R., and K.J. Luchessa. 1982. Using the historical record as an aid to salmonid habitat enhancement. Pp. 210-223 in N.B. Annantrout (ed.) Acquisition and utilization of aquatic habitat inventory information. Proceedings of a symposium held October 28-30, 1981, Portland, Oregon. The Hague Publishing, Billings, Montana, USA.

Sedell, J.R., P.A. Bisson, F.J. Swanson, and S.V. Gregory. 1988. What we know about large trees that fall into streams and rivers. Pp. 47-81 in C. Maser, R. F. Tarrant, J. M. Trappe, and J. F. Franklin (eds.) From the forest to the sea: a story of fallen trees. United States Forest Service, Pacific Northwest Research Station, General Technical Report PNW-GTR-229, Portland, Oregon, USA.

Sedell, J.R., and R.L. Beschta. 1991. Bringing back the "bio" in bioengineering. American Fisheries Society Symposium 10:160-175.

Shields, F. D., S. S. Knight and C. M. Cooper. 1995. Rehabilitation of watersheds with incising channels. Water Resources Bulletin 31:971-982.

Stanford, J. A. 1997. Toward a robust water policy for the western USA: Synthesis of the Science in Aquatic Ecosystem Symposium: A report to Western Water Policy Review Advisory Commission. Tempe: Arizona State University.

Stanford, J. A., and J. V. Ward. 1993. An ecosystem perspective of alluvial rivers: Connectivity and the hyporheic corridor. Journal of the North American Benthological Society 12:48-68.

Stanford, J. A. , J. V. Ward, W. J. Liss, C. A. Frissel, R. N. Williams, J. A. Lichatowich, and C. C. Contant. 1996. A general protocol for restoration of regulated rivers. Regulated Rivers, Research and Management 12:391-413.

Todd, D. K. 1959. Groundwater Hydrology. New York: John Wiley.

Trimble, S. W. 1974. Man-Induced Soil Erosion on the Southern Piedmont. 1700-1970. Ankeny, Iowa: Soil Conservation Society of America.

Trimble, S. W. F. H. Weirich, and B. L. Hoag. 1987. Reforestation and the reduction of water yield on the Southern Piedmont since circa 1940. Water Resources Research 23: 425-37.

Trimble, S. W., and K. P. Bube. 1990. Improved reservoir trap efficiency prediction. The Environmental Professional 12: 255-272.

Trimble, S. W., and S. W. Lund. 1982. Soil Conservation and the Reduction of Erosion and Sedimentation in the Coon Creek Basin. Wisconsin. U.S. Geological Survey Professional Paper 1234.

Trimble, S. W. 1993. The distributed sediment budget model and watershed management in the Paleozoic Plateau of the upper Midwestern United States. Physical Geography 14:285-303.

Trimble, S. W. 1997a. Contribution of stream channel erosion to sediment yield from an urbanizing watershed. Science 278:1442-1444.

Trimble, S. W. 1997b. Stream channel erosion and change resulting from riprarian forests. Geology 25:467-469.

Triska, F. J., and K. Cromack. 1982. The role of wood debris in forests and streams. Pp. 171-190 in R. H. Waring (ed.) Forests: fresh perspectives from ecosystem analysis. Proceedings of the 40th Biology Colloquium, 1979, Oregon State University, Corvallis, USA.

Turner, B. L., W. C. Clark, R. W. Kates, J. F. Richards, J. T. Matthews, and B. Mayer. 1990. The Earth as Transformed by Human Actions. Cambridge, Mass.: Cambridge University Press.

U.S. Environmental Protection Agency (EPA). 1996. Level III ecoregions of the continental United States (revision of Omernik, 1987) map M-1 (various scales). Corvallis, Ore.: US EPA, National Health and Environmental Health Effects Research Laboratory.

U.S. Environmental Protection Agency (EPA). 1997. Environmental Monitoring and Assessment, U.S. Environmental Protection Agency, Program (EMAP) Draft Research Plan. Washington, D.C.: US EPA, Office of Research and Development.

U.S. Geological Survey. 1970. The National Atlas of the United States of America.

Vervier, P. 1992. A perspective on the permeability of the surface freshwater-groundwater ecotone. Journal of the North American Benthological Society 11(1):93-102.

Wang, E. X., F. H. Bormann, and G. Benoit. 1995. Evidence of complete scavenging of atmospheric lead in the soils of northern hardwood forest ecosystems. Environ. Sci. Technol. 29:735-739.

Wang, S. Y., E. Langendoen, and F. D. Shields, eds. 1997. Management of Landscapes Disturbed by Channel Incision; Stabilization, Rehabilitation, and Restoration. University of Mississippi: Center for Computational Hydroscience and Engineering.

Ward, J. V. 1989. The four-dimensional nature of lotic ecosystems. Journal of the North American Benthological Society 8:2-8.

Water Information Center. 1973. Water Atlas of the United States. Port Washington, New York: Water Information Center, Inc.

Webb, J. R., B. J Cosby, F. A. Deviney, J. N. Galloway, M. E. Mitch, D. M. Downey, and K. N. Eshleman. 1997. Release of NO_3^- to Surface Waters Following Forest Defoliation by the Gypsy Moth. Preprint from Dept. of Environmental Sciences, University of Virginia. Charlottesville, Va.: University of Virginia.

Whitney, G. G. 1994. From Coastal Wilderness to Fruited Plain: A History of Environmental Changes in Temperate America from 1500 to the Present. Cambridge, Mass.: Cambridge University Press.

Whittier, T. M., R. M. Hughes, and D. P. Larsen. 1988. The correspondence between ecoregions and spatial patterns in stream ecosystems in Oregon. Canadian Journal of Fisheries and Aquatic Science 45:1264-1278.

Williams, G. P., and M. G. Wolman. 1984. Downstream effects of dams on alluvial rivers. U.S. Geol. Surv. Prof. Paper 1286.

Windom, H. L., J. T. Byrd, J. R. G. Smith, and F. Huan. 1991. Inadequacy of NASQAN data for assessing metal trends in the nation's rivers. Environ. Sci. Technol. 25:1137-1142.

Wolman, M. G. 1967. A cycle of sedimentation and erosion in urban river channels. Geografiska Ann. 49A: 385-395.

4

Data and Information

The effective integration of ecologic, economic, and social approaches to watershed management depends of the use of scientific methods, but those methods are no more successful than the data they employ. The previous chapter reviewed what we know about the natural and human systems that are important in watershed management. The application of that general knowledge in management, however, depends on the acquisition and skillful use of data about specific places and situations. This chapter explores the characteristics of available data and the state of our ability to use those data in the actual practice of watershed management. The chapter first reviews the types, sources, and management of available data to provide guidance on acquisition of existing information. Second, it explores two important aspects of data management: geographic information systems and special aspects of socioeconomic data. Finally, it identifies gaps in our scientific data, information, and knowledge as a guide for the investment of future research resources. (Later, Appendix B provides a brief guide to World Wide Web sites that provide data and information to watershed researchers, managers, and interested citizens.)

DATA

Four types of data are useful to watershed managers: 1) *abiotic,* such as weather and water discharge, 2) *biotic,* such as flora and fauna, and biomass statistics, 3) *social,* such as economic net returns, esthetics, and human values, and 4) *other,* such as land use and watershed history. These classifications are useful for communicating and managing data, although they are not mutually exclusive. The goal of data collection should be to provide decisionmakers with answers—what are the problems in a watershed, what are the causes of the problems, and what actions might lessen the problems (see Box 4.1).

The term information as used here connotes interpretation, synthesis, and communication of data. Knowledge connotes the translation of data, information, and ideas into explanations. Thus, explanations may be limited at the root by basic data. For instance, historical data for watersheds are often limited in coverage, of unreliable accuracy, or require significant assembly and interpretation (Trimble and Cooke, 1991). The usefulness of data, information, and knowledge is often limited because they are not offered to decisionmakers in forms that are appropriate.

Data Types

Traditionally, scientific questions concentrated on understanding specific processes and research was designed to provide focused data collection. For example, research to understand runoff processes required the collection of physical data to quantify such things as precipitation and soil characteristics. Current research efforts tend to be broader in scope and are directed toward integrating our understanding of specific processes to address problems at the watershed scale. As a result, data collection efforts now are more diffuse and include economic, social, and perceptual data.

Data Sources

There is a long tradition of collecting data in selected "experimental" watersheds, and these have provided the setting for the development of our current understanding of physical and biological watershed processes. Experimental watersheds that were initially instrumented to quantify hydrologic processes have become a valuable cornerstone on which to build integrated research programs addressing hydrologic, climatic, biotic, abiotic, and social factors, and their interactions. Until now, most experimental watersheds have been at sites where human influence is minimal. New experimental sites are needed in locations where social and biophysical systems interact significantly, and the addition of the Baltimore and Phoenix regions to the national Long-Term Ecological Research (LTER) program of the National Science Foundation is an important step. Current research to integrate multidisciplinary projects will build on the detailed data collection and process studies conducted at experimental watersheds. It is the strength of many of these watersheds that long-term data collection efforts can be used to quantify the year-to-year variability in natural processes, thus improving the scientific defensibility of interpretations based on the collected data.

Figure 4.1 summarizes active experimental watersheds in the United States (NRC, 1997). Most research watersheds receive support through the U.S. Forest

Box 4.1
White Clay Lake Watershed:
Science Guiding Management

Data are needed as a basis for decisionmaking because they provide answers about what causes problems and, in turn, what steps managers might take to resolve those problems, steps that might often not be intuitive. For instance, in the 1970s a series of studies conducted under the auspices of the White Clay Lake demonstration project in Wisconsin sought to understand the effects of agricultural runoff on the lake's water quality, prepare plans for reducing feedlot and runoff pollution from the watershed, and monitor the effectiveness of the pollution control measures that were implemented.

It came as somewhat of a surprise when researchers determined that surface water contributed only 35 percent of the water volume input to White Clay Lake, whereas groundwater discharging directly into the lake contributed 40 percent and direct precipitation contributed 25 percent. This meant that watershed management activities could influence only a fraction of the water inputs into the lake. But further research showed that surface water contributed a full 57 percent of the total phosphorus to the lake, illustrating that most of the nonpoint source pollution was contributed by the water source that managers could take management steps to improve. It also was learned that natural wetlands separating the lake from the uplands retained about 14 percent of the sediment and nutrient fluxes from the watershed, an amount that was equivalent to that retained by the various best management practices constructed in the watershed. The lesson was the importance of conserving the wetland in its natural state so that it could continue to provide this free environmental service.

The monitoring phase of the project also brought management lessons: researchers determined that a manure storage pit built according to sound best management specifications actually caused groundwater contamination that threatened a farmer's well water — showing the importance of monitoring implemented practices to ensure that they function properly and provide the intended benefits.

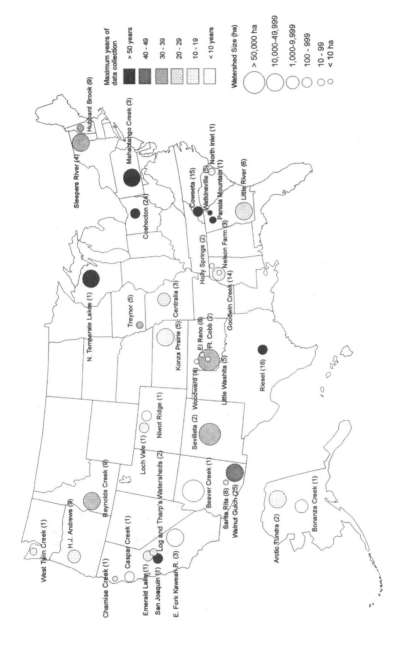

FIGURE 4.1 Locations of active experimental watersheds in the United States. Number of watersheds monitored is indicated in parentheses. Watershed size is indicated by the size of circle and maximum years of data collection for each watershed is indicated by the fill pattern of each circle. SOURCE: Data taken from NRC (1997).

Service, U.S. Department of Agriculture, and the National Science Foundation's LTER sites. The two LTER sites in urban areas added by NSF in 1997 are not shown. Other active research watersheds operated, for example, by university researchers are not included. Types of data collected include: meteorological, hydrological, surface water quality, ground water levels, surface water chemistry, ground water chemistry, soil, sediment, land use, vegetation, and animal data. All data types are not collected at all locations.

These experimental watersheds represent a wide range of ecosystem types across the United States, and they provide basic data for watershed knowledge from a national perspective. The number of monitored watersheds at these sites ranges from a minimum of 1 at several locations to a maximum of 25 at the USDA-ARS Walnut Gulch Experimental Range in Southeastern Arizona. The length of data collection ranges from 1 year at the most recently instrumented watersheds to as long as 75 years at North Temperate Lakes LTER site in Wisconsin.

The urban LTER sites are more than ecological studies that happen to be located in cities. USEPA and NSF, the sponsoring organizations, deliberately established the urban sites with the intention of fostering integrative research among practitioners of national science, social and economic sciences, and engineering. The measure of success for the urban LTER sites will be the degree to which they produce truly integrative results instead of purely ecological conclusions.

The purpose of watershed research, as implemented via experimental watersheds, is to collect, document, interpret and disseminate basic data, information, and knowledge of watershed processes and functions. These activities serve as a basis for design, implementation, monitoring, evaluating, and understanding watershed management practices and programs, and to predict watershed response to alternative land use and management practices. The need for prediction arises because all watersheds cannot be instrumented or monitored, and because we need to understand the potential impacts of watershed management before the programs and practices are implemented. Implicit in this need for prediction are interpretation of data and processes occurring on instrumented watersheds, along with development and scientific validation of simulation models to predict watershed response on non-instrumented watersheds.

Involving the Public in Watershed Monitoring

Concerned citizens represent a potentially valuable reservoir of human resources whose involvement in watershed monitoring can benefit management organizations and increase the overall level of public awareness of ecosystem health. Additionally, citizen involvement in coordinated monitoring activities can instill a sense of watershed ownership as people take an active interest in changes within the watershed and provide inputs to decisionmakers based on first-hand, objective observations. The result is a learning opportunity for those setting policy and public influence in watershed management decisions (Naiman et al., 1997).

Expectations of the abilities of concerned citizens to take samples and perform routine scientific tests must be tempered by the knowledge that the public lacks advanced technical training. A successful model is the American Association of Variable Star Observers, a network of skilled amateurs who provide a service by monitoring stars too numerous to be measured by professional astronomers. It is important that shared monitoring tasks focus on measurements that are readily understandable and do not require specialized skills. Lack of skill may preclude the collection of hydrologic data and biological samples. However, a number of monitoring activities are well within the abilities of average citizens, including the following specific examples.

Photographs

Time-series photographs are important contributions to understanding watershed changes. Often some of the most valuable information about historical condition is derived from old photographs, particularly those in which the location can be clearly identified. A network of reference photo points within a watershed is helpful in tracking long-term trends in both aquatic and terrestrial ecosystems. Reference photo points can also be used to display the effects of seasonal changes and large disturbances such as fires and floods. Historical photographs may already exist in family albums, or public collections, and public involvement can help bring these records to light.

Water Samples

Long-term trends in water quality require periodic, regularly-scheduled sampling, but the number of sites that can be routinely monitored by agencies is limited by the availability of automated sampling equipment and staff time. For example, the U.S. Geological Survey monitored water quality parameters in many watersheds after passage of federal water laws in the 1960s and 1970s, but was forced to abandon many of the sites in the late 1970s when funding for monitoring programs expired. Thus it is becoming more common for local volunteers to take samples.

Habitat Measurements

Stream morphology is an integrative measure of watershed processes. Pools, for example, are important habitat features for certain types of aquatic organisms, including many fish species. In streams with riffle-pool sequences, pool counts can be an important indicator of overall channel condition. Loss of large, deep pools over a 50-year period has been documented in Pacific Northwest watersheds with management histories that have included logging, agricultural, and grazing practices (FEMAT, 1993). While many environmental management agencies currently undertake habitat surveys, inventories of all streams within a watershed are often beyond their manpower capabilities. Citizen participation in simple habitat measures such as pool counts can increase the area of a watershed for which inventory information is available. Sportsmen's clubs and conservation organizations (including adopt-a-stream groups) are especially suited to this type of project.

Riparian Forest Surveys

The condition of riparian forests often goes unassessed, yet these areas are critical to watershed health. Riparian plots in which surveyors identify and count the number of plants within plot boundaries and periodically note changes in species composition, growth, and mortality yield useful information about the condition of streambanks and floodplains. Investigators can record causes of tree mortality such as human disturbance, beaver activity, streambank undercutting, or windthrow. Plots do not have to be revisited every year, as long as their locations are well documented; they can be resurveyed by the same group or rotated among several groups over longer periods. Information generated by these surveys can be useful for verifying remote sensing data, for providing riparian vegetation overlays in watershed Geographic Information Systems (GIS) mapping, and for teaching citizens about the dynamic nature of the interactions between water and land.

Public Outreach

Scientists and watershed managers can improve the transfer of knowledge of watershed processes and innovative management techniques to the public. Citizens and local interest groups usually act with the best intentions, but they do not always have the benefit of current scientific insights into ecosystem health and watershed productivity. The result can be projects that have a high probability of failing to achieve their objectives, or worse, that actually impair ecosystem functions (NRC, 1992).

There are very few widely available sources of information and advice on environmentally sound management practices that address watershed issues, apart from some limited water quality protection and soil conservation measures. Very few available sources truly address the problems of integrated approaches. Much of the ecological literature on watershed processes and land and water use impacts exists in a form that is largely unavailable (and not generally understandable) to citizens. The majority of technical information transfer occurs between agency staffs and the public. But agency involvement in watershed management is often limited to granting land and water use permits, with the emphasis on what *cannot* be done rather than what *can* be done. There are relatively few incentives for trying new things that could improve land stewardship. Instead, the focus of public activities tends more toward mitigation for lost habitat than toward stewardship.

Technology transfer must include the active participation of watershed scientists. Scientists can stress, among other things, the importance of land-water connections, the role of natural disturbances in maintaining ecosystem processes, and the need to view watershed management in terms of large landscape units. The success of agricultural and forestry extension services, in which the public can turn for advice to local extension agents familiar with the region, can serve as a model for the establishment of integrated watershed extension services. Watershed extension specialists could serve as local sources of the latest information, and can act as liaisons between small and large landowners, natural resource consumers, and management agencies.

Colleges and universities can also play a role in educating citizens about important watershed management issues. Although educational institutions sponsor many meetings, presentations at scientific conferences are often too technical for the public. A series of weekend or evening workshops aimed at communicating applied watershed science to a general audience would help facilitate increased public understanding of management options. These workshops could feature a combination of university faculty and other research scientists, as well as managers and environmental policy makers.

DATA MANAGEMENT

The advent of the computer has changed data management dramatically, from hand tabulations and paper files to electronic databases with the capability to rapidly organize, analyze, and display enormous amounts of data. Geographical Information Systems (GIS), for instance, offer the capability to manage and analyze spatially and temporally distributed data at the watershed level. Databases with a wide range of information such as streamflow data and precipitation rates can be obtained directly from a CD-ROM or even downloaded from the World Wide Web (see Appendix B for addresses). GIS information is now routinely available for watershed studies because many public agencies have developed the necessary coverages. Thus, a major challenge and opportunity for the future is to develop and incorporate efficient techniques for database management as part of the decisionmaking process.

As recognized by the U.S. Environmental Protection Agency and others (USEPA, 1993), the analysis and management of environmental, ecological, and other natural resource-related issues can best be addressed at the watershed level. Watersheds reflect natural systems, as compared to municipal and county boundaries which facilitate political and administrative decisionmaking. Watersheds

represent distinct ecosystems, or unique parts of ecosystems, and integrate phenomena such as material and energy transfer better than artificial man-made
boundaries.

Geographic Information Systems

GIS software is an especially effective tool for watershed management. GIS
software provides the ability to create a computerized database consisting of
spatial (map or image) data registered to some type of geographic coordinate
system (latitude/longitude, Universal Transverse Mercator, State Plane). Most
contemporary GIS software packages provide the capability to input spatial data,
manipulate it, and output the results in the form of various maps and/or tabular
products. In situations where complex environmental relationships exist, it has
been found that data concerning different aspects of the physical environment can
be used more effectively in combination than separately. One of the primary
functions of a GIS is the combination and evaluation of different spatial data sets
for the purpose of providing new composite information (see Box 4.2). Examples
of the products of some watershed-related GIS appear in color plates 1, 2, 3,
and 4.

GIS is a tool that is particularly conducive to watershed management because it integrates information on the basis of geography. Many workers in several of the disciplines that are typically brought together to address watershed
issues (e.g., geology, hydrology, chemistry, soil science, ecology, economics,
and management) are already familiar with the use of GIS for analyzing spatial
data. Because GIS provides the ability to manage and analyze data across spatial
and temporal scales, it effectively supports activities related to most, if not all, of
the watershed management elements mentioned above.

The development of GIS capabilities and databases have greatly facilitated
watershed research and planning efforts. Entire conferences, or major portions
thereof, have been devoted to the use of GIS in water resource management
(Goodchild et al., 1993, 1996; Kovar and Nachtnebel, 1996). An excellent primer
on the use of GIS in hydrologic applications has been published by UNESCO and
the International Institute for Aerospace Survey and Earth Sciences (Meijerink et
al., 1994).

The widespread availability of detailed Digital Elevation Models (DEM) has
contributed to the increased use of GIS in hydrology. Topography is the driving
force behind surface water movement through watersheds, so these detailed
elevation databases allow hydrologists to predict the location and amount of water
flowing over the land surface. Algorithms for flow routing and watershed boundary determination from DEM data (Jensen and Domingue, 1988) are now standard tools in most GIS software. The hydrologic modeling capabilities of GIS
may be used with or without linked hydrologic models.

Several other GIS databases are useful in watershed management. As discussed in Chapter 3, the U.S. Geological Survey has divided the nation into "Hydrologic Units," which are the watersheds for the major rivers and coastal regions of the United States (USGS, 1982). This system has been used since 1977 for the USGS National Stream Quality Accounting Network (Briggs and Ficke, 1977), and is widely used for a variety of other surface water applications. USGS has also developed digital land cover databases for the conterminous United States, derived from satellite imagery (Eidenshink, 1992). USEPA's digital "Reach File" divides the nation's rivers and streams into segments for which water quality data are collected and summarized. Medium-resolution (minimum mapping unit ~625 ha) digital soil maps are now available for the entire U.S. under the Natural Resource Conservation Service's STATSGO program (Lytle et al., 1996).

GIS provides an important tool for conducting watershed scale research (Johnston et al., 1988). For example, the location of wetlands relative to streams (Johnston et al., 1990) and lakes (Detenbeck et al., 1993) greatly influences their individual and collective capacity to improve downstream water quality. A wetland may have high potential for pollutant reduction, but it cannot realize that potential unless it is in a flow path located to intercept pollutants. A greater understanding of these watershed-scale relationships will lead to better watershed planning for maximum sustainability of watershed resources.

Socioeconomic Data for Watershed Characterization/Analysis

A variety of socioeconomic data are available from the decennial U.S. Census of Population and Housing. Individual and household data are aggregated into Census accounting units with geographic identifiers. These units are the building blocks for use of Census data in geographic information systems (GIS). The 1990 data have been formatted at the "block group" level for use with specific computer software, and are publicly available from the U.S. Census Bureau (and from many state agencies). Block group data can be aggregated to approximately cover a hydrologically defined watershed area.

Block groups are aggregations of Census data with a minimum population of about 200 households. The minimum population preserves anonymity. Aggregations of block groups may not correspond to watershed boundaries precisely, because the spatial boundaries of the basic block groups are fixed, but approximations to physical watersheds is often close. Block groups can accurately be aggregated to higher level political entities that fall within large watershed boundaries (places, congressional districts, cities, counties, metropolitan areas, states).

Variables in census data include a wide range of individual and household characteristics useful in describing the human population residing in watersheds, thus permitting analysis of potential human impacts to the physical and biological features of watersheds. The results of spatial analysis offer critical information resources for watershed planning. Aggregated characteristics of individuals in-

**Box 4.2
Finding Watershed Data:
The Pennsylvania Example**

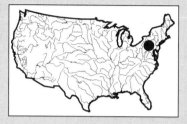

One tool for enhancing collaboration and effectiveness (and reducing duplication of data) among watershed managers, planners, and geographic information systems specialists is the development and maintenance of "clearinghouses" for spatial databases. Data clearinghouses save time and effort locating data and encourage the free and open exchange of critical shed management information. A spatial data clearinghouse provides a means to inventory, document, and share expensive spatial data. A clearinghouse allows data providers to advertise existing spatial data, the condition of these data, and instructions for accessing these data. Each data provider describes available data in an electronic text file and provides these metadata to the network using a variety of software tools. The clearinghouse may be a single repository, or a dispersed group of servers, all adhering to basic search and description standards. Even the data described in the clearinghouse's metadata may be located at the sites of data producers or, where appropriate, at sites throughout a region, state, or the country.

clude their place of residence (e.g., urban/rural, farm/nonfarm), demographic characteristics (age, sex race, place of birth), social characteristics (e.g., education, marital status, family type, etc.) work related information (employment, industry and occupation of worker, place of work, travel to and from work) sources and levels of income (earned, wage and salary, self-employment, farm, etc.) and poverty status.

Aggregate data are also available for a variety of household and housing unit characteristics, which can be particularly useful in watershed planning. These include location (urban/rural, farm/nonfarm), size and age, source of water, method of sewage disposal, and type of plumbing facilities.

Census data are also available on economic activities. The U.S. Department of Agriculture conducts economic censuses every five years for agriculture, construction, financial, insurance and real estate, manufacturers, mineral industries, minority and women-owned businesses, retail trade, service industries, transpor-

Where possible, a spatial data clearinghouse uses the Internet to link computer nodes that contain metadata and spatial data files. Using the Internet, data users can search the descriptions provided by producers to locate data that are suitable for their applications. WAIS (Wide Area Information Servers) software enables users to perform queries for data over the network using the Z39.50 protocol, which is emerging as an international standard. In addition, other features can be supported, such as an advertising area where producers can publicize data that are being prepared or are planned or for data seekers to solicit for data.

One example of a spatial data clearinghouse is the Pennsylvania Spatial Data Access (PASDA) system, developed as part of the National Spatial Data Infrastructure (NSDI) effort. PASDA can answer the question: "Where are data about watersheds in Pennsylvania?" PASDA was developed by the Pennsylvania Department of Environmental Protection in collaboration with Penn State University to improve watershed management through increased access to spatial data. PASDA consists of two resources: a metadata collection of over 2200 records configured to support distributed NSDI searches using the Federal Geographic Data Committee's standard wide area information server protocol and a World Wide Web site (www.pasda.psu.edu) that supports search and retrieval of GIS data and preview images in addition to the metadata collection. PASDA fosters communications between the users and producers, which encourages partnerships for data production and minimizes expensive duplication in data collection.

tation, and communication utilities. Each census provides data on the size and activities of enterprises covered, with specific characteristics reported that are relevant to each type of economic activity. These data are aggregated to the county level, providing less resolution than the Census of Population and Housing data aggregated into smaller Block Group units. Nevertheless, these data are available in dBase format for use in conjunction with GIS computer programs. Unfortunately, the counties may provide only a crude approximation of hydrologically defined watershed boundaries. In some cases, counties may be larger than watersheds of interest, and in others large counties may straddle watershed boundaries. In some instances, aggregations of counties can be used to approximate large river basins or the Water Resource Regions discussed in Chapter 3.

Files that summarize data from a variety of sources aggregated at the county level are also available. For example, the City and County Data Book and USA Counties are collections of a variety of social, economic and political data. These data are updated regularly and, like the economic censuses, are available in dBase format for use with GIS computer programs. Similarly, the Regional Economic Information System data file contains economic time series for data from 1969 to 1994.

CURRENT STATE OF KNOWLEDGE

Watershed science seeks to understand and explain the structure and function of complex ecosystems, which it delimits on the basis of watershed boundaries. It is a multidisciplinary field that integrates the biological, chemical, physical, and social sciences. It draws its identity from the system being studied, and thus is inherently complex. This complexity is a special challenge to watershed science that militates against easy predictive generalizations. One manifestation of complexity is the site-specific nature of watersheds. Since no two basins are exactly alike, extrapolating findings from one to another must be done with caution.

Watershed science overlaps considerably with limnology and aquatic science, and the broadest definitions of the three tend to merge. Traditionally, limnology focused on lakes and was rooted in biology. Today, the science extends to other surface water bodies, including streams and wetlands, and incorporates all the basic sciences (NRC, 1996). Still, the emphasis tends to be on the water bodies themselves, with contributing watersheds studied only secondarily. Watershed science differs from aquatic science mainly by always using drainage basins as the unit of study. Watershed science also tends to have a greater management orientation and tendency to include social dimensions.

Over the past century, progress has been made in understanding many of the components that influence the structure and function of aquatic ecosystems and their contributing watersheds, but we remain far from an integrated knowledge or a general predictive capability. Recently published studies indicate that despite extensive data and a solid foundation of knowledge, the ability to effectively manage watersheds is still impeded by significant information gaps (Naiman et al., 1997; NRC, 1997). Furthermore, the lack of reliable funding for research and a fragmented system for training aquatic scientists make the closings of gaps more difficult (NRC, 1996).

Watershed science has some overarching research needs. Most of these needs cut across disciplines and require synthesis of information from several basic sciences at a variety of spatial scales and at a high level of complexity.

Perhaps most fundamental is the need for reliable, representative environmental monitoring data across disciplines. Stream stage, water chemistry, species diversity and abundance, and habitat conditions all need to be measured in monitoring programs designed to evaluate regional environmental conditions and to provide benchmarks that can be compared to nearby sites. It is especially critical to sustain long-term (longer than 10 years) programs in order to identify natural trends and to evaluate the relative effect of human activities. Also, the

Much progress has been made in understanding many of the factors that influence the structure and function of aquatic ecosystems and their contributing watersheds, but much remains to be learned. There is a real need for reliable, representative environmental monitoring data across disciplines. Stream stage, water chemistry, species diversity and abundance, and habitat conditions all need to be measured in programs designed to evaluate regional conditions and such program should be long-term to identify trends and sort natural variability from the effects of human activities. Credit: USDA-Natural Resources Conservation Service.

highest possible level of quality assurance must be maintained, or the data may be useless. For the greatest utility, different watershed variable types (biological, chemical, physical) should be measured at the same monitoring sites. In addition, researchers must identify watershed indicators that reflect multiple variable types. Some current monitoring efforts, such as EPA's Environmental Monitoring and Assessment Program (EMAP), adopt these perspectives, but they represent only a beginning of what is needed.

So far, research has generally failed to integrate across disciplines at the watershed scale. This has occurred in part because most funding sources are discipline specific, so that multidisciplinary research must link separate projects, each of which has a low probability of funding success. This is especially true for integrating biophysical and social science research, even though this combination is exactly what is most needed to support watershed management decisionmaking.

One notable exception to the general lack of integrated, multidisciplinary research is the Water and Watersheds Program sponsored jointly by the National Science Foundation, the U.S. Environmental Protection Agency, and, as of 1997, the U.S. Department of Agriculture. This partnership program, initiated in 1994, emphasizes interdisciplinary research taking a systems approach to issues of water and watersheds. Its goal is to develop an improved understanding of the natural and anthropogenic processes that govern the quantity, quality, and availability of water resources in natural and human-dominated systems, and to improve understanding of the structure, function, and dynamics of the terrestrial and aquatic ecosystems that comprise watersheds.

Although the program is small and shrinking (making 36 awards in 1995, 12 awards in 1996 and 13 awards in 1997) (NSF/USEPA, 1998), the committee believes it is focusing attention on areas of great need. In 1997, when the program emphasized urban/suburban research, projects addressed the connection between ecosystem structure and function and human values and socioeconomic behaviors, integrating ecological and economic modeling of watersheds at multiple scales, and other innovative areas of study. In 1996, projects addressed topics such as developing an integrated approach to assessing water management options by extending a hydrodynamic-water quality model to include biological and political-economic components and studying the effectiveness of regulatory incentives for sediment pollution prevention. These are precisely the types of studies this committee believes are needed to enhance our ability to implement watershed management activities. No evaluation of the program has been done, however, to track whether the research has actually worked to increase the effectiveness of watershed management or benefit the environment, a common failing in watershed science.

Experimental watersheds also tend to be exceptions to the lack of integrated investigations because these sites are often the subject of interdisciplinary research. As a result, we have a superior understanding of the functioning of small, relatively pristine watersheds. This work needs to be continued and supported over long time scales. Just as importantly, there is a need to extrapolate to larger spatial scales and to consider systems that are strongly influenced or even dominated by human activities. In general, the importance of scale and of human interactions with watersheds are two critical areas requiring further study.

Little is known about how basic processes mesh at spatial scales ranging from molecular to global, linking aquatic systems at larger scales. Work is also badly needed to investigate the role of spatial heterogeneity and patchiness in the structure and function of watershed ecosystems, though this is becoming a significant area of research. Embedded in these questions is the role of disturbance regimes, both natural and anthropogenic, and how they influence watershed functioning.

Our understanding of the interactions between social and biophysical systems is in its infancy. The traditional view of human social systems as a perturbation of "natural" ecosystems is giving way to a model where human and non-human components interact through causal linkages at a variety of levels and in both directions. One critical area where this need is especially strong is in support of ecological restoration projects. The growing desire to rehabilitate, or even restore, degraded watersheds is leading to an increased necessity for the ability to predict the consequences of ecosystem manipulation, and to know what is possible in human influenced or dominated watersheds. Linked to this is the need to be able to evaluate what kind and level of development of a watershed is consistent with its sustainable carrying capacity, however that controversial phrase is defined.

Related to all of these information gaps is a necessity for improved predictive capabilities, usually in the form of mathematical models. Many current models are either "too good to be real" or "too real to be good." In the first case, oversimplification (dimensionally, through lumping of parameters, or by ignorance of key driving processes and feedbacks) undercuts the accuracy or generality of the results. And in the second case, the need for detailed data (which is usually lacking, and costly to acquire) renders the model impractical to apply except in a research setting. Most models tend to assess watershed components individually and thus to miss feedback linkages. They are empirical rather than process driven, and consequently require lots of costly site-specific data. They usually lack integration across disciplines and fail to have a sense of the big picture. Better models use linked modules (e.g., water quality, water quantity, soils, sediment, fish, benthic biota), but even these generally fail to account for complex feedbacks existing among these parts. In addition to complex numerical models, there also remains a need for elegant, simple models, such as Vollenweider's P loading model for lakes, that can be based on reliable existing data.

Finally, watershed management cannot wait for the resolution of all of these important questions. Often, there is a need to act now even if scientific understanding is incomplete. That requirement argues strongly for the use of adaptive management, where decisionmakers evaluate the effects of actions frequently to assess whether or not there is progress toward desired goals. Mid-course corrections may be possible before undesirable consequences become irreversible. If well-monitored, adaptive management can even serve as useful large-scale experiments, as cause and effect are documented in a range of watershed settings.

SCIENTIFIC GAPS

Gaps in Knowledge of Watershed Processes

Lack of knowledge about watershed processes is one of the key barriers to successful implementation of watershed approaches. Watersheds are complex systems with numerous components and complex relationships between those components, and yet too often our understanding of watersheds is uni-dimentional and overly simplistic. Understanding how system components interact, how complex systems react to change, and similar process questions remains as an unmet challenge. For instance, while we have made great strides in measuring precipitation, we are less able to follow water as it moves through the system and understand how water, soil, and associated chemical constituents interact under normal and abnormal conditions. We lack real understanding of how abiotic and biotic processes occurring throughout the watershed are related. Answers to such complex questions can take time and patience to develop, but it just is this kind of information that managers need if they are to find workable solutions to watershed-scale problems.

In the past, reductionist scientific approaches, in which processes and controlling variables are isolated as much as possible, have brought in-depth understanding of many aspects of watershed science. But the reductionist approach is less useful in the context of management decisionmaking, because managers need more than an understanding of individual parts; they need an understanding of the system as a whole. Reductionist and systems approaches to study are not mutually exclusive or competitive. Each has an important place in science. Fundamental data and knowledge gained from the reductionist approach is the scientific basis for understanding the components, for their interactions, and for their synthesis and integration.

One special challenge related to understanding the processes that operate in watersheds is integrating natural and social processes—that is, to understand the effects of human actions on the environment. Watershed science for managers and decisionmakers must be a judicial blend of natural science, social science, engineering, and planning. Additionally, we need to understand how these human, natural, and engineered processes operate at a variety of scales. What we learn at one scale may or may not be transferable to other scales.

Gaps in Data and Information

One of the most fundamental goals of watershed management is protection of water quality. Over $40 billion have been spent on measures to comply with point source pollution reduction since enactment of the Clean Water Act in 1972. Unquestionably, water quality has improved substantially over the last 25 years as a result, but do we know which contaminants have declined the most, and by precisely how much? Unfortunately, the answer is no. In spite of extensive water quality monitoring at a cost of billions of dollars (Hren et al., 1990), some studies indicate that past efforts have been "fragmented, duplicative and wasteful" (Blodgett, 1983).

Most past monitoring was directed toward evaluation of effluent quality. This was done, by design, in an effort to curb point source emissions, a goal at which it was very successful. The same data are of little value in measuring or predicting water quality conditions in receiving waters. Even when stream measurements have been made, often there was little effort to assure that sampling was representative of the entire stream cross section. In larger rivers, conditions can be very different in surface waters and near the streambed. This oversight is indicative of a larger problem; in general, analytical quality assurance/quality control has received much greater attention than the quality of sampling design and execution, even though the latter accounts for at least half of the utility of the final data.

Another problem is that most existing stream data are not coupled to parallel measurements of discharge, which is important for at least three reasons. First, most water quality parameters change dramatically with stream stage, some increasing in concentration and others decreasing. Only by knowing instantaneous discharge at the time of measurement, and the dependence of each parameter on flow rate, is it possible to fairly compare water quality data from different time periods. Second, without discharge data it is impossible to calculate total mass fluxes. These values are important both for calculation of global biogeochemical mass balances and as one of the best integrated measures of the success of clean water efforts, free from biases caused by changes in total discharge from year to year. Finally, links to other ecosystem components and predictions about the effects of future changes, such as climate, require an understanding of the systematic relation between water quality and quantity.

Another problem with most past measurements of water quality is that data on toxic contaminants are lacking or badly compromised. By far the most common assays performed have been for parameters such as pH, conductivity, and dissolved oxygen. These are easy to measure but tell virtually nothing about water quality except in the grossest cases of contamination, which generally have been eliminated in the United States. Toxic contaminants, and even nutrients, are considerably more difficult to analyze, but tell much more about the effectiveness of watershed management. Unfortunately, contamination artifacts and lack of sensitive, reliable methods render much of the existing data record useless for substances whose impact is felt at trace levels. For example, virtually all monitoring-based measurements of trace metals in surface and ground waters until the early 1990s are now considered invalid (Benoit, 1994; Windom et al., 1991). A great deal of valid trace substance data exists in the literature for recent years, but we will probably never be able to reconstruct water column conditions that existed in the past for most trace contaminants at most sites.

Other problems relate to consistency and accessibility of data. In the past, measurements by various agencies have targeted different parameters, used unlike analytical methods that are no longer acceptable, and stored results in formats that are not readily accessible. Also, well-designed strategies for collecting hydrologic data can be expensive to maintain over the long-term, although this long-term perspective is what makes them most valuable (Box 4.3).

Fortunately, there have been significant recent efforts at the national level to develop uniform sampling and analytical protocols, improve both field and labo-

Box 4.3
Improved and Enhanced Sediment Data from
Reservoir Surveys: The Example of the TVA System

Sediment yields, accumulation, and concentrations are important data in watershed management. Conventionally derived sediment yield data, which depend on stream sampling, are often of questionable reliability, expensive, and from only limited locations. A very large source of data which could greatly supplement conventional data is that of sediment accumulation rates in reservoirs. Using appropriate adjustments for sediment trap efficiencies, sediment yields and fluxes can be obtained (Figure 4.2). Further calculation from runoff data can give average sediment concentrations. Despite the value of reservoirs, two problems in obtaining these data have surfaced in the past two decades. First, many agencies no longer do as many reservoir sediment surveys as in earlier decades. Secondly, up-to-date data are no longer published on a regular and obtainable basis as was done up to 1975 (Dendy and Champion, 1978). Environmental management in general and, specifically watershed management, would be well-served by increased monitoring and publishing of reservoir sedimentation rates.

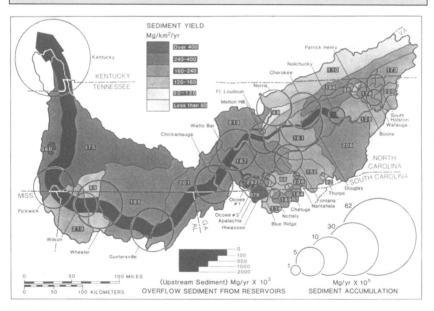

FIGURE 4.2 Sediment accumulation, yield, and overflow for the Tennessee River basin. SOURCE: Reprint, with permission, from Trimble and Bube, 1990. © 1990 by The Environmental.

ratory quality assurance/quality control procedures, and make resultant data widely available in standardized formats. Planning is under way to establish a National Water Quality Monitoring Council that would implement this strategy (Powell, 1995). The council has been preceded by an Intergovernmental Task Force on Monitoring Water Quality (ITFM). It will be important in future years to continue this integration effort and to avoid shortsighted cutbacks in monitoring programs, which supply critically needed data for watershed management programs nationwide. They also provide an invaluable gauge of the success or failure of costly regulatory programs.

It will be important then, to the extent possible, for future water quality monitoring efforts to incorporate the following improvements:

• Most fundamentally, monitoring efforts must seek to answer specific questions, and all parts of the monitoring programs must contribute to that goal. Increasingly, selection of which questions should be answered will be linked directly to societal concerns.

• Emphasize in-stream monitoring of water quality in addition to compliance-based measures of effluent quality. This will be especially necessary since nonpoint sources of pollution, which represent the dominant portion of today's loading, cannot be directly measured.

• Include both ground water and surface water samples.

• Develop consistent lists of analytes, their definitions, and their methods of analysis among agencies in order to facilitate data sharing.

• Establish uniform data storage formats and increase their accessibility among agencies and to the scientific and management communities as well as the general public.

• Use levels of QA/QC that are adequate to ensure reliable, accurate data. Also, apply these protocols to both field and laboratory components of the monitoring effort. Improperly collected samples or those taken without suitable sampling design cannot be compensated for by any level of care in the laboratory.

• Collect only data that serve a purpose. It would be better to have 10 sites with good data coverage, than 1000 with meaningless measurements of only conductivity and DO. Good coverage includes consideration of analytes (number and appropriateness), time (frequency, continuity, and duration), ancillary information (discharge, meteorology, etc.), and spatial coverage (river cross section and longitudinal representativeness).

• If sampling or methods must be changed, careful intercalibrations should be conducted to assure comparability over time.

• Especially needed are reliable long-term data at permanent sites with unchanging sampling and analytical protocols. Cost savings should probably be achieved by restricting sites rather than having fewer parameters, less frequent sampling, lower quality control, or inadequate measurement of key ancillary data.

Gaps in Simulation Modeling and Decision Support Systems

The current capabilities of computers and computer software, including the proliferation of complex natural resource simulation models, are advancing beyond our ability to efficiently use them for research and natural resource decisionmaking. The formerly common paradigm of formulating an equation to describe a portion of a point process and making a decision based on a single objective has been replaced by an approach in which point processes are linked together to form a natural resource simulation system and applied in a distributed manner often within a GIS framework. The simulation results from the system can then be used to aid in the decisionmaking process. Inherent within the linkage of process sub-components is interactions and feedback mechanisms that complicate the evaluation of the sub-components as well as their interactions.

The flexibility of simulation models with large numbers of output variables makes arriving at a decision difficult without a systematic methodology to evaluate the output. There is an urgent need to provide scientists with a bridge for the gap between the tools of technology needed for development (computers and computer software) and basic science (process description and understanding) which is the foundation of sound natural resource technology transfer. There is also an urgent need to provide decisionmakers with a means of applying the technology on a routine basis by closing the gap between simulation models and decisions.

At the same time that computer simulation models are powerful tools, they have very definite limitations. Modelers generally have a good sense of those limitations, while decisionmakers may not. Providing a user-friendly interface between computer models and decisionmakers runs the risk of encouraging over-reliance on imperfect modeling tools. Care must be taken to instill a proper level of caution and critical judgment when computer modeling tools are made more readily available to technically unsophisticated users.

Whereas the early focus of using computers was in developing and running models, attention has shifted to the related needs of database management, GIS application modules, and putting these tools together in an easy to use package called a decision support system (DSS). Reitsma at al. (1996) define a decision support systems as ". . . computer-based systems which integrate state information, dynamic or processes information and plan evaluation tools into a single software implementation." From a computer science point of view, the DSS can be generally partitioned into the following four subsystems: control system, database system, model system, and the report system. Functionally, this provides a link between a relational database, a GIS, simulation models, and management tools (Glover et al., 1992). Additional computer tools may be part of a DSS (e.g., optimization routines for resource allocation, artificial intelligence and expert systems, and object oriented structure).

As used here, an evaluation or planning decision support system is an interactive computer-based system that helps a decisionmaker, scientist, or manager use data and models to solve problems. In natural resource watershed applications, integral parts of a DSS are: (1) identification of a problem, (2) selection of the decision criteria which should include the impact on stakeholders' income as well as costs to the community if applicable, (3) selection of feasible management systems or design alternatives, (4) evaluation of the alternatives by simulation models and/or historic data, and (5) recommendation of a decision.

Operational DSSs require further work in the following areas: (1) expert systems to define the problem, aid in parameter estimation, and interpret output, (2) additional simulation models to evaluate a given problem and a set of alternative management systems using the best and most appropriate science and technology, (3) enhanced decision models that examine the effects of uncertainty in simulation model output and the propagation of uncertainty in the decisionmaking process, (4) data bases provide the DSS with the most up-to-date information available, and (5) GIS interfaces for spatially varying data, processes, and information.

Examples of smaller watershed scale, DSS development activities include systems for evaluation and design of shallow land waste disposal systems (e.g., Lane et al., 1991) and evaluation of alternative farm management systems for environmental and economic sustainability (Yakowitz et al., 1993).

The major benefits to science of the development of operational DSS would be the availability of objective methodologies to evaluate natural resource systems simulation models and to identify topics that require additional research. For decisionmakers, the benefits would be systematic decisionmaking tools which would couple the best simulation modeling with decision theory in repeatable, and thus, scientifically defensible manners.

Some major DSS development activities are under way. The Center for Advanced Decision Support for Water and Environmental Systems (CADSWES) at the University of Colorado is developing a workstation based DSS for the Tennessee Valley Authority, the Bureau of Reclamation, and the Electric Power Research Institute. Also, the Colorado Water Conservation Board is developing a DSS for water planning in the Colorado River Basin.

Several large efforts are under way to develop decision support systems for watersheds. As part of the South Florida restoration effort, a large DSS is being built to evaluate the watershed impacts of various control alternatives. The Watershed and River Systems Management Initiative between Bureau of Reclamation and USGS is supporting the development of computer models and fully integrated data management systems to help water managers and water users increase the environmental, economic, and social benefits of water systems and improve management of water resources facilities. These models were originally tested on the San Juan and Lower Colorado Rivers but are designed to be used on any Reclamation watershed (Bureau of Reclamation, 1997). A centralized and integrated data center for the Colorado River Basin would collect and disseminate comprehensive, reliable, scientific and economic data for all interested users. The existing Grand Canyon Monitoring and Research Center could be used as a model for this organization. McLaughlin Water Engineers and Aiken (1997) recommend the development of a DSS for the entire Platte River Basin to help resolve numerous technical issues about hydrology and water quality in the Platte River Basin. They cite how the Colorado River DSS was used in the Colorado River Endangered Fish Recovery Program. A common model and DSS would help reduce fear and mistrust among the states and federal agencies. They also recommend improved scientific studies to better understand the hydrology of the Platte River Basin. They cite the Missouri River Basin modeling as part of the Annual Operating Plan process as an example of how federal leadership with simulation models can help resolve conflicts.

Given the difficulties of using and interpreting complex natural resource simulation models and data at the watershed scale, it is necessary that we develop decision tools to assist decisionmakers in watershed management programs and to facilitate transfer of simulation modeling technology.

TMDL Development as an Illustration of Information Status and Gaps

One example of an area where data gaps limit the usefulness of a watershed management approach relates to implementation of Total Maximum Daily Load (TMDL) requirements. Under the precepts of Section 303(d) of the Clean Water Act (CWA), states must identify pollution-impaired streams and develop plans to reduce pollutant loads. They then set TMDLs for individual water bodies that account for both point and nonpoint sources of pollutants. Development of TMDLs requires a broad understanding of point and nonpoint sources, the processes that influence their magnitude, timing, transport to bodies of water, and attenuation en route, and how they affect aquatic biota. This procedure tends to be highly site-specific, and watershed managers are challenged by frequent gaps in data, information, and modeling in their efforts to comply with this section of the CWA.

Development of a TMDL presupposes that a water body has been classified as water quality impaired, that its condition has been ranked and prioritized with respect to other impaired waters within a state, and that standards for specific contaminants have been established. These initial steps already require substantial data collection and synthesis. A broad range of contaminants must be measured for all likely impaired sites, and their variation with season, discharge, and other factors monitored and understood. Questions regarding the relative importance of varying amounts of a range of contaminants at different sites must be answered; how can we compare the relative importance of nutrients, sediment, low oxygen, and toxic contaminants? Worst case conditions need to be determined. For locations that are influenced by both point and nonpoint sources, it may not be clear whether this should be under low flow (when point sources receive least dilution) or high flow (when nonpoint sources often make their greatest contribution). Many models are available to help in the identification and ranking process, ranging from simple mass balances and regressions, through steady-state numerical models, to dynamic computer models that predict both temporal and spatial variation in a range of contaminants. The simpler models generally require less site-specific data and produce simple and/or less reliable predictions. The more complex models have the capability of describing changing contaminant levels over broader scales of space, time, and other conditions, but may require considerable data input, and still need to be verified by extensive real world measurements.

Once standards have been established, TMDL development involves allocating loads among all point, nonpoint, and background sources within a watershed. A margin of safety needs to be added, and allowances may be made for future watershed development. Allocation requires a clear understanding of all the significant sources in a drainage basin and how they are linked to and influence water quality in the receiving body of water. For some point sources and contaminants, this maybe relatively straightforward, especially under baseflow conditions. But for nonpoint sources, contaminants with complex biogeochemical behavior, and stormflows, reliably relating inputs to final water quality pushes the limits of current understanding of watershed processes and how to incorporate them into the present generation of models. Models exist, but their ability to reliably predict contaminant loads from nonpoint sources, especially for unusual "worst case" conditions, is questionable. In spite of this uncertainty, watershed managers must make decisions, even if they are based on imperfect information.

As of this writing, USEPA makes available through the Center for Exposure Assessment Modeling a total of 21 models that collectively address aspects of urban runoff; leaching and runoff from soils; transport through soil and ground water; conventional and toxic pollution of streams, lakes, and estuaries; near-field mixing and dilution in rivers, lakes, estuaries, and oceans; cohesive sediment transport; river and tidal hydrodynamics; geochemical equilibrium; and aquatic food chain bioaccumulation. These models are based on the best available understanding of watershed processes, and they are constantly being refined and updated, but still remain an imperfect representation of the real world. In addition, these models are only as good as the input data that are available, and for the more sophisticated models, measurement coverage in time and space is rarely adequate. Furthermore, each model tends to focus on only a few elements of the web of processes that link the generation of nonpoint sources to water quality variations in space and time in a receiving water body. Linking these parts remains a manual task, which can become almost prohibitively time consuming.

Numerous additional considerations often are not addressed by the TMDL process. For example, in terms of their relative ecological importance, what is the tradeoff between setting standards in terms of ambient contaminant concentrations in a water body as opposed to the total load carried by a stream (normalized per area of contributing watershed)? What interactions exist among contaminants, either additive or antagonistic? How should dissolved and particulate forms of contaminants be compared considering the varying uptake pathways, aquatic habitat types, and life histories of different target organisms? What about exchange between dissolved and particulate contaminant forms under varying background conditions, and how should colloidal forms of contaminants be treated? At present, colloidal forms of contaminants are rarely measured, yet they can comprise a major portion of the filter-passing contaminant load. Furthermore, within the dissolved fraction, what is the relative effect on biota of various chemical species, and how can distribution among these species be predicted? These topics are the subject of active research today, and our predictive capabilities are rudimentary.

Partly because of existing data gaps and limitations in our knowledge of the structure and function of watershed ecosystems, development of TMDLs has proceeded slowly. So far roughly 500 TMDLs have been initiated and of these only 225 have been completed and approved. By comparison, the USEPA estimates that there are a total of 15,000 water quality impaired water bodies in the United States.

CONCLUSION

Watershed science seeks to understand and explain the structure and function of complex ecosystems, and thus it is inherently a multidisciplinary effort that integrates biological, chemical, physical, and social sciences. Implementation of watershed management activities requires more effective integration of ecological, economic, and social considerations, and such integration depends on the availability of appropriate data and information. More data and information are readily available to the interested citizen, manager, researcher, and decisionmaker than ever before—often free over the Internet (see Appendix B for examples). Geographic information systems are an especially valuable tool for watershed management. But despite significant progress over the past decade, there are still gaps in scientific understanding—gaps in basic data related to water quality, gaps in our understanding of watershed processes, and gaps in the capabilities of simulation modeling and decision support systems.

REFERENCES

Benoit, G., 1994. Clean technique measurement of Pb, Ag, and Cd in fresh water: A redefinition of metal pollution. Environ. Sci. Technol. 28: 1987-1991.

Blodgett, J.E., 1983. Summary of hearings on "National Environmental Monitoring". Congressional Research Service, Washington, D.C.

Briggs, J.C. , and J.F. Ficke. 1977. Quality of the rivers of the United States, 1975 water year based on the National Stream Quality Accounting Network (NASQAN). Open-File Report 78-200. U.S. Geol. Surv., Reston, Va.

Dendy, F. E., and W. A. Champion. 1978. Sediment deposition in U.S. reservoirs: summary of data reported through 1975. U.S. Department of Agriculture, Agricultural Research Service Miscellaneous Publication 1362.

Detenbeck, N.E., C.A. Johnston, and G.J. Niemi. 1993. Wetland effects on lake water quality in the Minneapolis/St. Paul metropolitan area. Landscape Ecology 8:39-61.

Eidenshink, J. 1992. The 1990 conterminous U.S. AVHRR data set. Photogrammetric Engineering & Remote Sensing 58:809-813.

Forest Ecosystem Management Assessment Team (FEMAT). 1993. Forest ecosystem management: an ecological, economic, and social assessment. Report of the Forest Ecosystem Management Assessment Team, USDA Forest Service, Portland, Oregon. 530 pp.

Glover, F., Klingman, D. and N. Philips. 1992. Network Models in Optimization and Their Applications in Practice. New York: J. Wiley.

Goodchild, M. R., B. O. Parks, and L. T. Steyaert (eds.) 1993. Environmental Modeling with GIS. Oxford University Press.

Hren, J., C. J. O. Childress, J. M. Norris, T. H. Chaney, and D. N. Myers. 1990. Regional water quality. Environ. Sci. Technol. 24: 1122-1127.

Jensen, S. K., and J. O. Domingue. 1988. Extracting topographic structure from raster elevation data for geographic information system analysis. Photogrammetric Engineering and Remote Sensing 54:1593-1600.

Johnston, C. A., N. E. Detenbeck, J. P. Bonde, and G. J. Niemi. 1988. Geographic information systems for cumulative impact assessment. Photogrammetric Engineering and Remote Sensing 54:1609-1615.

Johnston, C. A., N. E. Detenbeck, and G. J. Niemi. 1990. The cumulative effect of wetlands on stream water quality and quantity: a landscape approach. Biogeochemistry 10:105-141.

Kovar, K., and H. P. Nachtnebel. 1996. Application of Geographic Information Systems in Hydrology and Water Resources Management. IAHS Publication No. 235. International Association of Hydrological Sciences Press, Wallingford, UK.

Lane, L. J., J. Ascough, and T. E. Hakonson. 1991. Multiobjective decision theory—decision support systems with embedded simulation models. ASCE Irrigation and Drainage Proceedings, July, Honolulu, HI. pp. 445-451.

Lytle, D. J., N. B. Bliss, and S. W. Waltman. 1996. Interpreting the State Soil Geographic Database (STATSGO). Pp. 49-52 in M. R. Goodchild, L. T. Steyaert, B. O. Parks, C. A. Johnston, D. Maidment, M. Crane, and S. Glendinning (eds.) 1996. GIS and Environmental Modeling: Progress and Research Issues. Fort Coliins, Colo.: GIS World Books.

Meijerink, A. M. J., H. A. M. de Brouwer, C. M. Mannaerts, and C. R. Valenzuela. 1994. Introduction to the use of geographic information systems for practical hydrology. ITC Publ. No. 23. UNESCO International Hydrological Programme and the International Institute for Aerospace Survey and Earth Sciences (ITC), Enschede, The Netherlands.

Naiman, R. J., P. A. Bisson, R. G. Lee, and M. G. Turner. 1997. Approaches to management at the watershed scale. Pp. 239-254 in K. A. Kohm and J. F. Franklin, editors. Creating a forestry for the 21st century: the science of ecosystem management. Washington, D.C.: Island Press.

National Research Council (NRC). 1992. Restoration of Aquatic Ecosystems. Washington, D.C.: National Academy Press. 552 pp.

National Research Council (NRC). 1996. Upstream: Salmon and Society in the Pacific Northwest. Washington, D.C.: National Academy Press.

National Research Council (NRC). 1997. Watershed Research in the U. S. Geological Survey. Washington, D.C.: National Academy Press.

National Science Foundation/U.S. Environmental Protection Agency (NSF/EPA). 1998. Proceedings: 1998 Water and Watersheds Program Review. Arlington, Vir.: National Science Foundation.

Powell, M. 1995. Building a national water quality monitoring program. Environ. Sci. Technol. 29: 458A-463A.

Reitsma, R. F., E. A. Zoyana, S. C. Chapra, K. M. Strzepek. 1996. Decision Support Systems for Water Resources Management. Chap. 33 in L. Mays (ed.) Water Resources Handbook, New York: McGraw-Hill, pp. 33.1-33.35.

Trimble, S. W., and K. P. Bube. 1990. Improved reservoir trap efficiency prediction. The Env. Prof. 12:255-272.

Trimble, S. W., and R. U. Cooke. 1991. Historical sources for geomorphological research in the United States. Prof. Geographer, 43:212-228.

U.S. Environmental Protection Agency. 1993. The Watershed Protection Approach: A Project Focus. Draft. Washington, D.C.: USEPA Office of Water (WH-553).

U.S. Geological Survey (USGS). 1982. Hydrologic Unit Map of the United States (map, scale 1:5,000,000). Washington, D.C.: U.S. Government Printing Office.

Windom, H. L., J. T. Byrd, R. G. Smith, Jr., and F. Huan. 1991. Inadequacy of NASQAN data for assessing metal trends in the nation's rivers. Environ. Sci. Technol. 25:1137-1142

Yakowitz, D. S., L. J. Lane, and F. Szidarovszky. 1993. Applied Mathematics and Computation 54:167-181.

5

Connecting Science and the Decisionmaker

Significant scientific knowledge, data, and information are available to address watershed management problems. However, these scientific tools are not useful to the manager unless they are effective, readily available, and easy to use. The purpose of this chapter is to explore the connection between scientific efforts and the decisionmaker by outlining five important areas where science might reasonably be expected to aid management. We begin by illustrating the *major indicators* of watershed conditions as they are understood from a scientific perspective but that are also applicable by managers. We review at some length the promising approach of *ecological risk assessment* as a way of indicating how scientific thinking can improve the effectiveness of decisions. Watershed *restoration* is a venue for the interaction between science and management that illustrates both the strengths and weaknesses of scientific knowledge in the applied problem-solving arena. The case study of watershed management in the state of Washington provides an important object lesson on the *integration* of science, data, and diverse public policy goals. Finally, we turn our attention to the need for improved *process based research* to improve scientific tools for use by managers in addressing watershed problems.

INDICATORS OF WATERSHED CONDITION

One area that promises to improve watershed science is the effort to develop simulation models that can help predict watershed conditions. At the international level, the Organization for International Economic Cooperation and Development (OECD) has initiated a significant program to develop environmental indicators for the impacts of agriculture (OECD, 1997). The OECD program seeks to improve our understanding of the agricultural-environmental relationships affecting sustainability in agriculture so that managers can better develop, monitor, and assess agricultural programs that address the environmental problems.

The OECD's selection criteria for agricultural-environmental indicators include: (1) policy relevance, (2) analytical validity, (3) measurability, and (4) level of aggregation (i.e., scale issues, including both space and time). These criteria could be especially relevant to watershed management if the OECD definitions of various units of scale (i.e., field, farm, watershed, regional, national, and global) were modified so that watersheds were addressed.

In many areas in the American West, rangelands are critical components of watersheds. The National Research Council has defined rangeland health as "the degree to which the integrity of the soil and the ecological processes of rangelands are sustained" (NRC, 1994). The Natural Resources Conservation Service (NRCS), Bureau of Land Management (BLM), and other agencies and organizations charged with management of some 740 million acres (300 million hectares) of western rangelands (about a third of all U.S. land) have initiated programs to identify attributes comprising indicators for rangeland health, focusing on soil stability and watershed function. Research organizations such as the U.S. Department of Agriculture Agricultural Research Service (ARS) and the Land Grant Colleges in the West are also developing research programs to quantify watershed health and its indicators across a range of watershed scales and environments. Efforts to better quantify watershed health are under way in many areas, and one example is presented in Box 5.1.

ECOLOGICAL RISK ANALYSIS AND UNCERTAINTY

One ingredient that is built into successful watershed management is the use of "good science" in decisionmaking, but even the best science is inadequate to remove all uncertainty when dealing with environmental, economic, and social systems. The manager would prefer that the scientist or engineer provide hard and fast numbers with clearly understood implications, but despite the use of the best available models, data, and ideas, experts cannot offer precise understanding about the way watersheds and their components work. Risk assessment is one method of improving the usefulness of science for the decisionmaker because it provides improved understanding of the degree and types of uncertainty in management applications (NRC, 1993). Ecological risk assessments differ from environmental impact analysis and hazards assessments. The issue of uncertainty is of special importance to watershed managers because they often must work with incomplete information, and because watershed processes exhibit random, or stochastic, behavior. Environmental risk assessment is a scientific procedure that can augment the tool kit of the manager in dealing with an uncertain world where the objective cannot be to eliminate all risk. Success in watershed management is partly defined by the ability to account for risk and to succeed in spite of it.

Ecological risk assessment seeks to produce a scientific evaluation of ecological risk that enables managers to make informed environmental decisions (EPA, 1996). Ecological risk assessment is important for environmental decisionmakers because of the high cost of eliminating environmental risks associated with human activities and the necessity of making decisions in the face of uncertainty. Risk-based environmental decisionmaking seeks to balance the degree of risk to be permitted against the cost of risk reduction and against competing risks (Suter, 1993). The risk manager is given scientific information to consider along with the other factors (political, social, legal or economic) in selecting a course of action.

"Specifically, ecological risk assessment evaluates the likelihood that adverse ecological effects may occur or are occurring as a result of exposure to one or more stressors" (EPA, 1992). In this definition, stressors can be chemical, physical, or biological, and can affect organisms or an ecosystem function. The focus is on the ecosystem and the effects that human impacts cause. An ecological risk assessment attempts to predict what might occur as a result of a potential threat or to evaluate consequences of past actions. Regional organizations often use the method to evaluate series of complex problems (see Box 5.2).

In an ecological risk assessment, changes in ecological processes can be expressed as a function of changes in exposure to a physical, chemical, or biological stressor. The risk assessment can provide a basis for comparing and ranking alternatives on the basis of risk. An explicit evaluation of uncertainties is inherent in the ecological risk assessment, and the use of well-defined and relevant endpoints helps to ensure that the results will be expressed in a way that the decisionmaker can use them.

The process for developing an ecological risk assessment as laid out in the U.S. Environmental Protection Agency (EPA) Guidelines (1996) has three primary phases (Figure 5.1): problem formulation, analysis, and risk characterization. At the beginning of the process the risk assessor and the risk manager need to discuss the problem at hand. The risk manager is charged with protecting environmental values and needs to make sure that the ecological risk assessment will provide information relevant to that goal. The ecological risk assessor ensures that science is effectively used to address ecological concerns (EPA, 1996). Together they determine the purpose for the risk assessment by defining the decisions to be made in the context of the management goals. Because this would be a watershed-based, or regional ecological risk assessment, there needs to be a clear understanding of the scope of the assessment, with the watershed defining the regional scale.

The problem formulation phase identifies the goals, objectives, and clearly defined assessment endpoints. As explained by EPA (1996), "The ecological resources selected to represent management goals for environmental protection

Box 5.1
Willapa Bay Watershed Washington:
Quantifying Watershed Conditions

Quantification of watershed variables for research and management in the Willapa Bay Watershed of Washington provides an instructive example of the types and range of measurable indicators in watersheds. The Willapa Bay Watershed includes 1,180 sq. mi. of four western Washington counties. Its 1,470 miles of streams drain forested and agricultural lands, and supply water and nutrients to coastal wetlands. The long-term residents take pride in their management of lumbering, fishing, and farming, while short-term residents seek second-home and retirement amenities quite different from traditional pursuits. Since the early 1980s, increasing unemployment, protection of scenic amenities, declining commercial fish catches, and lumbering regulations have fueled discord among watershed residents. Two conservation organizations, Ecotrust of Portland Oregon and the Nature Conservancy of Seattle, have funded a nonprofit watershed coalition called the Willapa Alliance with the goal of promoting sustainable economic development with protection of environmental quality. The Alliance's first task, to define the means of measuring watershed health and changes, produced their first published report, "Willapa Indicators for a Sustainable Community."

The Alliance selected measures with the specific purpose of assessing economic, social, and environmental characteristics of the watershed. Although the parameters address particular needs of the Pacific Northwest watershed, they provide an example of the kinds of measures that may be useful in a range of settings across the nation. The indicators include the following:

are reflected in the assessment endpoints that drive the assessment process. Assessment endpoints often reflect environmental values that are protected by law, provide critical resources, or provide an ecological function that would be impaired (or that society would perceive as having been impaired) if the resource were altered." The endpoint also needs to be something that will be affected by the known or potential stressor. At a watershed scale there are multiple stressors and multiple endpoints, so the interactions become more complicated. The risk

Environmental:
- Water Quality—oyster conditions off shore and fecal coliform counts at river outlets
    - Land Use Patterns—map-based assessments of land use types
    - Species Viability—salmon and waterfowl census

Economic:
- Productivity—lumber production, cranberry harvests, oyster harvests, dairy cattle

Census:
- Opportunity—unemployment, housing, in- and out-migration
- Diversity—employment in various economic sectors
- Equity—income and poverty

Community:
- Education—high school graduation rates
- Health—average birthweight, hospital admissions, crime, mental health data
- Citizenship—voter turnout, citizen organizations
- Stewardship—waste disposal, electrical consumption

The Willapa Alliance has not yet solved every problem in the watershed, but it does have a better understanding of trends of change through these indicators. Most of the indicators are quantitative data readily available from county records or (in a few cases) from state or federal sources. Other watershed alliances might choose different specific measures, but the Willapa example demonstrates the sorts of indicators that are informative and easily obtained.

assessor must therefore recognize the possibilities for synergism, antagonism, and interference in the measurement of effects.

The definition of endpoints can provide a conceptual model that connects ecological entities, stressors, ecosystem processes, and responses. The model may be in text or visual form. The model also includes risk hypotheses, which are statements of assumptions about risk based on available information. An

Box 5.2
The Susquehanna River Basin:
Competing Problems and an Organizational Response

Problems in the Susquehanna River basin and the establishment of the Susquehanna River Basin Commission illustrate the kinds of issues and resulting organizations that give rise to the use of risk assessment in environmental management. The Susquehanna River Basin is the 16th largest in the United States, draining 27,500 sq. mi. of New York, Pennsylvania, and Maryland. The river flows 444 miles from mountain terrain through urbanized areas to the Chesapeake Bay, forming the largest riverine ecosystem east of the Mississippi. The river supplies 43 percent of the drainage to the Chesapeake Bay, one of the most productive estuarine ecosystems in the nation. Because the productivity of the bay is linked to the delicate balance between salt water from the Atlantic Ocean and fresh water from its inland tributaries, human impacts on the rivers, and especially the Susquehanna, have direct and long-term implications for the bay.

About 4 million people live in the basin, which has 65 percent of its area in forest, 30 percent in agriculture, and 5 percent developed for intensive uses such as urban activities. The basin has experienced chronic water quality problems that extend to impacts in Chesapeake Bay. The river delivers up to 132 million pounds (60 million kilograms) of nitrogen to the bay each year, with 93 percent coming from nonpoint sources including agricultural runoff, atmospheric deposition, septic systems, and urban runoff. These sources contribute smaller but problem-

analysis plan emerges from the combination of the conceptual model and the assessment endpoints.

The second phase is analysis, which includes measures of exposure, ecosystem properties, receptor characteristics, and effects. An *exposure profile* is developed by analyzing the measures of exposure; a *stressor-response profile* is developed based on an ecological response analysis of the effects measured. Risk characterization, the final phase, assesses these two profiles together.

Risk characterization requires making an estimate and a description of the risk and communicating those results to the risk manager. Risk estimation determines the likelihood of adverse effects to the assessment endpoints by integrating atic quantities of phosphorus. Additional water quality problems derive from acid mine drainage from coal mines.

Water quality is an issue at the outlet of the basin, but within the basin a major issue is water quantity. Generally there is an overabundance of water, but during drought periods water consumption in the basin of about 450 million gallons per day creates a myriad of problems. During the 1994-1995 drought, for example, surface flows were only one-third the normal flows, resulting in fish kills, high stream temperatures, low dissolved oxygen levels, significant crop losses, and severe restrictions on water use in 30 area water delivery systems. The drought was followed in 1996 by floods causing $600 million in damages and producing a massive influx of sediment to the bay.

The complex natural system and equally entangled administrative jurisdictions brought about the need for a regional decisionmaking structure. In 1971, federal, state, and local entities formed the Susquehanna River Basin Commission to develop and implement programs to address the basin's outstanding problems. The commission members include representatives from each of the states as well as the federal government. Their specific charge is to resolve problems related to:

- floodplain management and protection
- water supply
- water quality
- watershed protection and management
- recreation, fish, and wildlife
- cultural, visual, and other amenities

Environmental risk assessment has proven to be an important tool used by the commission as it examines options for addressing these varied goals.

exposure and effects data and evaluating any associated uncertainty. The ideal is to quantify all risk. However, sometimes a lack of specific information makes it necessary to express risks qualitatively using categories such as high, medium, and low.

There are other methods currently in use that seem very similar. They are Environmental Impacts Statements (EIS) as required by the National Environmental Policy Act 1969, risk assessments, and hazard assessments. Though there are some similarities, there are also major differences in focus among these approaches.

The EIS is a special form of the more general method of environmental

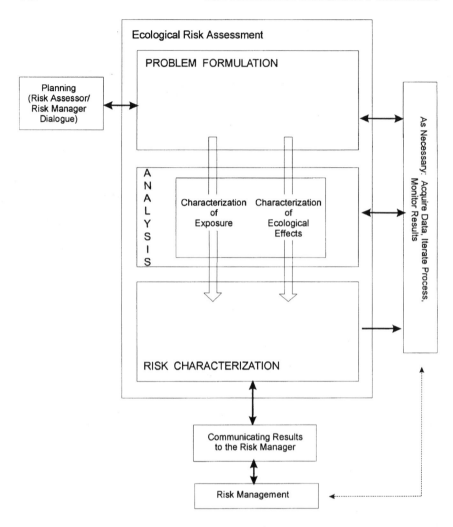

FIGURE 5.1 The framework for ecological risk assessment. Ecological risk assessment is shown as a three-phase process including problem formulation, analysis, and risk characterization. Important activities associated with ecological risk assessment include discussions between risk assessors and risk managers and data acquisition and monitoring. Ecological risk assessments frequently follow an iterative or tiered approach. SOURCE: EPA, 1996.

assessment. The EIS is performed only on major federal actions that would significantly affect the environment. It is a predictive exercise that compares effects on the environment from different alternatives, including a "no action" alternative. Because an EIS is a full disclosure document, it must identify a full range of the components in the affected environment. Temporal as well as secondary and tertiary effects are identified. This approach has tended to create a checklist or matrix of actions and possible impacts. A deterministic approach is taken, and though uncertainties should be identified, they rarely are. The assessment ends up being a discussion of species and site-specific interactions. Risk assessment grew out of the actuarial work of insurance companies concerned with estimating probability and magnitudes of undesirable events. It evolved partly to evaluate environmental risk assessments that arise or are transmitted through the air, water, soil, or biological food chain to man. It also includes effects of natural hazards such as floods, earthquakes, and landslides on people and on the natural environment. Risk assessment has generally emphasized risks to humans or their property and has ignored ecological effects. It sometimes falsely assumed that what protects human health automatically protects nonhuman organisms and thus ignored or underestimated many ecological risks. For instance, ammonia and chlorine are toxic to fish and bacteria at concentrations that are not harmful to humans.

Hazards assessment is a commonly used method for analyzing the effects of chemicals on the natural environment. It compares the expected concentration in the environment with the estimated toxic threshold, and makes a judgment whether the proposed release is safe, hazardous, or insufficiently characterized for making a decision. Hazards assessment does not use probabilistic methods, and does not attempt to predict the nature or magnitude of the effects (Suter, 1993).

One of the basic understandings of the scientific method is that reported results often contain some error and uncertainty. Yet scientific reports often omit any explicit statement about error, uncertainty, and assumptions made in doing the research, leading to misunderstandings and disagreements about what was found or what the data mean. A related problem occurs when technical professionals must report to general audiences, who are not accustomed to dealing with uncertainty as a ubiquitous and normal part of the natural world. In this case, discussions of kinds and levels of uncertainty can be mistaken for an admission of flawed analysis rather than evidence of careful inquiry. One of the basic underpinnings of ecological risk assessment is that uncertainty and assumptions will be clearly stated. Suter (1993) outlined three basic sources of uncertainty: the inherent randomness of the world (stochastic behavior); imperfect or incomplete knowledge of things that could be known (ignorance); and mistakes or execution of assessment activities (error). Incorrect measures, misidentification, data recording errors, and computational errors are issues of quality assurance. "Fundamental ignorance results in undefined uncertainty, the 'unknown unknowns' that cannot be described or quantified. More commonly, ignorance is simply a result of practical constraints on our ability to accurately describe, count, or measure everything that pertains to a risk estimate" (Suter, 1993).

EPA (1996) added other categories in its discussion of uncertainty. The authors note that along with descriptive errors, errors in the information itself, and variability (i.e., uncertainty about a quantity's true value and data gaps), unclear communication can also create uncertainty. Sources of uncertainty can also arise in the development and application of models, the structure of process models, and the description of the relationship between two or more variables in empirical models.

Methods for analyzing and describing uncertainties range from simple to complex. In some cases it is merely necessary to state the assumptions that went into the research. Classical statistical methods can describe uncertainty in measurable parameters. In simulation modeling, sensitivity analyses should be used. The availability of software for certain straightforward analyses has increased the use of probabilistic methods. Whatever method of ecological risk assessment one uses, the sources of uncertainty should be explicitly addressed. This will add credibility to the analysis and the information presented to the decisionmaker.

WATERSHED RESTORATION STRATEGIES

In response to policy direction from the Clean Water Act of 1977 and its revisions, government agencies at all levels have an increased interest in environmental restoration as a route to sustainable environmental quality while fostering economic vitality. Restoration is a fertile meeting ground for science and management. Scientists engaged in restoration research quickly learn that their abstract theories do not always play out well in the complex real world, and they must modify or simplify their thinking. Managers engaged in restoration work learn that the systems they try to influence are more complex and interconnected than at first seems the case.

In the vast majority of watersheds in the United States, population growth and natural resource development have altered the characteristics and functions of land and water ecosystems. The last two centuries, and particularly the last 50 years, represent a period of rapid transition for watershed ecosystems. Although the degree of alteration varies widely throughout the nation, significant habitat impacts and losses are common. The variety of impacts and social and economic constraints to restoration suggest that a diversity of strategies are needed to improve watershed conditions.

Where natural communities continue to survive and maintain healthy populations, the protection of intact aquatic and riparian habitats often represents a high priority in watershed protection or restoration efforts. When protection is the goal, human influences and stresses on ecosystem behavior are often prohibited or minimized.

Where watersheds have been degraded by human activities but have the potential to recover the characteristics and features that make them functionally similar to a pristine system, "restoration" may represent the preferred management strategy. These situations might include watersheds where a return to natural streamflow, nutrient, and sediment regimes is possible. Candidates for the restoration option often include areas that have experienced some adverse impacts from historical land and water management, but which are capable of self-recovery. If human disturbances can be modified to reduce or eliminate potential impacts to a watershed's hydrology and sediment production, the prognosis for long-term reestablishment of natural processes is favorable.

Management policies directed at the watershed restoration option can potentially proceed along two major pathways: (1) natural or passive restoration, where the watershed is allowed to recover naturally, and (2) active restoration, which involves human intervention to accelerate the recovery process. In natural restoration, removing the sources of anthropogenic disturbance is all that is necessary to restore the system. For example, where agricultural practices occur in riparian areas, eliminating such practices may allow the long-term reestablishment of riparian vegetation and associated ecological functions. Natural disturbances would combine with the establishment, growth, and succession of riparian plants to assist in restoring aquatic habitats. Similarly, the removal of grazing from streamside zones or a change to grazing policies that allow full recovery of riparian plants along streams may be all that is needed to restore aquatic and riparian functions for many rangeland streams. In forested watersheds that have been heavily logged, establishing no-harvest buffers may allow the restoration of natural plant and animal assemblages. The time required for restoration will vary depending upon local conditions (e.g., species of riparian plants, climate, geomorphic characteristics, and hydrologic disturbance pattern). However, natural restoration always seeks to use the natural abilities of physical (channel adjustments, bank building, scour and fill, etc.), chemical (nutrient transformations), and biological (plant establishment, growth, and succession) processes to functionally restore aquatic and riparian ecosystems.

The first step in active restoration also involves eliminating human activities that are causing environmental degradation. However, where monitoring or observation indicate that recovery will not be complete or may require a very large amount of time, additional management practices can be considered. Active restoration incorporates practices designed to fill an ecological void or accelerate natural recovery. For example, a forested riparian zone may have been harvested years ago, at which time large woody debris was simultaneously removed from the stream channel. Although the growth rates and species composition of the second-growth riparian forest may currently be providing the desired functions within the range of natural conditions, the scarcity of large wood in the stream may not be overcome for many decades. In this situation, placing large woody debris in configurations normally expected for the stream may speed restoration.

In other instances, riparian areas may have been previously used for crop production. Eliminating agricultural practices may initiate natural recovery of riparian functions and aquatic habitat, but because native plant species that would be characteristic of the local riparian system are infrequent, restoration might take an exceptionally long time. In this situation, planting native species of riparian plants obtained from locally adapted genetic stock might accelerate recovery. In rangeland areas where prolonged grazing or other practices have caused the disappearance of willows, cottonwoods, or other key riparian plants along streams, active management may be needed to reestablish a native vegetation community.

The types of practices used in active management can vary widely, but the intent is still the same—to assist or accelerate the restoration of ecological processes and related physical, chemical, and biological characteristics that support natural communities and maintain aquatic productivity. Such practices are intended to aid in reestablishing watersheds that will be, for all practical purposes, functionally equivalent to pristine conditions.

In many wetlands, streams, rivers, and estuaries where habitat alteration and loss have been extensive, restoration per se is no longer a feasible goal. Natural disturbance regimes may have been sufficiently altered that there is little opportunity for them to be restored. Such significant habitat alteration can occur in a variety of circumstances, including where hydrologic and sediment transport regimes are affected by dams, irrigation diversions, changes in fire frequency, or conversion of lands to agricultural practices; where introduced plants have replaced native riparian species; where channel incision has lowered local ground water tables and affected hyporheic interchanges with the stream; where estuaries have been filled; or where road construction, agricultural practices, or urban development have reconfigured channel sinuosity or shifted stream location. For many of these situations, watersheds still have the potential to provide habitat for some native species and provide high quality water and relatively natural conditions for humans to enjoy. However, realizing the potential might require increased levels of effort (time, money, and management persistence). In such cases management can be directed toward reestablishing conditions that are able to provide some (albeit not all) of the ecological processes that occurred historically, a strategy termed "rehabilitation." The rehabilitation option produces some natural habitats, but does not fully restore the watershed to predisturbance conditions.

The rehabilitation option does not seek to restore all of the ecological processes. For example, if a stream previously had a dike constructed along its edge, moving the dike back some distance from the channel would allow the return of streamside vegetation as well as restore some floodplain functions (e.g., temporary storage of floodwaters, sediment deposition on floodplains, and improved interactions between stream and ground water). However, the channel's ability to develop predisturbance sinuosity, density of side channels, or full floodplain functions might remain limited. Even though full restoration is not possible in this example, a major improvement in aquatic and riparian characteristics would be achieved by repositioning the dike. Rehabilitation projects often represent important and politically acceptable opportunities for developing improved and sustainable habitats for sensitive species.

"Substitution" approaches to watershed management are generally directed toward selectively creating, altering, or modifying habitat features to offset the effects of anthropogenic impacts, sometimes in a different location. While the term "enhancement" carries with it the implied message of improvement and betterment of a system, it is important to realize that if ecosystem needs are misinterpreted, a watershed enhancement project may actually shift an ecosystem from one degraded state to another (NRC, 1992; NRC, 1996). For example, fully spanning logs with bank revetments may be placed in a stream deficient of pools to provide additional pool habitat. However, if the new pools are without cover and losses to predation are increased, or if the logs create waterfalls that become barriers to juvenile or adult fish movements, or if the channel can no longer adjust to high flows and sediment transport by altering sinuosity or creating natural pools the enhancement will actually degrade the stream.

Where habitat losses are unavoidable, "mitigation" (i.e., replacement of lost habitat with habitat at another location) is a management option that attempts to minimize or offset the effects of habitat loss. Although the concept of mitigation is relatively simple, its application often is not. Losses of habitat that occur at a particular site are seldom balanced by mitigation at another site, because such mitigation rarely replaces all relevant ecological interconnections. If a key watershed feature is significantly altered or destroyed, there may be no suitable means of mitigating that impact elsewhere.

Watershed improvement projects tend to focus on the characteristics and needs of a particular site, but the condition of individual habitats, stream reaches, and entire tributary systems within a watershed must be considered for restoration planning to be effective. It may do little good to invest time and money restoring individual habitats (e.g., bird nesting sites, spawning gravels for fish) if other types of habitat are in short supply or downstream barriers to animal migration greatly limit accessibility to the improved site. Likewise, it may do little good to emphasize riparian restoration where excessive sediment production from land uses or water withdrawals upstream from the project prevent riparian recovery. Watershed managers should be aware of how conditions change as a result of a wide range of anthropogenic perturbations and natural disturbance patterns. This awareness can be greatly improved with a thorough watershed-wide assessment of the current range of conditions and disturbance history. The complexity of environmental factors and management options available presents a major challenge to the effective reduction of anthropogenic impacts, yet it is critically important that any strategy adopted accounts for the extent of watershed alteration and the potential for self-recovery.

All of the strategies discussed—passive and active restoration, rehabilitation, enhancement, and mitigation—require improved scientific knowledge and predictive capabilities to reach their full potential. Only through a better under-standing of watershed ecosystem structure and function will it be possible to decide which strategies are appropriate and whether the consequences of eco-system manipulation will be beneficial or harmful. Such scientific knowledge and understanding are still often lacking for many decisions regarding watershed restoration activities. Future research should put a high priority on integrative interdisciplinary research that can guide ecosystem restoration.

Watershed Analysis in the State of Washington

The integration of data, information, and science is one of the most difficult challenges of watershed management, and because of the variability from place to place in a nation as diverse as the United States, there is no one way to achieve integration. The experience of the state of Washington, however, provides an instructive example to watershed managers on how diverse sets of information, stakeholders, resources, and scientific ideas can be integrated into an effective watershed management strategy.

The state of Washington's approach to managing forestry operations in its watersheds illustrates current uses of data, information and science in watershed management decisions. In the early 1970s, Washington, like other states in the Pacific Northwest, enacted a Forest Practices Act to regulate forestry activities on the state's 12.5 million acres of state and privately owned forests. The Act's purpose was to protect fish and wildlife habitat, prevent soil erosion, maintain water quality, and ensure a sustainable supply of forest products by specifying prompt reforestation of logged areas. In part, the Forest Practices Act was a response to the federal Clean Water Act and its requirement that states formulate nonpoint pollution control plans, but it was also the result of increased public recognition that unregulated forestry operations had caused significant environ-mental degradation. During the 1970s and early 1980s the Act underwent several revisions in response to new scientific information, but the regulations only con-sidered forestry operations individually; it contained no provisions for regulating more than one operation at a time, and the law did not provide a watershed con-text. By the late 1980s it was clear that existing laws were not up to the task of controlling the environmental impacts of multiple activities within whole water-sheds.

The Washington Forest Practices Board, which sets forestry policies for state and private lands, recognized that the "one-size-fits-all" forest rules based on "Best Management Practices" could not effectively prevent the cumulative harm-ful effects of multiple forestry activities, defined as "the changes to the environ-ment caused by the interaction of natural ecosystem processes with the effects of two or more forest practices" (Washington Forest Practices Board, 1995).

In 1987 an agreement was reached between Washington state agencies, large and small private land owners, Native American treaty tribes, and environmental organizations. This agreement, called Timber/Fish/Wildlife (TFW), called upon various constituencies to act together to protect the state's natural resources on commercial forest land without having to continually resort to litigation. Although this agreement has had its share of successes and failures (Halbert and Lee, 1990), it has survived nearly a decade and continues to incorporate scientific information into the decisionmaking process. The original TFW agreement suggested an approach to addressing cumulative effects that contained five components: (1) state, regional, and basin goal setting, (2) use of risk assessment techniques to identify problems, (3) implementation of an adaptive management process, (4) monitoring and evaluation to determine if goals are being met, and (5) reevaluation of goals as new information becomes available (Washington Forest Practices Board, 1995).

From 1989 to 1991, TFW participants developed a process through which the chief regulatory agency—the Washington Department of Natural Resources—could specify what management practices were needed to minimize cumulative harm in forested watersheds. This process, termed Watershed Analysis, was meant to produce forestry plans tailored to individual watersheds and based on scientific understanding. The watershed analysis protocols developed by TFW participants were formally adopted into law in 1992. Part of the watershed analysis legislation divided Washington state into about 800 watersheds ranging from 10,000 to 50,000 acres (4,000 to 20,000 hectares).

In theory, Washington's approach to watershed analysis is meant to be an adaptive management approach based on biological and physical inventory. The protocol has three phases–resource assessment, prescription writing (rule making), and monitoring—each structured around the boundaries of a particular watershed. Guided by a series of key questions, a team of technical specialists initially develops information and interpretations of resource condition and environmental sensitivities within a watershed. These assessments include maps of sensitive areas as well as reports describing the nature of the sensitivity and the potential risk forest management poses to public resources. This information is fed into a prescription process, or rule-making, in which landowners and agencies develop tailored management plans for the watershed that respond to the resource concerns of the technical specialists. The public is then given an opportunity to review the study and prescriptions before the plan becomes final. Total time to completion is two to five months from initiation of the process to final approval, depending on the size and complexity of the watershed. Once the watershed plan is accepted, the findings are assumed to be valid for five years, after which time the process may be repeated.

In its current form, the resource assessment phase is strongly oriented toward determining the vulnerability of Pacific salmon populations, water quality, and capital structures to logging and road building activities. This orientation is reflected in the structured protocols of the process. Washington's watershed analysis procedure is divided into nine topic areas, or "modules," each conducted by assessment team members who must undergo a state certification process in one or more modules to participate. The modules are mass wasting (mass soil movements such as landslides), surface erosion, hydrology, riparian function, stream channel processes, fish habitat, potentially vulnerable capital structures (such as bridges), and water quality. (As of early 1998, the water quality module was undergoing development, and a tenth module pertaining to monitoring procedures has also not been completed.)

The state's watershed analysis procedures have been available for approximately four years. During that time only about 5 percent of the state's 800 designated watersheds have undergone a completed watershed analysis. Although this represents a small fraction of the area of state and privately owned forests, most stakeholders feel the approach should be retained. Many, however, have opted to continue operating under standard forest practices rules, thus choosing to forego the potential benefits of tailored, site-specific management plans. Although the reasons for this reluctance have not been fully examined, it appears that many landowners feel they cannot afford the assessment phase (costs of $1-2 per acre have been suggested) or are still somewhat uncomfortable with a process that provides for increased public input into policy decisions.

As a vehicle for bringing traditional adversaries together, watershed analysis in Washington state has been generally successful. For example, the Indian tribes and the environmental community have long complained of having little or no say in land use decisions, and have often used litigation to delay or stop projects they felt were harmful to watershed resources. The watershed analysis process, however, has brought them a seat at the table. As recognized stakeholders in watershed analysis, outside interest groups are free to bring whatever technical expertise they have to the assessment phase, and to provide input to the prescription phase. The importance of bringing everyone with a legitimate concern to the table cannot be underestimated. Not all conflicts have been resolved, but more often than not the prescriptions are based on consensus—a situation that is somewhat unique with respect to forestry operations on state and private lands in the Pacific Northwest.

It is still not clear, however, how well the watershed analysis process is working scientifically and how well its prescriptions are protecting the resources they are designed to safeguard. At its core, watershed analysis has lofty goals: to be an effective adaptive management strategy and to provide a framework for implementing ecosystem management at a watershed scale (Montgomery et al., 1995). Recently, Collins and Pess (1997a-c) have completed an examination of the first 20 watershed analyses with regard to their efficacy (1) as a cumulative effects assessment method, (2) as a framework for implementing ecosystem management, (3) as a watershed restoration tool, (4) as an adaptive management strategy, and (5) as a method for identifying and reducing the dominant direct effects of land management on aquatic resources. They identified a number of significant shortcomings in the process, many of which were related to a lack of monitoring and extensive use of untested assumptions and models in the hazard assessment process. These failures underscore the need for management informed by science.

Washington's watershed analysis procedure is noteworthy on several counts. First, it explicitly recognizes watershed boundaries as management units and provides a spatial definition of what these units are. Second, the process facilitates co-management of forests and aquatic resources, thus forestalling at least in part some of the bitter environmental disputes that have marked the practice of forestry in the region over the last two decades. Third, the procedure is meant to be adaptive and to be based on principles of ecosystem management. Fourth, the procedure is designed to incorporate the latest decision support technology, including GIS (slope stability, stream habitat, riparian condition) and simulation models (soil erosion, stream temperature changes, woody debris dynamics).

Application of watershed analysis has revealed some significant shortcomings, some of which are related to the newness of the process, some of which are related to lack of scientific information or failure to make use of it when it is available, and some of which are related to the policies of involved organizations (NRC, 1996). In terms of implementing watershed-wide management plans, the current process is limited to forestry operations on state and private lands. Both the agricultural community and some county and municipal land use organizations have resisted participating in watershed analysis. Washington does not have an Agricultural Practices Act similar to its Forest Practices Act. Federal land managers have implemented their own versions of watershed analysis, which usually leads to different, more environmentally restrictive management prescriptions. Lack of effectiveness monitoring severely limits adaptive feedback on site-specific prescriptions. The procedure makes few allowances for natural variability or the beneficial role of natural disturbances in creating and maintaining fish and wildlife habitat. Instead, it tends to impose uniform sets of environmental targets on watershed conditions, regardless of whether these targets are appropriate or achievable. Finally, the procedure lacks a clear rationale for targets that are set.

These shortcomings notwithstanding, Washington's watershed analysis approach incorporates most of the components of an adaptive management system. After several years of implementation, weaknesses of the procedure are becoming clear. The question now is: will participating organizations recognize these deficiencies and take appropriate steps to correct them, or will the watershed analysis protocols become "hardened" into a form that inhibits them from doing what they were designed to do in the first place—provide a decision-support tool flexible enough to enable sound management plans tailored to individual watersheds?

PROCESS-BASED WATERSHED RESEARCH

The goals of process-based watershed research are twofold: First, understand the physical, chemical, and biological processes in natural resource systems, and second, develop tools allowing decisionmakers to make use of that understanding. The overall goal of linking the understanding to decisionmaking tools is usually approached using simulation models, computer programs encapsulating our knowledge in a form useful to managers. These simulation models are especially important in making the connection between science and management because they are placed where the two actually meet and intertwine with each other in an interactive way. Table 5.1 is a summary of selected computer simulation models used in watershed research and development activities and in watershed management. These models were sponsored/developed by EPA, the U.S. Army Corps of Engineers Hydrologic Engineering Center (HEC), ARS, and the U.S. Geological Survey (USGS). These agencies developed and support these models in cooperation with other federal agencies, universities, state and local agencies, and consulting companies. Therefore, these models are widely used within these agencies and by other agencies and private organizations throughout the world. However, the models described below were selected to show a range of technology and of applications. No attempt was made to include all agencies, technologies, or applications and thus, the compilation is illustrative rather than comprehensive.

The development, testing, and parameterization of simulation models is not a trivial task, because the models are extremely complex; there is a lack of data for internal model verification, validation, and parameterization; objective criteria for model evaluation are not standardized; and model output (point or distributed) is often difficult to interpret. Wurbs (1994) summarized a large number of available water resources models. Most of these models are used to evaluate components of the watershed—for instance, there are ground water models, urban stormwater runoff models, water distribution system models, and nonpoint pollution models. The discussion of water resources models can be divided into the following categories (Wurbs, 1994):

- demand forecasting and balancing supply with demand
- water distribution system models
- ground water models
- watershed runoff models
- stream hydraulics models
- river and reservoir water quality models
- reservoir/river system operation models

Water resources handbooks edited by Maidment (1993) and Mays (1996) contain extensive information on water resources models. A contemporary watershed model should include simulation of the following features:

1. water quantity and quality
2. single event and continuous simulation

TABLE 5.1 Selected Hydrologic Models Used in Watershed Management

AGNPS - Agricultural Nonpoint Source Pollution Model. (Young et al., 1989)

The model was developed by the U.S. Department of Agriculture, Agricultural Research Service. The primary emphasis of the model is on nutrients, soil erosion, and sediment yield for comparing the effects of various best management practices on agricultural pollutant loadings. The AGNPS model can simulate sediment and nutrients loads from agricultural watersheds for a single storm event or for a continuous simulation. The watershed must be divided into a uniform grid (square cells). The cells are grouped by dividing the basin into subwatersheds. However, water flow and pollutant routing is accomplished by a function of the unit hydrograph type, which is a lumped parameter approach. The model does not simulate pesticides.

AGNPS is also capable of simulating point inputs such as feedlots, wastewater discharges, and stream bank and gully erosion. In the model, pollutants are routed from the top of the watershed to the watershed outlet in a series of steps. The modified universal soil erosion equation is used for predicting soil loss in five different particle sizes (clay, silt, sand, small aggregates, and large aggregates). The pollutant transport portion is subdivided into one part handling soluble pollutants and another part handling sediment absorbed pollutants. The input data requirements are extensive, but most of the data can be retrieved from topographic and soil maps, local meteorological information, field observations, and various publications, tables, and graphs provided in the user manual or references.

ANSWERS — Areal, Nonpoint Source Watershed Environment Response Simulation. (Beasley and Huggings, 1981)

The model was developed by the Agricultural Engineering Department of Purdue University. It is a distributed parameter model designed to simulate rainfall-runoff events. Currently the model is maintained and distributed by the Agricultural Engineering Department, University of Georgia, Tifton, Georgia. To use the ANSWERS model, the watershed is divided into a uniform grid (square elements). The element may range from one to four hectares. Within each element the model simulates the processes of interception, infiltration, surface storage, surface flow, subsurface drainage, sediment detachment, and movement across the element. The output from one element then becomes a source of input to an adjacent element. Nutrients (nitrogen and phosphorus) are simulated using correlation relationships between chemical concentrations, sediment yield, and runoff volume. Snowmelt or pesticides movement cannot be simulated. A single storm rainfall hyetograph drives the model.

BASINS — Better Assessment Science Integrating Point and Nonpoint Sources. (Lahlou et al., 1996)

This model is a multipurpose environmental analysis system for use by regional, state, and local agencies in performing watershed and water quality based studies. It was developed by the U.S. Environmental Protection Agency (EPA) to address three objectives:

1. To facilitate examination of environmental information
2. To support analysis of environmental systems
3. To provide a framework for examining management alternatives

TABLE 5.1 (continued)

A GIS provides the integrating framework for BASINS. The GIS organizes spatial information so it can be displayed as maps, tables, or graphics. Through the use of the GIS, BASINS has the ability to display and integrate a wide range of information (e.g., land use, point source discharges, water supply withdrawals) at a scale selected by the user. For example, some users may need to examine data at a state scale to determine problem areas, compare watersheds, or investigate gaps in data. Others may want to work at a much smaller scale, such as investigating a particular river segment. These features make BASINS a unique environmental analysis tool. The analytical tools in BASINS are organized into two modules. The assessment and planning module, working within the GIS, allow users to quickly evaluate selected areas, organize information, and display results. The modeling module allows users to examine the impacts of pollutant loadings from point and nonpoint sources. The modeling module includes the following: QUAL2E, Version 3.2, a water quality and eutrophication model; TOXIROUTE, a model for routing pollutants through a stream system; NPSM_HSPF, version 10, a nonpoint source model for estimating loadings. The latest versions of both QUAL2E and HSPF are included in the BASINS package.

HEC-1 Hydrologic Engineering Center, Flood Hydrograph Package. (Hydrologic Engineering Center, 1991)

The current standard version, Version 4.0, represents improvements and expansions to the hydrologic simulation capabilities with interfaces to the HEC Data Storage System (HEC-dss). The dss connection allows HEC-1 to interact with the input and output of other simulation models. New hydrologic capabilities in HEC-1 include: Green and Ampt infiltration, Muskingum-Cunge flood routing, reservoir releases input, and improved numerical solution of kinematic wave equations. This new release of this model also automatically performs numerical analysis stability checks for the kinematic wave and Muskingum-Cunge routings.

HSP-F Hydrologic Simulation Program - FORTRAN. (Donigian et al., 1984)

The HSP-F is a simulation model developed under EPA sponsorship to simulate hydrologic and water quality processes in natural and man-made water systems. It is an analytical tool that has application in planning, design, and operation of water resources systems. The model enables the use of probabilistic analysis in the fields of hydrology and water quality management. It uses such information as time history of rainfall, temperature, evaporation, and parameters related to land use patterns, soil characteristics, and agricultural practices to simulate the processes that occur in a watershed. The initial result of an HSP-F simulation is a time history of the quantity of water transported over the land surface and through various soil zones down to the groundwater aquifer. Runoff flow rate, sediment loads, nutrients, pesticides, toxic chemicals, and other water quality constituent concentrations can be predicted. The model can simulate continuous, dynamic, or steady state behavior of both hydrologic/hydraulic and water quality processes in a watershed.

PRMS - Precipitation-Runoff Modeling System. (Leavesley et al., 1983)

The Precipitation-Runoff Modeling System is a modular, distributed-parameter, physically based watershed model that was developed to evaluate the effects of various combinations of precipitation, climate, and land use on watershed response. Watershed response to normal and extreme rainfall and snowmelt can be simulated to evaluate changes in water-balance relations, flow regimes, flood peaks and volumes, soil-water relations, sediment yield, and groundwater recharge. Parameter optimization and sensitivity analysis capabilities are provided to fit selected model parameters and to evaluate their individual and combined effects on model output.

TABLE 5.1 (continued)

HUMUS - Hydrologic Unit Model for the United States. (Wang and Srinivasan, 1997)

The Resources Conservation Act of 1997 as amended (RCA), required the Department of Agriculture to appraise the status, condition, and trends in the uses and conservation of non-federal soil and water related natural resources. The HUMUS project has been designed to provide the technical basis for conducting the appraisal of water resources for the 1997 RCA Appraisal Report. It is intended to provide better information than has ever been obtained before about the uses of water on irrigated and non-irrigated agricultural lands and of the physical and economic effects of changing agricultural practices and cropping patterns on future water needs and supplies. The major components of the HUMUS project are: 1) a basin scale Soil and Water Assessment Tool (SWAT, Arnold et al., 1994) to model the surface and sub-surface water quality and quantity, 2) a Geographic Information System (GIS) to collect, manage, analyze and display the spatial and temporal inputs and outputs, and 3) relational databases needed to manage the non-spatial data and drive the models. The HUMUS project will simulate and validate approximately 350, 6-digit hydrologic unit areas (watersheds) that have been delineated by the USGS for the 18 major river basins in the U.S. Databases used in the analyses include: national resources inventory, national agricultural statistical survey, state soil survey data base, weather parameters, stream flow and reservoir operation data, agricultural census data, input and output of the simulation models and reports for the 350, 6-digit watersheds.

KINEROS - A Kinematic Runoff and Erosion Model. (Woolhiser et al., 1990)

The kinematic runoff and erosion model KINEROS is an event-oriented, physically based model describing the processes of interception, infiltration, surface runoff, and erosion from small agricultural and urban watersheds. The watershed is represented by a cascade of planes and channels; and the partial differential equations describing overland flow, channel flow, and erosion, and sediment transport are solved by finite difference techniques. Spatial variability of rainfall and infiltration, runoff, and erosion parameters can be accommodated. KINEROS may be used to determine the effects of various watershed management practices such as urban developments, small detention reservoirs, or lined channels on flood hydrographs and sediment yield.

SPUR - Simulation of Production and Utilization of Rangelands. (Wight and Skiles, eds., 1987)

The SPUR model is a comprehensive rangeland simulation model developed to provide information for research and management. SPUR is a physically based model designed to provide biophysical simulation capability for rangeland ecosystems. The model is driven by daily maximum and minimum air temperature, precipitation, solar radiation, and wind run. SPUR simulates the daily growth of individual plant species or functional species groups. Animal growth is simulated on a steer-equivalent basis, and net gain is used to calculate economic benefits. The hydrology component calculates upland surface runoff volumes, peak flow, snowmelt, streamflow, and upland and channel sediment yields. Two versions of SPUR address different levels of landscape resolution. The field-scale version was designed to simulate plant and animal interactions at a pasture or field level. The basin-scale version was designed to simulate small watershed processes.

3. physical, chemical, biological, socioeconomic, and institutional components
4. windows environment for use on personal computers
5. lumped or distributed parameters in the model
6. assistance with parameter selection (e.g., parameter optimization methods)
7. linkage to optimization models
8. linkage to decision support system
9. surface, vadose zone, and ground-water components

Unfortunately, no available model comes close to meeting all of these criteria. We continue to rely on models developed during the past 30 years and link them as best we can to perform some or all of the above functions. Links rarely take the form of active feedback loops, and the nature of such loops often remains a mystery.

The Hydrologic Engineering Center of the U.S. Army Corps of Engineers has made a major commitment to upgrade and integrate their models as part of their NEXGEN effort. HEC-RAS, an updated version of HEC-2, is the first output of this program (U.S. Army Corps of Engineers, 1995a and 1995b). Examples of existing models that are used in the absence of newer models are HSPF (Bicknell et al., 1992), SWMM (Huber and Dickinson, 1988), and SWRRB (Arnold et al., 1990), all of which are supported by the EPA's Center for Exposure Assessment Modeling, located in Athens, Georgia.

A major modeling effort is needed to develop and implement state-of-the-art models for watershed evaluations. In a review article, Goodrich and Woolhiser (1991) examined the state of the art in our understanding of entire catchment response. They concluded that even at watershed scales of up to roughly 200 sq. mi. (500 sq. km.), hydrologists lacked detailed and processes-based understanding, and thus also lacked the ability to develop simulation models to adequately describe hydrologic response. Notably, this failure is for a single, physical component of the functioning of the entire watershed, one that might be expected to be relative easy to describe and predict.

Results of attempts to model the hydrologic response of the 60 square mile (150 sq. km) Walnut Gulch Watershed in Arizona seem to support the need for improved models. Michaud and Sorooshian (1994) applied a distributed, kinematic cascade event model called KINEROS (Woolhiser et al., 1990), a simple lumped model (SCS, 1964), and a distributed version of the SCS model to Walnut Gulch. KINEROS and the distributed SCS model were comparable in their ability to fit measured data when calibrated, and both were superior to the lumped model. Also, KINEROS was more accurate when used without calibration. However, none of the models were able to accurately simulate peak runoff rates or runoff volumes. Nichols et al. (1994) used a distributed, continuous simulation model (SWRRB, Arnold et al., 1990) to simulate runoff from the same Walnut Gulch Experimental Watershed. When calibrated, the model accurately simulated average annual runoff volumes, but not maximum peak flows.

For the decisionmaker, implementing simulation models and interpreting their output is complicated by the complexity of the models and by the nature of natural resource decisions that often involve conflicting objectives. Although complex simulation models aid the decisionmaker by predicting the outcome of a particular management practice or system of practices, the abundance of information provided complicates the ability of the decisionmaker to analyze the information and come to a decision that satisfies more than one objective. A framework is needed that facilitates the efficient transfer of technology to user groups and gives the decisionmaker the ability to apply the technology easily and in a repeatable and scientifically defensible manner. Improved simulation models may be easier to use and more complete by taking advantage of newly developed geographic information systems. Effective simulation models must use GIS as a major platform not only for merely displaying data, but also for analysis. Research programs and the computerized models they use must be able to incorporate data with locational identifiers that are drawn from a geographically variable environment. Scientific research focused on incorporating these improvements in simulation models can only be effective if it is undertaken in concert with the managers who will ultimately use the models. Cooperation between researchers and users is paramount to a successful next generation of simulation models, and such cooperation requires innovative research funding arrangements.

CONCLUSION

To improve implementation of watershed management, efforts must be made to better connect science to decision-making. One of the primary goals of watershed science should be to increase our understanding of watersheds and how they function and present that information in ways that are useful to managers in practical settings. Risk assessment is one method for improving the usefulness of science because it provides improved understanding of the degree and types of uncertainty in management applications; the issue of uncertainty is of special importance to watershed managers because they must often work with incomplete information and because watershed processes inevitably exhibit some random behavior. One area of special promise is simulation modeling, because these can give decisionmakers interactive tools for both understanding the physical system and judging how management actions might affect that system.

Despite this wealth of data and a substantial scientific understanding of watershed components and their processes, our models and available methods for explaining the interaction of many components, predicting their future behavior, and especially for integrating ecologic, social, and economic approaches are inadequate and outdated. Decisionmakers have access to no truly integrated contemporary watershed models that satisfy minimum criteria for effectiveness, usefulness, and ease of application. Despite rapid advances in geographic information systems technology, in many cases users employ these powerful software packages only to create attractive maps, without extending their efforts to analysis and linkages with models. The nation needs from its scientific and engineering establishment new models that 1) link directly to geographic information systems and decision support systems, 2) incorporate social and economic science as integral parts rather than as afterthoughts, and 3) span a variety of scales for application. To serve public users, such models should be in the form of computer programs that are as easy to use as a typical word processor or spreadsheet so that they serve not only those who create them, but also those who truly need them: the managers and decisionmakers.

REFERENCES

Arnold, J. G., J. R. Williams, A. D. Nicks, & N. B. Sammons. 1990. SWRRB: A Basin Scale Simulation Model for Soil and Water Resources Management. College Station, Texas: Texas A&M Press.

Arnold, J. G., J. R. Williams, R. Srinivasan, K. W. King, and R. H. Griggs. 1994. Soil and Water Assessment Tool, USDA-ARS, Grassland, Soil and Water Research Laboratory, Temple, TX.

Beasley, D. B., and L. F. Huggings. 1981. ANSWERS Users Manual, EPA 905/982-001, U.S. Environmental Protection Agency, Chicago, Ill.

Bicknell, B. R. 1992. Hydrologic Simulation Program - Fortran: User's Manual for Release 10. Environmental Research Laboratory, EPA, Athens, Ga.

Collins, B. D., and G. R. Pess. 1997a. Evaluation of forest practices prescriptions from Washington State's watershed analysis program. Water Resources Bulletin 33(5):969-996.

Collins, B. D., and G. R. Pess. 1997b. Washington State's watershed analysis program compared to five management paradigms. Water Resources Bulletin 33(5):967-1010.

Donigian, A. S., Jr., J. C. Imhoff, B. R. Bicknell, and J. L. Kittle, Jr. 1984. Application Guide for the Hydrological Simulation Program—FORTRAN EPA 600/3-84-066, Environmental Research Laboratory, U.S. EPA, Athens, Ga.

Goodrich, D. C., and D. A. Woolhiser. 1991. Catchment hydrology. Rev. of Geophysics, Supplement, AGU, pp. 202-209.

Halbert, C. L., and K. N. Lee. 1990. The Timber, Fish and Wildlife Agreement: Implementing alternative dispute resolution in Washington State. Northwest Environmental Journal 6:139-175.

Huber, W. C., and R. E Dickinson. 1988. Storm Water Management Model, Version 4: User's Manual. Environmental Research Laboratory, EPA, Athens, Ga.

Hydrologic Engineering Center. 1991. Using HEC-1 on Personal Computer, User's Manual and Training Document No. 32, U.S. Army Corps of Engineers, Davis, Calif.

Lahlou, M., L. Shoemaker, M. Paquette, J. Bo, R. Choudhury, R. Elmer, and F. Xia. 1996, Better Assessment Science Integrating Point and Nonpoint Sources (BASINS), Version 1.0, User's Manual, U. S. Environmental Protection Agency, Washington, D.C. 20460.

Leavesley, G. H., R. W. Lichty, B. M. Troutman, and L. G. Saindon. 1983. Precipitation—Runoff Modeling System—User's Manual, Water Resources Investigation, Report 83-4238, Washington, D. C.: U.S. Geological Survey, 207 pp.

Maidment, D. R. Ed. 1993. Handbook of Hydrology. New York: McGraw-Hill.

Mays, L. W. Ed. 1996. Water Resources Handbook. New York: McGraw-Hill.

Michaud, J., and S. Sorooshian. 1994. Comparison of simple versus complex distributed runoff models on a midsized semiarid watershed. Water Res. Res. 30(3):593-605.

Montgomery, D. R., G. E. Grant, and K. Sullivan. 1995. Watershed analysis as a framework for implementing ecosystem management. Water Resources Bulletin 31:369-386.

National Research Council (NRC). 1992. Restoration of aquatic ecosystems. Washington, D.C.: National Academy Press.

National Research Council (NRC). 1993. A Paradigm for Ecological Risk Assessment. In Issues in risk assessment. Washington, D.C.: National Academy Press.

National Research Council (NRC). 1996. Upstream: salmon and society in the Pacific Northwest. Washington, D.C.: National Academy Press.

National Research Council (NRC). 1994. Rangeland Health: New Methods to Classify, Inventory, and Monitor Rangelands. Washington, D.C.: National Academy Press.

Nichols, M. H., L. J. Lane, H. M. Arias, and C. Watts. 1994. Comparative modeling of large watershed responses between Walnut Gulch, Arizona, USA, and Matape, Sonora, Mexico. In. Variability is Stream Erosion and Sediment Transport (Proc. of the Canberra Symposium, Dec. 1994, Ed. by L. J. Olive, R. J. Loughran, and J. A. Kesby). IAHS Pub. No. 224, pp. 351-358.

Organisation for Economic Co-operation and Development (OECD). 1997. Environmental Indicators for Agriculture. Paris: OECD Publications Services.

Soil Conservation Service (SCS). 1964. Hydrology. In SCS National Engineering Handbook, U.S. Department of Agriculture, Washington, D.C.

Suter, G. W., II. 1993. Ecological Risk Assessment. Boca Raton, Fla. Lewis Publishers.

U. S. Army Corps of Engineers. 1995a. HEC-RAS River Analysis Systems—User's Manual, Version 1.0. Davis, Calif.: Hydrologic Engineering Center.

U. S. Army Corps of Engineers. 1995b. HEC-RAS River Analysis System—Hydraulic Reference Manual, Version 1.0. Davis, Calif.: Hydrologic Engineering Center.

U.S. Environmental Protection Agency. 1992. Framework for ecological risk assessment. EPA/625/ 3-91/022. Washington, D.C.: Risk Assessment Forum, U.S. Environmental Protection Agency.

U.S. Environmental Protection Agency. 1996. Proposed Guidelines for Ecological Risk Assessment; Notice. 61 CFR 175 47552-47631. Washington, D.C.: U.S. Environmental Protection Agency.

Wang, H. and R. Srinivasan. 1997. WWW Publication of HUMUS — "HUMUS on Line", Annual Conference and Exposition Proceedings of the ACSM/ASPRS, Vol. 4, pp. 578-588.

Washington Forest Practices Board. 1995. Standard methodology for conducting watershed analysis under Chapter 222-22 WAC, Version 3.0. Olympia, Washington: Washington Department of Natural Resources.

Wight, J. R., and J. W. Skiles (eds.). 1987. SPUR—Simulation of Production and Utilization of Rangelands : Documentation and user guide.

Woolhiser, D. A., R. E. Smith, and D. C. Goodrich. 1990. KINEROS, A Kinematic Runoff and Erosion Model: Documentation and User Manual. U.S. Department of Agriculture, Agricultural Research Service, ARS-77, 130 pp.

Wurbs, R. A. 1994. Computer Models for Water Resources Planning and Management. Institute for Water Resources Report IWR 94-NDS-7. Fort Belvoir, Va.: U.S. Army Corps of Engineers.

Young, R. A., C. A. Onstad, D. D. Bosch, and W. P. Anderson. 1989. AGNPS: A nonpoint source pollution model for evaluating watersheds. J. Soil and Water Cons. 44:168-172.

6

Organizing for Watershed Management

Given the great variety of sizes and types of watersheds and the economic and political landscapes, what is the best organizational structure for implementing successful watershed management? Organizational structure can be either a barrier or an avenue to success. In the United States, regionally defined water management organizations have traditionally fared poorly (Newson, 1992), and agencies with missions focused on specific functions have dominated the scene. From time to time, commentators have speculated about shaping watershed management organizations and activities to more closely approximate watershed boundaries. Yet it is not necessarily clear that such watershed-defined organizations would be any more successful than present institutional arrangements. This chapter explores the structure and responsibilities of institutions and organizations seeking insight about organizational approaches to help integrate ecologic, economic, and social aspects of watershed management.

The current structure of federal involvement in water management traces its origins to the early 1800s, when the federal government became involved in navigation projects (Kenney and Rieke, 1997). During the depression years of the 1930s, the federal government greatly expanded water resource development, with a strong emphasis on using water projects to stimulate economic development. With a few notable exceptions such as the Tennessee Valley Authority (TVA), these federal investments were on a project-by-project basis, rather than on a watershed basis. Virtually all of the projects were constructed with major federal subsidies, including very low cost irrigation water in the West, subsidized flood control projects, provision of low-cost hydropower, and subsidized recre-

164

ation facilities. The most significant revenue generation is from sale of hydro-power.

Today we are in a much different economic situation and have different priorities for our water resources. Now, virtually all of the desirable dam sites have been developed, and flood control and navigation works exist on river systems throughout the country. These projects have brought major benefits to the citizens of the United States, but our past approaches to managing water resources also have imposed significant costs. They have at times encouraged inefficient practices such as wasteful use of water and energy and caused problems such as overdevelopment in floodplains; degraded water quality from return flows from urban, industrial, agricultural, and mining activities; and radically altered stream-flow hydrology due to hydropower generation. Current efforts to reexamine the structure and funding of the water agencies in light of the needs of the twenty-first century are appropriate.

Organizational fragmentation is often a major obstacle to effective watershed management. To begin with, divisions among levels of government—local, state, federal—may generate genuine disputes over the proper locus of taxing, spending, or regulatory authority. In addition, each governmental level may have different agencies pursuing apparent cross purposes. One state agency may advocate a new dam while another might oppose it; one local agency might advocate locating a new sewer outfall at a certain place while another may oppose it.

Such apparent contradictions among agencies are inevitable in a governmental structure that, by design, represents varied stakeholder groups. However, in general the various levels of government are in pursuit of common goals. Certainly, those empowered to act may have some jealousies about their authorities, but these conflicts are far less significant than the conflicts that arise over how the land and water of a watershed might be used. For example, a fisheries management organization will view (correctly) a decision by a water and sewer authority to locate a sewer outfall near an oyster ground as having a negative effect on their goals of promoting oyster production and harvester's income.

Governments must choose between legitimate but competing public purposes. Thus, general governments decide between the water and sewer authority's preference for locating a sewer outfall near an oyster ground, and the preferences of the fisheries organization.

Within this structure, decisions allocating watershed resources among competing uses are made through a bargaining process among the same levels of government as well as vertical organizations. Policy for any action results from the formal and informal ways organizations and their leaders seek to influence each other—by technical studies (economic assessments, environmental impact statements, water quality measurements, etc.), identification of policy constraints, exchanges of support, and exchanges of both threats and promises.

Throughout the nation's history, new agencies and new complexes of organizations have been created to make decisions about land and water use, and existing ones have been changed and reorganized to meet newly perceived needs. The present move toward watershed-based management is occurring in one such period of reassessment. The hope is that such changes would lead to coordination in spending and regulatory authority. In the following pages we assess the present organizational landscape in the United States, evaluate the various strategies for creating new American watershed management organizations, review the experiences of other nations, and offer a prescription to guide future organizational change in the United States.

THE AMERICAN ORGANIZATIONAL LANDSCAPE

Any effort to coordinate programs in support of effective watershed management must contend with the reality that formal authorities for regulating, taxing, and spending for land and water use are diffused throughout the levels of government, and the patterns of organizational responsibility vary greatly.

At the local level, primary responsibility for water often resides in a department of public works, which typically operates the drinking water system, sewer system, and wastewater treatment plant. Sometimes there is a separate department of water. These departments operate as enterprise accounts, where the fees collected must equal the costs of running the service. Many drinking water systems are privately owned, but few wastewater treatment plants or sewer systems are private. State agencies such as utility commissions usually set the rates for privately owned utilities, while elected officials usually establish rates for publicly managed services. Rates structures can encourage (or discourage) water conservation. Local public works agencies must often apply to state agencies for discharge permits and for certification of the drinking water system. Communities often become involved in issues of stormwater runoff, especially now that such runoff must be permitted and meet acceptable standards. Local governments are also involved in erosion and sediment control ordinances; street cleaning that removes oils, organic, soil, and bacteria from streets; and education to encourage residents to avoid overuse of fertilizers and pesticides. Local land use regulations governing floodplains and storage of hazardous and toxic materials also influence water quality. In rural counties, local government may set controls on livestock waste and use of pesticides and fertilizers, which are important for preventing surface and ground-water contamination. Most rural counties rely on septic systems for wastewater disposal and wells for drinking water, and both are usually regulated at the state or county level.

Ultimately, each state has its own organizational structure for dealing with watershed-related issues. In many states, a natural resource or environmental protection agency is responsible for water supply and quality, another agency handles recreation, a wildlife agency is responsible for aquatic life, and an economic development agency may regulate dam construction and navigation. Some states have coastal zone management plans to deal with land use in coastal river watersheds and estuaries. Other states have special wetlands boards to oversee wetland protection. Many states also have regional planning districts that address problems that go beyond one local jurisdiction's boundaries. Water is often one of their concerns, as well as air pollution.

The diversity of approaches to watershed-related issues is described in some detail in *Guide to State Environmental Programs* (Jessup, 1990), which notes:

- In 12 states, EPA has jurisdiction for administering the NPDES permits; the rest of the states administer their own permits.
- Twenty-six states have the same state agency handling point and non-point sources of pollution. Some of the remaining states rely on EPA to oversee point sources and a state agency covers nonpoint sources, while some states have separate state agencies for the two pollution sources.
- Most states have the same agency deal with ground water and surface quality issues; in Washington State, local governments handle ground-water protection.
- In the case of wetlands, 18 states have the Army Corps of Engineers handle permitting; 4 states have local governments work with the Corps and the rest have some mixture of state and Corps of Engineers programs.
- Coastal states use four different approaches to coastal zone management: two (California and South Carolina) have independent Coastal Commissions; eight use coastal agencies, nine have the coastal programs in their general environmental agencies, six handle coastal issues through their natural resources agencies, and three (Maine, New Jersey, and Washington) leave coastal issues to the local governments.
- Water allocation is handled by a separate department or agency in 29 states, while 17 states give responsibility for water allocation to their general environmental agency, Eight states give water allocation to their Departments of Natural Resources, while others give this to state engineers or a similar position. Illinois gives water allocation authority to its Department of Transportation, Florida to Water Management Districts, and Arkansas to its Soil and Water Conservation Districts.

The federal level offers similar organizational diversity[1]. Table 6.1 is a matrix of federal agencies and their associated watershed-related responsibilities. These agencies share responsibilities for numerous important functions. The division of responsibility is sometimes based on geographical boundaries. The Bureau of Reclamation's activities, for example, are restricted to the western

---

[1] The committee would like to acknowledge Katherine O'Connor, Orange County Water District, California, for her significant contributions to this section, which is based on her masters thesis, "Watershed Management Planning: Bringing the Pieces Together" (O'Connor, 1995).

TABLE 6.1   Major Water-related Responsibilities of Federal Agencies

Circle indicates some related responsibilities (○); filled circle indicates significant responsibilities (●).

Agencies	oceans and estuaries	wetlands	research and dissertation data	hydropower	navigation	recreation	preservation	wildlife	fisheries	flow regimes	ecological diversity/restoration	erosion/sediment control	water quality	flood risk management	water supply
Department of Agriculture															
Farm Services Agency		○										○	●		
Forest Service		○	○			●	●	●	●		●	○	○	○	○
Natural Resources Conservation Service		●									○	○	●	○	○
Agricultural Research Service												○	○		○
Department of Commerce															
National Marine Fisheries Service	●	○		○				○	●				○		
National Oceanic & Atmospheric Administration	●								●					●	●
Department of Defense															
U.S. Army Corps of Engineers	●	○		●	●					●	○	○	○	●	○
Department of Energy															
Federal Energy Regulatory Commission				●											
Department of the Interior															
Bureau of Land Management	●	○				○		●			●	●	○	○	
Bureau of Reclamation		○		●		○			○	○				●	●
Fish and Wildlife Service	●	○				○		●	●	●			●		
Geologic Survey	○	●	●						○	○	○	●	○	○	●
National Park Service	○	○				●	●	●	●				●	○	○
Bureau of Indian Affairs		○								○	○		○	●	○
Department of State															
International Boundary Commission		○											●	●	●
Other Federal Units															
Environmental Protection Agency	○	●	●			○	○	○	○	○	●	○	●		○
Tennessee Valley Authority		○	○	●	●	●	○			○	○	●	○	●	●
Bonneville Power Administration		○		●	●					○	●	○	●	●	●
Federal Emergency Management Agency														●	

SOURCE: Adapted from O'Connor, 1995. Circle indicates some related responsibilities; filled circle indicates significant responsibilities.

United States. In other cases, agency responsibilities are divided according to jurisdictional divisions, as explained below.

Department of Agriculture

The Department of Agriculture has several divisions that address watershed issues.

Farm Services Agency

The Farm Services Agency (FSA) (formerly the Agricultural Stabilization and Conservation Service [ASCS]) administers various land-use programs to protect, expand, and conserve farmland, wetlands, and forests. The FSA is mandated to administer programs to control erosion and sedimentation, and to encourage voluntary compliance with state and federal regulations to control point and nonpoint-source pollution, as well as other programs that improve water quality (EPA, 1993). Under the Soil Conservation and Domestic Allotment Act [16 U.S.C. 590] the FSA administers programs to control erosion and sedimentation related to agricultural practices, develops programs to solve nonpoint and point source pollution, and conducts various other water quality improvement programs. The Soil and Water Resources Conservation Act [16 U.S.C. 2001] established Resource Conservation Districts (RCDs) under the Secretary of the Department of Agriculture to promote federal, state, and local cooperative efforts to conserve water during times of drought, conserve surface water, preserve and improve the nation's wetlands, and increase migratory waterfowl habitat.

Forest Service

The Forest Service (USFS) manages the National Forests and Grasslands and regulates the use of forest resources on those lands, including the activities of commercial forestry and recreation. The original authority for the USFS was derived from the Organic Administrative Act of 1897, which created the National Forest Service System. The National Forest System originally had the dual purposes of preserving favorable conditions of water flows and ensuring continuous timber supply [16 U.S.C. 473-482]. The USFS participates in general forest protection and balances timber harvest with watershed protection for water quality and fish. The Multiple Use and Sustained Yield Act of 1960 [16 U.S.C. 528] requires the USFS to "manage watershed and fish resources as equally valuable resources with recreation, range (livestock grazing) and wildlife"[16 U.S.C. 528]. The multiple-use and sustained-yield objectives integrate consideration of physical, biological, economic, and scientific issues in resource management, and consider the resource needs of future generations (Doppelt et al., 1993).

Under the National Forest Management Act of 1964 [16 U.S.C. 1600], the

USFS undertakes forest management and "regulates timber harvest when watershed conditions will be irreversibly damaged or where water conditions of fish habitat will be seriously or adversely affect" (Doppelt et al., 1993). The Act requires that the USFS establish guidelines for riparian areas, soil, and water. The fish and wildlife habitats are to be managed to maintain well-distributed, viable populations throughout the forest system. Along with other federal agencies, the USFS nominates and manages river sections that are within national forest boundaries, and that have outstanding natural, cultural, or recreation features in a free flowing condition for designation under the Wild and Scenic Rivers Act [16 U.S.C. 1271]. The USFS also manages the majority of the nation's wilderness areas under provisions of the Wilderness Act of 1964 [78 Stat. 890, 16 U.S.C. 1131-36]

National Resource Conservation Service

The National Resource Conservation Service (NRCS), formerly the Soil Conservation Service (SCS), participates in cooperative resource management programs to develop and conserve soil and water resources. The NRCS offers technical assistance on agricultural pollution control and environmental improvement projects. Nearly three-fourths of the technical assistance provided by the agency goes to help farmers and ranchers develop conservation systems uniquely suited to their individual properties and ways of doing business. NRCS has helped producers develop and implement 1.7 million conservation plans on 143 million acres of highly erodible cropland (Rosenbaum, 1991). It provides assistance to farmers and ranchers to improve water quality and teaches them how to conserve water by irrigating more efficiently.

The NRCS and FSA work together under the Soil Conservation and Domestic Allotment Act of 1936 to encourage and improve state and local programs for resource conservation and development. The NRCS assists in planning soil and water conservation programs; provides leadership in conservation and development of soil, water and related resources programs; and provides water supply forecasts, data on climate, and soil surveys. Under the Soil and Water Conservation Act of 1977, NRCS also provides technical assistance to the Conservation Districts regarding soil, water, air, plants, and animals for watershed protection, flood prevention, fish and wildlife management, community development and other purposes. This program was designed so that the USDA could cooperate with state agencies, Resource Conservation and Development councils, local units of government, land owners, and land users. The nation's 3000 conservation districts (virtually one in every county) are the heart of the conservation delivery systems. They link the NRCS with local communities and local priorities for soil and water conservation. The Act recognized the importance of a coordinated appraisal and program framework, "since individual and governmental decisions

Technical specialists from USDA's National Resource Conservation Service work in the field with landowners to help them develop and implement sound conservation plans. Credit: USDA-Natural Resources Conservation Service.

concerning soil and water resources often transcend administrative boundaries and affect other programs and decisions. . ." [16 U.S.C. 2110, Section 2(3)].

NRCS administers a national watershed program that is integral to the USDA's National Conservation Program. Through this program, NRCS helps states, local units of government, tribes, and other sponsoring organizations address water-related and other natural resource issues, conduct studies, develop watershed plans, and implement resource management systems. The program includes projects carried out under the Watershed Protection and Flood Prevention Act of 1954 [PL 83-566] and the 11 watersheds authorized under the Flood Control Act of 1944 [PL 78-534]. Over 2000 plans covering 160 million acres in watersheds in every State, Puerto Rico, and the Pacific Basin have been completed or are under way. Authorized purposes for these NRCS-assisted watershed projects are watershed protection, flood prevention, agricultural water management, water based recreation, fish and wildlife habitat improvement, ground water recharge, water quality management, and municipal and industrial water supply.

Program objectives have changed over time in response to legislative direction, environmental concerns, and changing social values. The objectives of many of the original projects were to reduce flooding, improve drainage, and increase irrigation efficiencies. In the 1960s, high priorities were placed on projects that provided jobs to combat poverty and encourage rural development; many of these projects involved establishing recreation areas. In recent years, projects have focused on land treatment measures to solve natural resource problems, such as substandard water quality and loss of wildlife habitat. To meet new challenges, the watershed program is being expanded and strengthened to support the agency's new emphasis on locally led conservation. Locally led conservation is an extension of the agency's traditional assistance to individual farmers and ranchers for planning and installing conservation practices for soil erosion control, water management, and other purposes and is an effort to better tailor NRCS assistance to meet the needs of individuals and communities.

Department of Commerce

The U.S. Department of Commerce has two divisions that play substantial roles in watershed-related issues.

National Marine Fisheries Service

The National Marine Fisheries Service (NMFS) is responsible for marine habitat management and the protection and restoration of marine water quality. The agency reviews water quality criteria as they affect threatened and endangered species in the marine environment.

The NMFS also works with the U.S. Fish and Wildlife Service to implement the Fish and Wildlife Conservation Act of 1934 [PL 89-72] and the Endangered Species Act of 1973. The Fish and Wildlife Conservation Act states that "wildlife conservation shall receive equal consideration and be coordinated with other features of water resource development programs" [16 U.S.C. 661]. The NMFS is required to work with the USFWS to provide assistance and cooperation among federal, state, and public and private agencies managing fish and wildlife. The agencies are mandated to make surveys, investigate lands and waters, and accept donations of lands and funds to further the purpose of the management of wildlife resources. Under the Endangered Species Act (ESA), the two agencies make the final decision on whether or not to list a species as threatened or endangered. The NMFS is responsible for listings of marine species, including anadromous salmonids such as salmon, sea run trout, and steelhead (Doppelt et al., 1993). Section 2(b)(1) and (2) of the ESA requires that all federal departments and agencies use their authority to further the purpose of the act and "shall cooperate with state and local agencies to resolve water resources issues in concert with conservation of endangered species."

National Oceanic and Atmospheric Administration

The National Oceanic and Atmospheric Administration (NOAA) is responsible for describing, monitoring, and predicting conditions in the atmosphere, ocean, sun, and space environment. The agency is also responsible for managing and conserving living marine resources and their habitats, including certain endangered species and marine mammals.

Under the authority of the Coastal Zone Management Act [PL 92-482], NOAA assists 29 coastal states in promoting effective management of coastal zones by balancing competing demands on resources, protecting the public health and safety, public access, and economic development. The reauthorization of the Coastal Zone Management Act in 1990 required states to develop, with the aid of NOAA, coastal nonpoint-source pollution control programs to restore and protect coastal waters of the nation. Managing coastal watersheds has become a major focus since the reauthorization of the Act. NOAA administers this Act by encouraging states to exercise full authority over the lands and waters in the coastal zone and contributing funds for projects (1992 funding was $40 million). The agency also assists states in cooperation with other federal and local government agencies and other vitally affected interests to develop land and water use programs for coastal zones. Section 302 (k) states that "land uses in the coastal zone and the uses of adjacent lands which drain into the coastal zone, may significantly affect the quality of coastal waters and habitat." This statement emphasizes the importance of controlling land use activities in order to control coastal water pollution.

The Marine Protection Research Sanctuaries Act [PL 92-532] recognizes the long term consequences of human activities in the coastal zone, as well as the importance of assessing the ecological, economic, and social impacts of humans on the physical and biotic environment. Under this Act, NOAA assists agencies in developing management alternatives that minimize human impacts on coastal and marine resources (EPA, 1993). NOAA is also responsible for administering the National Estuarine Research Reserve System. Under this program, NOAA establishes and manages a national system of reserves representing different coastal regions and estuarine types that exist in the United States. These reserves not only preserve important ecological areas, but act as field laboratories for study of natural and human processes (EPA, 1993).

Department of Defense

The U.S. Army Corps of Engineers (USACE), under the Department of Defense, has wide ranging authority regarding water resources. The Corps' activities include: regulating of all construction permits in navigable waters; transporting and dumping dredged materials; developing, planning, and building dams and other structures to protect areas from floods; providing a supply of water for municipal and industrial use; creating recreational areas; improving water and wildlife quality; and protecting the shorelines of oceans and lakes.

The Corps is best known for its flood control facilities and major public works projects. It is authorized to construct and operate multipurpose dams and reservoirs for flood control and navigation. It also has authority over projects to protect public health, safety, and welfare; water quality; conservation; aesthetics; environment; historic values; and fish and wildlife values. The U.S. Army Corps of Engineers also helps communities with issues related to development and management strategies for flood control, coastal and shoreline erosion, outdoor recreation, environmental restoration, and water quality control (EPA, 1993). The Corps has become involved in major environmental restoration projects such as the Everglades Restoration Project in Florida and the Upper Mississippi Environmental Management Program (Eisel and Aiken, 1997).

Under the Rivers and Harbors Act of 1988, a permit is required from the Chief of Engineers for any activity that would cause physical alterations such as channelization in the nations' waterways (Portney, 1990). Later amendments to this law gave the Corps authority to control beach and shore erosion along public shores. Many such projects were designed and constructed by the USACE to assure that water pollution would not affect the public. The Corps' projects also involved some programs to provide recreational benefits and land enhancement.

Most of the various flood control acts adopted over the years provided for technical information and planning assistance by the USACE to local communities and involved cost sharing with local sponsors. The acts promote the development of projects that address flood hazards in land and water use planning for streams, lakes, and oceans [33 U.S.C. 701-709]. Ironically, section 1135 of the Flood Control Act of 1986 authorizes restoration in a watershed if a Corps project has directly contributed to a watershed problem, such as an area near a dam constructed by the Corps (EPA, 1993).

The Corps is the permitting agency for Clean Water Act section 404 permits for dredging or filling of wetlands. While the EPA has veto authority over the permits, the Corps does the day-to-day work in protection of wetlands. The Corps' manual also defines wetlands and how to delineate them (USACE, 1987).

Department of Energy

Federal law gives authority to license all nonfederal hydroelectric projects that use federal lands or affect navigable waterways to the Department of Energy's Federal Energy Regulatory Commission (FERC). Given its role in licensing hydropower facilities, FERC can have substantial impact on watersheds. Under the provisions of the Federal Power Act, FERC seeks to regulate the safe and efficient operation of hydropower facilities while also balancing other needs such as protection of fish habitat and provision of recreational opportunities (Rosenbaum, 1991). FERC can, for instance, require dam operators to meet instream flow requirements or make changes in operation protocols. FERC's authority is limited by the National Environmental Policy Act, the Clean Water Act, the Endangered Species Act, the National Wild and Scenic Rivers Act, and other statutes (Doppelt et al., 1993). Although FERC's procedures have evolved over the past decade to give more consideration to nonpower values, it is still sometimes criticized for favoring development of water resources over protection of environmental values and for being an inefficient mechanism for resolving complex conflicts over the use of water resources, FERC is moving to consider cumulative impacts of multiple hydropower projects within watersheds, but these efforts also can be controversial both to state and private interests uneasy with such federal oversight and to environmental organizations pushing for increased resource protection.

Department of the Interior

The Department of the Interior has several divisions that have a variety of authorities related to water and watershed management.

Bureau of Land Management

The Bureau of Land Management (BLM) administers significant acreage of public lands and the resources found therein. These resources include timber, minerals, oil and gas, geothermal energy, wildlife habitats, endangered plant and animal species, rangeland vegetation, recreation areas, wild and scenic rivers, designated conservation and wilderness areas, and open space lands (Rosenbaum, 1991).

The organic act for BLM, the Federal Land Policy and Management Act calls on BLM to manage its lands for multiple use and sustained yields, while taking into consideration resource needs of future generations and protection of environmental quality. BLM develops plans for its lands and controls activities that could threaten water quality and watershed values, such as timber harvesting, road building, livestock grazing, mining, water diversions, and motorized recreation. BLM designates areas of critical environmental concern in its land use plans, giving equal consideration to fish and wildlife resources, restoring natural systems, habitats, and water quality. The Act requires that BLM comply with state and federal pollution control laws governing nonpoint-source pollution that might be caused by forestry, grazing, mining, and roadbuilding.

Bureau of Reclamation

The Bureau of Reclamation (BOR) is authorized to develop and manage the water and power resources in the western states. Projects administered by the Bureau include flood control, regulation of river flows, outdoor recreation, fish and wildlife enhancement, and water quality improvements. The BOR constructs and operates federal multipurpose dams, reservoirs, and hydroelectric projects, and is responsible for managing the related natural resources (Doppelt et al., 1993). In addition, the BOR administers irrigation drainage programs and reclamation projects and develops other environmental enhancement projects.

To achieve its primary objectives, BOR exercises responsibility for protecting and restoring fish and wildlife resources, including endangered species and migratory birds, where water resources have been contaminated by pollutants resulting from irrigation. State and local projects receive federal assistance from the BOR for projects related to conservation of water, energy, the environment, and water quality. For instance, in the Platte River Basin, the BOR has revised project procedures and made other modifications to produce increased flows for wildlife habitat (Eisel and Aiken, 1997).

Fish and Wildlife Service

The U.S. Fish and Wildlife Service (FWS) regulates the development, protection, rearing, and stocking of wildlife resources and their habitats. The FWS is responsible for enforcing regulation of hunters, protects migratory and game birds, fish, and wildlife, threatened and endangered species, and preserves natural habitats of these resources.

FWS jointly administers the Fish and Wildlife Coordination Act of 1934 and (in partnership with the National Marine Fisheries Service) the Endangered Species Act of 1973. FWS has jurisdiction over terrestrial and native fresh water species. The FWS administers the National Wildlife Refuge System Act, and the refuges established under this authority provide for the conservation of fish and wildlife, including endangered and threatened species (Doppelt et al., 1993).

The Coastal Wetlands Planning, Protection, and Restoration Act authorizes FWS to facilitate the acquisition of coastal lands or waters for the restoration, enhancement, and management of coastal wetlands ecosystems and water quality. FWS administrators programs under this act for long-term conservation of coastal wetlands and the hydrology, water quality, fish, and wildlife dependent upon them (EPA, 1993). FWS also jointly administers the Wild and Scenic Rivers Act with BLM, the USFS, and the National Park Service, to preserve segments of rivers that have been designated part of the system. Other federal agencies involved in development, management, or policy relating to natural resources must work in consultation with FWS on potential impacts before implementation can begin.

United States Geological Survey

The U.S. Geological Survey (USGS) carries out comprehensive data collection and research and is responsible for classifying and managing the mineral and water resources on federal lands, including the outer continental shelf. Watershed research is conducted to expand understanding of basic hydrologic mechanisms and their responses at the watershed scale and to provide information that serves as the basis for the water and environmental management activities carried out by other governmental and private agencies. Although the value of watershed research is well recognized within the USGS, financial resources to support it are modest (NRC, 1997).

Related to watersheds, the USGS maintains the "Earth Resources Observation System Data Center," which conducts and sponsors research to apply data findings in mapping, geography, mineral and land resources, water resources, rangelands, wildlife, and environmental monitoring and is a major depository for aerial photography as well as satellite imagery. USGS also operates the National Stream Quality Accounting Network, a national system for gathering data on various measures of water quality (Portney, 1990). This program identifies emerging water quality problems by tracking the status of water bodies through long-term monitoring. The USGS has provided information on water quality since 1895, and maintains a water quality and water resources database from which one can interpret water quality trends.

Under its National Water Quality Assessment Program, USGS collects geological data and conducts appraisals of the nation's ground water and surface water resources. USGS publications and web sites provide consistent water quality and water quantity information for water resources decisionmaking at all levels of government. In addition, as a result of the Water Resources Research Act, USGS provides grants for limited research on water resources and water quality problems.

The USGS water resource program is financed by a combination of direct appropriations and reimbursable cooperative programs with other federal agencies and state and local governments (USGS, 1994). The fiscal year 1994 budget for the USGS water resources program was $400 million. Over half of these funds come from reimbursable sources. This high level of reimbursable support indicates a well developed network of cooperative interagency activities.

According to a recent review of watershed research at the USGS (NRC, 1997), the need for watershed science is considerable and diverse, and USGS, as a scientific nonregulatory agency, has important roles to play in generating knowledge, information, and data. To be most effective, the review notes, USGS should focus on areas that can provide key information on significant problems. Four areas merit increased attention (NRC, 1997): (1) relatively larger watersheds, (2) urban and urbanizing watersheds, (3) restoration of damaged watersheds, and (4) erosion and sedimentation processes in watersheds.

National Park Service

The National Park Service (NPS) administers programs to conserve the scenery, natural and historic objects, and wildlife in the nation's national parks. The parks are preserved for the enjoyment of the public and future generations.

Preservation includes protection of fish and wildlife, their habitat, and the management of water quality and quantity. The NPS provides for the protection and restoration of riverine ecosystems and aquatic habitats within parks (Doppelt et al., 1993).

NPS jointly administers parts of the Wild and Scenic Rivers and wilderness systems with BLM, USFS, and the FWS. The goal of the NPS is to create and maintain high quality recreational areas and facilities in the United States, which includes rivers and river access. NPS administers the "Rivers, Trails, and Conservation Program" of the Department of Interior to help citizens develop programs to conserve rivers and establish trails on lands outside national parks. Working in partnership with state and local governments, NPS provides guidance and technical assistance for planning and developing trails and river access and preserving the quality of the land and water resources (EPA, 1993).

Bureau of Indian Affairs

Established in 1824 in the War Department, the Bureau of Indian Affairs (BIA) became a bureau in the Department of the Interior in 1849. BIA is the principal bureau within the federal government responsible for the administration of federal programs for recognized Indian tribes and for promoting Indian self-determination. As a result of the various treaties and other agreements with Native American groups, the BIA also has trust responsibilities. The mission of the Bureau is to enhance quality of life for American Indians, promote economic opportunity, and carry out the responsibility to protect and improve trust assets of Indian tribes and Alaska Natives.

BIA provides federal services to approximately 1.2 million American Indians and Alaska Natives who are members of more than 557 federally recognized Indian tribes. The Bureau administers 43,450,267 acres of tribally owned land, 10,183,530 acres of individually owned land, and 417,225 acres of federally owned land held in trust in 257 Indian land areas. Developing forest lands, leasing mineral rights, directing agricultural programs and protecting water and land rights are among its activities. The Office of Trust Responsibility in the BIA works closely with the tribes, who have more control over these lands than in the past. Lands administered by BIA include parts of many important watersheds, especially in the western states, and Indian water rights (mostly still undetermined) have a direct bearing on watershed management.

Independent Agencies

There are several major independent national or regional entities with significant authority over water resources and watersheds.

Environmental Protection Agency

In 1970 the Environmental Protection Agency (EPA) was created by an administrative reorganization plan and then established by statute, taking bureaus from the Department of the Interior; Department of Agriculture; Department of Health, Education, and Welfare; and the Atomic Energy Commission. The new agency was given the task of environmental protection, including responsibilities for enforcement of the Clean Water Act, the Clean Air Act, the Resource Conservation and Recycling Act, the Superfund Program, the Toxic Substances Control Act, and the Federal Insecticide, Fungicide, and Rodenticide Act. EPA works through regulations, enforcement action, grants, and the setting of standards. It is involved in numerous water quality, water quantity, and pollution prevention activities.

EPA maintains a series of national hydrologic databases, known as reach files, that identify and interconnect the stream segments or "reaches" that comprise the country's surface water drainage system. Reach codes uniquely identify, by watershed, the individual components of the nation's rivers and lakes. The hydrologic transport network defined within the reach files allows the modeling and visualization of waterborne pollution coming from both point and nonpoint sources. Thus permit writers, emergency management personnel, and other environmental managers can "navigate" upstream and downstream when assessing the causes or implications of actual or potential pollution events. The agency also maintains a publicly available database, STORET, containing data on water quality throughout the nation.

Tennessee Valley Authority

The Tennessee Valley Authority (TVA) was created in 1933 as an independent federal agency to "improve the navigability and provide for the flood control of the Tennessee River; to provide for the reforestation and the proper use of marginal lands in the Tennessee Valley; to provide for the agricultural and industrial development of said valley; to provide for the national defense by the creation of a corporation for the operation of Government properties at and near Muscle Shoals in the State of Alabama" (Viessman and Welty, 1985). TVA, a $5.5 billion corporation, is the nation's largest power corporation, producing more than 130 billion kilowatt hours of electricity a year. Its power sales are financially self-supporting. TVA also manages 164 public recreation areas, including Land Between the Lakes, TVA's national recreation and environmental education area.

To achieve the two original primary purposes of flood control and navigation development, as required by the TVA act of 1933, the Tennessee River and its tributaries were developed into one of the most controlled river systems in the world. The series of dams and reservoirs built brought changes in water quality, aquatic habitats, fisheries, hydrology, and water uses. Initially, some of these changes were accepted as inevitable tradeoffs for the benefits provided, but over time the expectations of the people in the basin changed as the economy improved. The changing expectations caused TVA to evolve and respond, with its scientists and engineers working to understand the changing hydrology and conditions and looking for ways to facilitate multipurpose operations of the system of dams and reservoirs. A recent example of this is TVA's Clean Water Initiative, a way of focusing attention of smaller watershed units (see Box 2.1, Chapter 2).

Bonneville Power Administration

The Bonneville Power Administration (BPA) provides electric power, transmission, and energy services for the people of the Pacific Northwest. BPA is also responsible for conservation of fish and wildlife, energy, and renewable resources, and for enhancing the region's economic and environmental health. In 1995, BPA spent $399 million on fish and wildlife investments. Congress created the BPA in 1937 to market and transmit the power produced at Bonneville Dam on the Columbia River, but today, BPA markets the power from 29 federal dams and one non-federal nuclear plant in the Pacific Northwest. The dams and electrical system constitute the Federal Columbia River Power System, which services an area of 300,000 sq. mi. (including most of the Columbia River Watershed) and a population of 10.1 million people (BPA, 1997).

The BPA power system has produced significant benefits for the region, but these have come at a substantial cost to the fish and wildlife resources of the Columbia River basin. Salmon and steelhead populations have been reduced to historic lows, and many fish species in this region are or are about to be listed under the federal Endangered Species Act. Other resident fish and wildlife populations have also been affected. Native Americans and fishery-dependent communities, businesses, and recreationists have suffered substantial losses. In 1996, the governors of Idaho, Montana, Oregon, and Washington assembled a broadly representative, 20-member team to undertake a "Comprehensive Review of the Northwest Energy System." The goal was to reach consensus on how to shape change, ensuring that environmental goals are met and the benefits of the hydroelectric system are preserved for the Northwest. One of the recommendations was to hold the Northwest Power Planning Council, or its successor, responsible for Columbia River system governance (Steering Committee of the Comprehensive Review of the Northwest Energy System, 1996). However, the listing of salmon under the Endangered Species Act has resulted in re-regulation of river flow that has involved a multitude of federal and state agencies.

Federal Emergency Management Agency

A cabinet level independent agency, the Federal Emergency Management

Agency (FEMA) provides assistance to states and local communities struck by natural or other disasters. It does so by helping managers prepare for emergencies and disasters, responding to the disasters when they occur, helping people and institutions recover from them, reducing the risk of loss, and trying to prevent such disasters from reoccurring. FEMA's vision is that the nation "will have a public educated on what to do before, during, and after a disaster, to protect themselves, their families, their homes, and their businesses; structures located out of harm's way and built according to improved codes; government and private organizations with proven effective plans, necessary resources, and rigorous training for disaster response; and community plans, prepared in advance, for recovery and reconstruction after a disaster" (FEMA, 1996). FEMA works in partnership with federal, state, and local governments, nonprofit and private sector agencies.

FEMA manages the National Flood Insurance Program (NFIP). NFIP's major goal is to reduce flood losses by implementing floodplain management regulations to ensure the use of new and substantially improved construction in flood prone areas. Floodplain management is achieved primarily through local ordinances in over 18,000 participating communities. Participating communities adopt and enforce land use and floodplain management ordinances that meet NFIP minimum criteria. Flood insurance is available to property owners in participating communities. Communities use the agency's Floodplain Insurance Rate Maps (FIRM) to identify the 100-year floodplain which is the basis for the regulations. FEMA also provides a wide array of information and publications regarding NFIP construction requirements in 100-year floodplains (FEMA, 1997).

ORGANIZATIONAL STRATEGIES FOR WATERSHED MANAGEMENT: THE SEARCH FOR COORDINATION

The many agencies described in the previous section, along with hundreds of additional state and local agencies, as well as some transnational organizations, pose some important challenges to any attempt at integrated decisionmaking on watershed issues. Throughout the 20th century, water managers emphasized the need to control the timing and variability of river flows and overbank in order to advance the nation's material prosperity, and this emphasis drove the development of an increasingly complex administrative landscape. In the 1930s, massive public works programs such as TVA resulted in a rapid expansion of federal leadership and financial responsibility for water project development. The programs of the Bureau of Reclamation, the Corps of Engineers, the Soil Conservation Service grew significantly. It was also in this period that the Tennessee Valley Authority's water development program flourished. At the same time, the upland watershed programs of the Soil Conservation Service and Forest Service were being advanced as complementary programs that would help manage watersheds by improving forest and grassland cover on those areas not suited to farm cultivation. Constituencies for these agency programs grew, and strong stake-holder groups emerged with the purpose of advancing water development through the authorities and budgets of these federal agencies. As these water develop-ment programs grew and the federal role expanded, there were increasing calls for better interagency coordination.

The federal government began to establish interagency committees in the 1940s for the Missouri (1945), Columbia (1946), the Pacific Southwest (1948), the Arkansas-White-Red (1950), and the New York-New England basins (1950) (Featherstone, 1996). According to Featherstone (1996), these relatively informal committees were ineffective. Seven river basin commissions were formed in the late 1960s and early 1970s pursuant to Title II of the Water Resources Planning Act of 1965: New England, Ohio, Upper Mississippi, Souris-Red-Rainey, Missouri, Pacific Northwest, and Great Lakes. These commissions replaced the interagency committees (Featherstone, 1996). Each commission had federal and state members and a core staff of 20-30 employees. The federal government funded these commissions until 1981.

Three additional river basin commissions were formed for the Potomac, Susquehanna, and Delaware basins (Featherstone, 1996). The Interstate Com-mission on the Potomac River Basin was created as a nonregulatory agency to address water related issues throughout the basin. It is heavily involved in water supply management issues, water quality restoration issues, and planning projects throughout the watershed. The commission has been involved in coordinating the Chesapeake Bay nutrient reduction tributary strategies that are being devel-oped for the Potomac by Virginia, Maryland, Pennsylvania, and the District of Columbia. The commission's modeling work has been used in the development of tributary strategies throughout the Chesapeake Bay area. The commission is writing the Bay Program's Regional Action Plan to control toxic pollution on one of the Potomac's tributaries, the Anacostia River. And it has been involved in fish stocking, the construction of fish passages, and habitat restoration. The com-mission also does research, such as developing a plankton database for the Potomac and other parts of the Bay. Congress voted that 1996 would be the last year the commission would receive federal funds, which typically accounted for about 25 percent of the commission's budget (Bay Journal, 1996).

The Susquehanna River Basin Commission (see Box 5.2) was also given its last year of federal funding in 1997—$250,000, which makes up about 15 percent of its budget (Bay Journal, 1996). Formed by an interstate-federal compact in 1971, the Susquehanna Commission has the authority to regulate water use in the Susquehanna watershed in Pennsylvania and Delaware to ensure the supply is adequate for all users. In the face of increasing development in the watershed, the commission has been studying how much fresh water flow is required throughout the basin to protect critical habitats in the rivers and to supply the Chesapeake Bay. To avoid major changes in the Bay ecosystem and to make sure there is enough flow during droughts, the commission purchases water from federal reservoirs and sells it to utilities to help offset the discharges they need to run their power plants. The federal government has been an important partner in managing the river, and its several agencies (USACE, USGS, FWS and EPA) continue to make decisions that affect water management in the Susquehanna watershed.

Organizations for the Delaware River basin date to 1936 and the Interstate Commission on the Delaware River was formed because of the diversion of the river's flow by the city of New York. Low flows in the river during drought periods in the early 1960s spurred the creation of the Delaware River Basin Compact by the states of Delaware, New Jersey, New York, and Pennsylvania, with the federal government as a full member (Black, 1987). The compact has authority for planning, regulation, financing, construction, and operation of facilities that are agreed to by all the members. The Commission has succeeded in allocating water, a task especially important during periods of scarcity, but failed to build a major proposed reservoir. In cooperation with the Corps of Engineers, the commission proposed the construction of a large reservoir at the Delaware Water Gap on the border between New Jersey and Pennsylvania. The reservoir was to have augmented low flows, provided flood control, and offered an unusual recreational opportunity within a two-hour drive of New York City. The plan failed because some commission members objected because of environmental quality issues.

During the 1970s, studies of these and other large-scale watershed (river basin) organizations noted that the powers and duties expected of watershed organizations replicated some of those already existing within federal and (in some cases) state agencies (Ingram, 1973). Therefore, empowering these organizations required transferring some authority away from federal and state agencies. This, perhaps more than anything else, doomed these large-scale approaches.

> A regional organization is not created into an empty world. Instead, a web of relationships already exists among federal, state, and local agencies and interest groups. A regional organization must fit into, and if it is to have substantial impact, alter and redirect these relationships. A regional agency must possess and maintain support for its operations. . . . political considerations cannot be sidestepped by granting a regional organization more formal authority . . . decisions are going to be made by a process of negotiation and consent building, not by the fiat of a regional agency (Ingram, 1973).

Others have reached similar conclusions about the commissions and their parent organization, the United States Water Resources Council (Eisel and Aiken, 1997). However, an unwillingness to share power is only one source of the demise of the river basin commission concept. The commissions were largely developed to serve the budgeting and planning needs of the federal water development agencies, and were largely administered by those federal agencies. EPA was not an active participant in or supporter of the organizations. In fact, EPA was not convinced that the struggles of the council over issues such as cost sharing or water project planning guidelines were relevant to the execution of its water quality improvement mission.

The EPA attitude reflected a larger shift in the nation's water management concerns. As the nation's attention shifted away from water development and toward regulating water quality improvement, the mission and the membership of the Water Resources Council and the river basin commissions no longer served the role for which they were created. While this is understandable given the climate of the times, lost with the Water Resources Council was the last significant attempt to coordinate across federal agencies and political boundaries.

A new national vision for our waters was offered by the Federal Water Pollution Control Act Amendments of 1972 (generally known as the Clean Water Act or CWA), which called for restoring the "chemical, physical and biological integrity" of the nation's waters. Early in the 1970s and then in the 1980s, the principal program to restore the "chemical, physical, and biological integrity" of the nation's water was EPA's requirements and standards for wastewater treatment plant construction. Water quality programs focused not on the watershed and its streams, but on the quality of the discharge waters from specific sources. Publicly owned treatment works (POTWs) were designed by engineers to meet a fixed wastewater (effluent) standard. Industrial and commercial dischargers were expected to employ specified wastewater treatment technologies or to achieve wastewater discharge quality that was comparable to that produced by the mandated technology. As a result there was an ascendancy of the agendas and mission of the then relatively new EPA and some other long-standing federal agencies such as the Fish and Wildlife Service.

While organizations that supported the federal water project construction waned in influence, the federal role in setting environmental standards and paying for the programs necessary to achieve the standards expanded. New stakeholder constituencies formed to ensure that EPA's increasingly stringent effluent discharge standards were matched by a federal commitment to offset the cost of compliance. Such compliance was bought with generous federal grant subsidies to local governments. The federal tax code offered accelerated depreciation provisions for pollution control equipment as a financial incentive to the private sector.

Meanwhile, Section 208 of the Clean Water Act Amendments of 1972 defined substate watersheds in which nonpoint source (NPS) pollution control, along with the control of point source discharges by required technologies, was to be addressed by a watershed water quality plan. Although both point and nonpoint-source pollution are cited, no organizations were able to gain sufficient power to expand federal authority to enforce land use practices needed to reduce NPS contributions or increase the federal financial role in implementation of NPS controls. The traditional soil conservation payment programs were partly redirected toward water quality objectives, but only limited federal funds were provided to pay for implementing nonpoint-source controls. Without such funding, state and local efforts remained modest. As a result, attention to implementation of nonpoint-source controls languished during the 1980s, even as these sources came to contribute more pollution than did the more successfully controlled point sources.

In many ways the national approach to water quality protection and ecological restoration initially mimicked the historical approach to water development as federal agencies assumed leadership roles abetted by funding. However, in recent years several forces have challenged this federal agency dominated system, not only for water project construction and management, but also for water quality and general environmental management. Perhaps the initiating force was the decline in the federal financial commitment to expansion of environmental programs.

At the same time, the management capacity at state and local levels was expanding as state and local funding for water management increased, agency numbers grew, and expertise broadened. In addition, there was growing recognition nationwide that many pressing issues required solution through the exercise of powers reserved to non-federal levels of government. For example, a growing interest in restoring watershed ecological services sparked debates over low flows in rivers and to estuaries, and consequently over the wisdom of maintaining flood control and drainage projects that controlled flow in the nation's rivers.

While such issues were clearly related to water rights and water allocation, the legacy of the nation's water project construction program demanded a federal involvement. Of the total water storage capacity of reservoirs in the United States, 68 percent is controlled by three federal agencies: the Corps of Engineers (36.8 percent), Bureau of Reclamation (28.7 percent) and TVA (2.25 percent) (Federal Emergency Management Agency, 1996). These agencies have a major financial impact on water resource activities in the United States and exercise significant control over how water is used for municipal water supply, irrigation, flood control, hydropower, recreation, and in-stream flow needs.

USACE, BOR, and TVA project operations have had to serve new environmental restoration purposes in recent years. The largest claim on the Corps' future construction budget promises to be for environmental restoration efforts, such as recreating meanders in the Kissimmee River in Florida, reinitiating sheet flows in the Everglades, and securing the hydrologic regime necessary for downstream fish passage on the Columbia and Snake Rivers. Related issues focus on how to allocate water between off-stream consumptive uses and instream flows.

The emerging responsibilities of state and local governments include new emphasis on nonpoint-source discharges. With the decline of federal financing, contemporary watershed planning now includes a search for ways to advance the control over land use necessary for the control of nonpoint-source discharges, with less federal money and constrained federal regulatory authority. The burden of this effort must fall on local and state authorities.

Meanwhile another force is at work at the state and local levels. The public increasingly questions government agency powers and motives. The 1990s saw energized, locally based non-governmental groups advocate for improving the ecological conditions of watersheds where they live. Watershed management became synonymous for some with democratization of decisionmaking. Goals are set by "the people" and alternatives to achieve the goals are also selected in democratic process, informed by expert analysis. Sometimes, in the most extreme version, analysis has a limited place because watershed management transcends the resource itself. The following perspective offered by a keynote speaker at the *Watershed 96* conference is frequently heard in discussions of watershed management:

> Water is not a science issue, it is sociopolitical. Yes, we all want and need good science, but it is not enough. The challenge is to reconnect people who hold different values and restore civility. To depersonalize our conflicts, to create options for mutual gain, to each be a keeper of the other's dignity, to have open, conflicting discussions about experiences and values including pride, self-reliance, intergenerational equity, and yes, even fear.... Today, watershed planning may be as much about strengthening local communities and democracy as it is about resource management (Baril, 1996).

Successful water resource democracy requires that participants have a shared understanding of the resources and the administrative frameworks available to deal with the issues. The mistrust and disinformation that greeted the President's 1997 Executive Order on American Heritage Rivers crippled the efforts of some watershed groups in their attempts to participate in the program (Box 6.1) and provides an example of some of the problems that can arise when resource management enters the sociopolitical domain.

CONTEMPORARY ORGANIZATIONAL RESPONSES

As a result of the forces described above, various organizational arrangements have been developed in response to water quality and quantity problems. Partly because of the lessons of the river basin commissions, very few of these efforts have sought to transfer powers and authorities from existing agencies to a watershed authority. Instead, the organizational arrangements have evolved to mesh powers with existing authorities. Efforts of the once powerful TVA to advance water quality in the Tennessee River watershed illustrate this reality. TVA's original mandate—to use a series of dams and pools to create low cost hydroelectric power for economic development, control floods, and allow barge traffic to move goods—was accomplished with significant federal funding and by the exercise of significant powers vested in the agency.

One result of TVA's success in carrying out its original mandates is that a number of water quality problems developed, including low dissolved oxygen levels in the water and increased PCB levels. TVA's Clean Water Initiative has the stated objective of making the Tennessee the cleanest commercial river in the United States. Using a watershed approach, TVA pinpoints problem areas of nonpoint source pollution and establishes mitigation activities. TVA has taken a partnership approach, involving private landowners, soil and water conservation districts, local government, and state natural resource and fish and wildlife agencies in the projects. It finds itself working under many different local land use laws, wildlife laws, and approaches to water quality objectives. Because of the uniqueness of TVA's original legislation, it has some discretion in how it allocates the funds appropriated by Congress, but it works to keep local people informed about the problems and issues and involved in TVA's efforts. TVA, even as a federal agency, has had to rely on the powers and persuasion of local entities and the states to accomplish its water quality goals.

Intrastate Watershed Management Initiatives

Arrangements among management agencies vary greatly among states and regions. At least 20 states have organized their activities in varying degrees around watersheds, as listed in Table 6.2. By a watershed program, we mean that

TABLE 6.2 States That Have Watershed-Oriented Organizational Structures

State	Status
Alaska	In progress
Arizona	In progress
California	In progress
Delaware	Implemented
Florida	In progress
Georgia	Implemented
Idaho	In progress
Massachusetts	Implemented
Minnesota	Implemented
Montana	In progress
Nebraska	Implemented
New Jersey	In progress
North Carolina	Implemented
Oregon	In progress
South Carolina	Implemented
Tennessee	In progress
Texas	In progress
Utah	Implemented
Washington	Implemented
Wisconsin	Implemented

SOURCE: Reprinted, with permission, from Nagle et al., 1996. © 1996 by Water Environment Federation.

**Box 6.1
American Heritage Rivers and
the United Nations Plot**

The fate of President Clinton's American Heritage Initiative in some parts of the country illustrates the problems that can be generated by misinformation and extreme political positions. The Executive Order establishing the initiative on September 11, 1997 specified that the purpose was to "protect and restore rivers and their adjacent communities." The President ordered executive agencies to coordinate activities and resources to promote environmental restoration of waterways nominated for the program and economic restoration of the associated communities through partnerships with local authorities. In particular, the President ordered agencies to improve the delivery of federal services and programs and reduce procedural requirements and paperwork related to providing assistance. The policy directed that agencies make special efforts to coordinate federal planning and management efforts to protect the communities' goals, and to ensure that efforts for one community do not adversely affect neighboring communities. The focus of the program is to be a series of designated American Heritage Rivers that would be included in the system after nomination by local or state officials and citizens and demonstration of broad community support. The executive order specifically states as an objective the protection of private property rights.

analysis of the water quality and/or quantity is handled at some watershed scale. Many of these states have nonpoint pollution control as a primary objective. Actually, any state using a total mean daily loading (TMDL) approach for setting permit standards for National Pollutant Discharge Elimination System (NPDES) permits is taking a watershed approach, because that approach focuses on the quality of the receiving waters and quality is a function of all the land uses and discharges into the river upstream. Watershed-based water quality management provides a mechanism for pollution permit trading which recognizes that it may be more cost-effective to control agricultural nonpoint pollution than to control urban runoff pollution. These state-based watershed water quality programs are supported by reallocating existing state program moneys, some of which comes

Despite some support from communities desiring to better coordinate their activities, the initiative triggered hundreds of critical responses from newspaper articles to a flood of communications to the White House. Much of the opposition came from private property advocates who feared that the initiative was related to an attempt to usurp their rights and cede rivers to United Nations control. "The U.N. wants our river," claimed an editorial in a California newspaper, which went on to predict that if the initiative was not stopped, new property restrictions would be enforced by satellite surveillance. In congressional hearings, some speakers equated the initiative with socialism, communism, and treason. As reported by Wanich (1997), the opposition became strong enough to elicit congressional support, including a resolution to block implementation of the program.

Local watershed management groups also suffered from misinformation. In Arizona, for example, the Verde River Watershed Association considered applying for designation of the Verde River as part of the new program. Local opposition from residents fearing a take-over by distant authorities was strong enough to convince the association not to participate.

The response to the American Heritage Initiative is not an isolated instance of intentional disinformation. The response represents an example of a major barrier to effective watershed management because it is the product of a strong undercurrent of anti-federal sentiments. In the absence of accurate information, readily available to citizens and decisionmakers, fear of outside control is likely to derail many partnership efforts that otherwise might be productive in improving the natural as well as the economic environment.

from the EPA. Some of these state-organized watershed management programs have more traditional water resources development activities as their main mission. Nebraska, for example, formed 154 special-purpose districts and 24 natural resources districts (NRD) in 1969. (A 1989 merger reduced the NRDs from 24 to 12.) These NRDs are organized around river basin boundaries and deal with a wide variety of natural resource programs including water quality, water supply, flood control, soil conservation, habitat protection, and outdoor recreation. A property tax of 4.5 cents per $100 valuation funds the NRDs, which can also levy additional amounts for specific purposes.

Perhaps the oldest and most comprehensive state program is in Florida. Florida is a wet state with 53 inches of rain a year, yet 90 percent of its 14 million people depend on ground water. In the early 1980s, rapid growth and increasing water problems made it clear that the state had to take control of its water to achieve full beneficial use of the resource.

The Florida Water Resources Management Act of 1972 provided for the management of any and all water (surface and ground) and related land uses in five water management districts (WMDs) established along watershed lines. The WMDs, which are run by politically appointed boards, have the power to tax, make contracts, construct works, purchase land, establish basin boards, and regulate well construction. They also have the authority to survey water resources, establish minimum levels and flows for surface water courses and ground water in an aquifer, declare a water shortage emergency, promulgate rules for management and storage of water, and develop alternative water supply systems. They issue permits for consumptive use of water. To receive a permit, an applicant must show that the consumptive use is a reasonable and beneficial use, will not interfere with any existing legal right, and is consistent with the public interest. The Florida Department of Environmental Protection (DEP) administers the act at the state level. It develops a state water plan and supervises the WMDs and ensures their activities are consistent with state water policy (Dziuk and Theriaque, 1996).

The Florida water management districts provide instructive lessons about the utility of such watershed approaches and arrangements. Two generalizations emerge from their experiences. First, the WMDs hold their power fairly exclusively, so they rarely overlap with other agencies, and this reduces the potential for "turf battles." Making the power transfer to establish such authority is a major political task, and one that has rarely occurred in other states. If the powers are not transferred, however, watershed organizations risk repeating the unsuccessful story of the river commissions.

Second, the change in boundaries does not necessarily eliminate controversy or political problems. The Florida WMDs still face many of the same financial and political pressures.

Another example of watershed organization is the Blue Earth River Basin Initiative (BERBI) of Minnesota. Unlike the Florida example, BERBI is not part of a statewide overlay of watershed management organizations with dedicated powers and authorities. The Blue Earth River Watershed is 3,560 sq. mi. located in South Central Minnesota and North Central Iowa (Figure 6.1). It includes the LeSeur River, the Blue Earth River, and Watonwan River within its boundaries. The area is dominated by prime farmland in corn/soybean rotation and the main livestock enterprise is swine. The landscape is gently rolling and has an extensive drainage network. The major water quality issues include sediment, nitrogen, phosphorus, and bacteria, as well as water for the cities of Mankato and Fairmont.

In 1993, BERBI formed as a joint powers organization of the Soil and Water Conservation Districts (SWCD) in Blue Earth, Faribault, Martin, Waseca, and Watonwan counties under a Memorandum of Understanding from all five coun-

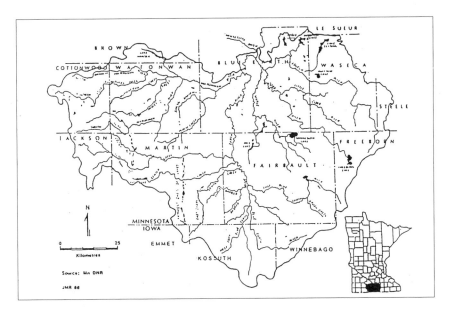

FIGURE 6.1 Blue Earth River Basin Watershed. SOURCE: Reprinted, with permission, from Meschke, 1997. © 1997 from Blue Earth River Basin Initiative.

ties. These five counties include about 80 percent of the Blue Earth River Watershed. Their goal is to improve the water quality of the Blue Earth River Basin through planning, coordination, and implementation of conservation practices and to share the water quality improvement strategies with others. Two committees make up the BERBI organization. A Policy Committee is made up of one supervisor from each of the five SWCDs plus a county commissioner, who serves in an ex-officio capacity. The Technical Committee includes a water planner and an SWCD staff member from each of the counties. This committee develops BERBI projects in each county. The SWCD staff works directly with landowners in their county on a regular basis to implement the projects. A coordinator writes and develops project proposals to secure funding and coordinates BERBI's work with the many other groups and agencies working within the region (Meschke, 1997).

Another Minnesota example is the Big Sandy Area Lakes Watershed (BSALW), a locally based watershed management organization with limited formal powers and authority. BSALW is an example of a watershed group working together, without benefit of formal organization structures, to practice stewardship over their region and their economy (Dziuk, 1997). BSALW covers 413 sq. mi. in portions of three counties in northern Minnesota, and includes 32 fishable lakes and 4 rivers that eventually feed the Mississippi River. The lakes in the BSALW have a surface area of about 14,996 acres and generate an estimated

$10,302,252 each year in customer purchases plus an estimated 247 jobs. Nearly 80 percent of the real estate taxes collected in Aitkin County are derived from shoreline property. Riparian lots on Big Sandy Lake alone have an assessed market evaluation of over $82 million. Clean water is needed for drinking, both in the area and downstream, and to support fishing and other recreation.

Between 1989 and 1992, it became apparent to citizens in the BSALW that the water resources required active management. In July 1993, citizen volunteers formed a partnership with employees of local, state, and federal governments to form a watershed management partnership that is citizen-driven, locally-directed, and agency-supported. The BSALW has no bylaws, no office, no bank account or payroll. However, in consultation with a committee of professional resource managers from local governments and state and federal agencies, two citizen committees recommended policies, planning, priorities, and budgets for area water management agencies and projects. The partnership is maintained by: (a) a determination to base decisions on wide consultation with citizens, (b) hard work, including a substantial amount of help from volunteers, (c) competent technical advice, science, information, and support, and (d) an ethic of treating partners as equals.

BSALW has encouraged the acceptance of voluntary best management practices (BMPs) by watershed landowners through informational workshops, newsletters, videos, meetings, local newspaper and TV stories. It promotes citizen participation in watershed committees, lake associations, and in a water quality monitoring network. BSALW has initiated 12 shoreland revegetation demonstration sites with partners from the University of Minnesota, done extensive water quality monitoring, sponsored writing and poster contests, seeded eroding areas, and produced and distributed a video "On Common Ground" schools, libraries, associations, and residents. BSALW finds that it spends a lot of time seeking ways to do projects without spending much money. It has found that getting governments to work with the organization as equal partners is very difficult, and that it is difficult for informed citizen volunteers to get elected officials to develop the political will to provide for sustainable development. The group is working to help counties find funds to identify and upgrade nonconforming septic systems and to educate planning commissioners on the impact of granting variances to such systems. Agricultural practices that degrade water quality need more attention, voluntary BMPs are not sufficient to halt the problems, and more financial incentives would strengthen the group's efforts.

Interstate and International Watershed Management

The Great Lakes Basin Compact is an effort to address the water quality issues in the Great Lakes Region within the structure of existing organizations. The Great Lakes stretch between the United States and Canada with a surface area of about 95,000 sq. mi. They contain about 20 percent of the world's surface fresh water supply, and 95 percent of the surface fresh water in the United States (MacKenzie, 1996). They provide an important inland waterway transportation system and have about 10,000 miles of inland coastline. Approximately 40 million Canadians and Americans live within the Great Lakes watershed.

The Great Lakes have suffered many water quality problems. Among the earliest was sediment pollution from logging and agricultural practices that caused a decline in fisheries in the late 1800s. For decades, the lakes also received direct discharge of industrial waste, sewage, vessel waste, and other products that were seen as benign because it was believed that the vast amount of water would dilute any discharge to insignificant levels. However, as population development increased along the shorelines in the early 1900s, pollution from the discharge of domestic sewage resulted in typhoid and cholera epidemics.

In 1909, the United States and Canada signed the Boundary Waters Treaty which established the International Joint Commission (IJC) as a permanent binational body. The IJC became a forum for international cooperation and dispute resolution regarding water quality, and it served as the regulator of water levels and flow between the United States and Canada. The IJC's Great Lakes Water Quality Board and Great Lakes Science Advisory Board also help in the administration of the lakes. However, despite the efforts of the IJC, pollution discharges into the lakes continued, and their biotic systems declined.

In 1978, the United States and Canada reviewed their Great Lakes Water Quality Agreement and expanded it to address toxic contaminants in the lakes through a watershed approach. The document stated its purpose:

> to restore and maintain the chemical, physical, and biological integrity of the waters of the Great Lake's Basin Ecosystem. In order to achieve this purpose, the parties agree to make a maximum effort to develop programs, practices, and technology necessary for a better understanding of the Great Lakes Basin Ecosystem and to eliminate or reduce, to the maximum extent practicable, the discharge of pollutants to the Great Lakes System.

The IJC Water Quality Board identified 43 tributaries or near-shore areas of the lakes with poor water quality. The board is developing remediation action plans to deal with problem areas around harbors, inlets, connecting channels, and major municipalities. Each action plan is expected to use an ecosystem approach that calls for a functional arrangement of organizations and interests as equal members of the team.

Evaluation of the action plans is ongoing, but MacKenzie (1996) reports that "creation of a successful ecosystem management plan turns on process-related issues. For example, success requires plenty of opportunities for meaningful participation by all interested stakeholders, real attempts to achieve consensus, and a commitment to quality of the ecosystem." MacKenzie also found that strong fiscal support was important, as well as nurturing political support. Considerable barriers to the ecosystem approach at both the individual and institutional levels continue to be a problem.

Another example of an international effort is the International Boundary and Water Commission, created in 1848 by the governments of Mexico and the United States to apply the provisions of the various boundary and water treaties and settle differences arising from such applications. The boundary between the United States and Mexico is one of the longest, stretching 1,952 miles (3,141 km). Because most of the border (1,278 miles) is marked by rivers, the role in river management has become important. The international nature of the setting complicates watershed management in such areas, whether dealing with water quality or quantity. The IWBC states that its "mission is to provide environmentally sensitive, timely and fiscally responsible boundary and water services along the United States and Mexico border" (www.ibwc.state.gov/index.html, 1997).

Another large-scale cooperative effort organized along watershed boundaries concerns Chesapeake Bay. The Chesapeake Bay effort has received international recognition as a cooperative program to restore the estuary. Located on the East Coast of the United States, the Chesapeake Bay is a large (193 miles long and 3 to 25 miles wide) fresh water estuary of the Savannah River, with headwaters in New York state. Major tributaries to the Bay come from New York, Virginia, Maryland, Pennsylvania, and Washington D.C. Efforts to restore the Chesapeake Bay are the results of voluntary cooperative efforts among Virginia, Maryland, the District of Columbia, the federal government, and the Chesapeake Bay Commission.

In 1980 Virginia and Maryland passed legislation creating the Chesapeake Bay Commission to coordinate interstate planning and programs. Pennsylvania joined the Commission in 1985, and it continues today as a part to the Agreement. In 1983, Virginia, Maryland, Pennsylvania, EPA, and the Bay Commission formally agreed to a cooperative approach to the restoration of the Bay. The opening paragraph of the 1987 Chesapeake Bay Agreement explains the effort (Chesapeake Bay Agreement, 1987):

> The Chesapeake Bay is a national treasure and a resource of worldwide significance. Its ecological, economic, and cultural importance are felt far beyond its waters and the communities that line its shores. Man's use and abuse of its bounty, however, together with the continued growth and development of population in its watershed, have taken a toll on the Bay's systems. In recent decades the Bay has suffered serious declines in quality and productivity.

The agreement set 8 goals, 45 objectives, and 29 commitments or tasks with deadlines. Each state passed legislation consistent with its own philosophy on how to accomplish the goals and deadlines. Virginia chose to require local governments to amend their comprehensive plans, zoning codes, and subdivision ordinances to require buffers around streams, rivers, and wetlands to prevent soil erosion and polluted runoff from reaching the Bay. Maryland set aside "critical areas" that met certain criteria. Intergovernmental committees continue to seek improved understanding of the ecosystem dynamics of the Bay and to define strategies that will accomplish the goals, but each state is left to decide on specific actions. This voluntary approach with commitments to goals and deadlines has so far been successful. Governors have agreed to continue to work toward the goals agreed to by their predecessors, although they may change methods.

By many measures, the health of the Bay is improving, but not all systems have returned to the quality levels of earlier times. Remaining problems include total suspended solids, nutrients, and toxic materials coming into the Bay from its tributaries. In response the Bay program states have initiated a tributary planning and implementation process with the intent of building water quality and habitat improvement from nonpoint-source controls from the small watershed to the larger Bay drainage area. The emphasis has been on a voluntary and cooperative approach with local governments and citizens, just as the overall program has been based on intergovernmental cooperation between state and federal agencies.

An older and more complicated regional watershed organization is the Colorado River Compact. This organization is part of a continuing effort to manage an "engineered hydro-commons," a water-use and allocation region that does not conform to the topographic boundaries of the river's watershed. This interstate cooperative effort concerns allocation of Colorado River water. It includes the upper basin states of Colorado, Wyoming, Utah, and New Mexico along with the lower basin states of Arizona, Nevada, and California. The river runs 1,440 miles to the Gulf of California and drains an area of 244,000 sq. mi.

In 1922, the seven states negotiated the Colorado River Compact which designated the upper and lower basins with a division on the Colorado River at Lees Ferry, Arizona. Under the assumption that the mean annual flow of the river was 15,000,000 acre-feet, the compact participants agreed that the upper basin states would deliver half that amount to the lower basin states. An additional later allocation was 1,500,000 acre-feet for Mexico as defined by a 1944 Treaty.

The Bureau of Reclamation manages the river primarily for hydroelectric power, irrigation, flood control, recreation, and navigation. A series of dams has been built, beginning with Hoover Dam in 1936 and continuing with Glen Canyon Dam in 1964, along with other structures on principal tributaries such as the Green River in Wyoming, the Gunnison in Colorado, and the San Juan in New Mexico. Parker Dam was built on the lower Colorado by the City of Los Angeles in order to transport more than 3,000 acre-feet (1 billion gallons) daily to southern California via a 250-mile open canal. Arizona takes its share of 2.2 million acre-feet per year via the Central Arizona Project canal to Phoenix and Tucson. The compact has been fraught with lawsuits over the amount of water sent to California and objections from Mexico regarding salinity of the water it receives. Rapidly growing Las Vegas has struggled to obtain more than its allocation of 300,000 acre-feet per year.

Although the Compact is a watershed approach with voluntary negotiations among its states to agree on the amount of water each can receive, it has proven to be inflexible in meeting needs not envisioned in 1922, such as demands from Mexico and population growth in Arizona and Nevada. Incentives from the federal government, such as dams, have helped the negotiations along, and judges have helped keep states from taking more than their share, so the compact has remained in force. But the use of the water probably is not optimal.

AN INTERNATIONAL PERSPECTIVE

Organizing government agencies to integrate environmental, social, and economic perspectives on watershed management is not a new idea. Although we can find examples of watershed management activities in many nations (e.g., Costa Rica), the focus here is on nations whose general legal and policy frameworks resemble those of the United States because of a shared heritage of British common law. Among such nations, the United States alone adheres to the dominance of agencies like the U.S. Army Corps of Engineers, the Environmental Protection Agency, and the Bureau of Reclamation, each pursuing its own mission defined by topic. The experiences of Australia, New Zealand, Canada, and Great Britain provide examples of water-resource management with organizational structures dominated by watershed organizations.

In Canada, provincial governments traditionally have organized their water and environment planning activities according to watersheds (Newson, 1992). In Ontario, for example, 38 "conservation authorities" promote integrated planning for development. The authorities are organized by local interests, often municipalities, and usually consider issues such as flood control, recreation management, water supply, and water quality together rather than separately. However, it has proven challenging to coordinate actions between these local conservation authorities and the larger-scale activities of the federal government, and to deal with the complexities of interbasin water transfers. A review of Canadian water policy outlined five strategies for improving the situation; these strategies emphasize water pricing, science leadership, integrated planning, larger scale legislation to span jurisdictions, and improved public participation (Pearse et al., 1985).

Australia's experience with watershed management is similar to that of Canada in that both countries have states (Australia) and provinces (Canada) that are large with respect to most of the nation's river basins, and both nations tend to emphasize water and watershed management at the state or provincial level rather than the federal level. Two legislative changes in the state of South Australia are of interest: the Catchment Water Management Act of 1995 and the Water Resources Act of 1997. The 1995 legislation is one in a series of laws that specify the management capabilities of local agencies called "catchment water management boards" (State of South Australia, 1995). These boards have responsibility for significant aspects of planning and implementing efforts to manage water, controlling flooding, dealing with recreation issues, and preserving and improving environmental quality. The boards, staffed by state governor appointees, are supposed to serve as management connections between watersheds and river channels, and they are empowered to purchase land in pursuit of their objectives.

Two such boards manage portions of the Adelaide area of South Australia: the Patawalonga and the Torrens Catchment Water Management Boards, each responsible for watersheds about of about 100 sq. mi. (250 sq. km.) The boards have produced comprehensive plans that account for water supply and quality as well as a full range of water resource uses (see Box 6.2).

The management plans emphasize the integration of ecological, environmental, and economic considerations on a geographic basis (BC Tonkin & Associates, 1996; Torrens Catchment Water Management Board, 1997). In Australia, larger projects such as the restoration of the River Murray require management by state officials (State of South Australia, 1995). Recent legislation in Australia has defined the role of the catchment boards as being resource management, while state and federal agencies have responsibility for standard setting and regulatory enforcement (Dyson, 1997).

New Zealand's use of watersheds as administrative units is instructive because of its exceptionally long record. Beginning in 1868, New Zealand established River Boards to deal with flooding and erosion problems, and by the late 1980s the nation had 20 Regional Water Boards. Each board administered about 5,200 sq. mi. (13,500 sq. km.) (Quinn and Hickey, 1987). The board's objectives included meeting water quality criteria defined at the national level by the 1967 Water and Soil Conservation Act. The regional boards were made up of local interests in pursuit of national standards, but each board also took into account issues specific to individual watersheds. For example, some boards were most concerned with water pollution from upland applications of fertilizer, herbicides, and pesticides (McColl and Gibson, 1979), while others were more concerned with land rights of the native population, the Maori. The nation has 82 hydroelectric dams, but their distribution is unequal so water board interest in them varies accordingly. The boards were organized by region rather than by legal function (Ministry of the Environment, 1989).

In 1989, local governments in New Zealand reorganized and consolidated to create 16 new regions defined by watershed boundaries (Dixon and Wrathall, 1990). These watershed boundaries were useful because many of them had served as River Board boundaries, so that administrators and citizens understood and accepted them as definable regions. Combining the local governments into watershed groupings supported the general belief "that decisions relating to resource allocation and use should be taken by communities most affected by those decisions, taking explicit consideration of their own specific geographies" (Furuseth and Cocklin, 1995). Technical specialists in the physical science and engineering professions moved directly into the new organizations from the old River Boards. The regional councils have sole responsibility over soil conservation, water and air quality, waste disposal, and geothermal resources. They share responsibilities

Box 6.2
The Patawalonga Catchment and the Murray-Darling Basin, Australia

The Patawalonga Catchment and the River Murray in southern Australia illustrate the successful matching of scales between a physical watershed resource and its responsible administrative unit. The Patawalonga Catchment is a watershed that includes a main drainage basin plus a small associated basin that drains directly to the sea. More than 50 percent of the catchment is urbanized as part of the Adelaide metropolitan area, so that stormwater drains augment its naturally defined stream system. The catchment also includes some agricultural areas in its headwaters area. Significant management problems in the catchment include water quality unsuitable for swimming, boating, or fishing; watercourses with eroded banks; stormwater that is piped directly to the sea rather than being used for other purposes; and urbanization that has increased downstream flooding on many tributaries (BC Tonkin and Associates, 1996).

The Catchment Water Management Act of 1995 provided the legal framework for the Patawalonga Catchment Management Board, which consists of nine members, four appointed by local government, four appointed by the state government, and a chairperson jointly appointed by local and state governments. Financial support for the board's activities comes from a catchment levy raised by local government based on property values, as well as borrowing authority for some capital works. The board has established and begun implementing a management plan that calls for preventing polluting discharges, constructing physical works to improve water quality, and establishing wetlands; replacing concrete channel linings with more natural beds and banks, and adding paths to create linear parks; detaining stormwater for aquifer recharge; mapping flood-risk zones; and acquiring flood-prone land for inclusion into linear parks.

with the central government for coastal resources and with local governments for natural hazards, noise, and cultural heritage.

The passage of the 1991 Resource Management Act (RMA) brought further changes to watershed management issues in New Zealand. The Act supersedes previous legislation (except for minerals and fisheries), and governs the manage-

These local scale activities contrast with simultaneous efforts at a regional scale for the basin of the River Murray and its principal tributary the Darling, a stream system draining 408,800 sq. mi. (about 1 million sq. km.) in the Australian interior near Adelaide. In this large basin, the management issues differ from those at the local scale for Patawalonga. The major problems are increasing salinity of the river's water, reduced economic vitality because of soil erosion and dryland salinity, lack of integrated management of flow regulation structures, lack of a regional perspective on stormwater runoff and urban effluent, loss of native bird populations, and declining health of riparian vegetation. These problems are so large scale, and the basin covers such a large geographic area (including parts of four states), that no single governmental entity can deal with them. The Murray-Darling Basin Initiative was created to bring together the state governments and the Commonwealth (federal) government in an organizational structure whose scale matches the basin scale. Established in 1985, the initiative began by maintaining the basin's physical water management structure, but the organization's new Murray-Darling 2001 project is designed to integrate ecological, economic, and social approaches to addressing the needs of the basin's natural and cultural resources (Brown, 1995). The primary proposed method of funding this broad effort is contributions from the participating state governments totaling about $150 million, with a matching contribution from the Commonwealth.

These Australian examples show that watershed problems are essentially regional in nature, and they can be best approached using organizations that are regionally defined. Small regions such as the Patawalonga Catchment require organizations of local governments and citizens, while large regions require consortia of larger governmental entities. Watershed problems are scale specific, with some, like the problem of linear parks along restored waterways best addressed locally and others, like basinwide salinity problems, best attacked by large-scale approaches. In each case, however, it is easiest to integrate the ecologic, economic, and social approaches by using regionally defined administrative units rather than units defined by restricted missions such as environmental quality, engineering, or reclamation.

ment of natural resources and environments (Furuseth and Cocklin, 1995). Two principles govern the RMA: sustainable management is the overall objective, and the mechanism for decisionmaking is to move from the central government to the regional and local levels. The RMA requires each region to formulate policy and vision statements to establish the local methods for reaching the goal of sustainable management. This policy process includes public participation and the involvement of the Maori. Territorial governments, in their land use plans and policies, as well as private resource owners and Commonwealth resource managers, must observe regional resource and environmental policies. The central government retains the responsibilities for setting national environmental standards, national policy, water conservation orders, heritage protection orders, and coastal policy.

In their evaluation of the reform process for New Zealand resource management, Dixon and Wrathall (1997) noted that implementation has largely been in the hands of local and regional councils, with minimal central governmental support. They indicate that while devolution of authority to the regional and local level should occur to improve management and control by local representatives, "there is no doubt that practitioners and councils would have benefited by more guidance from the center." They found that the new system is more complex than the former one, with several tiers of plans, often of variable quality. The New Zealand example shows that organizing according to watershed boundaries is a workable method for ensuring local control over water and water-related resources. The experience also shows that the natural boundaries must blend with previously established administrative boundaries, sometimes through aggregation of small administrative units to constitute regions approximating the watersheds. The New Zealand example also shows that there can be a logical division of responsibilities among local, regional, and national authorities.

Great Britain also has reorganized its regional approach to water and watershed management. In recent decades the nation has managed these resources through River Authorities, agencies with management responsibility for individual drainage basins ranging in size up to several hundred square miles, with jurisdiction defined by watershed boundaries. Recently these River Authorities have been folded into the national Environment Agency, but the subdivisions within the Agency remain defined by watersheds. The boundaries of jurisdiction have been modified somewhat to coincide with local government boundaries that approximate as closely as possible the natural boundaries.

These experiences in other nations show that management of water as a resource and as a subject of scientific inquiry can be accomplished with organizational structures that parallel the natural organization of watersheds. Often, the precise outlines of the natural watershed are not the most effective as an organizing principle, and the continuing adjustments made by New Zealand in its primary division, by Canada in its arrangements, and by Britain in its reorganization and continued adjustments of administrative boundaries show that concerns other than the physical environment must be taken into account. Political, social, cultural, or financial regions may be just as important as the physical region for definitional purposes. As an example, interbasin transfers of water or electrical power logically distort the drainage basin boundaries to fit the realities of the human use of the resource. In all the cases reviewed above, however, the use of geographically defined agencies has been critical to integrating ecological, economic, and social approaches. Yet for reasons of scale, complexity, governmental power, structures, and history, functionally defined agencies dominate the national organizational scene in the United States.

WATERSHED ORGANIZATIONS FOR THE FUTURE

New water and related land management organizations are developing across the nation. For example, according to McClurg (1997), several hundred watershed management programs are underway in California. In 1996, a new watershed initiative began to integrate water quality monitoring, assessment, planning, standard setting, permit writing, nonpoint source management, groundwater protection, and other staff work. Federal funding for some of these activities comes from modified administration of two EPA programs funded under sections 205(j) and 319(b) of the Clean Water Act.

Organizational structures for hydrologic resources and hydrologic research for watersheds in the United States are most likely to be effective if they follow watershed boundaries. Organizational structures for other resources and for integrated approaches, however, must often be more flexible, with the boundaries of organizational responsibility being defined by the issue at hand.

For the management of hydrologic resources, however, a nested hierarchy of hydrologic management organizations is preferable, with responsibilities for each organization dependent on the watershed scale of its responsibility (Table 6.3). This nested approach is required because the United States is large in terms of area (34 times larger than New Zealand, for example) and in terms of population (5 times more populous than Great Britain). This local to national continuum will help ensure the inclusion of all relevant stakeholders and provide an integrating framework.

Failing to match the scale of decisionmaking to the scale of the watershed can lead to two problems. If the decisionmaking body has authority over an area that is smaller than the watershed at issue, its policies will probably fail to take into account the impact that local decisions can have downstream. Those who benefit from such narrow decisions may not bear their true economic or environmental costs. If, on the other hand, a decisionmaking body has authority over an area that is too large or is dominated by federal interests, it will likely fail to take into account local interests that in the end must bear many of the ramifications of the decisions. Matching the decisionmaking authority with the watershed in question according to scale and geographic area thus helps resolve the questions of who benefits and who pays for watershed resources, including goods and services, and makes it easier to reach compromises.

We do not yet know how the nation's institutions need to change to achieve greater sustainability of natural resources (Cortner et al., 1996). In many cases, institutions that have served us well in the past have outlived their intended mis-

TABLE 6.3   Common Scales for Watershed Management Issues

Watershed Issues	Small Watersheds, Less than 2,500 km² (1,000 mi²)	Intermediate Systems, 2,500- 25,00 km² (1,000-10,000 mi²)	Larger River Basins, Greater than 25,000 km² (10,000 mi²)
Establish overall regulatory thresholds			√
Reservoir system management			√
Management issue and needs analysis	√	√	√
Goal, objective, and policy development	√	√	√
Hydrologic modeling for water quality	√	√	√
Management, water quality, point source	√	√	√
Public education	√	√	√
Flood-plain management	√	√	
Management, water quality, nonpoint source	√	√	
Participatory planning	√	√	
Stream bank stabilization	√	√	
Wetland management	√	√	
Lake management	√	√	
Surface water recreation management	√	√	
Fisheries management	√	√	
Rare and endangered species management	√	√	
Land use planning and zoning	√		
Construction site erosion control	√		
Drainage ditch management	√		
Greenbelt development and management	√		
Irrigation management	√		
Local flood-control works	√		
Shoreline erosion control	√		

sions and, in some cases, usefulness (Wilkinson, 1992). This is not to say these organizations and the laws they support were not sensible when they were created, during an era when resources were believed to be inexhaustible, but rather that societal values and needs have changed. The institutions responsible for managing our natural resources may well be the most significant barriers to the adoption of new, more integrated approaches to management (Kessler, 1992, 1994; Slocombe, 1993; and Grumbine, 1994).

Research is needed to provide a better understanding of how people and institutions can be more effective. Stankey and Clark (1992), in studying the social aspects of implementing new approaches in forestry, identified six general areas for research that are appropriate here as well: integrating social values; understanding public values for resources; public acceptance of management approaches; public participation mechanisms; structure, procedures, and values of natural resource organizations; and forums for debating issues. In a companion study on institutional barriers and incentives for ecosystem management, Cortner et al. (1996) identified five problem areas where social science research might help improve our ability to implement new approaches to management:

- the extent to which existing laws policies, and programs may constrain or aid implementation;
- institutional mechanisms for managing across jurisdictions;
- internal organizational changes and new arrangements among resource agencies and the public;
- theoretical principles underlying natural resource management; and
- methodological approaches for researching institutional questions.

Such research can help build our understanding of current social values and how these values can be integrated into management strategies.

CONCLUSION

Documentary histories, field visits, workshops, and the experiences of individual committee members lead us to several conclusions about organization for watershed management. While these conclusions apply in many cases, there are also many exceptions because of local or regional variation.

Organize according to watershed boundaries for direct hydrologic management and related scientific research. The inherent nature of the hydrologic system is that it is organized according to nested watersheds, so organizations that deal primarily with the water resource should be organized in the same fashion. Integrative scientific research focusing on water and closely related resources should take advantage of the natural geographic characteristics of hydrologic systems.

Organize decisionmaking boundaries to fit the issue at hand when dealing with engineered hydrologic systems where economic or social systems are involved. A slavish adherence to watershed boundaries can lead to missed opportunities and inefficient decisions when factors such as interbasin transfers of water and power create a hydrologic system that operates outside the natural watershed boundaries. No one arrangement fits all situations, and flexibility is important.

With respect to scale in dealing with hydrologic issues, the organization scale should fit the scale of the natural system. The management of water and closely related resources of small watersheds should be handled by local organizations, while larger scale organizations should deal with aggregations or nested hierarchies of smaller units. Larger, more encompassing organizations can help resolve local differences. Some functions, such as land use planning and zoning, are best left to local levels of governmental organization, while other tasks such as setting regulatory standards are best left to the national level. No one size fits all situations.

New organizational strategies must recognize the limitations of transfer of powers. The historical development of governmental organizations in the United States dictates a certain distribution of powers among levels and among agencies within the same level. Watershed management through newly defined organizations will not succeed unless there is a transfer of powers from these established agencies, often an unlikely scenario. Therefore, watershed management in the United States is often best accomplished through partnerships of existing agencies that work together in ad hoc arrangements for particular watersheds.

Watershed organizations are most successful if they are self-organizing from the grass-roots level, rather than having an organizational structure imposed by national fiat. In the United States, regional variations in the natural environment, customs, politics, financial resources, and existing distribution of powers are so great that a national overlay of proposed watershed organizations is unlikely to be successful. The most effective watershed organizations seen by the committee are those that developed from local needs focused on particular problems. Successful organizations often solved one initial problem before expanding their interests to attack other issues.

Individuals make a difference—they create organizations and drive their success. In field visits and workshops, the committee found that the most successful organizations were the product of the initial effort of one individual or of a small group of persons. These few individuals committed themselves to addressing a problem of local or regional extent and exerted enthusiasm and leadership to organize for a solution. We should not underestimate the power people have to identify problems and take action to solve them.

REFERENCES

Baril, K. 1996. Achieving results community by community. National satellite videoconference. In proceedings, Watersheds 96. Alexandria, Va.: Water Environment Federation.

Bay Journal. 1996. Susquehanna, Potomac commissions face funding cuts. Alliance for the Chesapeake Bay 6(9)(Jan-Feb).

BC Tonkin and Associates. 1996. Patawalonga Catchment Water Management Board Comprehensive Catchment Water Management Plan: Draft for Consultation. Adelaide, South Austrialia: BC Tonkin and Associates.

Black, P. E. 1987. Conservation of Water and Related Land Resources. 2d Ed. Totowa, N.J.: Roman & Littlefield.

Bonneville Power Administration (BPA). 1997. 1997 Annual Report. Portland, Oregon: Bonneville Power Administration.

Brown, D. 1995. Restoring the River Murray: Statement on the Environment. Adelaide, Austrialia: State of South Australia.

Chesapeake Bay Agreement. 1987. Chesapeake Bay Program Office, Annapolis, Maryland.

Cortner, H. J., M. A. Shannon, M. G. Wallace, S. Burke, and M. A. Moote. 1996. Institutional Barriers and Incentives for Ecosystem Management: a Problem Analysis. Gen. Tech. Rep. PNW-6TR-354. Portland, Oreg.: U.S. Dept. of Agriculture, Forest Service, Pacific Northwest Research Station.

Dixon, J., and A. Wrathall. 1990. The reorganization of local government: reform or rhetoric? New Zealand Journal of Geography 9:2-6.

Doppelt, B., C. Frissel, J. Karr, and M. Scurlock. 1993. Entering the Watershed: A New Approach to Save America's River Ecosystems. Washington, D.C.: Island Press.

Dyson, M. 1997. Navigating the South Australian Water Resources Act 1997. Adelaide, South Australia: South Australian Department of Environmental and Natural Resources.

Dziuk, H. E. 1997. Chairman, Steering Committee on Big Sandy Area Lakes Watershed. Personal communication.

Dzurik, A. A., and D. A. Theriaque. 1996. Water Resources Planning. 2d edition. Lanham, Maryland: Rowman and Littlefield Publishers, Inc.

Eisel, L. M., and J. D. Aiken. 1997. Final Draft Report for Platt River Basin Study. Denver, Co: Western Water Policy Review Advisory Commission.

Featherstone, J. P. 1996. Water resources coordination and planning at the federal level: The need for integration. Water Resources Update 104 (summer 1996):52-54.

Federal Emergency Management Agency. 1996. National Water Control Infrastructure: National Inventory of Dams. CD-ROM. Washington, D.C.: U.S. Army Corps of Engineers and Federal Emergency Management Agency.

Furuseth, O. and C. Cocklin. 1995. An institutional framework for sustainable resource management: the New Zealand Model. Natural Resources Journal 35(2):243-273.

Grumbine, R. E. 1994. What is ecosystem management? Conservation Biology 8:27-38.

Ingram, H. 1973. The political economy of regional water institutions. American Journal of Agriucltural Economics 55(1):10-18.

Jessup, D. H. 1990. Guide to State Environmental Program. 2d edition. Washington, D.C.: The Bureau of National Affairs, Inc.

Kenney, D. and B. Rieke. 1997. Resource Management at the Watershed Level: An Assessment of the Changing Federal Role in the Emerging Era of Community-Based Watershed Management. Report prepared for the Western Water Policy Review Advisory Commission, Denver, Colorado.

Kessler, W. B. 1992. New perspectives for sustainable natural resources management. Ecological Applications 2(3):221-225.

Kessler, W. B. 1994. Significant barriers to further progress of ecosystem management. Discussion paper for Institutional Problem Analysis Workshop; October 20-22, 1994; Stevenson, WA. On file with: Water Resources Research Center, 350 North Campbell Ave., Tucson, AZ 85721.

MacKenzie, S. H. 1996. Integrated Resources Planning and Management: The Ecosystem Approach in the Great Lakes Basin. Washington, D.C.: Island Press.

McClurg, S. 1997. Sacramento-San Joaquin River Basin Study. Draft Final Report. Denver, Co: Western Water Policy Advisory Commission.

McColl, R. H. S., and A. R. Gibson. 1979. Downslope movement of nutrients in hill pasture, Taita, New Zealand, III: Amounts involved and management implication. Journal of Agricultural Research 22:279-286.

Meschke, L. 1997. BERBI Facts. Fairmont, Minn.: BERBI.

Ministry of the Environment. 1989. Update on the Resource Management Law Reform. Wellington, New Zealand.

Nagle, D. G., G. W. Currey, W. Hall, and J. L. Lape. 1996. Integrating the point source permitting the program into a watershed management program. In proceedings, Watersheds 96. Alexandria, Va.: Water Environment Federation.

National Research Council. 1997. Watershed Research in the U.S. Geological Survey. Washington, D.C.: National Academy Press.

Newson, M. 1992. Land, Water and Development: River Basin Systems and their Sustainable Management. London: Routeledge. 351 pp.

O'Connor, K. A. 1995. Watershed Management Planning: Bringing the Pieces Together. M.S. Thesis. California State Polytechnic University, Pomona. 166 pp.

Pearse, P. H., F. Bertrand, and J. W. Maclaren. 1985. Currents of Change. Ottawa: Environment Canada.

Portney, P. R., ed. 1990. Public Policies for Environmental Protection. Washington, D.C.: Resources for the Future.

Quinn, J. M., and W. Hickey. 1987. How well are we protecting the life in our rivers? Soul and Water 23(4):7-12.

Rosenbaum, W. A. 1991. Environmental Politics and Policies. 2nd ed. Washington, D.C.: Congressional Quarterly Press.

Slocombe, D. S. 1993. Implementing ecosystem-based management: development of theory, practice, and research for planning and managing a region. Bioscience 4(9): 612-622.

Stankey, G. H. and R. N. Clark. 1992. Social Aspects of New Perspectives in Forestry: a Problem Analysis. Milford, Pa.: Grey Towers Press.

State of South Australia. 1995. Catchment Water Management Act of 1995. No. 37.

Steering Committee of the Comprehensive Review of the Northwest Energy System. 1996. Toward a CompetitiveElectric Power Industry for the 21st Century: Comprehensive Review of the Northwest Energy System Final Report. Portland, Oregon: Northwest Power Planning Council.

Torrens Catchment Water Management Board. 1997. Torrens Comprehensive Catchment Water Management Plan, 1997-2001. Adelaide, South Australia: Torrens Catchment Water Management Board.

U.S. Army Corps of Engineers (USACE). 1987. USACE Wetlands Delineation Manual. Environmental Laboratory, U.S. Army Waterways Experiment Station Technical Report Y-87-1.

U.S. Environmental Protection Agency (EPA). 1993. The Watershed Protection Approach: A Project Focus. Draft. Washington, D.C.: EPA Office of Water (WH-553).

Viessman, W., Jr., and C. Welty. 1985. Water Management Technology and Institutions. New York: Harper Row.

Wanich, J. 1997. River-cleanup plan alarms critics. Washington Post 29 September, 1997.

Wilkinson, C. 1992. Crossing the Next Meridian: Land, Water, and the Future of the West. Covelo, Calif.: Island Press.

7

Financing Watershed Organizations

Stable funding is one of the essential ingredients necessary to establish and maintain viable watershed organizations. In return, a truly integrated approach to watershed management offers the promise of improved economic efficiency and diverse benefits because it addresses multiple purposes and varied stakeholders. But the diversity that is the strength of watershed organizations is also a source of problems. It is difficult to assess each stakeholder a "fair share" of the cost of operating the organization and its watershed, and the identification of funding sources satisfactory to all participants is a major issue. This chapter, provided mostly for the use of managers, addresses three aspects of the financing of watershed organizations. First, it reviews the funding mechanisms currently in use, ranging from highly localized arrangements to federal approaches. Second, it explores the problem of cost allocation in watershed organizations. Finally, it briefly identifies potential financing options that may offer useful approaches for watershed groups. Because watershed structure and funding are often related, there is some overlap between this chapter and the previous one, as the different agencies and organizations are reviewed, but the emphasis here is on the problems and opportunities for funding watershed activities.

Ample precedent exists among federal water agencies in financing individual, multipurpose water resources projects. However, with the notable exception of TVA, little financial support has been provided by federal agencies for watershed-based organizations. Traditionally, federal funding has focused on the initial construction of facilities. After construction, the facilities were sometimes turned over to a local group to operate or sometimes a federal construction agency would operate the facilities. But the era of large-scale federal construction in water resources appears to be over (Worster, 1985; Reisner, 1986; NRC, 1996), and attention has shifted to management of existing systems. A key motivation behind many contemporary watershed programs is watershed restoration to reverse some of these detrimental impacts caused by water development and urbanization. However, restoration is a relatively new goal in most watersheds and financing for it is not well defined.

CURRENT FUNDING MECHANISMS

Current funding mechanisms for water resource management activities can occur at the local, regional, and country levels, as well as by agricultural district, by state, by interstate efforts, and by various specific federal agencies.

Local Funding Opportunities

Local water management activities can be funded at either city or multi-city levels.

City Utilities

Many local water-related institutions are funded as utilities or service districts. At the municipal level, separate utilities may exist for water and wastewater systems. In recent years, many communities have also established stormwater management utilities. Funding is based on assessing charges for services rendered. Water utilities, for example, typically assess charges for hooking up to the system, for fixed administrative costs, and for the quantity of water used. Most wastewater utilities charge in a similar manner, with the wastewater flow being estimated by the indoor water use. Wastewater utilities may also vary their charges based on the strength of the sewage. Stormwater charges can be based on the amount of impervious area associated with each customer. These charges usually are a fixed monthly rate. Although many utilities do not adhere to a zero net revenue goal, it is generally considered good practice to base charges on cost recovery so that utilities neither subsidize their services nor provide surplus revenues for other areas of government. Nelson (1995) provides a current overview of utility financing in the water, wastewater, and storm water areas. Local water, wastewater, and stormwater utilities can fund restoration activities as part of their charters if they are responsible for causing some of these impairments.

Metropolitan Utilities or Districts

Another popular local funding model is to form area-wide districts or utilities to serve specific purposes, like water supply, wastewater treatment, and stormwater management (e.g., the Denver Urban Drainage and Flood Control

District). The Environmental Protection Agency (EPA) encouraged area-wide wastewater management as part of its large construction grants program in the 1970s. Cities were required to demonstrate that any proposed area-wide waste-water management system was cost effective. Because of economies of scale, the analysis tended to favor the creation of larger area-wide wastewater control facilities as opposed to many smaller treatment plants. The federal government also nurtured the use of area-wide planning agencies, typically called Councils of Government (COGs), to encourage area-wide solutions to water, wastewater, stormwater, transportation, and other infrastructure problems. Much of their financing comes from the federal government. As with individual utilities, these agencies can fund watershed conservation or restoration activities if they view it as part of their responsibility.

The Anacostia River Watershed is a good example of federal agency involvement in an urbanized watershed (Interagency Ecosystem Management Task Force, 1996). This 170 sq. mi. (440 sq. km.) sub-basin of the Potomac River basin flows through parts of the Washington, D.C. metropolitan area, and the key water quality issues are degradation by urbanization and agricultural activities. Restoration activities are being facilitated by the Washington Council of Governments in cooperation with several federal agencies. The Interagency Ecosystem Management Task Force (1996) critiqued the funding aspects of these activities, and reached the following conclusions:

• Grant availability: The Task Force recommended creation of a federal clearinghouse to inform state and local governments of federal grants for environmental restoration.
• Grant scope: The allowable scope of grants tends to be too narrow.
• Matching fund requirements: Local people recommended the elimination of matching fund requirements, especially for financially strapped communities.
• Project operation and maintenance: The Task Force raised the issue that local communities may not have the resources to properly maintain projects, even if the federal government pays for installation.

County-Based and Agriculturally Oriented Districts

Some water organizations are formed around county boundaries. For example, Prince William County, Virginia, has established a three-county stormwater utility along the lines described for urban stormwater utilities (Pasquel et al., 1996). Some funds support watershed management , but in general counties are not significant funders of watershed activities.

Because of our nation's significant agricultural history and the importance of water to farming, a large number of agriculturally oriented districts have watershed responsibilities and provide some funding opportunities or in-kind services. The Natural Resources Conservation Service (NRCS) has developed water management programs for approximately 3,000 soil conservation districts covering virtually the entire United States. The NRCS also established hundreds of small watershed (<250,000 acres) programs as part of its PL 566 program, with the primary objectives of improving drainage and flood control.

Agriculturally oriented districts have a long history of federal involvement, although the assistance is more often technical than financial. Agricultural nonpoint pollution control programs rely primarily on financial incentives to encourage farmers to voluntarily adopt techniques that reduce nonpoint discharges. Thus, there is a strong tendency to expect the federal government to pay for watershed activities related to agriculture.

Funding for Regional and Interstate Watershed Organizations

Another level of spatial aggregation is by region within a state. This approach is typified by the five water management districts created in 1972 within Florida (described more fully in Chapter 6). Two of the districts, South Florida and Southwest Florida, already existed as drainage and flood control districts established as operating arms of large U.S. Army Corps of Engineers projects. Part of the St. Johns River Water Management District was also related to Corps of Engineers projects. The districts are funded by taxes, and each district sets its own tax rate. A comprehensive review of the water management districts was favorable (Water Management District Review Commission, 1995). For instance, the review notes that the Florida water management districts have moved aggressively into watershed management activities, especially the restoration of the Kissimmee River and the Everglades. These restoration projects are funded by a variety of sources, including the state, various counties, federal agencies such as the National Park Service and the Corps of Engineers, and taxes on agricultural operations in the Everglades Agricultural Area.

Other examples of regional approaches can be seen in the West. Kenney and Rieke (1997) surveyed western watershed management efforts to assess their evolution during the 1990s and found a wide variety of activities and financial strategies in use. For instance, the Verde Watershed Association in Arizona functions as an information dissemination organization, and it meets its modest financial needs by assessing annual dues on its members, including federal agencies. On a larger scale, the Animas River Stakeholder Group of the Upper Animas River (a tributary of the Colorado River) seeks to restore a viable brown trout fishery as its primary objective. The group receives most of its funds from EPA, in the form of Section 319 grants under the Clean Water Act, and from the Rocky Mountain Mine Waste Initiative. Other federal agencies have contributed resources such as in-kind services. A critical challenge for the Animas River group has been securing stable long-term financing for the planning process, in part because the effort lacks a statutory basis.

The Model Watershed Project of the Lemhi, Pahsimeroi, and East Fork of the Salmon Rivers in Idaho has as its primary objective the restoration of salmon runs by encouraging water users to modify their water use practices. Project funding comes from the Bonneville Power Administration as part of the Northwest Power Planning Council's Columbia River Basin Fish and Wildlife Program. Soil and water conservation districts also have had important roles in the program.

Another important example is the McKenzie Watershed Council of the McKenzie River in Oregon, often touted as the cleanest river in Oregon. This effort was stimulated when hydropower facilities on the river came up to be relicensed in 1991, and there was a call to investigate the potential for developing an integrated watershed management program in the basin. In 1993, the Oregon congressional delegation secured $600,000 in EPA funds to support the work. Additional funds included $500,000 from the NRCS and $100,000 from the Northwest Power Planning Council. However, as federal funds diminish, the Council will need to develop a more diverse base of federal, state, and local funding.

Not all efforts involve hundreds of thousands of dollars. The South Platte River Forum of the South Platte River in Colorado conducts annual conferences to inform interested people of watershed activities. Funding consists solely of members contributing $500 to $1,500 per agency. Similarly, the Clear Creek Watershed Forum of the Clear Creek Basin in Colorado has been funded primarily by EPA as part of mine cleanup activities. The Forum focuses on the noncontroversial role of sponsoring workshops, but it has not been successful in obtaining funding from sources other than EPA.

Another type of funding is exemplified by the Plumas corporation, a nonprofit group that funds the Feather River Coordinated Resource Management Group in California. Because of their interest in sediment control, Pacific Gas & Electric (PG&E) and the Forest Service have provided $4 million to the group. The most pressing present problem is to find new sources of funding to replace direct project funds from PG&E, which is becoming less interested in underwriting restoration projects. Possible alternatives include a unit tax on exported water and support from the State of California.

The Upper Carson River Watershed Management Plan was established to coordinate research and management activities among several agencies concerned with surface and ground water in this watershed in California and Nevada. EPA Section 319 funds support a watershed coordinator, with additional in-kind services from the Fish and Wildlife Service and NRCS.

Finally, the Rio Puerco Management Committee of the Rio Puerco Watershed (New Mexico) was formed to help manage serious sediment problems. This organization was established by section 401 of the Omnibus Parks and Lands Act of 1996. Congress has authorized approximately $7 million over the next decade for the organization through Section 401 of the Omnibus Parks and Lands Act of 1996.

In studying these and other western examples, Kenney and Rieke (1997) (see Box 7.1) drew the following recommendations about steps necessary top improve the financial side of watershed activities:

Box 7.1
The Changing Federal Role in the Emerging Era of
Community-Based Watershed Management

In 1995, the Western Water Policy Review Advisory Commission was chartered by the Department of the Interior to undertake a comprehensive review of federal activities in the 19 western states which directly or indirectly affect the allocation and use of water resources (WWPRAC, 1998). As part of the Commission's information-gathering phase, it commissioned experts to prepare a number of detailed reports on topics such as demographic trends, water use, land use changes, alternative dispute resolution, as well as special assessments of six key large watersheds.

One of these reports, Resource Management at the Watershed Level: An Assessment of the Changing Federal Role in the Emerging Era of Community-based Watershed Management (Kenney and Rieke, 1997) is especially relevant to this study. The report notes that one of the most striking trends of recent years is a focusing of water management activities at the watershed level, and it discusses this trend within an institutional and historical context. It presents 12 case studies of active watershed initiatives, looking primarily at smaller watersheds. The report offers the following overall findings:

• Managing water (and related resources) at a regional scale is an idea with a long history and sound theoretical basis, but it has never been so widely implemented as at the present time.

• Simplify and standardize the procedures and paperwork requirements associated with applying for federal support of watershed initiatives.

• Promote federal collaboration across substantive and geographic boundaries by simplifying interagency transfers of funds.

• Modify rules that inhibit allocating resources to projects on private lands.

• Provide greater flexibility in cost-sharing requirements to make it easier for watersheds without significant local sponsors to obtain federal funds.

• Modify contracting rules to make it easier for watershed groups to hire and retain watershed coordinators.

• Stable funding is needed for watershed activities that cross agency boundaries. The federal government should promote the establishment of stable funding systems that spread the costs of resource management equitably among the beneficiaries.

- The watershed initiatives of the West show tremendous variety in structures and functions, although the successful initiatives tend to exhibit several common qualities.
- A lack of formal authority for the watershed initiative usually does not hinder the functioning of the initiative; to the contrary, a reliance on "moral authority" is generally seen as a key asset.
- Most watershed initiatives are not closely linked to management programs at the larger river basin scale.
- The performance of most watershed initiatives is sufficiently positive to merit guarded optimism, and to justify greater support from all levels of government and the private sector.
- The federal government plays a significant and essential role in the effective functioning of most watershed initiatives.
- Most watersheds are more likely to suffer form a lack of federal support than from specific federal barriers; nonetheless, some barriers do exist.

The report goes on to provide recommendations, some pertaining to the federal role. For instance, it notes the need to train agency personnel in the theory and practice of collaborative watershed management and the great importance of reauthorizing the Clean Water Act and the Endangered Species Act, two essential but controversial statutes that support watershed initiatives.

Perhaps the best known federally-funded interstate watershed management organization is the Tennessee Valley Authority, which was created in 1933. The federal government attempted to establish other basin-scale organizations in the 1940s including the Missouri (1945), Columbia (1946), the Pacific Southwest (1948), the Arkansas-White-Red (1950), and the New York-New England basins (1950). These relatively informal committees proved to be ineffective (Featherstone, 1996). To replace them, Title II of the Water Resources Planning Act of 1965 created seven river-basin commissions to deal broadly with river basins in New England, Ohio, Upper Mississippi, Souris-Red-Rainy, Missouri, Pacific Northwest, and Great Lakes. As discussed in Chapter 6, each commission had federal and state members and a core staff of 20-30 employees. Lack of authority and an inability to come to grips with contentious problems led to the disbanding of the commissions in 1981. The Water Resources Council, the last vestige of attempts to coordinate water resources management across federal water agencies, has not been funded since 1981. The only three remaining interstate organizations are those managing the Delaware, Potomac, and Susquehanna river basins (Featherstone, 1996).

In spite of recent interest in watershed management, no other broad-based organizations at the very large watershed or river basin scale have been formed. McLaughlin Water Engineers and Aiken (1997) outlined the reasons when they recommended against creating a river basin commission for the Platte River Basin. (The principal author from McLaughlin Water Engineers was Dr. Leo Eisel, who as a former Director of the Water Resources Council brings a unique perspective to this question.) This report noted:

> The Title II River Basin Commissions failed to achieve their objectives in the past because of the reluctance by the states and federal agencies to provide authority to the river basin commissions to accomplish their missions. The reluctance still exists and, consequently, establishment of a river basin commission for the Platte River would probably not be successful today.
>
> The principal reason for the demise of the Water Resources Council was the general reluctance of the states and federal agencies to provide a single entity, such as the Water Resources Council, with sufficient authority and responsibility to meet its objectives. After reviewing the current water resources planning, management, and development situation in the Platte River Basin and elsewhere, it appears there is little indication of support from either the states or the federal agencies for a successor to the Water Resources Council, with sufficient authority to meet its goals and objectives.

Funding at the Federal Level

Numerous federal agencies have responsibilities related to water management. The division of responsibility is sometimes based on geographical boundaries (e.g., the Bureau of Reclamation's activities are restricted to the western United States), but more often the responsibility is based on the nature of the problem being addressed (e.g., 10 agencies play some type of role in water quality improvement). This structure traces its origins to the 1930s, when the federal government first became involved in water resources on a large scale.

Perhaps the most significant federal agencies for water and watershed issues are the Corps of Engineers and Bureau of Reclamation, which together are responsible for 66 percent of the total water storage capacity of reservoirs in United States (about 37 and 29 percent, respectively) (Ruddy and Hitt, 1990). Decisions related to management of this large amount of storage have a major financial impact on water resources activities in the United States. These agencies also exercise a large of amount of control over how water is used for municipal water supply, irrigation, flood control, hydropower, navigation, recreation, and instream flow needs. Financially, these agencies provide a significant source of the construction and operating support for these systems.

The following paragraphs describe the role of several key federal agencies in the funding of watershed-related activities.

Bureau of Reclamation

In 1990, the BOR provided 31.6 million acre feet of water to western farmers. Nearly 85 percent of this water was used for irrigated agriculture, and 11.4 percent was used for municipalities and industries. Although the estimated gross benefits from this water are over $4 billion per year, actual charges levied on users were only $39.9 million and the BOR shows a revenue loss in providing this water supply. Also, a significant portion of the cost of irrigation water comes from power revenues. Thus, the charges for water supply, especially irrigation water supply, are well below actual costs.

Hydropower generation is the "cash register" of western water development because it plays such a dominant role in generating revenue, and hydropower generation is the dominant source of revenue for the BOR. In 1984, the BOR's gross revenue from hydropower was $607 million and net revenue was $196 million, which was nearly 97 percent of the net revenue of the BOR that year. Recreation is of growing importance in BOR operations with 53.5 million visitors in 1990. If a unit value of $5/visitor day is assumed, then the gross benefits of recreation would be $268 million per year. However, this benefit is non-reimbursable. The BOR estimates that its projects have reduced flood damages by an average of $197 million per year for the period from 1951-90. Like recreation, this benefit is non-reimbursable. Given this funding picture, the BOR is very much dependent on power revenues to support its operations. According to Block and Shadegg (1996), federal power is sold at prices that are well below market rates. Thus, the revenues from BOR operations could be 50 percent higher and still remain within market rates.

The Bureau of Reclamation budgets $1,000,000 for its watershed and river systems management program, which supports the development of a Decision Support System that is intended to improve its ability to make management decisions involving complex hydrologic systems. The Bureau of Reclamation's FY 97 total budget was $651 million (BOR, 1997). Thus, the $1 million commitment to watershed activities is a minute portion of the Bureau's total budget.

U.S. Army Corps of Engineers

The total appropriation for the U.S. Army Corps of Engineers (USACE) was $3.7 billion in FY 1992 (USACE, 1992). The USACE estimates that its projects prevent an average of $15 billion in flood damages each year. USACE projects generate about 80 billion kilowatt-hours per year, which translates to an estimated revenue of $1.6 billion. About 200 million visitor days of recreation per year occur at USACE facilities and generate $1 billion per year. Water supply is not included in the USACE's national summary, although it is included in the summary of activities of the Missouri River Basin, discussed briefly below.

The Corps' Missouri River Basin is an example of a complex, multipurpose project. Many stakeholders are involved in determining the project's Annual Operating Plan (USACE, 1994). The estimated gross annual benefits for the Missouri River Basin are $1.1 billion. Water supply and hydropower are the primary benefits, with each accounting for about 44 percent of the total benefits. Flood control and recreation contribute about 10 percent each of the total benefits, with navigation contributing the remaining benefits (just under 2 percent).

Department of Energy

The Department of Energy (DOE) is a major player in water resources programs through its five Power Management Administrations (PMAs) (GAO, 1995). The service areas of these five PMAs and their FY 1994 revenues are shown in Figure 7.1. Bonneville Power Administration (BPA) is the largest (financially) of the five PMAs with annual revenues exceeding $2 billion per year. The Western Area Power Administration (WAPA) is the second largest PMA, with FY 1994 revenues of $714 million. The Southeastern Power Administration (FY 1994 revenues of $158 million) and the Southwest Power Administration (FY 1994 revenues of $109 million) are the third and fourth largest sources of revenue. The Alaska Power Administration (FY 1994 revenues of $10 million) is the smallest of the five PMAs. The Tennessee Valley Authority (TVA) operates both as a separate entity and as a partner with SEPA for part of its activities. These PMAs work in cooperation with the operators of the hydropower facilities. As shown in Table 7.1, these five PMAs and TVA account for nearly 10 percent of the nation's energy output. The output from these entities is sold at "cost" and results in charges of about 2 cents per kilowatt-hour, far less than the national average of 3.61 cents per kilowatt-hour.

These PMAs and the operating agencies (mainly the BOR and USACE) provide a wide variety of water resources functions (Table 7.2). Overall, over 78 percent of the appropriations are devoted to power generation. Irrigation accounts for 4.5 percent of the appropriations and other individual purposes are similarly less than 5 percent of the total appropriation. The power generation represents a $43 billion per year industry, with about $38 billion of that total generated by BPA and WAPA. By any comparative measure, hydropower is the national cash register of the water industry for federal agencies.

Environmental Protection Agency

EPA is a large agency with a diverse range of responsibilities, many related to water. One example of a relevant program is the State Revolving Fund, which can be used for financing watershed-based pollution control programs (Singells,

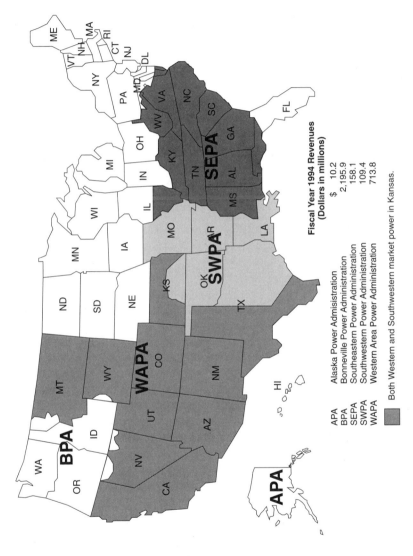

Fiscal Year 1994 Revenues
(Dollars in millions)

APA	Alaska Power Administration	$ 10.2
BPA	Bonneville Power Administration	2,195.9
SEPA	Southeastern Power Administration	158.1
SWPA	Southwestern Power Administration	109.4
WAPA	Western Area Power Administration	713.8

Both Western and Southwestern market power in Kansas.

FIGURE 7.1 Power Marketing Administration Service Areas. SOURCE: GAO, 1995.

TABLE 7.1 Average Revenue Per kWhr of Wholesale Power in DOE's Power Marketing Administrative Service Areas (PMAs), FY 1994

PMA	Energy delivered millions of kWhr	Revenue from sales millions of $	Average revenue cents/kWhr	Appropriation millions of $
APA[a]	406	10	2.46	0.2
BPA[b]	57,245	1,406	2.46	27.6
SEPA[c]	8,745	165	1.89	2.4
SWPA[d]	7,946	97	1.22	2.7
WAPA[e]	29,358	536	1.83	10.6
Total-PMAs	103,700	2,214	2.14	43.5
TVA Hydro	18,000	339		
Total-PMAs plus TVA Hydro	121,700	2,553		
Nationwide-wholesale	1,202,902	43,384	3.61	
PMAs plus TVA Percent of Total	10.1%	5.9%		

[a]APA: Alaska Power Administration
[b]BPA: Bonneville Power Administration
[c]SEPA: Southeastern Power Administration
[d]SWPA: Southwestern Power Administration
[e]WAPA: Western Power Administration

TABLE 7.2 Gross Appropriation Expended for Power and Non-power Purposes (1995)

Purpose	APA	BPA	SEPA	SWPA	WAPA	Total	Percent of Total
Power	$206.1	$25,331.0	$1,476.0	$1,007.6	$ 5,891.0	$33,911.7	78.1%
Flood Control	0.0	559.3	244.3	910.0	0.3	1,713.9	3.9%
Irrigation	0.0	409.2	0.0	0.0	1,558.4	1,967.6	4.5%
Navigation	0.0	815.8	320.9	231.7	0.0	1,368.4	3.2%
Recreation	0.0	113.8	231.3	402.3	28.6	836.0	1.9%
Fish and Wildlife	0.0	80.0	16.7	24.6	97.4	218.7	0.5%
Multi-purpose	0.0	0.0	0.0	0.0	2,801.6	2,801.6	6.5%
Muncipal and Industrial	0.0	0.0	0.0	0.0	197.6	197.6	0.5%
Other	0.0	244.2	14.3	121.1	6.1	385.7	0.9%
Total	$206.1	$27,553.3	$2,363.5	$2,697.3	$10,581.0	$43,401.2	100.0%
Percent of Total	0.5%	63.5%	5.4%	6.2%	24.4%	100.0%	

SOURCE: GAO (1995).

1996). The fund, which currently has $17 billion available, offers low-interest loans that can help save an estimated 30 to 50 percent of the cost of a project by reducing interest payments. EPA also provides significant support to state water pollution control activities including watershed-based systems and restoration projects. The agency also funds science and policy research by investing in state and university partnerships.

Geological Survey

The U.S. Geological Survey (USGS) has four major divisions, including geology, water resources, mapping, and biological resources. The Water Resources Division is financed by a combination of direct appropriations and reimbursable cooperative programs with other federal agencies, and state and local governments (USGS, 1994). The FY 1994 budget for the USGS water resources program was $400 million, with over half of the funds from reimbursable sources.

This high level of reimbursable support indicates a well developed network of cooperative interagency activities.

Natural Resources Conservation Service

The Natural Resources Conservation Service (NCRS) program directly linked to watershed-based approaches is the NCRS's PL-566 program, which promotes development of drainage and flood control projects for agricultural watersheds smaller than 250,000 acres (100,000 ha or about 390 sq. mi.). The current funding for this program is about $100 million per year. The PL 566 program has come under attack for promoting drainage of wetlands and subsidizing floodplain use. On the positive side, the program encourages watershed planning as part of the development activities. In addition to NRCS, other Department of Agriculture programs affect watershed funding, such as soil conservation districts.

National Oceanic and Atmospheric Administration

The National Oceanic and Atmospheric Administration's (NOAA) Coastal Zone Management program provides financial support for planning activities for watersheds that link interior areas with valuable coastal environments and affects 29 states (Robertson et al., 1996). This watershed-based program focuses on nonpoint pollution control and is conducted in cooperation with EPA. NOAA provides a significant financial contribution: in 1992, funding for the Coastal Zone Management Program was $40 million.

Hydropower production has long been the primary funding mechanism for water development projects, particularly in the West. Hungry Horse Dam, on the South Fork of the Flathead River in Montana, was built between 1948 and 1953 and was at the time of its completion the third largest concrete dam in the world. It was designed to provide flood protection and power generation, and contribute to downstream irrigation, navigation, and recreation. The powerplant can generate 285,000 kilowatts. Modifications were made in the early 1990s so that warmer water could be released to mitigate adverse impacts to downstream fish habitat. Credit: Bureau of Reclamation.

Hydropower Production and Watershed Financing

As noted earlier, hydropower production has long been the primary funding mechanism for water development, particularly in the West. This approach began in the 1930s when the federal government established the TVA and Power Marketing Administrations (PMAs) to sell subsidized power produced at federal hydroelectric plants in rural and underdeveloped areas. These organizations continue to function today even though electrification has been completed and many of the once-developing areas are now prosperous (e.g., Palo Alto, California, parts of Los Angeles and Kansas City, and Vail and Aspen, Colorado). Power from these federal dams is still sold at below market prices. According to Block and Shadegg (1966), the PMAs receive numerous subsidies including very low interest rates, extensive payback periods, unrealistic depreciation periods, and tax exclusions. These hydropower operations cause many watershed problems because of their major disruption of the normal hydrological cycles (Collier et al., 1996).

These low rates benefit only certain portions of the United States. For example, people on one side of Los Angeles who are served by Southern California Edison pay 12.10 cents/kWhr, while elsewhere in Los Angeles customers who benefit from the PMAs pay 9.85 cents/kWhr. In Northern California, residents of Santa Clara (7.30 cents/kWhr) and Palo Alto (5.46 cents/kWhr) pay much less than customers in the Bay Area, who pay 12.25 cents/kwhr (Block and Shadegg, 1996). Many of the communities receiving these subsidies are among the most affluent in the United States. The federal power operatives receive Congressional appropriations for their operations, and the power revenues are deposited in the general fund. Public agencies control over 60 percent of the hydropower capacity in the United States (Table 7.3).

WESTERN WATER POLICY COMMISSION

The Western Water Policy Review Advisory Commission (see Box 7.2) provides some excellent insights into financing mechanisms for watershed activities in the western United States (WWPRAC, 1998). The following paragraphs summarize some of the commission's findings that are particularly relevant to funding of watershed management.

In a report to the commission, MacDonnell and Driver (1996) recommend the creation of a new Colorado River Basin Commission that would assume responsibility for all federal facilities and the water deliveries to Mexico, and be self-supporting with income from hydropower revenues. Another report by

TABLE 7.3   Summary of Private and Public Hydropower Projects in the United States

Region	Number of Projects		Total Installed Capacity (MW)	
	Private	Public[a]	Private	Public
Northeast	146	12	4,194	4,119
South	80	60	7,330	5,669
Midwest	115	28	3,452	3,111
West	115	96	6,238	17,655
Total	456	196	21,214	30,584

[a]Public agencies consist of rural electric cooperatives, municipal utilities, state utilities, and federal projects.
SOURCE: Reprint, with permission, from Block and Shadegg (1996). © 1996 from The Progress Freedom Foundation.

Box 7.2
Water in the West: the Challenge for the Next Century

In 1995, the Western Water Policy Review Advisory Commission (WWPRAC) was charged to undertake a comprehensive review of federal activities in the 19 western states which directly or indirectly affect the allocation and use of water resources, whether surface or subsurface. The commission had 22 members including the secretary of the Interior, the secretary of the Army, 12 ex-officio members of Congress, plus citizens, lawyers, and the deputy administrator of the Bonneville Power Administration. The group set out to identify the challenges that western water managers face in achieving sustainable use of water resources. During two years of activity, the commission gathered information at public hearings, undertook a scientific review of the status and trends of water and related resources, and authorized production of assessments of water conflicts in six key basins and the capability of existing management institutions to resolve them. Although focused on the West, the commission addressed issues of wide national importance and used a process that might work or be tailored to work in other regions.

The Commission's report was still in draft form when this report was being written, so we cannot comment on it in any detail. However, the committee did have the opportunity to keep abreast of the Commission's activities and benefit from the basin assessments. Like this report, *Water in the West: The Challenge for the Next Century* (WWPRAC, 1998), com-

---

Pontius (1997) recommends establishing dedicated funding sources for financing programs for endangered species recovery, habitat restoration, and environmental enhancement in the Colorado River basin. Hydropower revenues already are being targeted for salinity control and fish recovery funding in the Upper Basin.

Volkman (1997) pointed out that the hydropower revenues from the Columbia River basin, which have supported a large salmon restoration effort, may dwindle in the face of competition from other low-cost power sources such as natural gas. He also concluded that watershed efforts need stable long-term funding if they are to be effective. In a related area, watershed activities in the Yakima River basin in the State of Washington address concerns about salmon habitat. Federal funding for the Yakima effort is from a congressional appropriation and matching funds from the Power Planning Council. The Umatilla River is Oregon illustrates a different funding approach for a somewhat similar basin. The State of Oregon, which has created 36 watershed or river basin councils, provides the funding.

ments on the maze of agencies and programs to deal with water issues and the conflicts caused by historic programs and laws aimed at developing water for economic purposes. They conclude that these problems cannot be resolved piecemeal, but rather must be addressed by fundamental changes in institutional structure and government processes. But this will not be easy, as they, too, note that the geographic, hydrologic, ecological, social, and economic diversity of the West will require regionally- and locally-tailored solutions.

The WWPRAC report sees potential for a new approach to governance of watersheds and river basins in the West based on hydrologic systems. In addition to opportunities for governance and management based on watersheds, the WWPRAC report identifies eight other key areas of challenge for western water managers, and addresses each at length in its report and its companion documents, including:

- sustainable water supply and water use
- meeting our water obligations to Native Americans
- aquatic ecosystems
- water quality
- flood and floodplain management
- protecting productive agricultural communities
- maintaining the federal water infrastructure
- data collection, research, and decisionmaking

In the Columbia River basin, a governing principle is that hydropower is partially responsible for funding fish and wildlife mitigation. The current agreement calls for Bonneville Power Administration to pay $252 million per year for fish and wildlife programs (Volkman, 1997). Hydropower is not the only cause of the salmon decline in the Pacific Northwest. Flood control, irrigation, navigation, and recreation also cause impacts, and these other activities are also subsidized by the federal government. From an equity point of view, should these other purposes be required to share in the cost of river restoration programs?

McLaughlin Water Engineers and Aiken (1997) recommend that federal funding and technical assistance for the Platte River Endangered Species Recovery Program be expanded to levels commensurate with other programs such as the Columbia River Restoration Program, the Upper Mississippi Environmental Management Program, the Everglades Restoration Project, and the Central Valley Improvement Program. They recommended that federal funding be based on a determination of federal interests in these projects. A proposed Memorandum of Agreement for the Platte River Basin calls for the federal government to pay 50 percent of the total $75 million cost of the recovery program, with Nebraska and Colorado each paying 20 percent and Wyoming paying 10 percent.

Agricultural water users in the Upper Rio Grande, for example, and most of the West receive irrigation water at subsidized costs (ECONorthwest, 1997). These subsidies include subsidized construction costs, shifting some of the irrigator's repayment obligation to others because the obligation exceeds the irrigator's ability to pay, and relieving irrigators of part of their repayment obligations in special circumstances, such as drought or economic hardship (GAO, 1996). The net result of these subsidies is that irrigators in the Upper Rio Grande pay less than 20 percent of the total cost of their providing irrigation water. One would expect reductions in irrigation if these subsidies were eliminated.

COST ALLOCATION AND WATERSHED MANAGEMENT

From the viewpoint of economic efficiency, it should be possible to take advantage of economies of scale, develop multi-purpose programs, and more fully exploit the benefits of integrated watershed management (Heaney, 1993). Unfortunately, as the size of the watershed organization and the number of purposes which it serves grows, it becomes increasingly complex to equitably apportion the benefits and costs. Is there a "correct" way to assign the costs of watershed activities among stakeholders? Some understanding of the conceptual approaches available is useful, although taking this information from the abstract to the concrete, where it can be implemented by managers, is of course a significant challenge (Heaney, 1997).

How costs are allocated is a long-standing issue in water resources management, and certainly an issue when it comes to financing watershed-based organizations. Cost allocation is required whenever an activity deals with multiple purposes and/or groups, with the underlying problems of allocating costs in ways that are both efficient and equitable. There are different methods available for cost allocation in the water resources field. The important question, in general, is the context in which cost allocation takes place. Each cost allocation problem has its unique history and set of agreements as to what constitutes a "fair" division of costs. The economic efficiency of water resource projects can be improved by taking advantage of various factors, including (Heaney and Dickinson, 1982):

- economies of scale in production and distribution facilities,
- the assimilative capacity of the receiving environment,
- excess capacity in existing facilities,
- multipurpose opportunities; and
- multi-group cooperation.

Unfortunately, when potential solutions to watershed problems are analyzed, the most economical strategy is typically a complex blend of management options. When the optimal economic solution is complex, it creates complex cost allocation problems since it is necessary to divide the costs among many purposes and groups. Thus, the search for improved economic efficiency exacerbates the difficulty of deciding how costs should be divided. The concept of equity is an essential part of the cost allocation problem. Young (1994a) defines a number of key terms to provide language to further the discussion. According to Young, an *allocation* is an assignment of the objects to specific individuals or groups. It is a decision about who gets a good or who bears a burden, and it is usually decided by a group or an institution acting on behalf of the group. An *allocation problem* occurs whenever a bundle of resources, rights, burdens, or costs is temporarily held in common by a group of individuals and must be allotted to them individually. *Exchange* involves many voluntary, decentralized transactions and can only occur after the goods and burdens have been allocated. As a result, *allocation* comes first, and *exchange* follows.

With regard to equity, Young (1994a) stressed that it is a complex issue:

> Equity is a complex idea that resists simple formulations. It is strongly shaped by cultural factors, by precedent, and by the specific types of goods and burdens being distributed. To understand what equity means in a given situation, we must therefore look at the contextual details.

According to Young (1994a), allocation rules usually exhibit one or a combination of three concepts of equity:

- Parity: claimants are treated equally.
- Proportionality: acknowledges differences among claimants and divides the goods in proportion to these differences.
- Priority: the person with the greatest claim to the good gets it.

The earliest reported literature on the cost allocation problem in water resources is a book by Ransmeier (1942), who reported on the results of several years of debate regarding how the costs of the Tennessee Valley Authority (TVA) should be divided among flood control, navigation, fertilizer production, national defense, and development of power. This debate was important because it represented the first time that public water projects would compete with private water development. In particular, there was strong concern that multipurpose public water projects could outcompete existing private hydropower development, because a significant part of the total cost could be assigned to other purposes. These deliberations produced five criteria for cost allocation (Ransmeier, 1942):

- An allocation method should have a reasonable logical basis.
- The method should not be unduly complex.
- The method should be workable.

- The method should be flexible.
- The method should apportion to all purposes present at a multiple purpose enterprise a share in the overall economy of the operation.

The TVA group could not agree on whether it was essential that total costs be paid but later groups supported this notion of assigning the full cost among the participants. Thus, the sixth condition would be:

- The method should apportion the entire cost of the project among the stakeholders.

Large-scale, federally sponsored water development after World War II brought attention to the need to develop cost allocation methods for water projects. The "separable costs, remaining benefits" (SCRB) method originated in this initiative (Federal Interagency River Basin Committee, 1950). A separable cost is the incremental cost of adding group i as the last member of a large coalition of N members. If economies of scale exist, a group incurs the lowest incremental cost if it joins last. If group i cannot pay at least its separable cost, then it will have to be subsidized by the other groups. In the SCRB method, each group is assigned separable costs—that is, the cost it would incur if it joined last, which will likely be less than if it was an original member of the coalition. The remaining non-separable costs are then apportioned based on each stakeholder's share of the total remaining benefits. Independent of the water resources field, game theorists have pondered the same questions of efficiency and equity using cooperative n person game theory (Aumann and Hart, 1994). Young (1994b) provided an explanation of game theory and cost allocation. Interestingly, the game theorists independently arrived at the same conclusions as did the professionals who evaluated the TVA problem (Heaney and Dickinson, 1982).

Importance of Context

For every cost allocation problem, it is essential to clearly define the context within which the calculations will be done. There is no single correct way to determine and allocate costs. However, some useful guidelines regarding the importance of context do exist. For example, Nelson (1995) describes various ways to determine System Development Charges (SDCs) for water, wastewater, and stormwater systems. SDCs are one-time charges paid by new system development to finance the construction of public facilities needed to serve it. Nelson (1995) describes the legal and other issues that have arisen in trying to establish "fair" charges for new developments. These lessons are applicable to financing watershed organizations.

Calculating Alternative Costs

An important component of cost allocation is to calculate the alternative costs for each participant. For example, assume that we have three stakeholders in a watershed organization. The following costs (C) need to be calculated:

1. The costs for each stakeholder if they act alone: C(1), C(2), C(3)
2. The costs for each pair of stakeholders if they act together: C(12), C(13), C(23).
3. The cost for all three stakeholders in the watershed organization: C(123).

In general, the number of cost combinations that must be calculated is $2^n - 1$ where *n* is the number of stakeholders. Thus, the number of combinations where *n* is 3 is 7, whereas it is 31 if *n* is 5, and 1023 if *n* is 10. Obviously, the transactions costs associated with large watershed organizations increase rapidly as the number of stakeholders increases. As the size of the group grows, transactions costs would be expected to increase even more rapidly due to factors such as multiple jurisdictions, growing administration costs, and more complex environmental impacts (Heaney, 1983).

A key question in determining the alternative costs is who gets to go first. Consider a three purpose project: navigation, flood control, and hydropower. If the three purposes cooperate, then a single dam will be built and they will share the costs, but how do we calculate the cost of building a dam to serve a single purpose such as flood control? Do the flood control system builders get to pick their ideal site along the river, or should they get to calculate their cost after the other two purposes have built their system? Depending on the answer to this question, the cost allocation will be cooperative or competitive.

Who Should Pay for Watershed Remediation and Restoration?

Much of the current interest in watershed organizations has been stimulated by groups interested in remediating and restoring watersheds to reverse years of decline due to dams, diversions, point and nonpoint pollution, hydropower operations, and other development. But who will bear the cost? One principle holds that polluters should pay. Thus those who altered the hydrology for hydropower releases, or made the river more saline due to irrigation return flows, or added contaminants due to mine drainage or municipal and industrial wastes, should pay for remediating this damage. Others argue that taxpayers should pay, since they have enjoyed the benefits of these economic activities or will enjoy the remediated watershed. In many cases, the federal government subsidized the original activities, but does that make the federal government responsible for cleaning up the subsequent waste problems? These issues are complex and are being hotly debated in many places throughout the United States. These equity issues are not related exclusively to environmental restoration. For example, federally financed flood control projects such as levees have caused significant external costs to other users. Who should pay to mitigate or eliminate these impacts?

Some degree of agreement exists as to what we mean by efficiency and equity and how to estimate "fair" ways to share costs. The importance of the context within which cost allocation takes place is, of course, critical. Participants may be willing to sacrifice a small gain in economic efficiency or choose not to accomplish all the intended goals to get a simpler cost allocation procedure. New institutions must be created to implement cooperative solutions. The associated transaction costs can offset the gains from a cooperative solution. The cost allocation problem is complex. Although practitioners have developed simple procedures for performing this task, the stakes are becoming higher as more competition enters the water resources field. It is essential that we fully understand the nature of and methods for properly answering the seemingly simple question, "How do we divide the cost of a watershed program?"

Financing Options

Given the great variation in watershed settings and the problems being addressed, no one approach to financing will fit all situations. One option for financing watershed organizations and activities is to maintain the status quo, and thus keep the current approach where different agencies have multiple responsibilities and programs and where the federal government plays an active role using water infrastructure develop as a way to stimulate economic development. This approach evolved over the past 60 years and has provided major gains in productivity for the U.S. economy, with the major return on the investment coming from hydropower revenues. A much larger return on the investment could be gained by assessing market rates for water supply, flood control, and recreation as well as hydropower production. At the other extreme are discussions of privatizing water resource management, an approach being tried for some purposes in a few U.S. locations and internationally (e.g., Great Britain). In between are various options for eliminating the federal water agencies and transferring control of watershed management to regional and local entities or creating major watershed agencies throughout the nation, along the lines of the old river basin commissions but with stable funding and actual management authority. Each of these broad approaches would require careful, detailed study before implementation to determine the associated advantages and disadvantages.

Much innovative thinking is occurring in the area of watershed management. For instance, MacDonnell and Driver (1996) suggested restructuring the governance of the Colorado River basin. Under the Colorado River Compact, the federal government paid most of the costs of developing the Colorado River to stimulate economic development and in return retained ownership and management of the facilities constructed. Hydropower revenues were the main vehicle to be used to repay the federal investment. But MacDonnell and Driver recommend establishing a regional governance for the Colorado River basin, one financially independent from the federal government. They suggest using power revenues and charges to those diverting water to finance the approach.

CONCLUSION

A steady source of revenues is essential to sustain watershed organizations. Existing watershed organizations typically are funded as part of single-purpose organizations. At the local level, these groups include water, wastewater, and stormwater utilities. Much of the current literature on watershed management deals with using watershed organizations to provide better nonpoint pollution control. Up to a point, these groups can use funds from a stormwater utility to accomplish broad water quality objectives, but they are not always ideal for addressing the full range of watershed activities. Similarly, water utilities can fund watershed programs as part of their source protection activities. The federal government's last effort to directly plan and fund watershed management was through the Water Resources Council, but it operated as an interagency coordinating group with a relatively small budget and little real authority. Both stable budgets and real authority would be needed if similar organizations were formed in the future.

At present, hydropower revenues are the dominant source of income for the water resources-related activities of federal agencies. Other purposes such as flood control, drainage, irrigation, water supply, recreation, fish and wildlife protection, and environmental quality control are funded from direct appropriations, and beneficiaries are seldom required to repay the total costs. The focus of most federal water management efforts since the 1930s has been to stimulate economic development, but this paradigm is changing (NRC, 1996) and must continue to evolve if federal agency financing methods are conducive to sustainable watershed management. Many examples can be cited of federal agency cooperation on individual water projects, but we are a long way from having meaningful integration of federal activities at the watershed scale.

With much of the stimulus for watershed-based programs being rehabilitation or restoration, it is essential to better define who is responsible for financing these activities. At present, there is no clear federal policy and each case is being negotiated separately. Hydropower revenues appear to offer a significant potential source of funding for watershed organizations, although privatization of the electric industry raises some uncertainty for the future. In addition, user charges for water supply, flood control, recreation, and other uses might provide substantial funding sources. Another potential source of funding might be penalties assessed on polluters, but this is a complex and controversial area in need of careful study and discussion because of concerns about both equity and efficiency issues.

Financing is a complex and yet critical element in the search for ways to implement watershed-scale approaches, and lack of funding opportunities continues to be a roadblock to many potentially useful activities.

REFERENCES

Aumann, R. J., and S. Hart., eds. 1994. Handbook of Game Theory, Vols. I and II. New York: Elsevier.

Block, M. K., and J. Shadegg. 1996. Lights Out on Federal Power: Privatization for the 21st Century. Washington, D.C.: The Progress Freedom Foundation.

Collier, M., Webb, R. H., and J. C. Schmidt. 1996. Dams and Rivers: A Primer on the Downstream Effects of Dams. U.S. Geological Survey Circular 1126. Tucson, Ariz.: U.S.G.S.

ECONorthwest. 1997. Water Management Study: Upper Rio Grande River Basin. Draft Report. Eugene, Oreg.: Western Water Policy Review Advisory Committee.

Featherstone, J. P. 1996. Water resources coordination and planning at the federal level: The need for integration. Water Resources Update, Issue 104, Summer: pp. 52-54.

Federal Interagency River Basin Committee. 1950. Proposed Practices for Economic Analysis of River Basin Projects. Washington, D.C.: Government Printing Office.

Heaney, J. P. and R. E. Dickinson. 1982. Methods for apportioning the cost of a water resource project. Water Resources Research 18(3):476-482.

Heaney, J. P. 1983. Coalition formation and the size of regional pollution control systems. In: Land Economics Monograph No. 6. Madison, Wisc.: University of Wisconsin Press.

Heaney, J. P. 1993. New Directions in Water Resources Planning and Management. Water Resources Update, Issue No. 93, Autumn.

Heaney, J. P. 1997. Cost Allocation. In Design and Operation of Civil and Environmental Engineering Systems: An Advanced Applications Text. New York: J. Wiley and Sons.

Interagency Ecosystem Management Task Force. 1996. The Ecosystem Approach: Healthy Ecosystems and Sustainable Economies. Volume I, PB95-265583, Volume II, PB95-265591, and Volume III, Case Studies. NTIS PB95-265609. Springfield, Va.

Kenney, D., and B. Rieke. 1997. Resource Management at the Watershed Level: An Assessment of the Changing Federal Role in the Emerging Era of Community-Based Watershed Management. Denver, Colo.: Western Water Policy Review Advisory Commission.

MacDonnell, L.. and B. Driver. 1996. Rethinking Colorado River Governance. The Colorado River Workshop. Phoenix, Ariz.: Grand Canyon Trust.

McLaughlin Water Engineers, Ltd., and J. D. Aiken. 1997. Platte River Basin Study. Draft. Denver, Colo.: Western Water Policy Review Advisory Committee.

Nagle, D. G., G. W. Currey, W. Hall, and J. L. Lape. 1996. Integrating the point source permitting program into a watershed management program. In: Proceedings, Watershed 96: Moving Ahead Together. Alexandria, Va.: Water Environment Federation.

National Research Council. 1996. A New Era for Irrigation. Water Science and Technology Board. Washington, D.C.: National Academy Press.

Nelson, A. C. 1995. System Development Charges for Water, Wastewater, and Stormwater Facilities. Boca Raton, Fla.: CRC Press.

Pasquel, F., O. Guzman, and M. Mohan. 1996. Funding mechanisms for a watershed management program. In: Proceedings, Watershed 96: Moving Ahead Together. Alexandria, Va.: Water Environment Federation.

Pontius, D. 1997. Colorado River Basin Study. Denver, Colo.: Western Water Policy Review Advisory Commission.

Reisner, M. 1986. Cadillac Desert: The American West and Its Disappearing Water. New York, N.Y.: Viking Press.

Ransmeier, J. S. 1942. The Tennessee Valley Authority. Nashville, Tenn.: Vanderbilt University Press.

Robertson, P., M. Jansen, and K. Walker. 1996. Progress in addressing nonpoint source pollution. In: Proceedings, Watershed 96: Moving Ahead Together. Alexandria, Va.: Water Environment Federation.

Ruddy, B. C., and K. J. Hitt. 1990. Summary of Selected Characteristics of Large Reservoirs in the United States and Puerto Rico, 1988. Open-File Report 90-163. Denver, Colo.: U.S. Geological Survey.

Singells, N. D. 1996. Financing priority watershed projects with the state revolving fund. In: Proceedings, Watershed 96: Moving Ahead Together. Alexandria, Va.: Water Environment Federation.

U.S. Army Corps of Engineers (USACE). 1992. 1992 Annual Statistical Highlights. Washington, D.C.

U.S. Army Corps of Engineers (USACE). 1994. Master Water Control Manual-Missouri River Basin, Draft EIS.

U.S. Bureau of Reclamation (BOR). 1990. Summary: U.S. Bureau of Reclamation Budget Justification. Denver, Colo.

U.S. Bureau of Reclamation (BOR). 1997. Bureau of Reclamation Responses to Western Water Policy Review Advisory Commission Questions. Draft. Washington, D.C.: U. S. Dept. of the Interior.

U.S. General Accounting Office (GAO). 1995. Federal Electric Power: Operating and Financial Status of DOE's Power Marketing Administrations. GAO/RCED/AIMED-96-9FS, October. Washington, D.C.: U.S. General Accounting Office.

U.S. General Accounting Office (GAO). 1996. Information on allocation and repayment of costs of constructing water projects. GAO/RCED-96-109, July.

U.S. Geological Survey (USGS). 1994. U.S. Geological Survey Yearbook. Reston, Va.: Government Printing Office.

Volkman, J. M. 1997. A River in Common: the Columbia River, the Salmon Ecosystem, and Water Policy. Denver, Colo.: Western Water Policy Review Advisory Commission.

Water Management District Review Commission. 1995. Bridge over Troubled Water: Recommendations of the Water Management District Review Commission. Tallahassee, Fla.:

Western Water Policy Review Advisory Commission (WWPRAC). 1998. Water in the West: Challenge for the Next Century. Washington, D.C.: Government Printing Office.

Worster, D. 1985. Rivers of Empire: Water Aridity, and the Growth of the American West. New York: Pantheon Books.

Young, H. P. 1994a. Equity in Theory and Practice. Princeton, N.J.: Princeton Univeristy Press.

Young, H. P. 1994b. Cost allocation. Chapter 34 in Handbook of Game Theory with Economic Applications. Amsterdam: Elsevier.

8

Planning and Decisionmaking

A key question underlying all watershed planning is: What is an effective process to relate science, policy, and public participation? Watershed planning demands integrated thinking and a coordinated approach. Perhaps the greatest contemporary concern is to provide meaningful public involvement in the process, because experience has shown that top-down planning can create a variety of implementation barriers grounded in the lack of public involvement at key points in the planning process. For instance, the public may oppose environmental regulations that are preceived to be unjust or ineffective. Or they may oppose a particular land use based on their perceptions of the risk involved, which may or may not be accurate. Although public concerns are often justified, at times they are rooted in the lack of accurate knowledge and lack of involvement in the analysis and decisionmaking process. Even when the public is involved in the planning process, it may still be ineffective if other factors are not integrated into the planning process at key steps along the way. One problem often cited is "getting the political process cart before the scientific horse." Naiman et al. (1995) characterize this situation as follows:

> Scientists, managers, and politicians are routinely called on to address competing demands on freshwater supplies and ecosystems, but they are increasingly unable to respond at scales commensurate with the issues. Why? Policy development and management activities are frequently undertaken without an adequate empirical foundation; inappropriately short-term, single focus approaches are accepted with little question; human-caused change is often difficult to distinguish from natural variation; and even when relevant data are available to guide decisionmaking, the legal and regulatory framework is inadequate.

Consequently, the criteria for effective management and policy decisions are ambiguous.

This chapter discusses some important considerations regarding the integration of science, policy, and public participation in watershed management. It considers the role of science and its relation to policy, as well as stakeholder involvement. Watershed planning and management is increasingly collaborative, raising questions about the nature of democratic decisionmaking, equity among stakeholders, and the need for the involvement of an informed public. This chapter considers these broad issues, presents six critical points that should be considered in the conduct of watershed planning, and reviews the planning procedures of six federal agencies in terms of these critical points.

RELATING SCIENCE AND DECISIONMAKING

Improving the interface between science and policy and between scientists and politicians remains one of the major challenges to watershed management. It is difficult enough to manage land and water resources at small spatial and short temporal scales, but to formulate management plans for the larger, longer scales often requires complex systems of governance and advanced science. It is common to hear scientists complaining that their voices are being ignored by policymakers.

Watersheds have taken on increasing importance in establishing a context for federal, state, and local policy. Some objectives are directly related to water, including water supply management, flood control, water quality protection, sediment control, fisheries conservation, navigation, and hydroelectric generation. Others are related but less focused on water, including maintenance of biological diversity, wildlife management, and general environmental preservation. Broader goals like recreation and economic development are also sometimes cast as watershed issues.

Which of these problems can be effectively addressed at the watershed level? Answering this question leads to an important first step in the planning process: defining the problem and setting clear objectives. Science plays an important role at this stage of the planning. The recent National Academy of Sciences report, *Understanding Risk* (Stern and Fineberg, 1996), provides a cogent summary of the challenge involved in integrating science into environmental management. First, the planning process must *get the science right*:

> The underlying analysis meets high scientific standards in terms of measurement, analytic methods, data bases used, plausibility of assumptions, and respectfulness of both the magnitude and the character of uncertainty, taking into consideration limitations that may have been placed on the analysis because of the level of effort judged appropriate for informing the decision.

Second, the planning process must get the *right science*:

> The analysis has addressed the significant risk-related concerns of public offi-
> cials and the spectrum of interested and affected parties, such as risks to health,
> economic well-being, and ecological and social values, with analytic priorities
> having been set so as to emphasize the issues most relevant to the decision.

Watershed planning and management makes some particular demands of
science. To begin with, science must play a major role in creating a robust knowledge base from which problems and objectives can be clearly defined and solutions effectively implemented. Comprehensive solutions also require interdisciplinary collaboration in the analysis and interpretation of watershed data.
While this process will yield clear answers to some questions, it may also lead to
new questions for which there are no unambiguous answers. When faced with
complexity and uncertainty, watershed planning and management must make provisions for ongoing monitoring and basic science research (Stanford and Poole,
1996).

Planning procedures seldom devote adequate attention to the integration of
science into the process. For example, as the EPA describes its "watershed approach," the process sounds analytical and seems well thought out. The watershed management plan emerging from this framework is expected to be founded
on "sound science," "efficient public program administration" and "broad participation of stakeholders" (EPA, 1993). The proposed approach, says EPA, will
analyze barriers to meeting water quality and quantity goals, define solutions in
land use and environmental planning strategies, and monitor progress in order to
adjust strategies as needed.

However, the EPA literature offers little definition of what is meant by good
science or what the technical requirements are. Nor does the literature tell how
the steps in planning are to be applied. The often unspoken message is that in
most cases we know what to do—we just need to do it. Watershed management
sounds like a world of few tradeoffs and no value conflicts other than those that
are misunderstandings. Conflict is accommodated by dialogue. Watershed planning exercises sometimes can be described as the accumulation of agreements to
support politically conceived projects. As a result there may be little interest in
scientific analysis or in the systematic and critical assessment of tradeoffs and
cost effectiveness in the utilization of limited resources. But these impressions
are at best simplistic and at times incorrect. Watershed management is both institutionally and scientifically complex, and there is significant need for new and
more in-depth knowledge on both fronts before we can be more effective implementing watershed approaches.

These are critical oversights, for the limited nature of watershed resources
cannot be ignored. Decision-support methods will need to be more widely employed to better search out cost-efficient ways to achieve goals. Decision-analysis
methods are formal protocols for manipulating and interpreting data in order to

provide information on the relationships between any alternative goals. The tools of decision analysis include cost/benefit analysis, risk assessments, and multi-criteria evaluation, but may also include less comprehensive assessments such as cost-effectiveness studies that identify the lowest cost means to achieve an objective, and/or evaluations of a solution's political and legal feasibility.

To make these tools work for decisionmaking, sound science is needed to predict the effects of alternative courses of action and policies on hydrologic, ecological, and social/economic parameters of interest. Whether the interest is in predicting sediment and nutrient transport, hydrologic and hydraulic effects of landscape alterations and restorations, or related problems, there must be attention to building and using predictive models that can address hydrologic, ecological, social, and economic outcomes of particular management actions. However, the incorporation of sound science in policymaking and planning is often easier said than done.

Lee (1993) points out that science and politics serve different purposes:

> The spectrum from truth to power places a crucial constraint on civic science: in learning to manage large ecosystems we cannot rely on philosopher-kings. So there must be a partnership between the science of ecosystems and the political tasks of governing. As in any partnership, the relationship between principal and agent is inevitably problematic at some points.

In politics the goal is the responsible use of the power to govern, and in democratic societies "responsible" means accountable to voters. In science the goal is to find truth, and accountability usually rests with one's peers. Figure 8.1 shows how scientists and policymakers are at opposite extremes.

As Lee observes, trouble often begins when one person attempts to play several roles simultaneously, for success is rarely achieved in more than one arena at a time. Attempts to move freely from one role to another often lead individuals away from their areas of expertise—a behavior that ultimately reduces both their knowledge *and* their power.

Yet it is not inappropriate role-playing alone that leads to management difficulties. Institutions are often not designed to incorporate scientific knowledge in an adaptive way. Table 8.1, adapted from Lee (1993), lists examples of institutional barriers to the principles of adaptive management.

There is increasing awareness of the need for adaptive strategies in the management in complex systems like watersheds. For example, Bella (1997) points out that the organizational systems of technological society are complex, adapting, and nonlinear. Organizational rigidity is often an unintended consequence of organizational functioning. Information that goes against current programs or beliefs, which represents a form of "disorder," tends to be selectively filtered out. The process is shown diagrammatically in Figure 8.2.

Consider how this paradigm might apply to watershed management. Institutional programs are designed, with the help of scientists, to improve resource

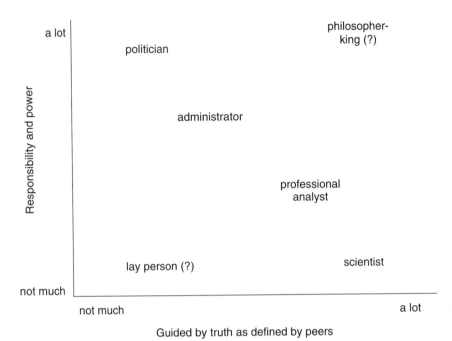

FIGURE 8.1 The Spectrum from Truth to Power. SOURCE: Reprinted, with permission, from Lee, 1993. © 1993 by Oxford University Press.

allocation or to mitigate environmental harm. Governing institutions or agencies fund projects and establish monitoring programs to determine project effectiveness. As long as data support the belief that a program is "working," decisionmakers are happy and scientists continue to be funded. But what happens when data do not support current programs or beliefs? In many cases, appropriate responses (additional studies to verify results, program changes, new management directions) are suppressed in favor of inappropriate responses (ignore the data, terminate monitoring, reassign the investigator). This pattern reflects an inherent institutional tendency to dampen disorder to nondisruptive levels. Bella (1997) suggests that organizational systems tend to be characterized by a dynamic tension between activities that sustain order and those that promote disorder (see Table 8.2).

Most politicians, administrators, and many professional analysts rely on behaviors that sustain order. Most scientists do, too, but sometimes their investigations result in data threatening to the established order. Then they are caught in a dilemma. Suppose, for example, a scientist found evidence that a fish hatchery was contributing to the decline of nongame fishes in a watershed. Further suppose that the scientist's agency was unwilling to accept the evidence or deliber-

TABLE 8.1 Barriers to Adaptive, Science-Oriented Management

Adaptive Management Principle	Barriers to Realization
There is a mandate and need to take action in the face of uncertainty.	Experimentation and learning are at most secondary objectives in large ecosystems management. Experimentation that conflicts with primary objectives will often be pushed aside or not proposed.
Decisionmakers usually recognize that they are experimenting.	Experimentation is an open admission that there may be no positive return. More generally, specifying the hypotheses that need to be tested raises the risk of perceived failure.
Decisionmakers care about improving outcomes over biological time scales.	The costs of monitoring, controls, and replication are substantial, and will appear especially high at the outset when compared with the costs of unmonitored trial and error. Individual decisionmakers rarely stay in office over periods of biological significance.
We have the ability to measure ecosystem-scale behavior.	Data collection is vulnerable to external disruptions such as budget cutbacks, changes in policy, and controversy. After changes in leadership, decisionmakers may not be familiar with the purposes and value of an experimental approach. Interim results may create alarm or a realization that the experimental design was faulty. Controversial changes have the potential to disrupt the experimental program.
Theory, models, and field methods are available to estimate and infer ecosystem-scale behavior.	Interim results may create panic or a realization that the experimental design was faulty. More generally, experimental findings will suggest changes in policy; controversial changes have the potential to disrupt the experimental program.
Hypotheses can be formulated.	Accumulating knowledge may shift perceptions of what is worth examining via large-scale experimentation. For this reason, both policymakers and scientists must adjust the tradeoffs among experimental and other policy objectives during the implementation process.
Organizational culture encourages learning from experience.	The advocates of adaptive management are likely to be staff, who have professional incentives to appreciate a complex process and a career situation in which long-term learning can be beneficial. Where there is tension between staff and policy leadership, experimentation can become the focus of an internal struggle for control.
There is sufficient stability to measure long-term outcomes; institutional patience is essential.	Stability usually depends on factors outside the control of experimenters and managers.

SOURCE: Modified from Lee, 1993.

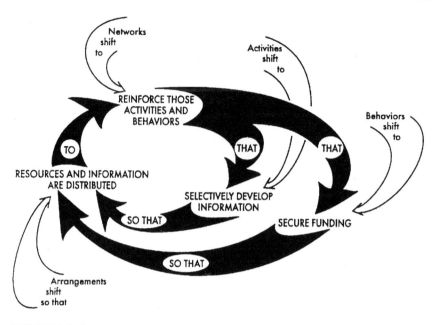

FIGURE 8.2 Dynamics of organizational change and function. SOURCE: Reprinted,
with permission, from Bella, 1997. © 1997 from Chapman and Hall.

ately chose to ignore it, arguing that the hatchery was politically popular and
funding for the hatchery program might be reduced if such findings became public. The scientist might have recourse to other ways of publicizing the data, but
doing so might jeopardize his or her job, promote a budget crisis, and upset those
in higher positions. In this case the scientist must choose between a course of

TABLE 8.2   Dynamic Tension Between Order and Disorder

Behaviors that sustain order (reinforced)	Behaviors that promote disorder (suppressed)
Securing and distributing funds to support revenue-producing activities.	Undertaking activities not promoting and possibly threatening the funding and support of activities.
Accommodating established arrangements, schedules, assignments, objectives, information channels, and authority.	Departing from established arrangements or schedules, going beyond assignments, going outside of information channels or around authority.
Gaining approval for activities; shaping behavior to performance evaluations.	Acting without and possibly contrary to prior approval; sustaining behaviors not favored by established performance evaluations.

SOURCE: Reprint, with permission, from Bella, 1997. © 1997 from Chapman and Hall.

action that favors order (but leads to continued harm) or one that favors disorder (but puts the individual and program at risk, perhaps leading to additional harm).

Institutions often respond to unfavorable scientific information by placing the burden of proof on the scientist or engineer who produced the data. A good example noted by Bella (1997) was the 1986 explosion of the space shuttle Challenger: because engineers could not prove beyond a doubt that the O-ring design was faulty in prelaunch safety meetings, the decision was made to launch even though there was reasonable doubt in the mind of key technical specialists. In many environmental decisions there is a very high level of uncertainty; scientists cannot predict outcomes with a great degree of precision. The result is a "war of scientists" or, perhaps more commonly, a "war of models" upon which scientists base forecasts. In most cases, the burden of proof falls on those challenging the status quo, and when they are unable to prove conclusively that they are correct, the decision is to continue in the current direction.

Providing a more balanced interface between science and policy will be key to better watershed management. Scientists must recognize the legitimate roles of politicians, administrators, and analysts, and maintain a strong loyalty to producing sound, unbiased data. Scientists must also respect the need for institutional stability. Funding for long-term monitoring, so important to adaptive management, depends on this stability. In turn, policymakers must realize that scientists provide the new information that, however uncomfortable in the short-term, yields insight into new policy direction and serves as a check on existing programs. Credible disorder will arise from goals that transcend assignments, incentives, and roles defined by established organizational systems. Watershed management that provides explicitly defined checks and balances between scientists and policymakers is likely to be the most robust over time.

Of course, the planning process must build commitments to action, in addition to providing analyses for selecting among alternatives. Science plays a crucial role in this selection of alternatives. As Stanford and Poole (1996) have noted, scientists offer the synthesis of "a central body of knowledge regarding the system and its components." Science provides data and analysis for watershed management, but ultimately policy is formulated on the basis of some societal values, and scientists must recognize this fact. Societies are diverse aggregations of individuals and groups representing a wide range of values. Experience has shown that watershed planning, and environmental management more generally, must take into account the values of all affected stakeholders. Management efforts that into account the complete range of interests will likely be more successful in avoiding concerted opposition and in soliciting public participation in the plan's implementation. However, it must be noted that not all stakeholders have the same political and economic power, and this complicates the process of reaching a solution that truly respects less powerful interests.

The revival of interest in watershed approaches to environmental management faces important budgetary constraints and this has led to increasing demands for inter-agency collaboration. Local communities are playing a much more central role in watershed management. Greater interest in inter-agency cooperation and the central role of communities presents the need for greater collaboration in the watershed planning process. We discuss these issues below, pointing out how they are related to broader societal issues like democratic decisionmaking and environmental equity. However, we also note that collaborative watershed planning will be most meaningful and effective if the public is educated about environmental issues and can play an informed role in the decisionmaking process.

IDENTIFYING STAKEHOLDERS AND GIVING THEM A VOICE

Successful collaborative planning requires careful attention to the nature of public participation. The report *Understanding Risk* (Stern and Fineberg, 1996) again provides us with a useful summary of key issues. According to this report, to be successful the planning process must *get the right participation*. When this happens, the report explains,

> The analytic-deliberative process has had sufficiently broad participation to ensure that the important, decision-relevant information enters the process, that the important perspectives are considered, and that the parties' legitimate concerns about inclusiveness and openness are met.

Second, the planning process must *get the participation right*; that is, it must

> ...[satisfy] the decisionmakers and interested and affected parties that it is responsive to their needs—that their information, viewpoints, and concerns have been adequately represented and taken into account; that they have been adequately consulted; and that their participation has been able to affect the way risk problems are defined and understood.

Involvement of relevant stakeholders is complicated by the common lack of corresponding political jurisdiction and watershed boundaries. This raises the question of how a community of interest within a watershed context is defined. When a watershed covers a large area, geographically dispersed and socially diverse groups must be brought together to solve a common problem—yet an institutional foundation to facilitate such community formation may not be available.

The mix of stakeholders may differ depending on specific watershed problems, and the community of interest must be defined on a case-by-case basis. This is a daunting task, given the usually uncertain nature of community formation. However, watershed plans can be effectively implemented only if such community definition and formation takes place. There is increasing recognition that if the watershed planning process is not carried out properly, its measures will fail. Many major, federally funded river system projects completed many scientific studies but resulted in little change in the way land is managed because they failed to take the human dimension fully into account (Moreau, 1994; Weatherford, n.d.). Small-scale issues are usually best resolved at the local level by involving all the relevant stakeholders in planning and decisionmaking.

What is needed is a new way of engaging local governments and involving citizens to take information generated by them and others to make changes that create long-term ecological improvements. Successful examples of this approach seem to be found in relatively small watersheds where the local population is convinced of the need for personal involvement in implementing changes that protect local resources but large watershed examples are rare (National Resources Law Center, 1996). Involvement often includes a long-term financial commitment on the part of local communities to a continuing program of watershed protection. The long-term success of a program may depend on local taxpayers, support. Such support cannot be forced on people, but must be achieved though an ongoing process of community involvement and collective learning. A recent nationwide study of ecosystem management found that personnel in about three-fifths of the cases studied considered collaboration to be a factor in facilitating their project's progress. Collaboration was considered important for progress by more project personnel than any other factor (Yaffee et al., 1996). How can such planning be brought about?

Collaborative Planning, Democratic Decisionmaking, and Environmental Equity

One approach to giving stakeholders voice is collaborative planning. A major focus of the next decade should be to design the institutions of collaboration. A basic feature of this effort is the development of an ethic of "shared leadership." When faced with significant issues, responsible agencies and interests will increasingly need to decide who should participate in a collaborative planning process to address the concerns at hand. The collaborative planning process looks much like the "scoping process" originally contemplated by the National Environmental Policy Act. This process focuses on a pressing issue and addresses related matters, provides for consultation with the affected constituency of interests, explores alternative futures and their impacts with appropriate studies and analysis, and narrows the range of acceptable alternatives to be considered by policymakers.

Collaborative planning involves diverse community interests within the watershed. It is a way of working together that honors a full spectrum of values and assumes that everyone is responsible for the group's success. There is no one leader and no outside expert telling people what is best for them. Rather, it is the collective effort to develop a vision and then make that vision become a reality.

Collaborative planning means bottom-up rather than top-down planning, so it taps collective energy, talent, and inspiration (see Figure 8.3). It means not

Planning Models

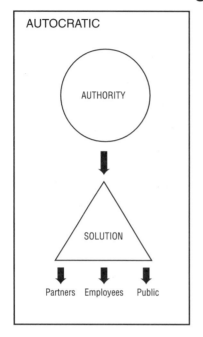

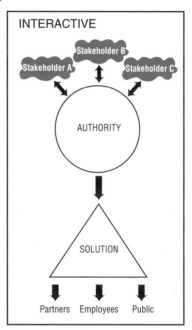

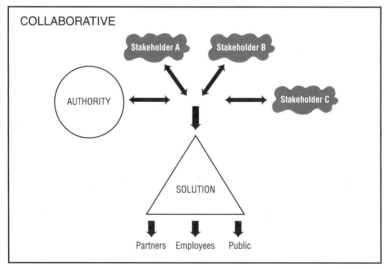

FIGURE 8.3 Illustrative planning models. SOURCE: USDA Forest Service, 1993.

waiting for the expert to come to town, but rather getting the stakeholders to take responsibility for their own future. Everyone has a seat at the table and is part of the discussion. It is most effective when community members come together to solve a specific problem.

Collaborative planning begins with trust building. The participants need to educate each other and explore their differences in values and interests to find a common ground. Newcomers and long-time residents can learn what they each see in the area, and that together they can enhance the area and have a greater opportunity to control their own destinies. Through dialogue, collaborators attempt to develop a shared community vision. It may be that not all agree, but all have had a chance to say how they see the world. Then there is often brainstorming or other means of creative problem solving to create an action plan. Recognizing that the future depends on each person's actions, can be empowering. As Margaret Mead is often quoted as saying, "Never doubt that a small group of thoughtful, committed citizens can change the world. Indeed, it is the only thing that ever has."

Collaborative and democratic decisionmaking demands that all persons with a stake in the outcomes of political decisions can represent their interests either directly or through duly elected political representatives. However, as noted above and in a National Research Council report (NRC, 1995), in the United States the question of democratic representation has usually been handled by drawing political boundaries based on a number of contingent and often arbitrary criteria. Problems best handled on a watershed scale do not respect these boundaries. The sources of problems may be in one location while the consequences appear in another.

Furthermore, stakes may be only indirectly related to the specific problem under consideration, and thus the range of stakeholders may not be immediately apparent. Thus decision tools used in the planning process must be sensitive to a wide range of possible interests. Relevant stakes may not be limited to costs and benefits directly associated with production and consumption activities. A more comprehensive cost-benefit accounting will identify the stakes involved in sustainable development and in doing so, extend the range of stakeholders. More socially and ecologically informed accounting demands greater attention to the overlap between political and natural boundaries, and will encompass all relevant stakes and stakeholders to establish the basis for effective democratic decisionmaking.

The expansion of the range of interests and values considered in watershed planning is the result of increasing integration of the decisionmaking process and environmental protection in public policy. For example, citizen involvement is an integral part of most major environmental legislation, beginning with the 1972 Federal Water Pollution Control Act. Some argue that this innovation created a potential institutional base for fundamental social change by encouraging greater citizen involvement in problem-solving (Priscoli, 1978; Rosenbaum, 1978).

Identifying all relevant stakeholders in watershed planning often creates an intersection of social and environmental concerns. "Environmental equity" is a term used to describe this convergence. In 1992, the EPA officially acknowledged environmental equity as a issue regarding the disproportionate distribution of environmental risk across population groups. This concern with the distribution of environmental benefits and burdens has further extended the range of stakeholder involvement relevant in watershed planning. All stakeholders, including the poor and minorities, need to be included so that watershed plans create an equitable distribution of benefits and burdens.

However, simply including a complete range of stakeholders does not ensure that all interests will be served. As we noted earlier in this chapter, in a context of limited resources there will be tradeoffs and conflicts between competing economic, social, and environmental interests. Decision-support tools must be capable of clearly identifying tradeoffs, and watershed planning must include means for dealing with conflicts. Methods of conflict resolution can help stakeholders create an acceptable balance between tradeoffs. However, the successful resolution of conflicts requires that stakeholders share a common knowledge base and a grasp of the big picture that unites them in the watershed context. Only then can they reasonably understand the tradeoffs involved in any solution (see Box 8.1).

The environmental movement has contributed to the development of an ethic of responsibility by drawing attention to the secondary consequences of private actions (Popovic, 1993). An environmental ethic of responsibility presupposes that individuals are aware of the consequences of their actions; education plays a key role in creating such awareness. The importance of expanding environmental awareness is widely acknowledged as an important element of planning. For example, the 1992 Rio Declaration on Environment and Development calls for:

> . . . the participation of all concerned citizens, at the relevant level. At the national level, each individual shall have appropriate access to information concerning the environment that is held by public authorities . . . States shall facilitate and encourage public awareness and participation by making information widely available (Popovic, 1993).

Education includes not only formal school curricula, but also media coverage and government dissemination of information. At a minimum, meaningful citizen participation is based on access to information, including the simple fact "that information exists and is available" (Popovic, 1993). Of cource, education alone will not increase the success of watershed management efforts, but it helps to create a more complete understanding of the consequences of local actions. Accordingly, it contributes to greater acceptance of both the decisionmaking process and the outcomes of that process (Dietz et al., 1989; Popovic, 1993). Given the range and complexity of many problems, public support for corrective policies requires an understanding of the "downstream" environmental consequences of local actions. This knowledge creates the potential for individuals

Box 8.1
Balancing Water Quality and Rural Community Viability: Management of the New York City Watershed

Management of the New York City (NYC) watershed provides a clear example of linkages between upstream and downstream popula- tions. Interests of the two may be very different, and actions that benefit some may create costs for others. In this case, maintenance of a supply of high quality drinking water for downstream NYC residents might be realized at the expense of viable rural communities upstream. The NYC Watershed Agreement is an attempt to balance the interests of upstream and downstream residents.

Physical Characteristics

NYC collects its drinking water in upstate watersheds covering over 1,900 square miles in eight counties. This surface water supply and storage system is one of the largest in the world. Water is collected from 3 separate reservoir systems made up of 19 reservoirs and 3 controlled lakes connected by tunnels and aqueducts. The system is an engineer- ing marvel that daily transports about 1.4 billion gallons of water to NYC almost exclusively by means of gravity from the reservoirs, some of which are more than 125 miles from the city. The system, with a storage capac- ity of 550 billion gallons, provides drinking water to more than 8 million city residents from watersheds inhabited by about 235,000 residents living in about 60 rural communities. Drinking water for the rural water- shed residents is mostly well water.

This water supply system has been built over the past century as an alternative to drawing water from highly polluted sources like city ground- water and the Hudson River. The system has enabled NYC to avoid filtering about 90 percent of its drinking water supply as would be re- quired under the Surface Water Treatment Rule issued by the U.S. Envi- ronmental Protection Agency under authority of the federal Safe Drinking Water Act. In 1993 NYC's estimates of construction costs for such filtra- tion facilities range up to $6 billion with annual operating expenses esti- mated at more than $300 million. To avoid filtration, NYC would, among other things, have to develop a watershed protection program to reduce the risks of waterborne diseases. This plan would have to address both

continued

Box 8.1 continued

cumulative and episodic impacts of pollution originating from environmentally insensitive land use and other behaviors in the watersheds.

Watershed Management Issues and Policy

In an attempt to meet the filtration avoidance conditions established by EPA, NYC began updating its Watershed Rules and Regulations, initially adopted in 1953 under the authority of the New York State Public Health Law. Certain land use restrictions would take effect under the revised Rules and Regulations. These would, for example, call for maintenance of buffer zones around water courses and reservoirs and restrictions on the siting and construction of sewerage and service connections. Such limitations would restrict the construction of roads, parking lots, and storage facilities for hazardous substances and wastes. NYC also considered acquiring watershed land. Under the most extreme scenario, NYC suggested an extensive land purchase program under which "all developable waste land in the entire watershed could be protected from further development by direct acquisition or conservation easements." However, this extreme land acquisition plan was never implemented and implementation of the revised Rules and Regulations was delayed because of strong opposition from the rural watershed communities. When plans to acquire just 80,000 acres were announced by NYC in 1993, the Coalition of Watershed Towns (CWT), representing about thirty watershed communities, filed suit to prevent NYC from implementing its filtration avoidance plans. CWT cited economic burdens on watershed residents resulting from restrictions placed on the use of privately owned lands. The CWT claimed that NYC would benefit almost exclusively from environmental measures imposed in the countryside.

The CWT lawsuit led to an impasse between the city and the watershed towns about a watershed management plan. In April 1995, New York State Governor George Pataki intervened by facilitating negotiations involving NYC, the CWT, EPA, selected county governments, and an ad hoc environmental coalition. In early 1997, the parties signed the Watershed Agreement for a comprehensive watershed protection plan. Under the terms of the agreement, EPA would permit NYC to avoid filtration of the currently unfiltered sources until April 2002, the city would invest up to $1.4 billion to protect its water over the next 15 years, the updated watershed Rules and Regulations would be implemented and enforced, and the city would purchase of environmentally sensitive land.

To balance the interests of upstream and downstream watershed residents, implementation of the revised Rules and Regulations, is accompanied with these important provisions:

(1) Land acquisition. NYC agrees not to take land by eminent do-

main, and instead acquire land "through the purchase of fee title to, or conservation easements on, environmentally sensitive, undeveloped land from willing sellers." These targeted purchases will be made at fair market value and the city will continue to pay property taxes on all land acquired. Almost $270 million have been allocated for land acquisition.

(2) Watershed Protection and Partnership Programs. About three-fourths of the almost $400 million earmarked for these programs are dedicated to infrastructure investments related to pollution prevention in the rural watersheds including the upgrade of public and privately-owned sewage treatment plants, septic system maintenance and rehabilitation, the construction of new centralized sewage systems and extension of sewer systems to correct existing problems, improved storage of sand, salt and de-icing materials, and stream corridor protection.

(3) Watershed Protection and Partnership Council. This forum is intended to aid in long-term watershed protection and the enhancement of the economic vitality of the watershed communities. The council will have no regulatory functions, but will assist in dispute resolution.

(4) Catskill Watershed Corporation. Watershed communities west of the Hudson River have also established a special relationship with NYC to carry out the Watershed Protection and Partnership Programs, carry out a comprehensive economic development study and administer NYC's $60 million contribution to the Catskill Fund for the Future. The latter will provide loans and grants for economic development projects that provide both job growth and watershed protection.

to recognize the common good that sometimes conflicts with their particular interests.

CRITICAL POINTS IN WATERSHED PLANNING

The purpose of watershed planning is to make practical choices from a full range of options that incorporate relevant economic, social, political, and ethical considerations. Such decisionmaking requires choosing between tradeoffs, but informed decisions can only be made when the tradeoffs are clearly specified. An accurate accounting of relevant alternatives and their tradeoffs requires the systematic observation and analysis provided by science. However, selection of particular options is often driven by values, and these may be in conflict (e.g., economic efficiency versus ethical considerations). To ensure that watershed management decisions are broadly understood and considered legitimate, all interested parties must participate in choosing between tradeoffs. Thus, effective watershed management must be based on a planning process that integrates both scientific analysis and public participation.

There is also growing consensus that planning processes should be organized to fit the specific context and problem at hand, and should not be linear or mechanistic, but rather recursive or iterative (Stern and Fineberg, 1996). Most planning models are similar, sharing four key steps: (1) defining the problem; (2) developing goals and finding alternative ways to reach the goals; (3) selecting the best alternative; (4) implementing the plan.

Figure 8.4 illustrates a model of a desirable watershed planning process that incorporates these basic steps. A central message provided by Figure 8.4 is that scientific uncertainty about the theory and tools of environmental management is a persistent concern that establishes the need for an iterative planning process. The success of a particular management plan may not be ensured without experimenting on the watershed to better understand the relationships among features and processes and to secure the data needed to build the necessary models of the system. Recognizing this uncertainty may influence the way plans are formulated and evaluated.

Also, the decisionmaking approach itself may need to be modified to deal with uncertainty. This accommodation has been termed "adaptive management." Adaptive management recognizes the limitations of current knowledge and data as a guide to decisionmaking. Adaptive management makes knowledge creation an objective (Lee, 1993). Adaptive management is akin to the research process, where the purpose of the activity is to cause change and simultaneously learn about relationships among unknown variables. But more than this simple notion of research is applicable, because the very questions being asked will change based on shifts in social priorities and on knowledge gained.

Gaining information through adaptive management means that there will be a watershed planning process that has a long time horizon in which actions will

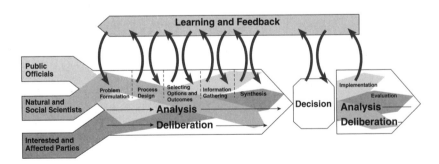

FIGURE 8.4 Schematic view of an integrated and iterative planning process. SOURCE: Stern and Fineberg, 1996.

be taken, monitoring will occur, and, based on that feedback and the new insights gained, adjustments to the plan will be made. Adaptive planning and management is a learn-by-doing approach to decisionmaking, and plan formulation and evaluation is affected by this reality.

Adaptive management places a premium on avoiding irreversible decisions. It means more than spending and hoping for some desired outcome. Decisionmaking must respond to new insights about social and economic priorities given by the interplay of interest groups in the decisionmaking process, and by a new appreciation of scientific understanding of watershed systems and new technologies. Numerous authors on policymaking have long advocated this concept of decisionmaking as the best combination of both the possible and the desirable (Simon, 1954; March and Simon, 1958; Lee, 1993; Stern and Fineberg, 1996).

With these general points in mind, there are several specific considerations that should be taken into account in any watershed planning process. Watershed planning should explicitly specify processes for identifying:

- the watershed problem and objectives for its resolution,
- the appropriate watershed scale,
- relevant stakeholders,
- tradeoffs among alternative solutions,
- shared values guiding selection of alternatives, and
- best actions to balance among tradeoffs.

These considerations provide a set of criteria for evaluating existing watershed planning frameworks.

Defining the watershed problem and objectives for its resolution. As stated earlier in this chapter, for watershed planning and management to be meaningful, the problem must be one that is best solved within a watershed framework. These are typically problems directly related to the use or value of the water resource. Careful statement of the problem to be addressed is essential to gathering appropriate science in analyzing the problem and alternative solutions. The problem should be formulated in such a way that it adequately addresses the concerns of those affected and is conducive to the specification of clearly measurable objectives for its solution (National Research Council, 1992; Shabman, 1996; Stern and Fineberg, 1996). Problem definition is a critical and difficult task that should that involve both scientific analysis and critical feedback from affected parties. Effective problem definition requires inputs of relevant interests and experts. Stakeholders, scientists, decisionmakers, and managers all need to participate in problem definition.

Identifying the appropriate scale. Watersheds can be defined at different scales, and smaller watersheds are nested within larger ones. The appropriate scale for watershed management effects should be selected on the basis of the problem at hand. The attempt to match problem and scale should address questions like the following: 1) What scale is optimal for solving the problem identified? 2) Can managers effectively influence critical areas, given the scale selected? (If the source of critical problems falls outside the watershed boundaries, management within the watershed will be ineffective.) 3) Is the scale selected large enough so that the problem and its solution can be effectively evaluated? 4) Is management at the selected scale politically feasible and economically affordable (National Research Council, 1992)?

Involving the relevant stakeholders. As mentioned earlier in this chapter, top-down planning has been widely criticized. These critiques have been based on normative, substantive, and instrumental grounds. The normative criticism of top-down approaches is based on the democratic principle that citizens have the right to meaningful participation in public decisions. Substantively based critiques of top-down planning note that more extensive public involvement better captures the collective wisdom of society. Thus effective stakeholder involvement helps ensure that problems are addressed more comprehensively and that solutions better address the needs of affected parties. Finally, in this chapter, top-down planning and management has often created in conflict and limited trust in public officials. As noted in *Understanding Risk* (Stern and Fineberg, 1996), "Simply providing people an opportunity to learn about the problem, the decision-making process, and the expected benefits of a decision may improve the likelihood that they will support the decision. Even if participation does not increase support for a decision, it may clear up misunderstandings about the nature of a controversy and the views of various participants. And it may contribute generally to building trust in the process, with benefits for dealing with similar issues for the future."

Specifying tradeoffs among alternative solutions. As noted above, science provides a basis for identifying alternative problem solutions. Scientific input provides information for stakeholders to identify tradeoffs between alternatives. This task requires the application of engineering, biological, and behavioral sciences to predict or measure the consequences of any of the alternatives under consideration. Economic valuation may be used to estimate the values of those outcomes. Specific accounting methods have been used for particular classes of outcomes. Unfortunately, no widely shared methods for the valuation of non-market goods have been developed. This led the Government Accounting Office, in a report on the Federal Energy Regulatory Commission, to conclude, "Given that the costs and benefits of various alternatives could not be fully quantified, we believe that the selection of one alternative over another is essentially a public policy decision in which the value judgements must be made about the costs, benefits, and any tradeoffs" (Shabman, 1996).

Identifying shared values that guide the selection of alternatives for problem resolution. Stern and Fineberg (1996) note, "Analysis can gather useful information about which tradeoffs citizens as individuals would prefer, but scientists cannot and should not be expected to make decisions that involve societal values." The identification of shared values that can guide decisionmaking raises the difficult question of the relationship between individuals and society. To what extent are individual values an expression of the person's embeddedness in society and its structures, or simply idiosyncratic ideas? If the former, then public hearings and public opinion surveys can be used to determine the dominant social values in the watershed that would make compelling the selection of certain alternatives. In this case, a set of values may constitute a cultural model or a sphere of values widely subscribed to within a particular community.

However, individuals often confront new problems without firmly established values, and only form the relevant values through a process of social interaction. When this is the case, the planning process must provide opportunities for interaction within the affected community. No one form of interaction will create a cultural model for making decisions, rather, a wide range of opportunities for interaction regarding the watershed problem is needed. These might include public hearings, citizen advisory committees, task forces, citizen juries or panels, opinion surveys, focus groups, meetings involving computer-assisted models, environmental education, and media exposure.

Taking action and balancing among tradeoffs. Most decisions will create winners and losers. Watershed management can proceed more smoothly and more equitably if it includes some mechanisms to compensate those who suffer significant losses from management decisions. It is important to address the costs incurred by some stakeholders in the watershed management process, because they may serve as disincentives to action. Past research has shown that short-term economic losses outweigh the effects of education and heightened awareness in inducing landowners to solve environmental problems (Napier et al., 1998). Prospects of economic loss can create a foundation for more widespread public opposition, which has been shown to be one of the most important obstacles to progress in ecosystem management nationwide (Yaffee et al., 1996). A number of such compensation mechanisms that may be useful in watershed context have been developed to deal with this barrier to positive changes in environmental behavior.

Over the past two decades, environmental regulation has evolved to better recognize tradeoffs involved in the implementation of management plans. Government policies have been under pressure to become more flexible, turning away from "one size fits all" command-and-control regulation to more flexible performance standards, fees and charges as incentive systems, and more recently, watershed-based effluent trading systems (EPA, 1996).

There are different means for dealing with costs and benefits associated with the implementation of watershed plans. At small scales, where financial and opportunity costs are modest, voluntary actions may be motivated by education about watershed conditions and the alternatives available to change those conditions. Basic information may encourage people to voluntarily change behaviors;

that is, they will not see making the behavioral change as a cost, because their values are changed by education. However, implementation through education usually needs to be supplemented with other implementation tools.

Acceptance of regulation is often purchased with cash transfers. Also, "voluntary" changes in behavior are often the consequences of receiving cash payment or tax subsidy. Successful transfer payment systems require a measurable environmental goal and a governmental willingness to pay for its achievement.

As a result, securing funds for watershed management has been an important theme in federal policy implementation for much of this century. Financing watershed management for such transfers and for program administration is a central challenge that must be addressed in the face of changing social objectives for watersheds and changing intergovernmental responsibilities.

Programs that fund compensation payments to adversely affected landowners and owners of water rights are promising options for application in watershed management. To preserve an existing land use, blocks of land may be designated as off limits to certain development, with landowners compensated for giving up those development rights. Under purchase of development rights (PDR) programs, landowners are compensated with public funds. Such programs can be very expensive.

To implement such programs without major expenditures of public funds, transfer of development rights (TDR) programs have been developed. TDR programs compensate landowners for lost development rights by assigning a certain number of transferable development credits from land in a preservation area to an area deemed more capable of sustaining high levels of development. Landowners in the designated development areas are required to buy development credits from the preservation area, and in return are allowed to develop properties at densities exceeding the limits set by current zoning restrictions. The market price of development credits times the number of credits held by each landowner determines the level of compensation. Unlike a PDR program, the buyer of development rights (credits) is not a public agency. Instead, payment for the development credits is secured through the market created for these development credits. Thus when specifying a growth area, TDR administrators must ensure that adequate demand will exist for development credits. Also, program administrators must ensure that each landowner in the preservation area is issued an acceptable number of development credits. Finally, program administrators need to overcome transaction costs or other factors inhibiting free negotiations. For instance, the administrators might ensure the legal legitimacy of development credits or facilitate buyers' and sellers' contacts and subsequent negotiations through a central TDR bank. Although not yet widely used, the TDR concept has been used in many habitat conservation plans under the Endangered Species Act recently, and in some state-level environmental preservation programs as well (Pfeffer and Lapping, 1994).

An alternative to regulating land use and creating "losers" is to create positive incentives for land use change. The promotion of new markets for nontraditional watershed services, such as hunting leases, to encourage and reward habitat protection is one example. Finally, trading in various "rights" (e.g., development rights or effluent allowances) can provide a means of minimizing losses suffered by any particular party as a result of watershed management decisions. Box 8.2 describes the importance of collaborative decisionmaking in an ecosystem management context, as well as other elements considered essential to effective planning and implementation.

Planning Protocols of Selected Agencies

Federal agencies have historically played a central role in watershed management (Adler, 1995). Even with the current explosion of local watershed management efforts, federal agencies continue to play an important role in these collaborative planning processes (Kenney and Rieke, 1997). At least six federal agencies are likely to have a continuing involvement in watershed management (the Environmental Protection Agency, the Forest Service, the Bureau of Reclamation, the Natural Resources Conservation Service, the Army Corps of Engineers, and the Tennessee Valley Authority), and their planning protocols are described here.

Environmental Protection Agency

The Environmental Protection Agency (EPA) has advocated a watershed approach to water quality and more general environmental protection since 1991. In contrast to earlier top-down regulation, EPA's more recent watershed planning attempts to deal with environmental management on a community- or watershed-specific basis. This approach is intended to best address specific watershed needs in context. EPA intends watershed planning to be comprehensive, incorporating a complete range of scientific expertise and a full range of interests, or stakeholder concerns. The "watershed approach framework" advocated by EPA addresses most of the critical points in watershed planning identified above.

EPA has identified a set of coordinated management activities to identify watershed problems and objectives for their resolution. One of these activities is "problem prioritization and resource targeting," which takes into account stakeholder concerns within the relevant watershed unit. Closely related is "goal setting," which ideally begins with established water quality standards but reviews and (if appropriate) revises those standards to better meet expectations within the local watershed. These activities are informed by data that accurately assess the watershed's aquatic resources; baseline parameters and evaluative standards are based on existing water quality goals. These data are provided by a comprehensive monitoring program that maintains an up-to-date record of local conditions, but which inventories references of already existing key data.

EPA attempts to base the geographic scope of management units on hydro-

Box 8.2
Effective Ecosystem Management

There are significant similarities in the philosophies behind watershed management and ecosystem management, and current thinking about ecosystem management has lessons to offer to watershed managers. A major document outlining the principles of ecosystem management (Keystone Center, 1996) noted six elements that the workshop members believed would help promote the success of ecosystem management initiatives:

- Use a collaborative decisionmaking process.
- Use an adaptive process.
- Make the best use of science and data.
- Incorporate regional and national interests into locally driven initiatives.
- Emphasize market-based incentives.
- Use an ecosystem-based approach when developing on-the-ground management strategies.

According to the group, collaboration among the organizations and individuals involved in the initiative is critical to success because it allows all parties' concerns to be aired and potentially resolved. The report contains a detailed discussion of the collaborative process, but some of the elements of effective collaboration include: that participant roles and authorities be clearly defined, trust built among participants, and leadership promoted; that participants approach the process with an open mind and willingness to learn; that organizers recognize limits on participants' time and resources; and that cultural differences and power imbalances be addressed.

Regarding the use of adaptive management, the group notes that it is a mechanism for allowing informed decisionmaking and addressing uncertainty by structuring initiatives as experiments in which the results are used to continually correct course. Active adaptive management results in a faster rate of learning and greater accountability to management goals. Science and the information it generates are also integral to effec-

logical considerations, although the agency considers other factors such as political boundaries as well. Although EPA acknowledges that watersheds may be defined at different scales and that the scale identified has implications for the roles of political authorities and relationships between stakeholders, it does not explicitly link problem and scale identification. EPA seems to be most concerned

tive management because credible, objective, relevant information helps support decisionmaking. Comprehensive monitoring, too, is essential as support for adaptive management.

The stakeholders involved in planning are likely to hold disparate views, including sometimes a collision of national interests (as expressed through law, regulation, or agency action) with the economic and lifestyle interests of the local communities. The report suggests ways to integrate local and non-local interests. It notes that not all participants will see consensus solutions as the goal, so the group must be broadly representative and convinced that its course is appropriate to keep divisive outside influences to a minimum.

The report recognizes that regulations have a role in motivating change, but stresses that they may not always be the most effective way of proceeding. The workshop participants see increased emphasis on market-based incentive approaches as having significant potential to reduce conflict and provide landowners and members of the business community with reasons to contribute to solutions. Such incentives might include programs to support conservation banking, forest certification, and forest stewardship. Tax reductions for open space can encourage protection of priority resources and changes in property appraisal procedures (to not tax on the highest potential use) can remove disincentives to retaining open space. Effluent trading in watersheds can be used to achieve economic efficiencies while still meeting national water quality standards and local water use goals.

Finally, the report addresses using an ecosystem-based approach when developing on-the-ground management strategies. It notes that ecosystem management builds on traditional multiple use and sustained yield principles but goes further in considering how commodity and noncommodity resources are used.

In addition to discussing elements of effective ecosystem management, the Keystone report provides a significant overview of this emerging field, addressing definitions, steps for implementation, participation, the collaborative process, and policy recommendations.

SOURCE: Keystone Center, 1996

with the identification of "geographic management units," that is—spatial units within which watershed policies are implemented and monitored.

The importance of broad stakeholder involvement in the planning process is heavily stressed by EPA, which urges that watershed planning and management partnerships include representatives from all levels of government within the watershed's boundaries as well as representatives of conservation districts, public interest groups, industries, academic institutions, private landowners, concerned citizens, and any others with an interest in the management of the watershed. Effective stakeholder involvement, according to EPA, should create not only environmental protection, but community building and lasting solutions as well.

Sound management relies on scientific inputs in problem identification and goal setting as well as in the development of solutions. The EPA encourages watershed partnerships between stakeholders to develop plans that are consistent with applicable regulations of relevant levels of government and the needs and concerns of all stakeholders (EPA, 1997). Any effort to incorporate such a broad array of parties is likely to encounter conflicts of interest in the development of management plans.

EPA does not acknowledge this problem, however, and offers no procedures for identifying tradeoffs between different options. This omission implies that an optimal and mutually acceptable solution can be developed and that a common set of values will lead to a conclusion. This assumption leads EPA to understate the need for compensation tools to address unequal burdens shouldered by some interests in the implementation of watershed management plans.

Forest Service

The Forest Service is mandated by the National Forest Management Act (NFMA) to give comprehensive notice and allow for comment on forest planning and project-level decisionmaking. The products of this process are approved "Land and Resources Management Plans (LRMPs)," or "Forest Plans." These plans consist of ten steps: (1) identifying purpose and need; (2) planning criteria; (3) inventorying data and information; (4) analyzing the management situation; (5) formulating alternatives; (6) estimating effects of alternatives; (7) evaluating alternatives; (8) recommending preferred alternatives; (9) approving the plan; (10) monitoring and evaluation.

The NFMA requires the Forest Service to continuously monitor, evaluate, and adjust these plans. The plans establish broad multiple-use goals and objectives for administrative units. The LRMPs are comprehensive plans that establish the direction for future management of forests. More specific problems, goals, and objectives are established under particular projects that are carried out within the framework of LRMPs and the National Environmental Policy Act.

LRMPs must comply with site-specific requirements associated with federal environmental laws like the Clean Water Act (CWA). Watershed management provides a means by which the Forest Service addresses CWA provisions for nonpoint source pollution control. Watersheds are considered one of the multiple uses of forests in addition to outdoor recreation, range, timber, wildlife and fish, and wilderness. Thus the identification of the watershed scale is a secondary consideration subsumed under the multiple-use goals and objectives of Forest Service administrative units, and there are no provisions for watershed scale

assessments. Doppelt et al. (1993) note, "Planning for nontimber surface resources including riparian and flood plain management, is to a large degree determined by limitations on timber production—despite the fact that the NFMA re-
peatedly directs that the forests be managed for 'multiple use' of renewable
resources."

The Forest Service planning process solicits public comment on proposed
plans and projects through standard NEPA procedures (e.g., environmental impact statements). But stakeholder inputs are also solicited as a first step in the
planning process, as well as in the EIS draft review. In response, about 1000
administrative appeals and 20 to 30 lawsuits are filed annually in response to
Forest Service timber plan decisions and NEPA compliance. Consequently, the
courts provide an important mechanism for identifiying tradeoffs between alternative courses of action, as well as the means for selecting final actions (U.S.
Forest Service, 1997).

Bureau of Reclamation

The Bureau of Reclamation (BOR) has developed a guidebook, *Achieving
Efficient Water Management* (U.S. BOR, 1996), which details a five-step planning process. This process begins with problem definition and information gathering. The guidebook emphasizes that these activities go hand-in-hand and are
intended to uncover information gaps and uncertainties about problems. This
phase of the process considers the physical setting, water rights, permits and contracts, lands and crops, district operation and operating policies, water pricing
and accounting, the inventory of water resources, other water uses, and existing
water management and conservation programs. Goals and priority are closely
related to problem identification in the BOR planning process, and are intended
to chart a direction for water management and to establish yardsticks by which to
measure progress in meeting goals.

The BOR planning process does not address the issue of appropriate watershed scale. BOR water management is centered around districts, not watersheds.
This organizational artifact diverts BOR planning from addressing watershed issues directly. BOR planning guidelines do, however, stress the importance of
stakeholder involvement in creating effective and credible plans. BOR seeks to
include water users, local community leaders, state and federal agency staff, and
representatives of various interest groups in the planning process. According to
the BOR, stakeholder involvement: (1) seeks to build credibility, (2) identify and
understand the diverse concerns and values of parties potentially affected by the
plan, and (3) develop a consensus among divergent interests.

A critical evaluation of alternative solutions is the third step in the BOR
planning process. This phase considers such factors as costs, water savings, flow
and use patterns, environmental impacts, legal and institutional considerations,
and political acceptability. At this stage the acceptability of certain solutions

should be considered, as well as possible revisions of the candidate solutions. The BOR planning guidelines state explicit criteria to consider in the selection of alternatives. The list of criteria provided suggest alternative values to be considered in the selection of particular solutions. The suggested criteria include relative implementation costs, ease of implementation, costs and benefits of water saved, environmental effects, and the extent to which proposed measures complement or conflict with other measures already in place. While the BOR planning guidelines acknowledge potential conflicts or tradeoffs associated with the implementation of a particular plan, they provide no compensation measures in conjunction with plan implementation. Implicit in the guidelines is the assumption that a plan can be developed and implemented that avoids unacceptable tradeoffs between different interests.

Natural Resources Conservation Service

The Natural Resources Conservation Service (NRCS) provides conservation planning and technical assistance to individuals, groups, and units of government and lays out basic planning guidelines in its *National Planning Procedures Handbook* (U.S. NRCS, 1996). These procedures are intended to assist in the development of plans based on ecological, economic, and social considerations. NRCS presents a three-phase planning process with nine steps. The process is intended to be used in a dynamic, iterative mode. It can be used for a number of planning purposes, one of which is the development of "area-wide conservation plans" for watersheds.

The first phase in the NRCS planning process (containing four steps) is data collection and analysis. The initial step in this phase is to identify resource problems, opportunities, and concerns in the watershed. Once the problem has been identified and clearly defined, the next step is to determine specific objectives. These objectives should incorporate the needs of watershed stakeholders and their values in the watershed's management. The third step in the planning process is to collect natural resource, economic, social, and other relevant data on the watershed. Analysis, the fourth step, is intended to provide a basis for the developing and evaluate alternative solutions. NRCS calls for a scientific approach in this step, which establishes cause-and-effect relationships related to the problem under consideration. Results of this analysis may be used to redefine the problem.

The collection and analysis of data in the first phase is intended to provide a benchmark for subsequent analysis of progress in problem resolution. Missing, however, is explicit consideration of the appropriate watershed scale related to the problem identified. The failure to directly address this issue might be because the *National Planning Procedures Handbook* is a generic document that was not written specifically for watershed management. It would seem that explicit consideration of the appropriate watershed scale could be incorporated into Step Four, "analysis," and into the problem reformulation emerging from the analysis.

NRCS labels the second phase of its planning process, "decision support." This phase begins with the critical fifth step of "alternative formulation." The purpose of this step is to "develop alternatives that will achieve the objectives of the . . . stakeholders, solve identified problems, take advantage of opportunities, and prevent additional problems from occurring (U.S . NRCS, 1996)." The NRCS explicitly calls for the development of multiple alternatives that allow for choices based on various criteria that address the cultural, social, ecological, and eco-nomic conditions of the watershed. These criteria are identified by means of active stakeholder involvement that includes the public, special interest groups, and state and federal agencies. To this end, NRCS advocates "coordinated re-source management," a collaborative, nonadversarial decisionmaking process. According to NRCS (1996), "A guiding principle of coordinated resource man-agement is that those who live, work, and recreate on a given piece of land are the people most interested in and capable of developing plans for its use."

Step six is the evaluation of alternatives. This evaluation considers tradeoffs between the alternatives taking into account social, economic, and ecological fac-tors. The seventh step in this phase of the planning process is decisionmaking.

According to the NCRS handbook, decisions are taken by the responsible party after public review and comment are obtained. Implicit in the NRCS plan-ning process is the assumption that an alternative can be found that does not disproportionately burden any stakeholders with costs. Consequently, the NRCS planning process does not explicitly discuss compensation measures. NCRS does acknowledge the need to carefully consider social and economic considerations in the planning process. For example, NRCS (1996) notes, "Some social and ethnic groups have land use ethics that may conflict with some NCRS conserva-tion practices." However, the NRCS planning handbook gives the impression that merely taking these factors into consideration will ensure success.

Once a plan is chosen, the process enters Phase Three, "application." The two steps in this phase are plan implementation and evaluation. According to NRCS, the plan is to be evaluated upon implementation to determine if it is meet-ing objectives. Plans are adjusted based on the results of evaluation. Such evalu-ation is expected to be an ongoing process.

U.S. Army Corps of Engineers

The U.S. Army Corps of Engineers (USACE) has longstanding planning pro-cedures. These consist of four principal elements. The first of these elements is problem definition and the statement of planning objectives that will establish both the desired direction for change in the watershed and measurable criteria of that change. This element of the Corps' planning procedures recognizes that clear statement of objectives is essential to the formulation of alternative solu-tions. The Corps does not explicitly state procedures for identifying appropriate watershed scale. Instead it uses general planning procedures, which can be applied to watersheds.

The second element in the Corps' planning process is the formulation of alternatives, which seeks to consider all measures available for addressing the planning objectives. The formulation of alternatives is followed closely by another element of the planning process, the measurement of the effects of alternatives on the planning objectives. Measurement of these outputs provides data for the final element in the USACE planning process, formal valuation of the alternatives.

Like all federal agencies the USACE uses the *Economic and Environmental Principles and Guidelines for Water and Related Land Resources Implementation Studies* (U.S. Water Resources Council, 1983). This protocol is intended to summarize measured effects of the adoption of a given alternative in four accounts: 1) national economic development, 2) regional economic development, 3) environmental quality, 4) other social effects. The Principles and Guidelines protocol provides an interesting mechanism for systematically considering different values and identifying a shared understanding of their relative importance. The Corps' planning process does not, however, specify a process for balancing the tradeoffs involved in implementing of a given alternative. Shabman (1996) explains the importance of the Corps' planning process in providing support to decisionsmakers: "In the future, . . . planning will be focused as much on building external agreements on the 'value' of the preferred alternative as on documenting value through computation called for by the agency budget authorities."

Tennessee Valley Authority

The Tennessee Valley Authority (TVA) launched its Clean Water Initiative (CWI) in 1992. The CWI is a programmatic alternative to regulatory and enforcement solutions to water quality problems (Poppe and Hurst, 1997). This alternative focuses on integrating local residents, businesses, and government agencies in watershed protection efforts. The key organizing feature of TVA's watershed planning approach is the River Action Team (RAT). This organizational feature won praise from Water Quality 2000's Model Watershed Committee. In evaluating TVA's CWI, the committee concluded, "The River Action Team concept should be expanded, promoted and replicated in other watersheds (Model Watershed Committee, 1994)." RATs are multidisciplinary teams made up of water resource experts like biologists and environmental engineers as well as community specialists and environmental educators. Team members ideally serve long-term assignments to specific watersheds to allow them to work closely with stakeholders building trust and to gain a deep knowledge of resource conditions in the watershed. The watershed is the RAT's fixed geographic area, and it may transcend various political boundaries. Watersheds are conceived of on a large scale (e.g., river basin) by TVA, so RATs have a high degree of flexibility in identifying the appropriate scale for dealing with particular problems. However, the variation of watershed scale to address specific problems in not dealt with explicitly by TVA's CWI guidelines.

RATs are expected to be able to deal with problems as they evolve. To do so, RATs muster resources (funds, staff, and expertise) and stakeholder support. TVA strongly emphasizes the latter point, stating a strong commitment to include all stakeholders—critics as well as supporters—in the watershed planning process. At the same time, TVA stresses development of partnerships to solve watershed problems. These partnerships are important tools in the leveraging of resources.

Problems are identified with help from continuous resource assessment based on TVA's ecological monitoring program. These assessment data are analyzed and used to identify specific problems and measurable objectives and to prioritize problems for treatment. These data and analyses drive TVA's use of a project selection matrix to prioritize projects. In making such analyses, TVA takes into account tradeoffs made in selecting some projects over others. While the same principles could be applied to the selection of alternative solutions to a particular problem, TVA does not discuss this type of analysis. An implicit assumption is that there will be an unambiguously best solution to any problem. However, TVA does recognize that not all stakeholders will be equally informed about watersheds, and that lack of awareness and understanding of the functioning and value of aquatic ecosystems is an important source of environmentally harmful behaviors and lack of support for watershed management. CWI strives to involve stakeholders in watershed projects as a means of increasing knowledge, changing behavior, and revealing shared values regarding the environment and the need for watershed management. However, as noted earlier, even widely held values are unlikely to be held by everyone in a community or watershed. And while many interests may be served by a given plan to solve a watershed problem, other interests may suffer. Like the other agencies reviewed here, TWA has not specified mechanisms by which those adversely affected by watershed plans will be compensated (Ungate, 1996; Poppe and Hurst, 1997).

In concentrating this review of watershed planning guidelines on major governmental institutions, we have not addressed the most profound development in the past decade, the growing number of local, often voluntary watershed organizations. One study identified 76 ongoing watershed efforts in just 11 of the western states, these efforts all had significant local citizen involvement (Natural Resources Law Center, 1996). Such organizations are found nationwide, and their numbers have increased substantially in the past decade. This trend closely parallels the growth of grassroots environmental organizations since the early 1980s (Freudenburg and Steinsapir, 1992). While much of the grassroots movement has been concerned with environmental contamination, local watershed initiatives are focused on "resource management problems related to the allocation, use, or quality of water" (Natural Resources Law Center, 1996).

Because of a lack of comprehensive data on local watershed initiatives, this report cannot evaluate their planning procedures. Depending on the type of local watershed group and its mission, planning activities may be more or less formal. In any case, the critical points regarding the watershed planning procedures of the more formal agency efforts described above can serve as useful guidelines to more informally operating groups. And formal planning procedures are of direct relevance to watershed initiatives led by government agencies or working closely with them. Increasingly, local watershed initiatives involve multiagency collaboration. Kenney and Rieke (1997) conducted case studies of a dozen local watershed initiatives in the western United States and found that most had active involvement from some federal government agency. Most of the 76 local watershed initiatives in the West mentioned above also had significant federal involvement (Kenney and Rieke, 1997).

Given the importance of federal involvement in watershed management, it is useful to review critical points in planning addressed by the agencies reviewed above. Table 8.3 shows how these agencies addressed (or failed to address) critical points of watershed planning. All the agencies' planning procedures gave substantial attention to identification of the problem and objectives for its resolution. Tieing the problem to the appropriate watershed scale was a weak point for all the planning procedures. This weakness may be overstated, however, because the agencies follow planning guidelines issued for general purposes and not specifically for the treatment of watersheds. Nevertheless, watershed scale is not typically treated as a variable component in the planning process. The importance of involving stakeholders in environmental planning has received increasing attention, especially given the growth of NIMBY (Not-In-My-Backyard) opposition to the siting of environmental hazards and property rights protests against environmental regulation. Our review shows that agencies generally are aware of the importance of stakeholder involvement, and that planning procedures increasingly include explicit mechanisms for it.

Some planning procedures include very strong mechanisms for identifying tradeoffs associated with solutions to watershed problems. Most of these rely heavily on scientific analysis. In marked contrast, some protocols fail to address the distribution of costs and benefits associated with alternative solutions—a failure that stems from the assumption that widely accepted solutions are the norm. This shortcoming may lead to an inability to recognize sources of conflict embedded in any particular alternative. Recognizing that some stakeholders may disproportionately bear the costs of watershed management practices and developing mechanisms to address such inequalities can help avert or resolve such conflicts.

It is extremely difficult, however, to account for costs and benefits associated with watershed management, because many "goods" are incommensurable (Anderson, 1993). To reach agreement on who bears the greatest burden and who reaps the most benefits, there must be some agreement on the applicable accounting unit. Most commonly this accounting is done in monetary terms, but such

TABLE 8.3 Critical Points in Watershed Planning As Addressed by Selected Agency Planning Protocols

Clearly Specified Processes for Identifiying the:	EPA[a]	FS[b]	BOR[c]	NRCS[d]	USACE[e]	TVA[f]
(1) Watershed problem and objectives for its resolution	YES	YES	YES	YES	YES	YES
(2) Appropriate stakeholders	NO	NO	NO	NO	NO	NO
(3) Involvement of relevant stakeholders	YES	YES	YES	YES	YES	YES
(4) Considerations tradeoffs among alternative solutions	NO	YES	YES	YES	YES	NO
(5) Shared values to guide selection of alternatives	NO	NO	YES	YES	YES	YES
(6) Best actions to balance costs and benefits among tradeoffs	NO	NO	NO	NO	NO	NO

[a]EPA: Environmental Protection Agency
[b]FS: Forest Service
[c]BOR: Bureau of Reclamation
[d]NRCS: National Resources Conservation Service
[e]USACE: U.S. Army Corps of Engineers
[f]TVA: Tennessee Valley Authority

accounting is not preferred or accepted under all circumstances. While the agency planning procedures review did provide some mechanisms for identifying of shared values that might help select solutions, these mechanisms were weak and may not provide adequate guidance for determining the relative importance of different values in the decisionmaking process.

Even if there is agreement on the relative importance of different values, and decisions are made based on such consensus, some stakeholders may still bear a disproportionate share of the costs. None of the planning procedures addressed how appropriate compensation could be considered and then carried out. Given growing concern with environmental equity and the development of compensation mechanisms, it is surprising that agency planning procedures give so little attention to this point.

CONCLUSION

This chapter began by posing a key question in watershed planning: what is an effective process in relating science, policy, and public participation? One key conclusion is that science play a prominent role in any watershed planning process. Planning on a watershed basis and demands robust, interdisciplinary scientific inputs that not only answer key questions, but offer insights into the limitations of our understanding of watershed processes. Acknowledgment that knowledge is incomplete establishes the need for continuing scientific inputs in an adaptive, or recursive, planning process. Sound science provides the basis for establishing realistic limits on what can be accomplished and identifies tradeoffs associated with different alternatives. However, the choice of particular solutions to adopt is ultimately a political one. The role of science is to respond to the information needs of policymakers and the public, and to inform the formulation of watershed management policy. Thus, there are clear roles for scientists and policymakers. Watershed management plans that provide explicitly defined checks and balances between scientists and policymakers are likely to be the most robust over time.

Science provides information, but it cannot determine which values should guide watershed management policies. These values must emerge from the watershed planning process through public participation. Contemporary watershed planning increasingly involves a broad array of stakeholders. However, meaningful stakeholder involvement is often difficult to achieve within existing institutions. Political representation often is organized in jurisdictions where the boundaries do not correspond to those of watersheds. Thus established mechanisms of political involvement may be ineffective in a watershed context, and planning must therefore be seen as part of a process that strives to create a watershed community. In the long run, effective watershed management will encourage changes in personal behaviors and land management practices that threaten the local resource base.

Creating a sense of community in a watershed can be a difficult task, but there are some important approaches and considerations that can increase the likelihood of success. One approach is collaborative planning, which consists of bringing together all the interests in the watershed and working together to come up with the solutions. The basic idea is asking not how you should change to accommodate me, but how I should change to accommodate the others in the group so that we reach our goal. Effective collaborative planning acknowledges that solutions to watershed problems do not affect all interests equally; some benefit and others incur costs. Effective collaboration in watershed planning acknowledges these disparities in order to reach just and equitable outcomes. Collaborative planning works best when all those affected have a reasonable understanding of watershed problems, alternative solutions, and the tradeoffs involved in choosing some solutions over others. Thus, education about watershed processes, legal and institutional constraints, and opportunities is an important element in collaborative planning. Education about the watershed should promote and support the integration of science, policy, and public participation. Sound, integrated policy can only be achieved when the education about the watershed assures that watershed management decisions are broadly understood and considered legitimate by the public. It is also necessary that all parties participate in making the choices between tradeoffs, and that those tradeoffs are fully understood and supported.

Watershed planning may be organized in a variety of ways to address these issues. But whatever the organizational form chosen, the planning process should address six critical points: 1) the identification of the watershed problem and objectives for its resolution; 2) the appropriate watershed scale; 3) involvement of stakeholders; 4) tradeoffs among alternative solutions; 5) values guiding the selection of alternative solutions; 6) best action to balance among tradeoffs.

As indicated above, current federal agency planning procedures are strong on many of these critical points. All have clear procedures for identifying problems and objectives for their solutions, most pay careful attention to stakeholder involvement, and most consider tradeoffs involved in selecting between alternative problem solution. However, the agencies need to better match the watershed problem being solved to the appropriate watershed scale for intervention, and all agencies should give more attention to the identification of different values held by watershed stakeholders that can lead to conflicts over possible solutions. Many of the planning procedures seem to assume that general consensus about the preferred solution already exists or can be easily achieved. This assumption seems unrealistic. Failure to acknowledge fundamental differences in values can undermine the search for an acceptable means to address these differences. This point is closely related to another shortcoming in agency planning procedures: the identification of mechanisms to compensate those who bear a disproportionate share of the costs associated with the implementation of a watershed management plan. None of the agency planning procedures provided a means by which compensation could be considered and then carried out. By addressing these weaknesses, agencies could greatly strengthen their planning procedures and move watershed planning to a higher level of sophistication.

REFERENCES

Anderson, E. 1993. Value in Ethics and Economics. Cambridge, Mass.: Harvard University Press.

Bella, D. A. 1997. Organizational systems and the burden of proof. Pp. 617-638 In Stouter, D. J., P. A. Bison, and R. J. Naiman, (eds.) Pacific Salmon and Their Ecosystems: Status and Future Options. New York: Chapman and Hall.

Dietz, T., P. C. Stern, and R. W. Rycroft. 1989. Definitions of conflict and the legitimation of resources: The case of environmental risk. Sociological Forum 4(1):47-70.

Doppelt, R., M. Scurlock, C. Frissell, and J. Karr. 1993. Entering the Watershed: A New Approach to Save America's River Ecosystems. Washington, D.C.: Island Press.

Freudenberg, N., and C. Steinsapir. 1992. Not in our backyards: The grassroots environmental movement. Pp. 27-38 in American Environmentalism. Philadelphia: Taylor and Francis.

Kenney, D., and B. Rieke. 1997. Resource Management at the Watershed Level: An Assessment of the Changing Federal Role in the Emerging Era of Community-Based Watershed Management. Boulder, Colo.: University of Colorado, Natural Resource Law Center.

Keystone Center. 1996. The Keystone National Policy Dialogue on Ecosystem Management: Final Report. Keystone, Colorado: The Keystone Center.

Lee, Kai N. 1993. Compass and Gyroscope: Integrating Science and Politics for the Environment. Washington, D.C.: Island Press.

March, J. G. and H. A. Simon. 1958. Organizations. New York: Wiley.

Model Watershed Committee. 1994. Evaluation of a Watershed Approach to Clean Water: A Site Visit to the Tennessee Valley Authority and Evaluation of Their Clean Water Initiative. Alexandria, Va.: Water Quality 2000.

Moreau, D. H. 1994. Watershed Planning—What's New? What's Old? The Wayne S. Nichols Memorial Lecture. Ohio State University, November 17.

Naiman, R. J., J. J. Magnuson, D. M. McKnight, J. A. Stanford, and J. R. Karr. 1995. Freshwater ecosystems and their management: A national initiative. Science 270:584-585.

Napier, T. L., S. M. Napier, and J. Turdon. 1998. Soil and Water Conservation Policies and Programs: Successes and Failures. Ankeny, Iowa: Soil and Water Conservation Society Press.

National Research Council. 1992. Restoration of Aquatic Ecosystems: Science, Technology, and Public Policy. Washington, D.C.: National Academy Press.

National Research Council. 1995. Criteria for Watershed Sustainability. Washington, D.C.: National Academy Press.

Natural Resources Law Center. 1996. The Watershed Source Book: Watershed Based Solutions to Natural Resource Problems. Boulder, Colo.: University of Colorado, Natural Resources Law Center.

Pfeffer, J. J., and M. B. Lapping. 1994. Farmland preservation, development, rights and the theory of the growth machine: The views of planners. J. Rural Studies 10(3):233-248.

Popovic, N. A. F. 1993. The right to participate in decisions that affect the environment. Pace Environmental Law Review 19(2):683-709.

Poppe W., and R. Hurst. 1997. TVA's clean water initiative: A partnership approach to watershed improvement. WQI March/April 1997:39-43.

Priscoli, J. D. 1978. Implementing Public Involvement Programs in Federal Agencies. Pp. 97-108 in Langton, S. (ed.) Citizen Participation in America: Essays on the State of the Art. Lexington, Ky.: Lexington Books.

Rosenbaum, W. A. 1978. Public Involvement as Reform and Ritual: The Development of Federal Participation Programs. Pp. 81-96 in Langton, S. (ed.) Citizen Participation in America: Essays on the State of the Art. Lexington: Lexington Books.

Shabman, L. 1996. Environmental Restoration in the Army Corps of Engineers: Planning and Valuation Changes. Manuscript.

Simon, H. A. 1954. Administrative Behavior. New York: MacMillan.

Stanford, J. A., and G. C. Poole. 1996. A protocol for ecosystem management. Perspectives in Ecosystem Management 6(3):741-744.

Stern, P., and H. V. Fineberg, eds. 1996. Understanding Risk: Informing Decisions in a Democratic Society. Washington, D.C.: National Academy Press.

Ungate, C. D. 1996. Tennessee Value Authority's Clean Water Initiative: Building Partnerships for Watershed Improvement. Journal of Planning and Management 39(1):113-122.

U.S. Department of Agriculture, Forest Service. 1993. the Power of Collaborative Planning: Report of the National Workshop.

U.S. Department of Agriculture, Forest Service. 1997. Overview of Forest Planning and Project Level Decisionmaking. Internet: http://www.fs.fed.us/forum/nepa/decisionm/index.html.

U.S. Environmental Protection Agency (EPA). 1993. The Watershed Approach. Annual Report 1992. EPA840-S-93-001. Washington, D.C.: U.S. EPA.

U.S. Environmental Protection Agency (EPA). 1996. Draft Framework for Watershed-Based Trading. EPA 800-R-96-001. Office of Water. Washington, D.C.: U.S. EPA.

U.S. Environmental Protection Agency (EPA). 1997. The Watershed Approach. Internet: http://www.epa.gov/OWOW/watershed/wa1.html.

U.S. Natural Resources Conservation Service. 1996. National Planning Procedures Handbook. NRCS 180-vi-NPPH, Revision 1. Washington, D.C.: USDA.

U.S. Water Resources Council. 1983. Economic and Environmental Principles and Guidelines for Water and Related Land Resources Implementation Studies. Washington, D.C.: U.S. Government Printing Office.

Weatherford, G. D. N.D. From Basin to Hydrocommons: Integrated Water Management Without Regional Governance. Western Water Policy Project, Discussion Series Paper, No. 5. Natural Resources Law Center, University of Colorado, School of Law.

Yaffee, S. L., A. F. Phillips, I. C. Frentz, P. W. Hardy, S. M. Maleki, and B. E. Thorpe. 1996. Ecosystem Management in the United States: An Assessment of Current Experience. Washington, D.C.: Island Press.

There is a need to stabilize, enhance, and restore to some degree the nation's aquatic and riparian ecosystems, and particularly to restore more natural discharge regimes and ensure habitats for native species. One step toward these goals is to reduce pollution and protect riparian zones with ecologically sound management practices such as these contour buffer strips in Iowa. Credit: USDA-Natural Resources Conservation Service.

9

Conclusions and Recommendations

The Committee on Watershed Management began this study with the hypothesis that a watershed perspective is the best framework for integrating social, ecological, and economic aspects of water and water-related management issues. In this analysis, we found some cases where our hypothesis was true, and some where it was not. We also identified ways the watershed approach could be improved in its application. We confirmed that uncertainty associated with a watershed perspective was least at small scales and in relatively simple systems and greatest at large scales and in complex systems. Overall, the committee finds that the philosophy of watershed management is sound but there still is significant uncertainty associated with how to implement it, particularly in large watersheds. There is a real need to motivate changes in institutional behavior to make watershed approaches more effective, and for continued research targeted to fulfill the promise of watershed management.

This chapter summarizes the committee's analysis of how to improve the nation's implementation of watershed management, including some important general principles that place watershed management in a broad context, comments on reauthorization of the Clean Water Act, and recommendations for various agencies and others involved in watershed-related activities.

SUCCESSFUL WATERSHED MANAGEMENT

It is not possible, or necessarily desirable, to restore the nation's waters and watersheds to completely natural conditions to provide healthful water resources. But there is a need to stabilize, enhance, and restore to some degree our aquatic and riparian ecosystems—that is, to achieve more "normative" ecological conditions. Normative conditions occur where more natural discharge regimes predominate and where aquatic and riparian habitats are present in sufficient quantity, quality, and diversity to sustain food webs dominated by native species (Graf, 1996; Stanford, 1997; Stanford et al., 1996). Normative does not imply pristine conditions. Rather, the goal is to normalize key ecosystem attributes and processes to the extent that goals relating to water quality and quantity, fish production, biodiversity, and other watershed goods and services are met and sustained.

Successful watershed management strives for a better balance between ecosystem and watershed integrity and provision of human social and economic goals. Stanford (1997) discussed several general objectives that can be managed within a watershed context which can help the nation achieve more normative watershed conditions:

Reduce pollution sources by developing watershed water quality standards, such as using the concept of total maximum daily loads to control nonpoint source pollutants. Federal, state, and local laws provide water quality standards that safeguard drinking water, but they do not necessarily protect ecosystems or watershed integrity. One example is the drinking water standards for nitrate and nitrogen, which were designed to prevent methemoglobinemia in infants (blue baby syndrome), but which in many cases allow dissolved nitrogen levels high enough to cause excessive algae growths in streams and lakes.

Protect and enhance riparian zones with ecologically sound management practices such as buffer zones. The vegetation that grows along the edges of waterways, especially wetland vegetation and floodplain vegetation, provides critically important borders that buffer lakes and streams against upland pollution and streambank erosion. These riparian zones provide ecological functions, support native plants and animals, and can increase property values. Yet there are tremendous differences among the riparian protection requirements for different types of land use (NRC, 1996). Forested headwaters often receive far greater protection than urban or agricultural floodplain areas. Controls and incentives for riparian conservation practices are needed to prevent overgrazing, excessive logging, road building, invasions of exotic plants, and encroachment of urban and industrial development in important buffer areas.

Recognize in law and regulations that ground and surface waters interact. Connections between ground and surface waters are poorly appreciated, especially in legal frameworks. Yet many aquifers are constantly exchanging water with streams and rivers. In floodplains and riparian zones, ground water that upwells from alluvial aquifers can produce a diverse array of habitat types.

Recognize in land management activities that rivers need room to roam, and their floodplains are inherently subject to flooding. Floodplains act as storage sites for floodwaters, and the ability of floodplains to store and moderate high flows is strongly influenced by the width of the floodplain, the development of an overflow channel system, and the condition of riparian vegetation. Lateral change in the channel—meandering—is an essential feature of streams in alluvial valleys, yet we have systematically attempted to straighten and confine rivers in an attempt to increase water conveyance, confine flows, and protect property. Recent large floods, however, serve to remind us that dams and levees have limits and cannot contain increasingly large floods that occur at least in part as a result of watershed and floodplain alterations.

Recognize that dams change rivers and their ecosystems, but some of the negative consequences of dams can be mitigated through operational strategies that create more normative discharge and temperature regimes. Dams can alter seasonal availability and temperature of water extensively, reducing stream productivity and diversity. Large, erratic base flows create a dead zone along the river margin where plants and animals are either washed away or desiccated and reduce near-shore shallow water habitat that is crucial for juvenile fishes and emerging insects. Simply establishing minimum flows as mitigation for lost habitat or extirpated species is insufficient to maintain the physical and biological integrity of rivers. Periodic flushing flows are needed to scour river bottoms, build gravel bars, replenish woody debris, and also minimize proliferation of non-native biota. It is also important to reduce the erratic nature of base flows associated with daily hydropower operations and irrigation withdrawals. Restoration of more natural discharge regimes in regulated rivers and lakes is one of the most pressing needs in maintaining normative watershed conditions.

Conserve and promote native species by creating native biota reserves, restoring and reconnecting critical habitats, and minimizing conditions that favor invasions of non-native species. Native biota can serve as sentinels of ecological change and reductions in the abundance of native species can indicate degradation. Watershed planning can incorporate steps to protect and even restore habitat, including designating reserves for remaining intact assemblages of native plants and animals (Moyle and Yoshiyama, 1994; Sedell et al., 1994) and is especially suited for mobile organisms that require a network of interconnected habitats.

Promote best management practices for upland and riparian land uses as a means of controlling pollution, but recognize that the best practices for one watershed in one region of the country may differ from other watersheds in other regions. Many agencies and organizations, including the U.S. Department of Agriculture, have implemented a variety of forestry, grazing, and agricultural initiatives to limit water pollution and loss of biodiversity. Rigorous scientific evaluation of best management practices is required, however, before they are widely accepted in place of legal standards (Bisson et al., 1992).

REAUTHORIZATION OF THE CLEAN WATER ACT

Implementation of the 1972 Clean Water Act (CWA) has had profound impacts on state and federal regulatory programs related to water quality and on funding for construction of treatment plants, planning, research, and training. After more than 25 years of activities under the Act, the nation's most polluted waters have experienced substantial improvements in quality. But legislation that was appropriate more than two decades ago does not necessarily address today's needs. In spite of attempts within the CWA framework to address nonpoint pollution concerns, much less progress has been made in controlling nonpoint pollution than in controlling point sources and it is widely agreed that nonpoint sources now account for the great majority of degraded surface waters (Patrick, 1992; Brezonik and Cooper, 1994; Postel et al., 1996). And although the CWA has done much to stem the trend of declining conditions in the nation's surface waters, much remains to be done to restore their quality and integrity.

When the CWA was first passed, the driving issues were related primarily to human health and human use of surface waters, thus explaining the goal to make all waters "fishable and swimmable," and the pollutants of concern were those typically found in municipal and industrial wastewater (organic matter, suspended solids, microbial pathogens, nutrients). In contrast, the driving forces today are broader—ecosystem health, integrated management of water quality—and the pollutants of concern have expanded to include synthetic organic compounds and selected heavy metals which may be toxic to aquatic organisms as well as people. The primary sources of the contaminants have changed, with more impacts now from urban and agricultural runoff and atmospheric transport (Brezonik and Cooper, 1994). Congress and the President are faced with the difficult task of reauthorizing the Clean Water Act so it better meets today's needs. The reauthorization process provides an important opportunity to address the nation's need for improved water management.

There appears to be a developing consensus that many problems caused by the past fragmented approach to water resource management might be better addressed from a watershed perspective. For instance, a revised CWA might help solve some problems caused by the fragmented approach of water managers dealing independently, and under separate legal authorities, with surface water, ground water, wastewater, and drinking water, with too little recognition of the interrelationships. For instance, under the precepts of Section 303(d) of the Clean Water Act, states must identify pollution-impaired streams and develop plans to reduce pollutant loads. This approach relies on setting total maximum daily loads (TMDLs) for individual water bodies that account for both point and nonpoint sources of pollutants. When a waterbody exceeds its TMDL, however, water managers have traditionally targeted point sources for pollutant reduction because of the ease with which these sources can be monitored and manipulated. Nonpoint sources, on the other hand, are dispersed and diffuse and so are more challenging to manage.

Fragmented consideration of ecological, economic, and social concerns in water resource management has not served the nation well in either science or management. Research sometimes is focused on single issues or disciplines when a broader context might led to very different conclusions. This causes managers who rely on the science to address problems piecemeal. Too often, decision-makers see themselves forced to make "either/or" trade-offs between economic vitality and environmental quality rather than striking a balance. Lack of integrated thinking produces single-problem solutions where a balance of objectives might have been pursued.

The shortcomings of the existing Clean Water Act, and the advantages offered by a watershed approach to achieve some water related goals, should be addressed during the reauthorization of the Act. This committee, and many other people in the scientific and management communities, believes that the Clean Water Act should explicitly recognize that:

• Components of the landscape are connected, and that surface water, ground water, and drinking water are directly related resources that must be managed together rather than separately. Water is most effectively managed using an integrated approach, including consolidation of authority in watersheds where possible.

• Clean water is a function not only of natural processes, but also of responsible social behavior by citizens and integrated and coordinated management by government agencies. Management of waters and closely related resources requires understanding that the human dimension, including economic and social processes, are components of the overall system that should be accounted for in research, planning, and management.

There is considerable support for making a watershed approach a critical aspect of the Clean Water Act, as evidenced, for instance, by many policies and guidance documents already in place under the Environmental Protection Agency, such as the Administration's recent Clean Water Action Plan (1998). A reauthorized Clean Water Act should provide for partnerships between federal agencies with water and watershed management responsibilities and the National Science Foundation in developing priorities and funding scientific research related to watersheds, especially research emphasizing the integration of ecological, economic, and social concerns. One goal of the Clean Water Act should be to encourage ecological restoration: the Act should be a visionary statement that gives national emphasis to the conservation and enhancement of watersheds because of the many important functions and values they provide, and it should give authority to the relevant agencies for implementing that goal.

CONCLUSIONS

In addition to the previous suggestions to guide reauthorization of the Clean Water Act, the Committee on Watershed Management offers the following conclusions concerning other mechanisms to steer the nation toward improved strategies for watershed management. These conclusions address basic guiding philosophy (1 and 2), management processes (3 to 8), research (9 to 12), and support functions (13 to 15).

1. Watersheds as geographic areas are optimal organizing units for dealing with the management of water and closely related resources, but the natural boundaries of watersheds rarely coincide with political jurisdictions and thus they are less useful for political, institutional, and funding purposes. Initiatives and organizations directed at watershed management should be flexible to reflect the reality of these situations. (For more information, see Chapters 2, 6, and 8.)

2. Specific watershed problems must be approached in distinctive ways, and determining the appropriate scale for the resolution of any problem is an essential first step. Both the structure of watershed management organizations and the nature of the activities undertaken should be matched to the scale of the watershed. The range of stakeholders varies with scale and must be clearly defined so that the costs and benefits associated with any plan are fully taken into account. Watershed approaches are easiest to implement at the local level; they can be most difficult to implement at large scales where the political, institutional, and funding decisionmaking grows especially complex. (For more information, see Chapters 2, 6, and 8.)

3. Risk and uncertainty are parts of the natural as well as institutional settings for watershed management, and they can limit the effectiveness of applying the watershed approach. One important need for advancing watershed management is to develop practical procedures for considering risk and uncertainty in real world decisionmaking. Scientists and managers should strive to educate the public by specifically outlining potential uncertainty so that expectations of research and decisionmaking are reasonable. (For more information, see Chapter 5.)

4. Watershed management plans should be viewed as the starting point and not the end product of a management cycle. The cycle should include formulation of a problem statement, identification of an agreed-upon set of goals, identification of the scope of activities appropriate to the issue in question, negotiated action steps, implementation, feedback, evaluation, and appropriate adjustments made as a result of lessons learned (i.e., adaptive management). (For more information, see Chapter 8.)

5. Scientific and technical peer review of watershed improvement activities conducted by qualified independent professionals can provide objective evaluations of their impact. Scientific or technical review groups can help design and evaluate monitoring programs and help prioritize locations for intensive study. Such groups also can inform policymakers about the relative uncertainty associ-

ated with implementing management alternatives. (For more information, see Chapter 8.)

6. For too long, agencies have viewed their polices and projects in isolation. In their normal course of work, the U.S. Army Corps of Engineers, Bureau of Reclamation, U.S. Department of Agriculture, and Environmental Protection Agency should examine the watershed-wide implications of their policies, programs, rules, and permitting processes to take into account the regional and downstream ecological, social, and economic consequences of their actions, rather than using a limited project-by-project approach. (For more information, see Chapter 8.)

7. The Committee was impressed with the information-gathering aspects of the Western Water Policy Review Advisory Commission. This kind of regionally based analysis of watershed resources provides a comprehensive evaluation of the current management of American watersheds and guidance for the future, and should be duplicated for other regions as a means of gathering information and evaluating the potential of the watershed approach. (For more information, see Chapter 8.)

8. Watershed management seeks to develop careful, long-term solutions to problems and provide sustainable access to resources and thus it benefits the nation. The President and Congress should consider establishing some stable mechanism to fund the federal contribution to watershed management partnerships, such as a revenue sharing strategy or trust fund. This funding should be available to state, regional, and local organizations for research, planning, implementation, and ongoing peer evaluation of watershed initiatives. (For more information, see Chapter 7.)

9. Because water is a strategic national resource and sustainable use of water resources is a national priority, watershed management decisions must be based on the best possible science. More research is needed to provide the data, knowledge, and technology necessary to support effective watershed management, especially work focused on integrating social, economic, and ecological elements. There is a special need for research and monitoring that is long-term and integrated across scales and timeframes, as well as for specific problem-solving research and theory and model development One specific step to greatly improve scientific understanding of watersheds is for Congress to increase funding for the National Science Foundation in areas that can improve understanding of the human dimensions of watersheds. Moreover, new problems and challenges such as human alteration of watersheds, volatile world economies, and global climate change will require new and innovative centers of research excellence in watershed science and management, and more effective technology transfer and lead-

ership, at scales ranging from local to regional. (For more information, see Chapters 4, 5, and 6.)

10. Although our understanding of fundamental physical, biological, economic, and social processes needs improvement, an even greater need is improved understanding of how all these components operate together within watersheds. Watershed researchers should emphasize the integration of environmental, economic, and social perspectives, with more attention to the linkages and what they imply for management and overcoming barriers to implementation. Science and policy must function together for watershed management to be successful, so there also must be more attention to the role of politics in decisionmaking. (For more information, see Chapter 5.)

11. Process-oriented research is research that extends beyond description and measurement; it addresses structure, function, and the how and why of the processes operating within a watershed. Process-oriented research is particularly valuable because it leads to enhanced predictive capabilities, better understanding of cause-effect relationships, and a firmer foundation for planning and management. The National Science Foundation, Environmental Protection Agency, U.S. Geological Survey, U.S. Department of Agriculture, and other federal agencies involved in process-oriented watershed research should reorient their efforts to close critical information gaps that hamper effective implementation of watershed management. Important gaps include:

• linkages among watershed components (rivers, wetlands, ground water, atmosphere, floodplains, upland areas);
• integration across disciplines (especially biophysical and social sciences);
• feedback among processes operating at different spatial and temporal scales;
• inexpensive, useful indicators of watershed conditions and quantitative methods to evaluate land use and watershed management practices;
• advanced watershed simulation models (especially models that link natural and social attributes) that are useful to and can be operated by managers who are not scientific experts; and
• understanding of risk and uncertainty in the decisionmaking process. (For more information, see Chapter 4.)

12. A solid scientific foundation of basic and applied research is needed to provide the data, information, and tools necessary for effective implementation of watershed management activities. Federal resource management agencies should form partnerships with the National Science Foundation in jointly funded research, with agencies identifying critical areas needing investigation and NSF ensuring high quality, peer reviewed work in both short-term and long-term

projects. Agencies might include the Forest Service, Bureau of Reclamation, Corps of Engineers, Bureau of Land Management, National Park Service, U.S. Geological Survey, and Tennessee Valley Authority. Universities and non-governmental organizations can be key partners in this process. (For more information, see Chapter 4.)

13. The Federal Geographic Data Committee (FGDC), as the organization charged with primary responsibility for establishing the National Spatial Data Infrastructure (NSDI), should assume a leadership role in establishing a capability for collecting spatial data on watersheds by creating national data standards, designating a central clearinghouse, and maintaining a single national watershed database. Other federal agencies should be encouraged to coordinate efforts and electronically link related databases. In particular:

• The USGS should, in accordance with the NSDI initiative, continue to develop the Watershed Data Clearinghouse to provide a detailed catalog service of watershed data with support for links to databases on the Internet. The clearinghouse site can provide data searches by watershed and enable users to directly download the digital data sets. When necessary, the USGS should also act as a digital data repository of last resort for watershed information that will no longer be stored and/or served by the original data owner.

• The FGDC should actively promote and coordinate a spatial data standard that defines the digital representation of watershed features, accuracy requirements, and the graphical representation of these features supported in a variety of system formats. Features to be defined include wildlife habitats, environmentally sensitive areas, and special use areas. The standard also should provide a convention for related data tables and define the minimum data to be kept about the feature.

• States should establish and maintain state-wide databases in a GIS format, available to local watershed managers through the Internet. These databases should contain ecological, social, and economic data with spatial attributes organized and presented according to watersheds of convenient size within each state. (For more information, see Chapter 4.)

14. Data collection efforts provide baseline information for increased scientific understanding of watershed processes, for analyses and interpretation of problems and causes, for assessing the status of watershed resources and detecting and predicting trends, and for decisionmaking in watershed management. Stream gaging and monitoring network design should emphasize adequate temporal resolution, sampling of storm events, measurement of appropriate ancillary hydrological and biogeochemical data (e.g., meteorological data with hydrological data or biological surveys with water quality parameters), and should use the highest possible quality of sampling and analysis. It is increasingly expensive to

maintain data collection and monitoring efforts. As the USGS, NOAA, and other federal and nonfederal organizations engaged in collecting watershed data evaluate their monitoring sites, they should prioritize the remaining sites to ensure continuation of sites that are most effective in helping managers understand water quality trends. Particular emphasis should go to maintaining sites with exceptionally long-term records. In some instances, monitoring sites should be retained to provide adequate geographic representation and geographic areas with dense coverage might lose some sites without loss of data. Sampling schemes should be designed to answer specific questions about the status and trends of watershed resources rather than simply collect broad-based data. (For more information, see Chapters 3 and 4.)

15. Effective watershed management requires integration of theory, data, simulation models, and expert judgment to solve practical problems and provide a scientific basis for decisionmaking at the watershed scale. The engineering and scientific communities should develop better, more user-friendly decision support systems to help decisionmakers understand and evaluate alternative approaches. These improved approaches should help decisiomakers understand and convey the concepts of risk and uncertainty. A decision support system (DSS) is a suite of computer programs with components consisting of databases, simulation models, decision models, and user interfaces that assist a decisionmaker in evaluating the economic and environmental impacts of competing watershed management alternatives. The technical challenges in developing DSS technology for watershed management include linking models for all of the components of an extremely complex system to estimate the effect of management alternatives on all of the criteria of interest. (For more information, see Chapters 5 and 8.)

CLOSING THOUGHTS

This report began with the hypothesis that watersheds are the most appropriate way to integrate ecological, economic, and social approaches to resource management. The hypothesis was confirmed in many cases, but with several important limitations.

- variability of the human and natural ecosystem prevents a single standardized approach,
- external connections expand watershed boundaries into problem-sheds,
- there is a local to national continuum of scales, each with a different behavior pattern,
- there are numerous social, economic, and political barriers to effective watershed management,
- science has provided inadequate support for and ineffective connection to policy,

- the effectiveness of management is rarely measured or evaluated,
- societal values continually change, changing the objectives of management, and
- financial considerations are a major limiting factor.

Differing levels of government have varying financial, technical, and political capabilities with respect to watershed management. The scale of the organizational capabilities and responsibilities must match the scale of the problem. Although some caution is necessary to avoid taking these observations too strictly, the committee offers the following thoughts about the relative roles of federal, state, local, and regional levels of decisionmaking in a watershed approach context:

- Local organizations are best positioned to take primary responsibility for staffing, planning, and implementing projects, and, in particular, for facilitating citizen involvement.
- State governments are best positioned to facilitate coordination, research, and technical assistance; to ensure application of standards and water use regulations; to conduct evaluation of projects; and in some cases to provide financial support to local governments, either with their own funds or funds dispensed to states by the federal government.
- The federal government and its agencies are best positioned to take primary responsibility for watershed management affecting the interstate scale, as well as for supporting research, providing technical assistance, and providing financial support to state and local entities. The federal role should include designing incentives to encourage state and local initiatives, conducting evaluations where appropriate, and representing national interests in watershed discussions.

Two recurrent themes appeared throughout the committee's deliberations. First, one overarching lesson from the nation's long history of interest in watershed management is that "one size does not fit all." Watersheds in the United States reflect tremendous diversity of climatic conditions, geology, soils, and other factors that influence water flow, flora, and fauna. There is equally great variation in historical experiences, cultural expression, institutional arrangements, laws, policies, and attitudes. No single model could fit with all the existing governmental arrangements found at the state and local levels, and it would be a mistake to impose a standard model from the federal level.

Second, fragmentation of responsibility and lack of clarity about how to resolve disputes caused by conflicting missions among federal agencies inhibits the success of the watershed approach. For example, during the course of this study the committee identified 22 federal agencies that deal with the hydrologic cycle, although often with dramatically different perspectives. To the public, these confusing and sometimes conflicting approaches to water management are baffling. There is no one consistent voice for the water resource.

As an intellectual and organizational tool, watershed-scale management can be useful in many circumstances, especially for managing biological and geophysical resources and especially for local and some regional applications. The value of watershed management as a means for truly integrated efforts to achieve a balance of ecological, economic, and social goals remains a hypothesis that has not yet been completely proven. But flexible application of watershed principles can improve the joint efforts of researchers, managers, decisionmakers, and citizens in their search for a sustainable economy and a quality environment.

REFERENCES

Bisson, P. A., T. P. Quinn, G. H. Reeves, and S. V. Gregory. 1992. Best Management Practices, Cumulative Effects, and Long-Term Trends in Fish Abundance in Pacific Northwest River Systems. Pages 189-232 in Watershed Management: Balancing Sustainability and Environmental Change. New York, N.Y.: Springer-Verlag

Brezonik, P. L. and W. Cooper. 1994. Reauthorization of the Clean Water Act: important issues for water quality scientists. Water Resources Update, winter 1994: 47-51.

Graf, W. L. 1996. Geomorphology and Policy for Restoration of Impounded American Rivers: What is Natural? Pp. 443-473 in The Scientific Nature of Geomorphology. New York: John Wiley and Sons.

Moyle, P. B., and R. M. Yoshiyama. 1994. Protection of aquatic biodiversity in California: a five-tiered approach. Fisheries 19(2):6-18.

National Research Council (NRC). 1996. Upstream: Salmon and Society in the Pacific Northwest. Washington, D.C.: National Academy Press.

Patrick, R. 1992. Surface Water Quality: Have the Laws Been Successful? Princeton, N.J.: Princeton University Press.

Postel, S. L., G. C. Dailey, and P. R. Ehrlich, 1996. Human appropriation of renewable fresh water. Science 271:785-788.

Sedell, J. R., G. H. Reeves, and K. M. Burnett. 1994. Development and evaluation of aquatic conservation strategies. Journal of Forestry 92(4):28-31.

Stanford, J. A., J. V. Ward, W. J. Liss, C. A. Frissell, R. N. Williams, J. A. Lichatowich, and C. C. Countant. 1996. A general protocol for restoration of regulated rivers. Regulated Rivers 12:391-413.

Stanford, J. A. 1997. Toward a Robust Water Policy for the Western USA: Synthesis of Science. Pages 1-11 in Aquatic ecosystem symposium: A report to the Western Water Policy Advisory Commission. Tempe, Arizona: Arizona State University.

Appendixes

Appendix A

Water Quality Management in the United States: Major Related Legislation

The following is an historical overview of the evolution of the institutions and legislation for water quality in the nation.[1] This institutional framework is complex, given that many agencies, and many programs within agencies, have some responsibilities related to water quality.

RIVERS AND HARBORS ACT OF 1899

This act, also referred to as the "Refuse Act," is the first statute that addressed water quality conditions in the United States, if only originally for purposes of navigation. The act states that "It shall not be lawful to throw . . . any refuse matter of any kind or description whatever, other than that flowing from the streets and sewers and passing there from in a liquid state, into any navigable water of the United States" [33 U.S.C. 401, Section 13].

Any activities that could impact the navigable waterways, by obstructing excavations, filling navigable waters, discharging of refuse matter, or causing injury to harbor or river improvements or flood control devices required a permit from the Chief of Engineers of the Army Corps of Engineers. The act had only an indirect relationship to water quality. It is apparent from the materials excluded from the act—"matter . . . other than that flowing from the streets and sewers and passing therefrom in a liquid state"—that urban runoff and municipal sewage

---

[1]The committee would like to acknowledge Katherine O'Connor, Orange County Water District, California, for contributing this overview. It is adapted from her masters thesis, Watershed Management Planning: Bring the Pieces Together (O'Connor, 1995).

discharges were not yet an issue. The so-called "Refuse Act" was not really directed at regulating industrial or municipal sources of water pollution. Most of the water pollution control permits issues under Section 10 of the Act were U.S. Army Corps of Engineers (USACE) permits for physical alterations such as channelization (Portney, 1990).

WATER POLLUTION CONTROL ACT OF 1948

This Act, enacted 50 years after the Refuse Act, dealt explicitly with water pollution control [P.L. 80-845]. It authorized the federal government to conduct research on water pollution problems. It also authorized the federal government for the first time to make loans to municipalities for the construction of sewage treatment facilities, although no actual funds were appropriated (Portney, 1990). At this time, the responsibility for compliance and enforcement of water pollution control was left entirely to the state and local governments. There were no federal requirements in the form of goals, limits, or guidelines. The Act stated that it was the policy of Congress to "recognize, preserve, and protect the primary responsibilities and rights of the states in controlling water pollution" (WEF and Kovalic, 1993).

WATER POLLUTION CONTROL ACT—AMENDMENTS OF 1956

In this Act, federal involvement was still limited to the investigation of water pollution problems and intervention in cases dealing with interstate water quality issues [P.L. 89-660]. The federal government entered into cost-sharing agreements with local municipalities and supplied up to 55 percent of the cost of constructing municipal wastewater treatment plants (WEF and Kovalic, 1993). Primary responsibility for water pollution control was still left to the states. This Act initiated a goal-oriented approach, and each state was authorized to establish its own criteria for desirable levels of water quality (Portney, 1990). The role of the states was increased by this legislation, which allowed them to take abatement action against polluters (WEF and Kovalic, 1993).

WATER QUALITY ACT OF 1965

This Act increased federal intervention in water quality control (P.L. 89-234]. For the first time, the states were mandated by the federal government to establish ambient water quality standards and develop implementation plans for controlling pollution from individual sources to meet those standards (Portney, 1990). This Act also created the "Federal Water Pollution Control Administration," which set general guidelines for the state's standards and had oversight authority to approve the standards and the implementation plans set by the states (WEF and Kovalic, 1993; Water Quality 2000, 1992). Under the Act, the water quality standards established by the states could vary for different bodies of water throughout the state depending on the benefits and costs of attaining certain levels of water quality. The states still bore the primary responsibility for issuing discharge permits to individual sources of pollution, and could impose fines and take enforcement action against violators (Portney, 1990).

FEDERAL WATER POLLUTION CONTROL ACT OF 1972

The Federal Water Pollution Control Act (the Clean Water Act or CWA) adopted in 1972 was, to date, the most extensive piece of federal legislation regulating water quality. It instituted a national program for cleaning up the nation's water. The set of guidelines in the act was to be administered by the recently formed Environmental Protection Agency (EPA). The requirements of the Clean Water Act signified that the federal government was assuming primary direction of water pollution control for the nation (Portney, 1990). The Clean Water Act developed an objective, goals, and policies for the nation, and required state programs to be put in place to achieve them.

In Title I, The Declaration of Goals and Policy, the CWA established the overall objective to restore and maintain the chemical, physical, and biological integrity of the nation's waters (P.L. 92500, Section 101 (a)]. Title I continues by setting two national goals to meet this objective: (1) eliminate the "discharge of pollutants into the navigable waters" of the nation by 1985 (often called the "zero discharge" Goal) and (2) achieve an "interim goal of water quality which provides for the protection and propagation of fish, shellfish, and wildlife and provides for recreation in and on the water" by 1983 (the "fishable and swimmable" goal) [Section 101(a)(1) and (2)]. Additionally, Title I sets four national policies for reaching these goals and objectives, which are: (1) prohibit discharge of toxic pollutants in toxic amounts, (2) provide federal grants for the construction of Publicly Owned Treatment Works (POTWs), (3) develop area-wide wastewater treatment management planning, and (4) research and develop technology to eliminate the discharge of pollutants into the nation's waters [Section 101(a)(3) through (6)]. States were responsible for meeting these goals and for developing programs to "prevent, reduce, and eliminate pollution" [Section 101(b)].

The basis for the enforcement of the programs of the Clean Water Act was the "National Pollutant Discharge Elimination System" (NPDES), which created a national system for issuing permits to dischargers [Section 402(a)(1)]. This permitting program is central to the Clean Water Act. The NPDES permits set effluent limitations for point source dischargers. All municipal dischargers were required to achieve secondary wastewater treatment by the year 1977 [Section 301 (b)(1)(B)]. Industrial dischargers of toxic pollutants had strict discharge standards using the best available technology [Section 301(b)(2)(B)]. The states could take over responsibility for administering the permitting program, with EPA oversight and approval.

In addition to the NPDES permits, the states were also granted permitting authority under Section 401 of the Clean Water Act. Section 401 requires that in order for a discharger to obtain a federal permit or license for any activity "including construction or operation of facilities" that would result in a discharge to navigable water, a "water quality certification" must by received from the state in which the discharge is to occur [Section 401(a)(1)]. The 401 permit certifies that the discharge complies with the state's water quality standards, and must be obtained from or waived by the state before the issuance of any permit, including: NPDES permit, a permit for dredged and fill material by the U.S. Army Corps of Engineers, a Section 9 &10 permit under Rivers and Harbors Act, or a license for hydroelectric power from the Federal Energy Regulatory Commission (RWQCB 1994).

From the point of view of watershed management, perhaps the most relevant portion of the CWA is section 303(d), which defines an approach known as Total Maximum Daily Load (TMDL). This method, which was refined in later regulations, is a water quality-based standard. It strives to assure water quality through a series of steps that, in effect, require a watershed approach. Under federal oversight, states: (1) identify water bodies with impaired water-quality, (2) establish a priority ranking of these sites, (3) allocate maximum total loadings of various contaminants among point and nonpoint sources (waste load allocation, or WLA, and load allocation, or LA, respectively), (4) implement control measures, and (5) assess the results. In most cases, step 3 of this process virtually mandates a watershed approach, since waters are impaired by multiple dischargers and pollutants, and these derive, to a considerable extent, from nonpoint sources distributed over broad regions. EPA even recommends that TMDLs be developed on a geographical basis, e.g., by watershed. A virtue of the TMDL approach is that it is flexible and considers water quality to be a function of an extensive range of sources distributed across the landscape. It is so flexible that physical and biological stressors, like water temperature and habitat alteration, can be considered within the same management framework. A disadvantage is that enforcement options are limited, mainly to restricting point sources through the NPDES permitting process.

THE CLEAN WATER ACT OF 1977

These 1977 amendments were the first major revision of the CWA of 1972 [Public Law 95-217]. The amendments encouraged states to manage the construction grants program for POTWs under Section 205, as well as the standards and enforcement responsibility of the NPDES permit program under Section 402 (Portney, 1990; WEF and Kovalic, 1993). The 1977 amendments made quite a few changes to Section 301 of the CWA, the Standards and Enforcement section. The restrictions of municipal wastewater treatment discharges under Section 301 were weakened to allow for waivers from full secondary treatment of wastewater to coastal dischargers [Section 301(h)]. In addition, extensions for reaching the treatment limitations were granted to industrial discharges. The EPA reclassified and revised the toxic pollutant list to arrange toxins in three Groups: (1) "conventional pollutants" such as biological oxygen demand (BOD) and suspended solids, (2) "non-conventional pollutants" such as phosphorus and nitrogen, and (3) priority pollutants, or toxic pollutants, such as synthetic organic chemicals [Section 301(b)(7 (C)].

MUNICIPAL WASTEWATER TREATMENT CONSTRUCTION GRANT AMENDMENT OF 1981

The primary goal of these amendments (Public Law 97-117) was to reform the federal construction grant program for municipal wastewater treatment plants, which had been creating major reductions in federal financial assistance to the local governments for the construction of wastewater treatment facilities. The amendments also extended the national deadline for meeting full secondary treatment deadlines to 1988 (Portney, 1990; WEF and Kovalic, 1993).

WATER QUALITY ACT OF 1987

This final set of major amendments to the federal Clean Water Act brought the policies for water quality programs full circle to the policies before 1972. The amendments reaffirmed the states' primary authority and responsibility for developing and implementing programs to meet federal water quality goals [Section 101(b)]. In addition, the discharge requirements for many water bodies went back to being based on water quality, instead of uniform technology-based standards for the nation. Previous technology-based limits and standards for municipal and industrial DPES permits had been issued without regard to the quality of the receiving water. The move back to water-quality-based standards based the discharge limits on the designated use of the water and the standards required to sustain that use. States were also granted the authority to decide themselves on the programs for meeting water quality based standards (WEF and Kovalic, 1993).

The major responsibilities, including financial ones, for wastewater treatment facilities were also handed down to the states. A schedule was developed to gradually eliminate federal grants for POTW construction and replace the program with state revolving fund loans (Portney, 1990; Water Quality 2000, 1992; WEF and Kovalic, 1993).

One of the most significant amendments to the Clean Water Act was the addition of a fifth national policy in Title 1, the national policy for control of nonpoint sources (NPS) of pollution [Section 101(a)(7)]. Under Section 304, EPA sets the guidelines for controlling NPS pollution, and the regulation of activities that cause "diffuse and intermittent flows of pollutants." This section also identifies the programs of other federal agencies that may be affected by the provisions of the national NPS policy, such as the U.S. Army Corps of Engineers, the U.S. Department of Agriculture, and the U.S. Department of the Interior [Section 304(k)(L)].

The NPS policy requires each state to assess its water pollution and determine which water bodies fail to meet the water quality objectives because of NPS pollution [Section 319(a)]. The state is then to develop a state management plan and implementation measures to reduce the pollutants [Section 319(b)]. The states have primary control over the NPS program and are authorized under Section 3 19(h) to use funds from state revolving fund loans for statewide NPS management plans, and for programs to protect ground water from NPS pollution as well [Section 3 19(l)] (WEF and Kovalic, 1993).

REFERENCES

Portney, P. R., ed. 1990. Public Policies for Environmental Protection. Washington D.C.: Resources for the Future.

Regional Water Quality Control Board, California (RWQCB). 1994. Water Quality Control Plan: Santa Ana River Basin M. Riverside: Santa Ana Region VIE.

Water Environment Federation (WEF) and J. M. Kovalic. 1993. The Clean Water Act of 1987. 2nd ed. Washington, D.C.: The Bureau of National Affairs, Inc.

Water Quality 2000. 1992. A National Water Agenda for the 21st Century. Final Report. Alexandria, Va.: Water Environment Federation.

APPENDIX B

Watershed Data and Information on the Internet

Information of interest to watershed managers, researchers, and the general public is available free of charge on the Internet through World Wide Web. The number of Web sites that address watershed issues and information is so great that it is impossible to provide a complete catalog. The purpose of this appendix is to provide a brief list of sites representing examples of the types of information available. Links embedded within these sites allow the user to access other related sites. The following list includes sites that are primarily data sources as well as examples of sites maintained by watershed management agencies from the local to the national level. All the sites were active as of September 30, 1998.

EXAMPLES OF FEDERAL SITES—AGENCIES

Army Corps of Engineers Hydrologic Engineering Center: http://www.wrc-hec.usace.army.mil/.

Bureau of Land Management Geospatial Homepage: http://www-a.blm.gov/gis/.

Environmental Protection Agency, Surf Your Watershed (a major data source): http://www.epa.gov/surf.

Environmental Protection Agency, Watershed Program: http://www.epa.gov/OWOW/watershed.

Natural Resources Conservation Service (watershed data and technical information): http://www.nrcs.usda.gov/NRCSProg.html.

Pacific Northwest Bureau of Reclamation, Dams, Facilities, Electrical Power: http://www.pn.usbr.gov/dam/index.html.

National Atmospheric and Oceanic Administration (climate data by states): http://www.cdc.noaa.gov/USclimate/states.fast.html.

National Aeronautics and Space Administration, Earth Observing System, including normalize differentiated vegetation index and land biosphere images: http://xtreme.gsfc.nasa.gov.

EXAMPLES OF FEDERAL SITES— GEOGRAPHIC INFORMATION SYSTEM DATA

Geological Survey National Geospatial Data Clearing House: http://nsdi.usgs.gov/nsdi/pages/nsdi004.html.

National Spatial Data Infrastructure: http://fgdc.er.usgs.gov.

U.S. Geological Survey, Hydrologic Unit Boundary Maps: http://water.usgs.gov/public/GIS

U.S. Geological Survey Water, Land, and Population Data: http://water.usgs.gov/lookup/getgislist

EXAMPLES OF FEDERAL SITES—ECONOMIC AND SOCIAL DATA

Bureau of the Census, Demographic and Business Data: http://www.census.gov.

Federal Reserve Bank System, Economic Data, Northern Plains Example: http://woodrow.mpls.frb.fed.us.

Regional Economic Data, Upper Mid-West Example: http://www.frbchi.org/econinfo/midwet_econ/midwest_econ.html.

Regional Economic Data, Links to all Regions of the Country: http://www.woodrow.mpls.frb.fed.us/info/sys/banks.html.

Department of Transportation, Bureau of Transportation Statistics, Links to Databases and GIS: http://www.bts.gov.

Securities Exchange Commission, Corporation Data for Companies with Public Stock: http://www.sec.gov.

EXAMPLES OF FEDERAL SITES—REMOTE SENSING IMAGERY

Central Intelligence Agency Satellite Imagery: http://edcwww.cr.usgs.gov/dclass/dclass.html.

Geological Survey EROS Data Center: http://edcwww.cr.usgs.gov/eros-home.html.

Jet Propulsion Laboratory, Space Platform Imagery: http://www.jpl.nasa.gov.

EXAMPLES OF FEDERAL SITES— PHYSICAL ENVIRONMENTAL DATA

Agricultural Research Service Water Data Base, Precipitation and Streamflow Data from Experimental Watersheds: http://hydrolab.arsusda.gov/arswater.html.

Geological Survey Real Time and Historical Stream Flow, Water Quality, Water Use Data: http://h2o.usgs.gov.

Geological Survey National Stream Quality Accounting Network: http://water.usgs.gov/public/nasqan.

National Oceanographic and Atmospheric Administration, Guide and Links to Federal Data Bases for Environmental Information: http://www.esdim.noaa.gov.

National Climatic Data Center: http://www.ncdc.noaa.gov.

National Oceanographic and Atmospheric Administration Environmental Information Services Links to Data Bases: http://esdim.noaa.gov.

EXAMPLES OF FEDERAL SITES—BASIC REFERENCES

Library of Congress: http://www.loc.gov.

Federal Laws: http://www.legal.gsa.gov.

EXAMPLES OF STATE-BASED SITES

California Watershed Projects Inventory:
http://ice.ucdavis.edu/California_Watershed_Projects_Inventory.

Environmental and Natural Resources Data for Nebraska:
http://www.calmit.unl.edu/calmit.html.

Links to Online Iowa Digital Cartographic and Environmental Data:
http://www.cgrer.uiowa.edu/iowa-environment/Iowa-environment.html.

Pennsylvania Spatial Data Access (PASDA): http://www.pasda.psu.edu.

EXAMPLES OF WATERSHED-BASED SITES

Great Lakes Information Network: http://www.great-lakes.net.

Verde River Watershed Association: http://www.verde.org.

St. Johns River Watershed: http://www.riverpage.com.

EXAMPLES OF OTHER SITES WITH DATA AND MAPS
USEFUL TO WATERSHED MANAGERS AND RESEARCHERS

Watershed Maps for the entire United States: http://water.usgs.gov/nsdi/usgswrd/huc2m.html.

American Planning Association, Policy and Organizational Data by State:
www.planning.org/plnginfo/growsmar/gsindex.html.

Know Your Watershed Program: http://www.ctic.purdue.edu/cgi-bin/KYW.exe.

High-Resolution Infra-Red Imagery for Weather and Climate:
http://ssec.wisc.edu/data/.

Hydrologic Links: http://www.us.net/adept/links.html.

Appendix C

Acknowledgments

The preparation of a report such as this one takes input from many people. The committee wishes to extend its sincere appreciation to all the people who shared their time and expertise with us during the study process. This includes the many people who participated in our information-gathering workshop in Minnesota, led us on field trips in California and Tennessee, spoke with us at meetings, helped with our research, provided documents, and contributed to our study in other ways. In particular, we would like to thank the following people for their important contributions:

Jim Addis, Wisconsin Department of Natural Resources, Madison, WI
Robert Adler, University of Utah College of Law, Salt Lake City, UT
Joyce Altobelli, Cornell University, Ithaca, NY
Wayne Andersen, Minnesota Pollution Control Agency, St. Paul, MN
Todd S. Bacastow, The Pennsylvania State University, University Park, PA
Brian Baharie, Orange County Water Districts, Fountain Valley, CA
Paul Barrett, U.S. Fish and Wildlife Service, West Carlsbad, CA
Greg Beck, United Community Action Alliance, Chattanooga, TN
Don Brady, Environmental Protection Agency
Curtis Brown, Western Water Policy Review Advisory Commission, Denver, CO
Anne Buckley, Lose and Associates, Nashville, TN
John Burt, USDA Natural Resources Conservation Service
Susan Carpenter, Common Ground Planning, Riverside, CA
Lee Carter, Tennessee Valley Authority, Land Management
Corina Chaudhry, Orange County Sanitation Districts, Fountain Valley, CA

Tim Cody, BASS, Chattanooga, TN
Lee Colten, Kentucky Division of Water
James Colston, Orange County Sanitation Districts, Fountain Valley, CA
Steve Cordle, Environmental Protection Agency, Washington
Tom Davenport, Environmental Protection Agency, Chicago, IL
Craig Denisoff, California Resources Agency, Sacramento, CA
Lucy Dunn, The Koll Company, Newport Beach, CA
Harold Dzuik, Big Sandy Lake Association, McGregor, MN
Theresa Eclov, Mississippi River Headwaters Board, Walker, MN
Barry M. Evans, The Pennsylvania State University, University Park, PA
Rebecca Fawver, California Resources Agency, Sacramento, CA
Robert Feenstra, Milk Producers Council, Ontario, CA
Robert Finley, Redwood-Cottonwood Rivers Control Area, Redwood Falls, MN
Jim Frierson, River Valley Partners, Chattanooga, TN
Jack Frost, U.S. Natural Resources Conservation Service
Willis Gainer, Office of Surface Mining, Knoxville, TN
Don Glaser, Western Water Policy Review Advisory Commission, Denver, CO
Homer Gray, Tennessee Valley Authority
Stephen Hansen, Minnesota River Joint Powers Board, St. Paul, MN
Warren Harper, U.S. Forest Service
Linda Harris, Tennessee Valley Authority, Clean Water Initiative
Tex Hawkins, U.S. Fish and Wildlife Service, Winona, MN
Mariano Hernandez, USD-ARS and University of Arizona
Janet Herrin, Tennessee Valley Authority
Ray Herrman, U.S. Geological Survey
Lee Hill, Tennessee Valley Authority, Clean Water Initiative
Linda Hixon, Friends of North Chickamauga Creek Greenway, Hixon, TN
Stephen Hughes, Aitkin County Soil and Water Conservation District, Aitkin, MN
John Izbicki, U.S. Geological Survey, Water Quality Division, San Diego, CA
Kate Jackson, Tennessee Valley Authority
Bruce Johnson, Fox Wolff 2000, Appleton, WI
Kat Kulhman, Environmental Protection Agency, Region 9, San Francisco, CA
Rick Lance, Tennessee Valley Authority, Land Management
Raleigh Leef, U.S. Army Corps of Engineers
Victor Leipzig, Bolsa Chica Conservancy, Huntington Beach, CA
Steve Light, Minnesota Department of Natural Resources, St. Paul, MN
Ron B. Linsky, National Water Research Institute
Greg Lowe, Tennessee Valley Authority
Joe Magner, Minnesota Pollution Control Agency, St. Paul, MN
Lindell Marsh, Siemon, Larsen & Marsh, Irvine, CA
Dave Matthews, Bureau of Reclamation
Tom Matthews, County of Orange, Environmental Management Agency, Santa
    Ana, CA

Teresa McDonough, Tennessee Valley Authority
Dan McGuiness, MN-WI Boundary Area Commission, Hudson, WI
Linda Meschke, Blue Earth River Basin Initiative, Fairmont, MN
Amy Middleton, Citizens for A Better Environment, Minneapolis, MN
Craig Miller, Orange County Water Districts, Fountain Valley, CA
Drew Miller, Tennessee Valley Authority, Clean Water Initiative
Brenda Milsaps, Emma Wheeler Residents Association, Chattanooga, TN
Allene Moesler, Cannon River Watershed Partnership, Inc., Fairbault, MN
Patrick Moore, Land Stewardship project, Montevideo, MN
Gary Myers, Tennessee Wildlife Resource Agency, Nashville, TN
Ron Nargang, Minnesota Department of Natural Resources, St. Paul, MN
Mary Nichols, USDA-ARS, Southwest Watershed Research Center, Tucson, AZ
Donna Norton, Tennessee Valley Authority, Land Management
Katherine O'Connor, Orange County Water Districts, Fountain Valley, CA
Dana Oldenkamp, Milk Producers Council, Ontario, CA
Larry Pauls, County of Orange, Environmental Management Agency, Santa Ana, CA
Stan Ponce, Bureau of Reclamation
Dan Ray, The McKnight Foundation
Galen Reetz, Minnesota Pollution Control Agency, St. Paul, MN
James Robbins, Bolsa Chica Conservancy, Huntington Beach, CA
Frank Robinson, Newport Beach, CA
Lianne Russell, Tennessee Citizens for Wilderness Planning, Oak Ridge, TN
Bruce Sandstrom, Minnesota Board of Water and Soil Resources, St. Paul, MN
Joanne Schnieder, Regional Water Quality Control Board, Santa Ana Region VIII Riverside, CA
William Schaoling, Cornell University, Ithaca, NY
Harold Sharp, Fishing Talents, Inc., Chattanooga, TN
Suzanne Smith, Orange County Sanitation Districts, Fountain Valley, CA
Bill Stokes, Natural Resources Conservation Service, St. Paul, MN
Shelley Struss, Whitewater Joint Powers Board, Rochester, MN
Reid Tatum, Tennessee Wildlife Resources Agency, Crossville, TN
John Tettemer, John Tettemer & Associates, Ltd., Costa Mesa, CA
Gerard Thibeault, Regional Water Quality Control Board, Riverside, CA
Dough Thomas, Minnesota Board of Water and Soil Resources, St. Paul, MN
Ken Thompson, Irvine Ranch Water District, Irvine, CA
Ron Tippets, County of Orange, Environmental Management Agency, Santa Ana, CA
Leslie Turrini-Smith, Tennessee Department of Environment and Conservation, Nashville, TN
Christopher Ungate, Tennessee Valley Authority
Richard D. Urban, Signal Mountain, Tennessee
Bill Vorley, Institute for Agriculture and Trade Policy, Minneapolis, MN

Linda Wagenet, Cornell University, Ithaca, NY
Mary Walker, Walker and Associates, Lookout Mountain, TN
Robert Wallus, Tennessee Valley Authority, Clean Water Initiative
Michael Wehner, Orange County Water Districts, Fountain Valley, CA
Martha J.M. Wells, Tennessee Technological University, Cookeville, TN
Kathleen Williams, Tennessee Greenways, Nashville, TN
Dan Young, U.S. Army Corps of Engineers, Los Angeles, CA

APPENDIX D

Biographical Sketches of Committee Members

William L. Graf, *Chair*, is Regents Professor of Geography at Arizona State University. He obtained his Ph.D. from the University of Wisconsin, Madison, with a major in physical geography and a minor in water resources management. His specialties include fluvial geomorphology and policy for public land and water. His geomorphologic research and teaching has focused on river-channel change, human impacts on river processes and morphology, and contaminant transport and storage in river sediments, especially in dryland rivers. In the area of public policy he has emphasized the interaction of science and decisionmaking, and resolution of conflicts between economic development and environmental preservation. He has published more than 100 papers, articles, book chapters, and reports. He has served the National Research Council in numerous capacities, including membership on the Water and Science Technology Board.

Clifton J. Aichinger is administrator of Minnesota's Ramsey-Washington Metro Watershed District and one of the founding partners of the Phalen Chain of Lakes Watershed Management project, a pioneering initiative in an urban-suburban watershed. He previously served as an environmental planner for the city of St. Paul and a natural resources planner for the Dakota County Planning Department. He received a B.S. in Recreation Resource Management from the University of Minnesota in 1971.

Blake P. Anderson received a B.S. in civil engineering from California State Polytechnic University, Pomona, and has pursued graduate work at California State University, Long Beach, and California State Polytechnic University,

Pomona. He is a registered civil engineer and a certified wastewater treatment plant operator in California. Mr. Anderson is the Chief Operations Officer for the County Sanitation Districts of Orange County. He has been a leader of the Watershed Management Committee of the Association of Metropolitan Sewerage Agencies, and in this role has testified before Congress and written on the concept of watershed protection as a management tool for state and local governments. He is a member of the American Society of Civil Engineers and the Water Environment Federation.

Gaboury Benoit is an associate professor in the School of Forestry and Environmental Studies at Yale University. His research includes trace metal chemistry, chemical spectation, nonpoint source pollution, aquatic chemistry, environmental colloid chemistry, and watershed management. He received a B.S. in geochemistry in 1978 from Yale University; an M.S. in civil engineering (water resources) from Massachusetts Institute of Technology; and a Ph.D. in chemical oceanography in 1988 from Massachusetts Institute of Technology and the Woods Hole Oceanographic Institution.

Peter A. Bisson is an aquatic biologist at the Forestry Sciences Laboratory of the USDA Forest Service in Olympia, Washington. His research includes studies of fish populations and communities, stream habitats and food webs, riparian zones, and land–water interactions. Dr. Bisson is president of the Western Division of the American Fisheries Society and holds affiliate faculty appointments at the University of Washington and Oregon State University. He received a B.A. in environmental biology from the University of California, Santa Barbara in 1967 and an M.S. and a Ph.D. in fisheries and wildlife from Oregon State University in 1969 and 1975, respectively.

Margot W. Garcia is an associate professor in the Department of Urban Studies and Planning at Virginia Commonwealth University. She was chair of the department from 1989 to 1992. She has done research in the area of environmental and natural resource planning and was vice-chair of the Water Quality 2000 steering committee. She has written numerous articles and is co-editor of the book *Public Involvement and Social Impact Assessment.* She majored in botany at the University of California, Berkeley, until 1960, received a B.S. in biology from the University of New Mexico in 1961, an M.S. in botany from the University of Wisconsin, Madison, in 1966, and a Ph.D. in watershed management from the University of Arizona in 1980.

James P. Heaney is a professor in the Department of Civil, Environmental, and Architectural Engineering at the University of Colorado, Boulder. He was formerly in the Department of Environmental Engineering Science and director of the Water Resources Research Center at the University of Florida. As a water resources engineer, he has a long-term interest in applying systems analysis techniques to water resources and watershed planning. His research interests include water resources and environmental decision support systems, risk management and engineering design and operation, and optimization of water and environmental systems. He received a B.S. in civil engineering from the Illinois Institute of Technology in 1962 and an M.S. and Ph.D. in the same field from Northwestern University in 1965 and 1968, respectively.

Carol A. Johnston is a senior research associate at the Natural Resources Research Institute of the University of Minnesota, Duluth. Her research in landscape ecology, geographic information systems, and the biogeochemistry of wetlands and watersheds has been funded by the National Science Foundation, the Environmental Protection Agency, Sea Grant, the National Park Service, the National Aeronautics and Space Administration, and other organizations. Her professional experience includes positions at Cornell University, the Wisconsin Department of Natural Resources, and the U.S. Environmental Protection Agency. She has served NRC as a member of the Committee on Characterization of Wetlands and as vice-chair of the Water Science and Technology Board. She received M.S. and Ph.D. degrees in soil science from the University of Wisconsin-Madison in 1978 and 1982, respectively.

Leonard J. Lane is a hydrologist with the U.S. Department of Agriculture's Agricultural Research Service and an adjunct associate professor of renewable natural resources at the University of Arizona. His research interests include the hydrology of semiarid watersheds, runoff and sedimentation simulation models incorporating geomorphic features, and improved erosion prediction technology. He received a B.S. in 1970 and an M.S. in 1972 from the University of Arizona and a Ph.D. in civil engineering from Colorado State University in 1975.

Carolyn Hardy Olsen received a B.S. in civil engineering from the University of Wyoming in 1963. She received an M.S. in environmental engineering from the Southern Illinois University in 1976. She has over 25 years of experience in planning, design, and construction of water and wastewater projects. She served as Commissioner of Water and Pollution Control for City of Atlanta for six years and was responsible for the treatment and distribution of potable water, treatment of wastewater, and the long-range water resources and water conservation programs. Ms. Olsen is a member of the Water Quality 2000 Committee and the National Drinking Water Advisory Council. Her experience includes extensive environmental work with major governmental jurisdictions and a state environmental protection agency. She is a registered civil engineer in California and a registered professional engineer in Illinois and Georgia.

Gary W. Petersen is a professor of soil and land resources in the Department of Agronomy in the College of Agricultural Sciences and co-director of the Office for Remote Sensing of Earth Resources in the Environmental Resources Research Institute at The Pennsylvania State University. His research interests have been primarily in the areas of pedology, landscape and watershed processes, land use, geographic information systems, and remote sensing. He has worked closely with the Natural Resources Conservation Service in the areas of mapping, correlation, characterization, and interpretation. He is president of the Soil Science Society of America. He received a B.S. in soils in 1961, an M.S. in soil chemistry in 1963, and a Ph.D. in soil genesis and morphology in 1965 from the University of Wisconsin.

Max J. Pfeffer is an associate professor in the Department of Rural Sociology at Cornell University. His research has focused on the social aspects of agriculture, the environment, and development planning. He has done work on the social dimensions of watershed planning within the New York City watershed. He received a B.A. in sociology from the University of Colorado, Boulder, in 1976 and an M.S. and a Ph.D. in sociology from the University of Wisconsin, Madison, in 1979 and 1986, respectively.

Leonard Shabman is professor of resource and environmental economics and director of the Virginia Water Resources Research Center at Virginia Polytechnic Institute and State University. Dr. Shabman has conducted economic research over a wide range of topics in natural resource and environmental policy, with emphasis in six general areas: coastal resources management; planning, investment, and financing of water resource development; flood hazard management; federal and state water planning; water quality management; and fisheries management. He was an economic advisor to the Water Resources Council in 1977-1978 and scientific advisor to the Assistant Secretary of the Army, Civil Works in 1984-1985. He received a Ph.D. in agricultural economics in 1972 from Cornell University.

Jack Stanford is director of the Flathead Lake Biological Station and Bierman Professor of Ecology at the University of Montana. He is an expert with extensive field experience in the ecology of lakes and streams. He has done research on many aspects of limnology with a special focus on nutrient cycling by algae and heterotrophic bacteria, benthic ecology, and hyporheic ecology. He received a B.S. and an M.S. from Colorado State University in 1969 and 1971, respectively, and a Ph.D. in limnology from the University of Utah in 1975.

Stanley W. Trimble is a professor of geography at the University of California, Los Angeles. He specializes in human-induced soil erosion and associated stream changes with particular emphasis on water and sediment budgets. He has been visiting professor at the Universities of Chicago, Vienna, Oxford, and

London (University College), and was a research hydrologist with the U.S. Geological Survey from 1973-1984. He is presently joint editor of *Catena*, an international journal of soils, hydrology, and geomorphology. Since 1978, Trimble has owned and managed a 200-acre farm in Tennessee. He received a B.S. in chemistry from the University of North Alabama and an M.S. and a Ph.D. in geography from the University of Georgia in 1969 and 1973, respectively.

Index

U.S. Army Corps of Engineers (USACE), 3, 6,
    8, 28, 32, 210
  funding through, 214-216
  Hydrologic Engineering Center, 160
  planning protocols of, 259-260
  water-related responsibilities of, 173-174
U.S. Department of Agriculture, 6, 8, 41, 122,
    126, 271
  regionalization scheme of, 81
  water-related responsibilities of, 169-172
U.S. Department of Commerce, water-related
    responsibilities of, 172-173
U.S. Department of Defense, water-related
    responsibilities of, 173-174
U.S. Department of Energy
  funding through, 216-219
  water-related responsibilities of, 174-175
U.S. Department of the Interior, water-related
    responsibilities of, 175-178
U.S. Fish and Wildlife Service (FWS), 29, 82,
    172, 176
U.S. Forest Service, 8, 81, 113, 116
  planning protocols of, 256-257
  water-related responsibilities of, 169-170
U.S. Geological Survey (USGS), 2, 8-9, 32, 52-
    53, 117, 176-177
  "Earth Resources Observation System Data
    Center," 177
  funding through, 219
  "Seasonal Land Cover Regions," 81
U.S. Water Resources Council, 51, 53, 183
University of Minnesota Department of
    Landscape Architecture, 18
University of Montana Flathead Lake
    Biological Station, 23
Uplands, linked with downstream areas, 1
Upper Carson River Watershed Management
    Plan, 211
USEPA. *See* Environmental Protection Agency

V

Verde Watershed Association, 210

W

Washington Department of Natural Resources,
    153
Washington Forest Practices Board, 152-153
Waste load allocations (WLAs), 286

Wastewater treatment plants, 101, 104
Water and Watersheds Program, 126
Water consumption, 18-19
*Water in the West: The Challenge for the Next
    Century,* 222-223
Water Pollution Control Act of 1948, 284
  Amendments of 1956, 284
Water quality, 20, 76-81
  problems with data on, 129
  related U.S. legislation, 283-288
  of stormwater, 91
Water Quality Act of 1965, 284-285
Water Quality Act of 1987, 287-288
Water resource democracy, 186
Water Resources Council, 213-214
Water Resources Planning Act of 1965, 213
Water resources regions, 51-52, 123
Water Resources Research Act, 177
Water sampling, 117
Waterscape, defined, 2
Watershed and River Systems Management
    Initiative, 133
Watershed approach
  rationale for new, 31-33
  to wide ranging problems, 1, 5-6, 14-17
Watershed-based Internet sites, 292
Watershed boundaries, 203
Watershed condition, indicators of, 139-140
Watershed 96 (conference), 186
Watershed data and information
  finding, 122-123
  on the Internet, 32, 289-292
Watershed Data Clearinghouse, 277
Watershed management. *See also* Ecosystem
    management
  barriers to adaptive, 237
  cost allocation for, 224-229
  defined, 14
  effective, 3, 9
  funding, 4, 7, 30, 32
  guiding philosophy for, 5-6
  international, 192-201
  issues of scale, 202
  need for flexibility in, 10, 279
  organizational structure of, 164-207
  processes of, 6-7
  succeeding at, 269-271
  terminology used, 33-34
Watershed management plans, 1, 6
  barriers and challenges to implementing,
    28-29